A Forged Glamour

Landscape, Identity and Material Culture
in the Iron Age

Melanie Giles

Windgather Press
is an imprint of
Oxbow Books, Oxford

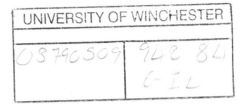
ISBN 978-1-905119-46-2

A CIP record for this book is available from the British Library

This book is available direct from

Oxbow Books, Oxford, UK
(Phone: 01865-241249; Fax: 01865-794449)

and

The David Brown Book Company
PO Box 511, Oakville, CT 06779, USA
(Phone: 860-945-9329; Fax: 860-945-9468)

or from our website

www.oxbowbooks.com

Printed by
Berforts Information Press

This book is dedicated with grateful thanks to:

Maggie and Norman Damerell,
who started all of this

Pat Wagner, whom I have been privileged
to call both mentor and friend

and in loving memory of
Christopher Godwin Giles

Contents

List of Figures

List of Tables

Preface and Acknowledgements

....

Beauty's also a matter of power,
a way to say, *Look, this I make,*
What's identity but a forged glamour?
Isn't it style that mocks death?
Mark Doty Emerald

This book takes as its title part of a poem written by Mark Doty. In a reflection on the death of a friend, Doty focuses on the things that we make or curate, as palpable expressions of enduring existence. Sitting in the archives of the Hull and East Riding Museum, feeling the weight and heft of an iron mirror, it is easy to sense the hand of the past reaching out in defiance of time, through this exquisitely crafted object. Yet as Mark Doty reminds us, beauty also concerns power, and the status and identity of people in the past. His use of a powerful metaphor to convey this ... the 'forged glamour' of performance and display ... is an inspiring and apposite way to begin a study of ironworking communities renowned for their spectacular material culture, who lived in modern-day East and North Yorkshire, between the 4th and 1st centuries BC.

At its simplest, this book is an exploration of their lives and deaths. It evaluates settlement and funerary evidence, analyses farming and craftwork, and explores what some of their ideas and beliefs might have been. It situates this regional material within the broader context of Iron Age Britain, Ireland and the near Continent, and considers what manner of society this was. In order to do this, however, it makes use of theoretical ideas on personhood, and relationships with material culture and landscape, arguing that (as Mark Doty's poem goes on to suggest) the making of identity always takes work. It is the character, scale and extent of this work (revealed through objects as small as a glass bead, or as big as a cemetery; as local as an earthern-ware pot or as exotic as coral-decoration) which enables archaeologists to investigate the web of relations which made up their lives, and explore the means of power which distinguished their leaders.

This book is aimed at several audiences. I hope it will be useful to the excavator of a new sword burial or someone who discovers an Iron Age brooch, enabling them to find out its approximate date, how to describe it, and where other examples have been found. At the same time, it is an interpretive account, which, no doubt, varies from the stories others have told (or might yet tell) of the so-called 'Arras culture'. Each generation gets the past it deserves, we are often told, and I have undoubtedly brought my own interest in age and gender, or the relationship between craft skill and power, to bear on this rewarding material. I hope at the very least, to highlight the remarkable quality, international significance, and compelling fascination of this archaeology, to both old and new audiences.

The book began life as a PhD funded by the AHRC, under the direction of both Mike Parker Pearson and John Barrett – my thanks go to both of them, as to Mark Edmonds, whose creative approach to archaeological writing continues to inspire. It was completed through a research sabbatical from the University of Manchester, and matched Research Leave funding from the AHRC: for this generous grant the author is most grateful. The reconstruction drawing by Aaron Watson was funded by a Research Small Grant from the University of Manchester.

The work that has gone into this book rests squarely on the shoulders of many renowned archaeologists. Key amongst these is John Dent: director of the excavations at Wetwang Slack, who has been unfailingly generous in allowing access to unpublished material, and courteous in sharing his extensive knowledge of Iron Age East Yorkshire. Also Ian Stead, director of the British Museum excavations in the Great Wold Valley, whose meticulous archival research, inspiring excavations and incisive interpretations form the foundation of much material presented here. His successors at the British Museum, J. D. Hill and Jody Joy, have likewise been unfailingly supportive of this project, providing access to archival material and unpublished reports on the Wetwang Village chariot burial. Adrian Havercroft, Rod Mackey and Kate Dennett also gave invaluable insights into this excavation as well as the broader East Yorkshire material. Other researchers who have kindly shared their time, ideas and insights include: Cathy Stoertz, Val Rigby, Mandy Jay and Janet Montgomery, Kate Waddington, Chris Fenton Thomas and Bill Bevan. Throughout, Paula Gentil, curator of the Hull and East Riding Museum, has been unfailingly generous with her time and access to excavation material. Caroline Rhodes (Collections Curator, Hull Museums) kindly photographed key objects and provided other illustrations. Adam Parker of York Museums Trust kindly helped with image enquiries. Stephen Harrison's inspiring research on the antiquarians John and Robert Mortimer, has also been invaluable. Oxford Archaeology North kindly gave permission to visit the Ferry Fryston burial under excavation. I have also greatly benefited from the staff and expertise at Humber Field Archaeology, particularly the wisdom of Dave Evans and Pete Didsbury, whilst Jim Fraser and Sophie Tibbles facilitated access to the Caythorpe excavations, courtesy of the developer Centrica. Victoria Brown, SMR Officer at Hull, provided invaluable information at short notice, whilst Linda Smith facilitated archival access for North Yorkshire. In terms of expertise, Andrew Chamberlain offered invaluable advice on the demographic analysis and Sonia O'Connor kindly shared ideas and information on the Ferry Fryston metalwork. The collaboration with the artist Aaron Watson to produce the chariot burial reconstruction, has been especially rewarding (and thanks to Joan and Medwin Giles, for participating in the making of this special image). Meanwhile, Jo Wright has been unfailingly patient in the production of all other illustrations and line drawings in this volume. I have also been privileged to benefit from insightful conversations and fascinating research produced by three key PhD students: Sarah King, of Bradford University, Gala Argent of Leicester University and Greta Anthoons of Bangor University. Meanwhile, a broader group of prehistoric scholars have patiently listened to, debated and critiqued much of the argument presented here: thanks especially to Duncan Garrow, Bob Johnston, Chris Gosden, Niall Sharples, John Collis, Barry Cunliffe, Tim Champion, Andrew Fitzpatrick, Colin Haselgrove, Richard Bradley, Raymond Karl, Miranda Aldhouse-Green, Adrian Chadwick and Jonathan Last.

Writing a book is a long process, and the ideas presented here have been developed through the inspiring academic institutions of the University of Sheffield, University College Dublin, the University of Leicester and particularly, the University of Manchester. I want to thank Siân Jones and Chantal Conneller, Gabriel Cooney, Aidan O'Sullivan and Graeme Warren, and Simon James and David Mattingly, for being such supportive and rewarding colleagues to work with. Joanna Brück was the inspirational mentor for an IRCHSS funded research sabbatical at UCD, whose approach and interpretations of prehistory continue to shape my own. My touchstone for the book has been Pat Wagner, who first took me up to Vessey Pastures and introduced me to the Wolds. Thanks also to the many discussions with colleagues from the MA in the Archaeology of Landscape at the University of Sheffield (led by Mark Edmonds) through which a community of friendship and ideas continues to thrive: Rowan May, Anna Badcock, Graham and Heidi Robbins, John Roberts, Emily LaTrobe-Bateman, Jon Bateman, Judith Winters, Anwen Cooper, Willy Kitchen and Andy Wigley. Thanks in particular to Emily and John for allowing me to write in the inspirational environment of Glandwr Terrace. Particular thanks to Mark Doty for giving permission to cite his poem in the title of the book: *Emerald* from 'Sweet Machine' by Mark Doty (© Mark Doty 1998), published by Jonathan Cape, reprinted by permission of The Random House Group Ltd and HarperCollins publishers (thanks particularly to Sarah McMahon for facilitating this).

The illustrations are the work of Jo Wright, based on originals in publications by Ian Stead, John Dent, J. D. Hill and Cathy Stoertz, as well as Oxford Archaeology North, Humber Field Archaeology, the British Museum and English Heritage, who have all kindly given permission to redraw and modify their originals. All images supplied by the following institutions are acknowledged gratefully: the British Museum (© Trustees of the British Museum), the Hull and East Riding Museum (© Hull and East Riding Museum: Hull Museums) and York Museums Trust. Thanks to Marcus Abbott for the book cover design. Special thanks to Julie Gardiner and Tara Evans for their editing and preparation of the publication.

Finally, this book would not have been possible without the unfailing support and critical advice of two individuals: my twin, Kate Giles, and my husband, Danny Hind. To them, especially, I owe a great debt of love and thanks.

All errors and omissions remain the responsibility of the author.

A note on site names and codes

In the rest of this book, burials are identified by the following site codes followed by the number of the burial: Wetwang Slack (WS), Garton Slack (GSl), Wetwang Village (WV), Rudston (R), Burton Fleming (BF), Garton Station (GS), Kirkburn (K), Arras (A or W), Danes Graves (DG).

CHAPTER ONE

Archaeological Approaches to Landscape, Identity and Material Culture

Introduction

September 1985. Sifting through the fill of a square barrow burial, in a shallow chalk valley near Garton Station, the digger's trowel hit something hard and metallic. Carefully easing away the silt, flakes of decayed iron fell away from the stump of an object. It was the circular end of a spearhead, embedded tip-down in the grave fill. Working carefully but eagerly, the rest of the grave was emptied. In total, 14 spearheads were recovered, perched in the soil at many different levels (GS10, Stead 1991, 224). Traces of mineralised wood suggested the shafts of the spears were intact when they were thrown into the fill of the grave. Near the base of the pit, six of these were embedded in the tightly crouched body of a young man, who was aged between 25–35 years old when he died. The spears seem to have splintered and pierced through a hide-covered wooden shield which had been laid over the rib-cage, and an iron sword lay just behind his back. Although there were no obvious signs of injury on the skeleton, deep flesh wounds, strangling or poisoning would have left no mark, nor would many common but dangerous infections.

Piecing together the evidence, the director of the excavations, Ian Stead, realised that this burial had been the focus of an elaborate funerary ritual. The grave had been cut into the bed of the local stream – the Gypsey Race (pronounced with a hard 'g') – probably when the waters had dried up, or were running shallow (Figure 1.1). Perhaps it had been a long, hot summer, when either tempers had flared or disease had run rife through the local community. Whatever the cause of death, the loss of this man in the prime of his life, must have been deeply felt. By this age, he would have become a respected father, farmer, hunter or fighter: skilled at wielding a spear. From the trajectory of the weapons, we can guess that at least four individuals took turns to cast their weapons into his body, as the grave was rapidly backfilled. Why 'kill' someone who was already dead? Was this a mark of honour or a gesture of fear? Whatever the motivation, the shafts of their spears would have stuck out of the resulting barrow mound, like bristles or spines. Taking years to decay, they would have become a long-lasting and dramatic reminder of the events that had taken place there.

This individual was not alone: there are four further burials interred in this manner in the cemetery, adjacent to each other (GS4, GS5, GS7 and GS10, Stead 1991, 22). They may have died together, or months or years apart: we have

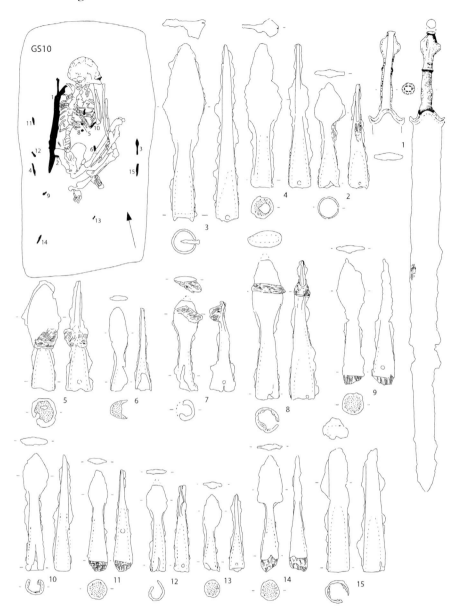

FIGURE 1.1. Burial of GS10. Based on Stead 1991, 223, fig. 124.

no way of knowing. What binds them together is the fact that they are all adult males, ranging from their late teens to early 30s. They were all associated with 'martial' objects: spears, bone points, shields and a sword. And it is clear that the place of burial – in the very bed of the local chalk stream, running along the base of the valley – was also significant.

The three themes highlighted by this burial – the place where they were buried, the identity of the dead and the objects they were buried with – form the core of this book. *'A forged glamour'* is an archaeological study of the lives and deaths of the Iron Age inhabitants of the Yorkshire Wolds, who are renowned for their square barrow cemeteries, and the rare but impressive chariot burials which are occasionally found within them. It seeks to interpret the drama of these funerary rites within the context of everyday life: the more mundane landscape of settlements, stock-raising and craftwork, through which their concerns, fears and ambitions took shape. Each chapter of the book will focus on a different theme or area of those lives. Weaving between these chapters will be a study of the relationship between the living and the dead.

We only come to know these people through the traces they left behind: the material culture of banks and ditches, roundhouses and barrows, human and animal remains, and artefacts, which they made and deposited in this landscape. Whilst the classical authors refer broadly to habits of the pre-Romanised Britons, we have no account of East Yorkshire until names of places and tribes are listed by Ptolemy in the 2nd century AD. This first chapter is thus a study of how we know what we know: a history of research in the area, from the days of the earliest antiquarians to the modern era of developer-funded contract archaeology. Throughout this first section, I will consider how the three key themes of the book – landscape, identity and material culture – were viewed by each generation of archaeologists, evaluating how and why their ideas changed, and outlining the challenges we still face. First, it is vital to appreciate the landscape which both shaped these later prehistoric communities and was simultaneously transformed by them.

The Yorkshire Wolds

Introducing the landscape

The Yorkshire Wolds form a crescentic arc of chalk hills, rising at Hessle on the northern shore of the river Humber, and turning gently eastwards, to outcrop at Flamborough Head, on the North Sea coast (Kent 1980). They are located within the counties of both East and North Yorkshire (Figure 1.2). To the west of the Wolds lies the relatively flat Vale of York, and – close to the foot of the Wolds itself – the Foulness Valley: dissected by the headwaters of the Humber and its tributaries. To the north, the Vale of Pickering stretches out towards the Howardian Hills and the North Yorkshire Moors, watered by the river Derwent. Finally, to the east is the gently undulating land around the River Hull, sinking into the low-lying Vale of Holderness. The rapidly eroding coastline fringes the region to the east.

From a distance, the Wolds form an impressive block of land, rising out of the surrounding vales, but their unitary appearance is deceptive. The scarp edge of the Wolds, especially in the north-west, consists of extensive 'swells and plains' (Leatham 1794, cited in Woodward 1985, 34): broad, open Wold 'tops' dissected by sharp, 'v' shape dry valleys. Many of these dales (as they are known locally) were formed when faults in the chalk were worn open by glacial activity, which often left deposits of moraine (crushed chalk and worn flint gravels) in their bases. These gravels are often overlain by several metres

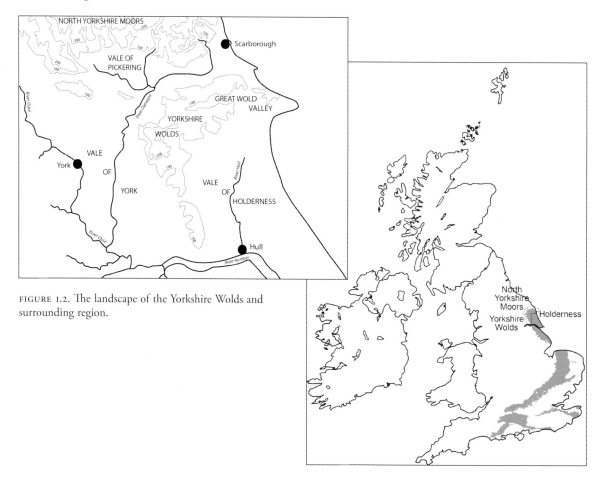

FIGURE 1.2. The landscape of the Yorkshire Wolds and surrounding region.

of hillwash ('colluvium', Hotson 1985): the result of the natural erosion of the land surface, exacerbated by centuries of cultivation (Foster 1987; Evans 1992) and the aerial denudation of soils (Reid 1885; Furness and King 1978). The high, sharp sides of these valleys form long, sinuous corridors, with frequent side dales and steep valley heads. In places, they feel almost claustrophobic. In contrast, the exposed Wold tops in between these dales are open to the wide canopy of the sky. The brilliance of the stars up here on a clear, autumn night is awe-inspiring.

As you move down from these highest parts of the Wolds onto the eastern dipslope, the topography becomes less severe. The Great Wolds Valley, which dissects the eastern arm of the Wolds, has a broader base, rising to slighter hills on each side. Further south, these are called 'slacks', as at Wetwang and Garton. Gradually, they give way to more undulating land, as the chalk of the Wolds meets the Holderness Plain. Here, glacially deposited bars of tills and fluvio-glacial gravels (Reid 1885; Van der Noort and Ellis 1995), are punctured by kettle holes: formed as these capping deposits collapsed into hollows left by melting ice blocks.

Today, after centuries of drainage, canalisation, reclamation and land improvement, it is hard to appreciate what the lower-lying later prehistoric landscape around the Wolds would have looked like. In Holderness in particular, it would certainly have been wetter: a mosaic of richly-vegetated marsh and submerged forests, rising peat deposits, small spring-fed streams, seasonal floodplains and more permanent meres, as at Hornsea. To traverse certain areas of this landscape would have required intimate local knowledge of safe routes across slightly higher ground, as well as the use of water transport, such as the Brigg rafts and Hasholme boat (Millett and MacGrail 1987; MacGrail 1990; Wright and Churchill 1965; Wright 1990). By the early Iron Age, some clearance of the Holderness landscape is suggested (Dinnin in Van der Noort and Ellis 1995) although grazing and cultivation may have been limited to better drained areas of sand and gravel (Didsbury 1990).

It is unlikely that later prehistoric communities were restricted to one area of the landscape. Whilst the Wolds may have had a distinct identity arising from its bedrock, soils and topography, as well as its commanding views, communities from it moved down into the surrounding Vales, to meet with others, exchange resources and news, and make use of seasonally available foodstuffs, pasturage or water (Fenton Thomas 1999). Equally, groups from off the Wolds made journeys up into the hills, for similar reasons. The evidence for this will be discussed later in the book, but it is important not to see the Wolds as an isolated region, but rather a distinct yet internally varied zone, set within a diverse broader landscape utilised by many communities.

History of archaeological research

The Yorkshire Wolds have been well-investigated by archaeologists over the nineteenth to twenty-first centuries. There are several reasons for this. A highly visible set of monuments (long, round and square barrows, a massive standing stone at Rudston and kilometres of linear earthworks) attracted the interest of a series of antiquarians. Initially they were collectors, such as Thomas Kendall of Pickering, but others, such as Jas. Silburn and Barnard Clarkson actively investigated these ancient monuments (Marsden 1999). Some were of independent financial means (such as Canon Greenwell, who also worked extensively from North Yorkshire to Northumberland, 1877). Others (such as John and Robert Mortimer) were funded in part through the patronage and encouragement of local landowners (the Sykes of Sledmere, in particular), as well as the profits of their business activities (Giles 2006). Their research was facilitated through a vigorous, and often aggressive agricultural regime, which saw the large-scale ploughing-up of earlier pastoral regions known as 'sheepwalks', during a major period of land improvement (Harris 1996). Vast quantities of surface finds, particularly lithics, were recovered by agricultural labourers, and sold for financial reward (Sheppard 1929, iii). Other activities resulted in the accidental discovery of remains, such as the creation of the

Malton to Driffield railway (Mortimer 1905a, 194), quarrying for chalk or clay digging (*ibid.*, 238) and road-mending (Mortimer 1889). Sometimes, farmers or labourers reported the finds that had been disturbed as they cut into or even levelled ancient barrows (Mortimer 1905a, 113, 359). Both Greenwell and Mortimer solicited news of such finds, rushing to record the discovery and collect whatever artefacts remained (Greenwell 1906; Mortimer 1869). However, these barrow-opening activities sometimes had unintended consequences, as reported in the *Driffield Times and General Advertiser* for Saturday 6 December 1862 on page 3. A labourer who had previously assisted an unnamed antiquarian took it upon himself to open another barrow 'actuated by a desire of profit', but rather than uncovering valuable artefacts to sell he made an 'unfortunate sepulchral discovery', much to the horror of the landowner as well as the editor of this local newspaper!

The archaeology of this region became much more widely known and appreciated through an assiduous programme of public speaking at local institutions and regional societies by Greenwell and Mortimer, as well as another interested amateur: the local vicar of Wetwang Slack, E. Maule Cole. The subsequent publication of these lectures in the associated proceedings helped disseminate their discoveries and ideas, as did the longer articles and major monographs by both Greenwell (1877) and Mortimer (1905a). John Mortimer's *Driffield Museum of Antiquities and Geological Specimens* also made his collection available to fellow scholars, even if access to the general public was more restricted (Giles 2006, 290). By bequeathing his collection to the British Museum, Greenwell's material gained a much wider audience upon his death. In contrast, the purchase of Mortimer's collection by the Hull and East Riding Museum in 1913 (engineered by the curator Thomas Sheppard) respected the wishes of its creator by ensuring it remained in the district in which it had been collected (Harrison 2001). By the early twentieth century, it was evident that the Iron Age archaeology of East Yorkshire had a considerable role to play in narratives of both regional and national identity (Giles 2006).

By the middle of the twentieth century, archaeological techniques – particularly the use of aerial photography – were transforming knowledge of the underlying prehistoric landscape. The light chalk soils which cover the Yorkshire Wolds, are easily worked, and the post-war increase in arable production, enabled by the use of new machinery and artificial fertilizers, made the area particularly profitable for recording soil and crop marks (Stoertz 1997, 1). In addition, large tracts of grazed pasture still contained upstanding earthworks, and dry summers helped reveal further sites through ploughed-out parch marks (*ibid.*). From the 1950s–1990s, the Royal Commission on the Historical Monuments of England (RCHME), took thousands of aerial photographs, which resulted in another seminal archaeological publication: the comprehensive mapping programme undertaken by Cathy Stoertz, and published in 1997. Alongside the work of other local flyers, these images began to stimulate further programmes of archaeological research. These were undertaken by individual local researchers such as Terry

Manby and Tony Pacitto, amateur rescue archaeologists such as the Granthams of Driffield, as well as institutions such as the British Museum, whose impressive programme of research was directed by Ian Stead. In addition, the large-scale gravel quarrying activities at Garton and Wetwang Slack led to a co-ordinated programme of excavation, initiated by T. C. M. Brewster and carried forward by John Dent. Other research programmes have included the work of Dominic Powesland, on the edge of the Wolds at Heslerton; survey and excavation in the Foulney Valley by Peter Halkon and Martin Millet; long-term excavation by Rod Mackey at the villa site of Welton Wold; the work of the East Riding Archaeology Society; and research by the Wharram Landscape Project, directed by Colin Hayfield. University-driven research by departments of archaeology at Sheffield, York, Hull and Manchester, have also enriched knowledge of the region. More recently, developer-funded work on both housing and pipeline projects have yielded fascinating results both on and off the Wolds, undertaken by various units, including the locally based Humber Field Archaeology, Northern Archaeological Associates and On-Site Archaeology.

The result of all of this research is a vast body of archaeological data relating to the Iron Age, investigated to different standards and under different agendas. Caution is needed when comparing the records of antiquarians with contemporary archaeological investigation carried out under the guidance of current planning guidance (*PPG*16, *PPS*5). Even then, many of the more recent excavations – particularly those at Wetwang Slack and Wetwang Village – have yet to be published, or exist merely as a microfiche report (e.g. Brewster 1980). However, as a result of this work by many individuals, the general character of the Iron Age archaeology can still be confidently outlined.

The character of the Iron Age landscape

It is the funerary evidence which dominates accounts of the region. From around the fourth century BC to the mid-first century BC, inhumations became increasingly numerous. Small groups of square barrows (such as Cowlam) or isolated graves, contrast with larger cemeteries at Arras, Danes Graves, Burton Fleming, Rudston and Wetwang/Garton Slack. The largest cemeteries are usually found in the base of valleys at the edge of the Wolds dipslope, or clustered along the Great Wolds Valley (Figure 1.3). However, smaller cemeteries are also found in Holderness and the most northerly barrow cemetery has been recorded at Slingsby in North Yorkshire, with outlying chariot burials discovered on the North Yorks Moors and in West Yorkshire.

Some burials were deposited on the ground surface but later inhumations were generally interred in grave pits (Stead 1991, 228). They were commonly surrounded by a square enclosure ditch, with the up-cast spoil used to create a small covering mound or barrow. However, by the 1990s, it was recognised that some graves had a circular enclosure ditch, whilst others had none (Stead 1991, 7). The body was generally crouched or contracted, with the head commonly

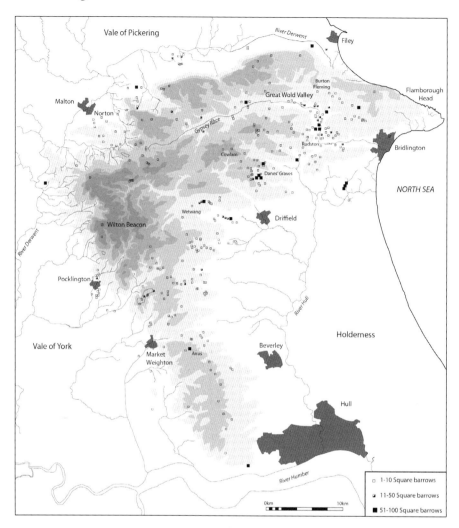

FIGURE 1.3. Square barrow cemetery distributions. 1. Wetwang Slack; 2. Garton Slack; 3. Garton Station; 4. Kirkburn; 5. Eastburn; 6. Cowlam; 7. Danes Graves; 8. Burton Fleming (BF1-22); 9. Rudston (190–208); 10 Rudston (Makeshift, R1-189); Burton Fleming (Bell Slack BF23-64); 12. Grindale (Huntlow). Based on Stoertz 1997, 34, fig. 15.

orientated towards the north end of the grave, facing east (*ibid.*). Grave goods were scarce but included brooches, items of jewellery, and small earthern-ware jars which sometimes contained a joint of mutton. Rarer artefacts included tools and weapons (Stead 1979). However, the most impressive burials within these cemeteries were the 'chariot' or 'cart' burials: inhumations surrounded by the remains of two-wheeled vehicles with a central pole shaft, originally pulled by a pair of ponies. The trappings of these chariots were frequently arranged around the body: horse-gear and decorative ornaments, as well as personal items such as swords and mirrors. From the antiquarian writers onwards, these chariot burials have been seen as the graves of the local chiefly Celtic elite. Their similarities with burials on the Continent have led to the assumption that the burial rite itself is the result of a migration from Iron Age Europe: an interpretation which will be extensively discussed throughout this book.

Alongside this rich material is the scanter evidence for settlement:

roundhouses, four and six-post structures, pits, gullies, enclosure ditches, track-ways and fence-lines, as revealed in the extensive open area excavation along the Wetwang and Garton Slack valleys. Smaller windows into settlement activity have been provided at villa sites such as Rudston (Stead 1980) and other late Iron Age–early Roman farmsteads, where an early phase of occupation frequently underlies later activity. In contrast, 'hillforts' are rare and diverse in form: they largely appear to be a late Bronze Age/earliest Iron Age phenomena and as the scope of this book focuses on the middle–late Iron Age, they are not discussed in detail here (see instead Giles 2007c). Evidence for agricultural activity is scarce: there are no well-preserved field systems, so environmental evidence (of both flora and fauna) is particularly valuable (Wagner 1992). However, the landscape is framed by a series of impressive linear earthworks, which seem to date to the late Bronze Age but continue to be modified throughout the first millennium BC (Giles 2007c) and these can be used to gain a (speculative) insight into patterns of landscape use.

Summary

So far, this chapter has introduced the Iron Age landscape of the Yorkshire Wolds, and it has briefly reviewed the history of investigation in the region. Returning to the discovery at the beginning of the chapter, it is now time to delve a little deeper into the work and ideas of these key researchers, to explore the ways in which this material has been used by them to explore one of the three key concepts of this book: *identity*. Since its formal origins as a social science, archaeology has prided itself on being able to contribute to understandings of humanity through a long-term perspective on the past. In the late nineteenth and early twentieth centuries, the discipline made claims about the nature of different human races, the spread of particular cultures, and the degree of civilisation they represented, which unfortunately helped underpin and justify colonial and nationalist programmes of expansion, invasion and exploitation (Jones 1997). By the mid-20th century, these debates had turned to the pressing issue of the indigenous or invasionary origin of Britain's inhabitants, when again the East Yorkshire material was used to exemplify conflicting ideas. The rest of this chapter explores the changing paradigms within which such opinions were formed, challenged and revised.

I will suggest that the problems with approaches such as racial analysis or culture history stem from their simplistic attitude towards the relationship between people, place and objects. The latter part of the chapter will then explore these three key concepts, advocating an approach which places social relationships at the heart of what it meant to be human in later prehistory. It will also emphasise the importance of practice in reproducing relations with other people, animals, places and things, and outline a methodology with which to investigate these issues.

Archaeological approaches to identity, landscape and material culture

'Decidedly British': the excavations at Arras

Between 1815 and 1817, a small number of local gentry, assisted by a group of labourers, excavated a series of barrows on the high escarpment of the Yorkshire Wolds at Arras. This was to become the 'type site' for the Iron Age in this region, after which the later prehistoric culture was named. It was a dramatic setting: from the vantage point of this square barrow cemetery, the land fell away, giving views across the plain of Holderness, towards the River Hull. Whilst this pastime of 'barrow opening' and the acquisition of relics for private collections was gaining popularity amongst the educated classes, it was regarded very sceptically by the general public (Giles 2006, 282). A locally known jibe was to be 'as fond [meaning 'as foolish'] as Barnard Clarkson' (Hicks 1978, 26) – a key member of the excavation party. However, the group also included respectable individuals such as the vicar of South Cave, the Rev. Edward William Stillingfleet, and the dig was certainly visited by Thomas Hull, a doctor with a local practice in Beverley (Stead 1979, 7). Given the full-time occupations of these men, it is perhaps not surprising that nothing was published on their discoveries until 1829, when an account by Clarkson and a letter from Dr Hull were quoted in Oliver's *History and Antiquities of the town and minster Beverley*. Stillingfleet's own account took thirty years to publish, prompted by a temporary exhibition associated with the 1846 York Meeting of the Archaeological Institute (Stead 1979, 7), in which he displayed the 'most interesting portable articles which fell to my share' (Stillingfleet 1847, 3). By this time, there was increased interest in both the artefacts and the burials from which they came.

Stillingfleet and his colleagues noted several repeated traits in the burials – that they were commonly crouched inhumations, with heads often orientated towards the north, seldom accompanied by grave goods. Some of the barrows appeared 'empty', probably since the burials were placed on the land surface or in a shallow grave, and had already been ploughed out. Interestingly, Stillingfleet describes the barrows as generally 'circular' in shape (*ibid.*, 3) and in fact, this is the profile which many of the square barrows take on, following the erosion of the central mound. It was only later that the distinctive square form of the surrounding ditch was fully appreciated (Stead 1979, 10).

The three most interesting burials from Arras were quickly given memorable names by the gentry who peered into their grave pits, and divided the finds up amongst themselves. There was the Queen's Barrow, containing a crouched inhumation accompanied by a necklace of nearly 100 blue and green glass beads; a red amber ring found at her neck or breast; a bronze brooch which adorned this 'fair wearer' (Stillingfleet 1847, 4); a round bronze plaque or pendant; two bracelets; a nail cleaner and pair of tweezers, and a gold finger-ring. Stillingfleet noted that this latter object was 'by no means of despicable workmanship' (*ibid.*). There was also the burial of an elderly man associated with an offering of wild boar and the trappings of a vehicle: the iron tyres and bronze nave-hoops of two wheels still had traces of wood adhering to the metal. Uniquely, these wheels overlay the remains of two ponies, of around 13 hands (1.32 m) in height: flanking the charioteer, their heads close to his. Although the bridle-bits were easily recognised, it was the workmen who identified the 'linch-pins' which secured the wheel to the axle (*ibid.*, 5). Stillingfleet commented that the grave of this 'uncivilised Brigantian' was a 'concealed mausoleum dedicated to his memory and fame' (*ibid.*, 6). It was simple yet durable, speaking to 'other years' of his 'character, rank and celebrity' (*ibid.*). The labourers would not be gainsaid: this was surely the burial of a King, and thus it became known as the 'King's Barrow'. A second chariot burial discovered by the group was instead distinguished by the name of 'the Charioteer', again associated with iron wheels and nave hoops, horse-bits and two probable linch-pins made of antler, as well a bronze case which may have enclosed the end of the cart pole. Stillingfleet described this individual as lying on the remains of a shield, defined by a series of bronze bosses, fragments of wood and parts of its iron rim (*ibid.*, 6). Although Stead did not agree with this interpretation, parallels for shields within chariot burials have been found more recently at Wetwang Slack (Dent 1985, cart burials 1 and 3).

What motivated these early barrow diggers? Stillingfleet's comments about the barrows as a means of commemorating and celebrating the deceased are insightful. But it is clear that he felt their excavations were also of 'historical value' (1847, 8) in collating a 'mass of evidence' that in conjunction with research on the northern Continent, could be used to reconstruct 'the customs of various tribes, who have peopled Britain, in different eras' (*ibid.*, 7). Similarly, Oliver's reading of Hull and Clarkson's accounts gave him to believe that the burials were 'decidedly British' (1829, 3), as opposed to later incursions of Romans or Danes. In these accounts, there is already a sense of different peoples or 'tribes' whose successive occupations contributed to the history of Britain. Stillingfleet describes the Arras inhabitants as 'uncivilised', also indicating some sense of a trajectory from primitive to modern, but his concept of a 'tribe' remains rather nebulous. It was the next generation of antiquarians who were to take up these ideas and develop a racial history of Britain.

Race and craniology

When Stillingfleet exhibited his Arras finds at the 1846 meeting of the Archaeological Institute in York, they caught the eye of a local surgeon, William Proctor, and John Thurnham, the director of the forward-thinking mental asylum 'The Retreat': a Quaker institution, located near York. Both men had a strong interest in archaeology (Ramm 1971, 68–9): Thurnham had been elected a member of the Yorkshire Philosophical Society in 1840–1, and in 1849, these two men formed the 'Yorkshire Antiquarian Club', with Proctor acting as secretary (Stead 1979, 10).

They initially targeted a new site for investigation, at Danes Graves, near

Driffield. This was, in fact, the first Iron Age barrow cemetery ever to be investigated – by a group from Kilham parish in 1721 – and the site had also been described earlier by both Leland and Camden (Mortimer 1897, 286). Local folklore held that there were originally over 500 barrows in this cemetery (Stead 1979, 16) but the 1st edition Ordnance Survey map only recorded 197 barrows – largely preserved in the nearby woodland plantation – the rest having been ploughed out (East Riding Archive and Library Service ref. no. 01/144). By 1979, 212 had been plotted on the ground but aerial photographs confirm over 400 barrows once existed (Stead 1979, 16). The purpose of the Yorkshire Antiquarian Club's excavations of six of these barrows was more clearly defined than those of the previous generation's barrow-opening gentry. Thurnham had a strong interest in the ways in which aspects of identity, particularly ethnicity, could be identified through the technique of craniology: the study of the shape and form of the human skull. As he later put it, he believed that 'typical ethnic peculiarities' inherent in the skull were 'not transmutable in the different Races' (Davis and Thurnham 1865, 2). Given his medical background, it is perhaps not surprising that like many antiquarians, Thurnham believed in a physiological basis for racial difference, and had an explicit interest in the science of ethnology (Morse 1999). He was in good company: in 1843, Prichard had recommended that skulls from British barrows could be used to illuminate 'the races of people by whom they were erected' (1843, 192), in order to compose 'a sequence of races based on cranial types' (*ibid.*, 1). Working with the ethnologist Joseph Barnard Davis, Thomas Bateman took up this challenge in 1848, combining craniology with an early use of the Three Age System in his analysis of prehistoric burials from the Peak District (finally published in 1861: Morse 1999). Daniel Wilson also used craniology alongside historical and linguistic ethnology, and ethnographic analogy, to compose a racial history of Scotland (1851). In this ferment of new antiquarian methods, Thurnham was desperate to acquire more examples to test this technique, but the ambitions – and field techniques – of the Yorkshire Antiquarian Club were regarded scornfully by a contemporary critic:

> that pack of asses Thurnham and co. intended to go to Driffield on Monday night and commence early on Tuesday morning, finish the barrow by noon, fly over to Danes' Graves, open four or five of them and return to York by the last train.
>
> William Bowman, cited in Marsden 1999, 86.

Undaunted by such concerns, Thurnham and Proctor opened six barrows at Danes Graves in 1849, and in 1850, moved on to Arras, where the Club excavated three more burials. Although two of these had previously been disturbed by Stillingfleet and Clarkson, one was pristine (Stead 1979, 10). The Arras and Danes Graves skulls were beautifully illustrated in Thurnham's collaboration with Davis, *Crania Britannica* (1865), supported by drawings of contemporary grave goods from the 1815–1817 Arras excavations. Material culture was beginning to be allied with skeletal evidence, to identify and characterise racial type. In addition, Proctor had noted that one of these tumuli was surrounded by a 'square instead of a round fosse' (1855, 182), an architectural feature also noted in the barrow cemetery at Skipwith which the Club had examined (*ibid.*, 188), though here the burials themselves had decayed. Despite the exhaustive measurement of the Arras and Danes Graves material and other skulls from long barrows, round barrows and stone cairns across Britain, Davis and Thurnham (1865) were divided on the significance of the results. Whilst Thurnham believed they represented two races: a long-headed ('dolicocephalic') Stone Age race, which was replaced by a round-headed ('brachycephalic') race (1865, 230), Davis was not so sure. In any case, their analysis was presaged with a lengthy historical ethnology (drawing on Ptolemy's account of Britain) to suggest that, whilst they showed 'an identity of race' with other 'British tribes' (*ibid.*, II, section xiii, pls 6–7, 8), the Arras and Danes Graves skulls belonged to a 'small maritime tribe ... who occupied a great part of the East Riding of Yorkshire ... [and who] have been traced to the Parisi of the continent where they occupied a territory either side of the Seine, and may almost be regarded as Belgic Gauls' (*ibid.*, I, 146). The amateur archaeologist and local vicar of Wetwang Slack, Maule Cole, supported this identification of the Parisi as the proper tribal inhabitants of Holderness and the Wolds dipslope (1897, 301). Thus by the second half of the nineteenth century, archaeologists were using both human remains and material culture to construct their racial account of Britain's past, but this primary evidence was consistently framed by the classical sources, regarded as the first reliable 'histories' of Britain.

Thurnham and Davis' work inspired other local archaeologists to further test these ideas. Canon Greenwell and John Mortimer sought to add to the available skeletal data and number of craniological reports, through their own excavations. Both felt that the site of Danes Graves was key. Greenwell gained permission to dig fourteen more barrows here in 1864 (1906, 258) but his lack of care in backfilling these graves, as well as the activities of other barrow diggers, riled the landowner. When Greenwell's local rival, John Mortimer, asked to dig on the same site, he was refused permission, since – as the landowner W. H. Harrison Broadley's response indicates in 1871 – the previous work had been carried out 'so recklessly, so thoughtlessly, and even so indecently' that he could not permit further investigation (Mortimer 1899, 296). In fact, Mortimer circumvented Harrison Broadley's refusal by surreptitiously investigating two burials disturbed by tree-fall in the woodland in 1881. His wistful regret at not being allowed to dig further was justified by the fact that more needed to be known about 'the distinctly marked community of men (as shown by the crania)' who raised these barrows (1897, 298). In the meanwhile, he contented himself with investigating six mounds at Scorborough, near Beverley, concluding that they were of a similar date to Arras, Danes Graves and the recently excavated chariot burial found by Greenwell at Beverley Westwood in 1875 (Mortimer 1895). However, when a further chariot burial was found in a chalk pit at Arras in 1876 (the 'Lady's Barrow' complete with iron mirror), it was Greenwell who gained the credit for it, by speaking with the labourers, recording the burial and collecting the finds (1877).

John, and his brother Robert, already had a history of dispute with Greenwell, over the nature of his excavation techniques. Commenting on the Canon's excavation of the Butterwick round barrow, John noted that 'it would have been more satisfactory had the Canon himself been present at the opening of this rich and interesting barrow' (Marsden 1999, 133). When the three collaborated on the excavation of Esh's barrow (Greenwell's British Barrow XLIX), it was Robert who complained that:

> as night approached, the barrow was being rapidly completed and unsatisfactorily explored … turned over with four-tined forks and shovels in a hurried manner … a method not at all suitable for making antiquarian researches on a scientific principle
>
> Letter in the Hull and East Riding Museum, Mortimer collection: cited in Marsden 1999, 135

John and Robert were so concerned by the inadequacies of this rushed probing, that they returned to the site later on, re-excavating the foundations to disclose a complex conjunction of long and round barrow. Two months after the excavation, a furious Canon Greenwell wrote to his friend, John Evans, complaining bitterly that:

> that scoundrel Mortimer has been spreading calumnious reports, to the effect that I am destroying all the Wolds barrows and missing half the interments … to stop me getting leave. His conduct … has been that of a rascal, and I only wish I could get authority to walk in on him. I may possibly have to get you to give me a testimonial as to my mode of barrow opening
>
> Cited in Marsden 1999, 135

A series of further letters from 1867 between Greenwell and Evans continue to refer to the dispute (P. Graves, pers. comm.). However, such disagreements were evidently put aside when the opportunity arose to collaborate on a return to Danes Graves, following the death of the original Harrison Broadley in 1896. From 1897, working with both the Canon and another antiquarian, Thomas Boynton, they excavated 53 barrows between 1897 and 1898. A fascinating photograph from 1898, reproduced as part of Mortimer's posthumously published account of the site (1911a), shows the three archaeologists crouched in the open grave-pit of one of the burials. It is a rather solemn and formal image, which hints at ongoing tensions between these men. Although Greenwell was responsible for making records (whilst Boynton and Mortimer directed the actual excavations), the latter noted defensively 'I also took notes!' (*ibid.*, 30). Mortimer may have doubted the accuracy of Greenwell's observations or suspected he might not be granted access to them at a later date: either way, he wanted his own record of the discoveries. He may well be the shaded figure scribbling in the background of a quite different representation of the dig, published in *The Yorkshire Weekly Post* for 7 August 1897, 11 (Figure 1.4). These intimate sketches, made by his young daughter Agnes

FIGURE 1.4. Agnes Mortimer's sketches of the Danes Graves excavations. *Yorkshire Weekly Post*, 7 August 1897, 11.

(whose watercolours vividly illustrated his 1905a monograph, Giles 2006, 286) capture the popularity and excitement of the excavation, as well as something of the gender and class relations inherent in the project. In a second image, a plump woman sits on the baulk, flanked by one of the directors and an elegant young lady: they gaze into the grave pit below, where – on their knees – labourers scrape away the earth from a new chariot burial; their faces hidden and backsides turned to the viewer. The brimmed hats of the directors contrast with the soft caps of the labourers, and shovels lean against the sides of the trench, abandoned in favour of trowels, as the burials are carefully uncovered.

From 1899–1909 Mortimer continued by himself, opening a further 26 graves (Stead 1979, 17). This split may have been occasioned by John Mortimer's public lecture in October of 1897: '*A Summary of what is known of the so-called Danes Graves, near Driffield*' to the Yorkshire Geological and Polytechnic Society. Rather unwisely, perhaps even provocatively, Mortimer read aloud an excerpt from Harrison Broadley's initial letter of refusal. Mortimer's lecture was published two years later in the society's proceedings, and this may explain the end of the collaboration in 1899. Danes Graves was a site of both contest and friction, of revelation and insight, and it allows us to compare how two different antiquarians interpreted the same set of results. For a start, they were divided over the implications of the craniological analysis. Like Thurnham, the Canon believed in an early race of long-headed people (which he thought were associated with long barrows) and a later race of round-headed people (associated with round barrows, 1877). He also believed that the distinctive skull form found in the smaller barrows of Arras and Danes Graves, associated with iron grave goods, were the result of interbreeding between these earlier populations (1867). Following the dig, he argued that the sheer number of graves, and inclusion of women and children in the cemetery, were indicative of 'a settled population and not of any mere invaders' (cited in Mortimer 1897, 293 n. †). His interpretation may well have been influenced by the moderate comments of Maule Cole, who had visited the dig that summer. Maule Cole argued that the 'peculiar grouping' of the graves, being densely clustered and respecting the 'ancient British way' of a local linear earthwork, were the result of a '*settled occupation*' (original emphasis), not the result of a battle massacre (1897, 300). In contrast, Greenwell's own craniological specialist, Wright, suggested that the remains were the result of a more recent invasion … 'immigrants from the Continent … living in a tribal fashion' (Wright in Greenwell 1906, 323, 314). Mortimer's craniologist, Garson, concluded that the skulls were 'dolichocephalic' in form (Garson in Mortimer 1905a, 30–9) smaller in stature but more uniform in type (or 'racially pure') than the preceding 'mixed community' of the Wolds (Garson in Mortimer 1911b, 314). Comparative analysis with other burials led him to confirm their 'racial kinship' with people buried at Arras and Cowlam (Mortimer 1897; 1898, 125). In short, Mortimer believed he was dealing with a new ethnic group: evidence of an Iron Age invasion.

Ethnicity and artefacts

Mortimer's interpretation of this skeletal analysis cannot be separated from the way in which he viewed the associated material culture. Back in 1847, the translation of Worsaae's work by Thoms held out the promise that a 'history of the earliest state of the European nations' might be achieved 'by means of the antiquities alone' (1849, 328). Yet as Morse has pointed out, the Three Age system of Stone, Bronze and Iron (originally developed by Thomsen) had largely been taken up in Britain by ethnologists interested in organising their cranial specimens into a temporal sequence (2005). It was only in the latter half of the nineteenth century that the value of artefacts began to be appreciated independently of this evidence by individuals such as John Evans, the archaeologist, and Joseph Anderson (Keeper of the Museum of the Society of Antiquaries of Scotland). Anderson used the Rhind lectures to promote the study of the 'culture' of different ages through a study of ornament (1883; 1886, cited in Morse 1999, 13). But although studies of technological and stylistic change were being undertaken, and the first archaeological typologies began to emerge, antiquarians were divided on how to explain such phenomena. As early as 1851, Daniel Wilson had expressed doubt as to whether technological innovation resulted from 'the gradual improvement of the aboriginal race, or by the incursion of foreign tribes' (1851, 144). Wilson was a monogenist (Morse 1999), who was open to the idea of independent development in each race, as well as the possibility of change arising through the intermixing or exchange of peoples and ideas. But he was opposed in these beliefs by the polygenists, such as Robert Knox, who believed in the discrete and limited potential of each race (Giles 2006, 293). Both groups were influenced by the experience of colonialism, and the perceived analogies between the ancient past and contemporary 'primitive' societies who were effectively regarded as being 'stuck' in time, having failed to progress or evolve (see Fabian 1983). Whereas the monogenists believed such races could be encouraged to develop, polygenists had a much more negative attitude towards what they saw as innately inferior colonised peoples, such as Knox's antagonism towards the 'Irish Celts' (Morse 1999, 11). Antiquarians such as Pitt-Rivers therefore believed that a close analysis of material culture could help resolve the 'monogenesis or polygenesis of certain arts: whether they are exotic or indigenous' to the countries in which they were found (cited in Stocking 1971, 386).

Mortimer had access to a large body of material with which he could investigate these issues. Alongside his own collections and those in the possession of Greenwell (from the small square barrow cemetery at Cowlam as well as the Beverley chariot burial), he was a regular visitor to the British Museum, and had seen objects such as the Battersea and Witham shields, Iron Age material from the Christy collection, and some of the original Arras finds, acquired in 1877 and 1880. In addition, he had himself recorded the accidental discovery of an Iron Age burial at Grimthorpe in 1868, which included a decorated scabbard, iron sword and shield fittings. Although he had initially identified it as Anglo-Saxon (Mortimer 1869), by 1905, he had recognised its proper date and affinities, and linked it to other Iron Age sword burials such as North Grimston (1905a), as well as the chariot burials of Arras, Danes Graves and Cawthorn Camps (1905b). By 1911, he could add Pexton Moor as a further example of this rite (Mortimer 1911a).

What did he make of this material? Mortimer had chosen to join the Anthropological Society of London: the splinter group founded by the polygenists, who had broken from the Ethnological Society in 1863. The influence of their model of human progress is evident in his interpretation of the changes in art and technology observed in the horse-gear and chariot technology at Danes Graves. This 'greater advance in mechanical skills and the decorative arts' meant that he was 'strongly not in favour of their independent native origin' (1905a, 354), but instead saw it as 'a somewhat sudden introduction of a higher state of civilisation' (1905a, lxxv). Underlying all of these accounts was an implicit belief in a social evolutionary trajectory: a motif prevalent in most Victorian discourses, drawn in part from biological metaphors which treated society as an 'organism' (Bowler 1989). Drawing on the commonly perceived effects of colonialiam, many archaeologists believed that sudden change could *only* come about through the influence of a superior race which imposed its more developed, civilised ideas upon the conquered nation. Writing in the late nineteenth century, when cremation (as a means of disposing of the body) was being morally contested, Mortimer even saw the Iron Age rite of inhumation itself as a mark of social progress. In sum, he concluded, these burials were the result of:

> invaders of a comparatively recent period, say a few centuries before the Roman occupation of this country ... [because] there seems to be ... too great a leap in advances of ornamentation and the art of working in metals between the barrows containing bronze only and those which contain iron.
>
> 1898, 125–6

Mortimer's opinion again contrasted with that of Greenwell, who believed that:

> no new people had come in with iron, but that acquaintance with and use of this metal were gradually developed amongst an originally bronze-using people, either according to the natural process of improvement characteristic of man, or through knowledge gained by contact and intercourse
>
> 1877, 212.

Greenwell was supported in this conclusion by Boyd Dawkins who also believed that in contrast to other eras, the Iron Age did not represent a racial transition (1880, 496). However, Greenwell's excavations with Mortimer at Danes Graves gave the Canon occasion to slightly revise his ideas. He still believed in some form of population continuity but also appreciated the cultural affinities between art styles and burial rites on the Wolds and those from northern Continental Iron Age Europe. He cautiously concluded:

> The apparatus of war, the instruments and luxuries of ordinary life, even rites of burial, have so often been taken over by one people from others, where there was no relationship by blood that it would be unwise to argue in favour of identity of race upon this basis alone. But on the other hand, unless the evidence to the contrary is abundant and trustworthy, where such things ... are found to be similar in two districts, the presumption is strong that they were in the main occupied by people who were united by the affinity of blood ... the tribe who dwelt in that part of Yorkshire where these cemeteries are situated, may be regarded as kinsmen of that family of Celts who occupied the north-eastern and adjacent part of Gaul, as they were related to some sections of the population of Britain itself.' 1906, 307.

This interpretation was still favoured by R. A. Smith in his 1925 *British Museum Guide to Early Iron Age Antiquities* (1925, 112). Mortimer also argued that that Danes Graves was 'the graveyard of a comparatively well-to-do community of peaceable settlers who had, for a somewhat lengthy period, dwelt near by, a charming spot' (1898, 125) but were derived 'from over the sea' (1911b, 316). In his later publications, he less favourably depicted these peoples as 'squatters, that is waifs and strays from across the ocean ... immigrants from the Continent' (1911a, 51–2), but in general he thought they represented 'a great advance in civilisation' (1911b, 315) compared with the indigenous inhabitants, 'rather than a gradual transition from one stage of culture to the other' (1898, 126). This last phrase is very telling, for by the turn of the twentieth century, the central interest of archaeology was moving away from ethnology and race, towards the paradigm of culture history.

Culture history

The problems associated with trying to identify race on the basis physiological criteria led to its gradual abandonment by archaeologists. However, the belief that humanity evolved through different *social* stages, gradually improving over time, still underpinned early concepts of culture (Jones 1997, 45). The socio-evolutionary anthropologist, Tylor, expressed this as a three-fold development in cultural stages from savage to barbaric and finally civilised life (1888, 269). What was significantly different about this approach was the shift towards the cultural aspects by which such progress might be charted:

> Culture, or civilisation... is that complex whole which includes knowledge, belief, art, morals, law, custom, and any other capabilities and habits acquired by man as a member of society
>
> Tylor 1871, 1

This definition began to direct archaeologists to aspects of behaviour which might be characterised and defined by their material signatures. The further development of conceptualising cultures as distinctly organised and patterned ways of life was introduced through the German concept of *Kulturkreise* (culture circles), developed by Ratzel to describe the distinct 'culture areas' he defined on geographical and ethnological grounds (Jones 1997, 46). It was championed by another anthropologist Frank Boas, who was vehemently opposed to social evolutionism. He saw an alternative method of categorising people not according to a sequence of inevitable cultural stages, but on the basis of 'a plurality of historically conditioned, distinct cultural wholes' (Jones 1997, 46). Boas' work was vital in challenging racially-deterministic models, and he advocated a close-grained, particularist methodology which resulted in ethnographically rich accounts of different groups. He explained these shared systems of belief and common life-ways as the result of both historical conditions and learned social behaviour (Rapport and Overing 2000, 95): a subtle approach which was never fully taken up in archaeological circles of the time. Instead, back in Germany, a school of archaeologists and ethnologists were using Montelius' idea of artefact types to trace the origins, history and geographic distribution of distinctive ethnic groups (Jones 1997, 15). Their most famous proponent was Gustav Kossina, who formalised this notion of distinct 'cultural provinces' on the basis of archaeological type forms. His ideas were taken up by Gordon Childe, who further refined the notion that archaeological culture areas coincided with recognizable peoples or tribes:

> We find certain types of remains – pots, implements, ornaments, burial rites, and house forms – constantly recurring together. Such a complex of associated traits we shall call a 'cultural group' or just a 'culture'. We assume that such a complex is the material expression of what today would be called a people.
>
> Childe 1929, v–vi

Childe's objectives differed notably from the ethnic agenda of Kossina, whose motive was to trace the prehistoric origins of contemporary 'superior' races: work which was later used to justify expansion into their supposed hereditary homelands (Trigger 1989). Unfortunately, such archaeological studies of material culture retained an association with race or ethnicity, long after the techniques of craniology had been discredited (Morse 1999, 14). Despite this, the concept of culture history swiftly gained popularity in British prehistory and remained at the core of its approach to the past until the 1970s.

In Iron Age studies, one of the earliest occurrences of the term was in Cyril Fox's study of the Cambridge region, in which he used two Iron Age type sites from the Continent to distinguish between a 'Hallstatt culture' or 'pre-La Tène iron culture' (1923, 85). However, it was Christopher Hawkes who first attempted to define a long-term cultural sequence for the first millennium BC. In his 1931 version of the 'ABC' model Hawkes did not explicitly use the word 'culture' – for which he apologised in 1959, since this was '[w]hat I meant' (1959, 174). The system was based upon the notion that Britain could be divided into a series of five 'Provinces' whose boundaries were 'physiographically clear' (1959, 172). Hawkes opted not to define these boundaries in detail, referring readers to the topographical detail of the forthcoming Ordnance Survey *Map of Southern Britain in the Iron Age*: not very helpful for those working outside of this core research region! These 'Provinces' could be further subdivided into 'lesser natural divisions' called 'Regions' (*ibid.*):

> These regions seem to me at once the largest and smallest that will contain, consistently with physiographic boundaries, an Iron Age archaeological entity in every case – whether well attested or not.
>
> 1959, 174.

Overlying this geographic framework was the 'A, B and C' system, which stood for 'cultures not periods' (1959, 174). Hawkes did not mean to imply that these were 'ages' nor 'periods' or 'phases' and yet of course, he recognised that they needed to be defined by some sense of chronology. Hence the alphabetical suffix was preceded by terms such as the Iron Age 1 or 'First Iron Age' (*c.*550–350 BC), Iron 2 'Second Iron Age' (*c.*350–150 BC) and Iron 3 'Third Iron Age' (*c.*150 BC to the 'beginnings of Romano-British culture, varying regionally from AD 43/4 onwards', 1959, 174). Thus Hawkes created a grid, with fixed regional and chronological parameters, into which future scholars could place – and subsequently shift or move – the 'manifestation' of particular cultures, as they were recognised in the archaeological record. He literally wanted to 'stitch' cultures onto the 'net of absolute time' (1959, 176). In terms of his understanding of culture change, Hawkes distinguished between what he saw as 'mere infiltration' from 'outright colonisation' (1959, 177). The 'Arras culture' was placed in the 'Eastern Second B', and dated approximately to 300–50 BC. Interestingly, Hawkes suggested that the art and metalwork associated with this period might arise from an 'amalgamated culture': the result of Continental influence *and* internal development (*ibid.*, 179–80).

Hawkes' 'ABC' was driven by 'the need for some common scheme of terminology' in the face of burgeoning settlement and hillfort excavations, and increasingly diverse assemblages of Iron Age material culture (1959, 171). It was thus a way of classifying complex spatial and temporal variation (Trigger 1978, 86). In addition, Hawkes wanted to invent a technical shorthand as distinctive as the Romano-British chronology in which finds were simply related to the period of rule of the Emperor in question: 'Claudian', 'Flavian' etc. (1959, 174). He actually created a complex alpha-numeric system which became increasingly unwieldy as archaeologists debated where and when to place certain cultures, and tried to further sub-divide his categories to fit the entities they believed they were seeing in the material record.

Nevertheless, many Iron Age scholars took up the scheme. In his popular account of *Prehistoric England*, Grahame Clark referred to the 'Iron Age B overlords of East Yorkshire' whom he saw as 'immigrants' (1948, 127). In the same year, the Council for British Archaeology's *Survey and Policy of Field Research in the Archaeology of Great Britain* (whose authors included Piggott and Hawkes) also referred to the dense settlements of these invaders, who had conquered the 'feebler native substratum' (CBA 1948, 46). Hawkes and Hawkes' *Prehistoric Britain* also saw these newcomers to the Yorkshire Wolds as successful colonists:

> La Tène chiefs [who] ruled their followers and the native population with an absolutism that allowed them to maintain more of their Continental habits and standards

> 1958, 127.

Not everyone was happy with Hawkes's scheme: both Daniel and Wheeler had their reservations (cited in Hodson 1960, 138). Strict culture historians such as Hodson objected to the topographical basis of his 'provinces' and 'regions', arguing that culture groups could only be defined on the basis of object type fossils or site types (*ibid.*). A similar emphasis on topography featured in Fox's *Personality of Britain* (1943) in which he divided England into a Lowland and Highland zone. He argued that the nature or 'personality' of the country (determined by soils, weather, topography, climate and natural resources) were primarily responsible for the location and 'success' of different invasions, as well as the subsequent spread of ideas and habits (cultural diffusion) and resulting character of these communities. Whilst on the surface it presented a more subtle and integrated landscape account, it retained an uncomfortable sense of the relationship between ethnicity and land which was redolent of the 'blood and soil' paradigm that had characterised German National Romanticism, and underpinned Nazi ideology ('*blut und boden*'). At best, its environmental determinism foreshadowed some of the problematic models of Iron Age society which will be discussed below. The Yorkshire Wolds, in any case, was seen as fluctuating 'in its allegiance' between the two zones: vulnerable to invasion, as in the case of the Early Iron Age 'B', which was the result of a number of 'irruptions from overseas' (1943, 34). In the case of Eastern Yorkshire, these were 'attributed to the Parisii and culturally related groups' (*ibid.*).

Hodson's ongoing criticism of the 'ABC model' was levelled not at its practicality but its very validity, and he was annoyed by the implication that archaeologists could no longer simply describe a culture group without simultaneously 'announc[ing] its ancestry and affiliations' (1960, 138). He highlighted 'Yorkshire, with its chariot burials' as an example which seemed 'quite distinct culturally and economically' from southern sites, yet was linked to them through the concept of the 'B' culture (*ibid.*, 139). The 1953 guide to

Later Prehistoric Antiquities of the British Isles in the British Museum, dubbed these groups the 'Marnian culture', making their Continental origins explicit (Brailsford 1953, 48). However, true to his culture historical background (and Childe's 1940 outline of British Prehistory) Hodson used the term the 'Arras La Tène culture' in his diagrammatic representation of Iron Age culture groups, based on the key type site (1964, 108, fig. 1). The core of Hodson's seminal 1964 article revolved around the definition of three distinct Iron Age cultures, of which the 'Early Iron Age La Tène group centred on east Yorkshire' was the first, complemented by the 'Late Iron Age … Aylesford Culture', both of which were notable for their Continental affiliations. The rest of Britain was characterised by a whole series of regional groups (based on the analysis of ceramic styles) loosely called the Woodbury culture. This was characterised by the 'type-fossils' of the round house, the bone weaving comb and ring-headed pin (1964, 108). Hodson argued that the considerable '*cultural archaism*' demonstrated in the bulk of the British Iron Age, and its independent, insular features, suggested that these were not, by and large, the result of cultural invasions but rather the product of continuous occupation from the late Bronze Age, which diverged from Continental habits through local 'inventiveness' (*ibid.*, 105, original emphasis). Hodson's ideas were echoed in the work of Clark, who by 1966, had come to believe in the largely indigenous development of later prehistoric peoples. He criticised Hawkes' 'ABC' as being part of an 'invasion neurosis', in which 'A … was in effect defined by 'Halstatt' invasions, the B by the 'Marnian' invasions and the C by the 'Belgic' invasions' (1966, 185). He rejected such histories of the British Isles in which these hypothetical invasions, rather than the archaeological material itself, became the basis of classification (*ibid.*, 173). Underlying this critique however, was a move towards a more insular narrative of British prehistory:

> when all is said, the object of British archaeology is surely to tell us about the lives of the people who, generation by generation, age by age, *in unbroken succession* occupied and shaped the culture of the British Isles.
>
> *ibid*, emphasis added

Where did this leave the Arras culture? In most interpretations, it was excluded from this new narrative of indigenous continuity and self-improvement, and was still seen as evidence of a cultural migration. An interesting qualification of this model is the 1953 account of the exhibits in the British Museum, in which Brailsford (following Childe) explained the contrast between the 'richness' of the chariot equipment and weaponry from East Yorkshire, and the 'rough and poor' ceramic jars that were also found in these burials, as indicating 'the invaders came over without their womenfolk' (1953, 49)! This extremely crude interpretation of the material culture, complete with its assumptions about the gendered nature of craftwork, illustrates the literal way in which culture history was being applied to the artefactual record. In a rather different model of invasion, Piggott argued that the similarity between a group of decorated Irish scabbards and some of those from East Yorkshire (such as Bugthorpe) represented 'the plantation of Ulster by Yorkshire charioteers' (1950, 16), presumably moving on after their successful colonisation of the Wolds! The political implications of such a theory (which could be read as an attempt to naturalise later colonialism and Home Rule through historical precedent) are extraordinary. Fortunately, this theory has been roundly criticised on grounds of date (Harding 2007, 113) though some form of privileged connection between the two regions might still be feasible (Raftery 1994). Clark argued that the appearance of 'exotic' objects in the archaeological record should generally be interpreted as increasing wealth on behalf of native leaders rather than automatically interpreted as the 'signs of replacement by an invading aristocracy' (1966, 188). Yet as even Hodson interpreted the Arras material as an 'unambiguous Iron Age culture of continental type' (1964, 101), Clark also made an exception in this instance:

> The invaders with La Tène culture *for which a reasoned case has been made* ... were the offspring of the Parisi who introduced the Arras culture to East Yorkshire.
>
> Clark 1966, 186, *my emphasis*

It was Hodson's PhD student, Ian Stead, who explored this issue in more detail. In his first review, *The La Tène Cultures of Eastern Yorkshire*, he supported his mentor's approach that cultures should be identified 'by recurring groups of type fossils' (1965, 1). In its companion volume, *The Arras Culture* (1979), he confirmed that this is what he had identified, through both burial and settlement evidence: 'an assemblage of archaeological types regularly associated in a limited area' (*ibid.*, 89). Stead defined this geographic region by topographic features: the North Sea to the east, the Humber to the south, the North Yorkshire moors to the north and the River Ouse to the west (*ibid.*, 89). Yet initially, the culture history paradigm had led him to believe he was dealing with two cultures: a northern suite of 'sword' burials such as North Grimston, and a south-eastern group of square barrows with occasional 'cart' burials, like Arras (1965). By 1979, his own excavations had convinced him that the sword burials were simply a variant on the main rite (probably later Iron Age in date), and he admitted 'what had seemed a clear distinction between two cultures has now been eroded: the material belongs to a single culture, the Arras culture' (Stead 1979, 5). In 1979, he was still prepared to accept an exotic origin for the distinctive burial rite within the context of historically attested movements of Celtic peoples, but by this time, he was at pains to point out its subsequent isolation, independence and divergence from Continental traditions (*ibid.*, 92–3).

Over the 1950s–1960s (particularly in the pages of the Journal *Antiquity*) the debate over the indigenous or invasionary origins of culture groups raged back and forth. Hawkes responded angrily to Clark's critique of his 'ABC' by arguing that 'indigenous evolution' had to be clearly demonstrated (1968, 298). Clark clearly felt that Hawkes was out-of-date and out-of-step with recent thinking: archaeologists should be open to 'alternative explanations for the appearance of exotic traits' (such as cultural diffusionism and trade) and be receptive to the idea of the 'inherent dynamism of economic and social life' (*ibid.*, 299). This was certainly at odds with Childe's original vision, in which cultural distinctiveness was the result of stability and conservativeness in prehistoric life (1956, 8). Arguably, these tensions arose from problems with the very concept of 'culture'.

Culture history assumed that people lived in homogeneous social wholes, bounded in space, adhering to culturally approved norms of behaviour and material practice (Jones 2000), which were handed down through successive generations relatively unchanged. As we have seen, these units were often naturalised by arguing they had distinctive geographical limits. This model of social life was a fallacy. Archaeological cultures were the product of archaeologists identifying patterns in material culture (in time and space) rather than representing any social reality as perceived by those groups (*ibid.*). The question of self-perception lay at the heart of the issue. In 1969, the anthropologist Barth proposed a new approach to ethnicity, which did not rely on the identification of cultural similarity or difference by the analyst, but instead sought to reveal the 'categories of ascription and identification' articulated by the social groups themselves (1969, 10). His ethnographic work had convinced him that there was considerable cultural variability *within* groups, which was often suppressed in accounts of what bound them in common. This variability was negotiated by people who used a variety of symbolic practices to engender a sense of commonality and belonging (work which had much in common with that of Cohen, 1985). The relationship between ethnicity and cultural practice was far from simple or self-evident, Barth argued, partly because it was always embedded in complex economic and political relations that informed the choices of affiliation people made (Jones 2000). These were not fixed but fluid and dynamic: people could change their sense of identity, according to historical circumstance, rather than being determined by it. In other words, people did not live in 'cultures' but rather *acted culturally* (after Ingold 1994, 330). The implications for archaeological studies of identity were far-reaching. By the 1970s, the challenge facing Iron Age archaeologists was to find new ways of understanding these complex social dynamics.

Iron Age societies

The seminal publication of *Iron Age Communities in Britain* by Barry Cunliffe in 1974, altered the terrain of later prehistoric studies. It retained the regional and temporal structure of Hawkes' analysis, as well as the legacy of culture history, in its recognition of 'groups' but acknowledged from the start that patterns of economic exploitation, material culture styles, belief systems, settlement traditions and patterns of trade, constituted 'overlapping systems' (Cunliffe 1978b, xviii). Cunliffe relied on aspects such as pottery, coinage and metalwork to determine 'style zones' whilst settlement, burial and environmental evidence were used to identify 'socio-economic systems'. This resulted in a portrayal of Britain characterised by regional diversity yet bound together through exchange. It is clear from Cunliffe's language that he was influenced by systems theory, which envisaged social and economic organisation, material culture and religious beliefs as interdependent aspects of a complex cultural and environmental whole (Clarke 1968). Each attribute of society was seen as adaptive to change in another part of the system, in order to maintain a dynamic equilibrium. Clarke's conceptualisation of this system is similar to that of an electronic flex, composed of intertwined cables (Giles 2008a, 337). Perhaps this is not surprising, as with the advent of early computerisation, sophisticated methods of data analysis could be used to test different models of human behaviour, and compare them with the archaeological data. However, since the 'system' was supposed to tend towards homeostasis, it became hard to explain processes of change other than through overarching external pressures (such as environmental pressures) or foreign cultural influences. Hence Cunliffe's account of the rise of hillforts in Wessex is set within a model of climatic deterioration, which affected crop yields and grazing regimes, leading to agricultural intensification, soil depletion, and stock/crop pressure (1995a, fig. 41). Coupled with the effects of population growth, he saw competition over resources leading to endemic violence, resulting in centralised, defended settlements (the hillforts), which were maintained through hierarchical social organisation. In contrast, his account of Iron Age East Yorkshire suggests that there was some kind of 'intrusive folk movement', perhaps of small bands, which introduced 'alien' burial traditions to the indigenous communities (1991, 77–78). In the latest edition of *Iron Age Communities*, he argues that the archaeological evidence suggests 'small bands arriving, with little more than their personal equipment, and settling down among the natives… When time came for burial, they maintained their own rituals' (2009, 86). Amongst this broader population, the chariot burials are seen by Cunliffe as a means of distinguishing status by the elite (1991, 503–4).

The change which Cunliffe brought about through his study was to shift the object of analysis away from the culture group to that of society (Giles 2008a, 337). This was a product in part, of the influence of sociology and anthropology, particularly the work of Marshall Sahlins and Elman Service (1965). They had outlined a new social evolutionary scheme, which replaced Tylor's vision of savage-barbaric-civilised life with more specific social formations: band-tribe-chiefdom-state (*ibid.*, 37). Their underlying premise was similar however, arguing that over time, societies tended towards more complex forms of organisation, both economically and politically. Archaeology's task was to characterise the form of society represented in the past, thus identifying successive stages of social evolution. It was commonly believed that by the Iron Age, northern Europe had progressed towards the 'chiefdom' stage of society (Fried 1967; Earle 1978). In his model of this kind of society, Cunliffe proposed that the elite held sway over the labouring client classes through systems of tribute and redistribution (1983). The generation of an economic surplus enabled the growth of a warrior class and religious and craft specialists, who helped fuel high-status competition and rivalry, manifest in displays of fine material culture, gift-giving and ritualised conspicuous consumption – feasting and votive deposition (Frankenstein and Rowlands 1978). This pyramidal vision of Iron Age society was not only attractive (see James' illustration of this model, 1993, 53), it appeared to be supported by both the Roman authors' accounts of Iron Age Gaul and the colourful annals of early Medieval Ireland, complete with stories of chariot races and cattle raids (Cunliffe 1983, 166). Some authors believed the latter literally represented a 'window onto the Iron Age' (Jackson 1964), where the character of society may have survived, culturally untainted by 'the heavy hand of Roman imperialism' (Cunliffe *ibid.*).

This vision of Celtic society remains dominant in both public interpretations of the Iron Age as well as much Continental scholarship (though see critique by Gwilt 1996 of Arnold and Gibson 1995). However, archaeologists working within Britain became increasingly critical of this model, not least because of its neo-social evolutionism, which implied that state formation represented the epitome of historical 'civilisation'. As Fabian has argued, this was a view constructed from the perspective of Western modernity, which regarded alternative forms of social organisation as effectively stuck in the past: labelling such societies as failures since they had not progressed as quickly and successfully as others (1983). Within Britain, scholars experienced problems with finding the archaeological correlates of such chiefdoms, particularly convincing evidence for a landscape hierarchy of central places and client farmsteads, which were tied into an organised system of redistribution (see critique summarised in Hill 1995a, cf. Cunliffe 2000). Alternative models of society were proposed which challenged this evolutionary schema (Hill 1995a; 2006; Sharples 2010), and new studies of hillforts and other forms of settlement indicated they had very different histories of use and meaning, which changed over time (Barrett, Freeman and Woodward 2000; Lock *et al.* 2005). In addition, there were very few instances where there seemed to be any distinction in housing or burial practice, suggesting the existence of a warrior chieftain class. The most recent revision of Wessex during the middle Iron Age depicts a society defined instead by a commitment to community which suppressed individual expressions of prestige (Sharples 2010). Despite this, the material culture associated with the later Iron Age in particular – especially its metalwork – has been taken as evidence of the growth of powerful 'noble classes', 'emergent élites' (James 1999, 92–3) or a 'hierarchical class system' (Pryor 2003, 411) concerned with aristocratic activities such as feasting, horse and chariot-riding, and warfare (Creighton 2000).

In contrast to many other areas of Britain, the middle Iron Age archaeology of Eastern Yorkshire, with its chariot burials and 'rich' grave goods seemed to provide the perfect example of this society, where 'status' or 'social stratification' was being expressed through the burial rite (see Cunliffe 1991, 501–2; James 1993, 102; Pryor 2003, 345). Most recently, Sharples uses the Yorkshire Wolds burials to argue for the existence of an elite culture whose burials 'personify what is felt to be the classic warrior chief', due to the remarkable objects made to be carried or worn by individuals (2010, 242–3). Sharples ideas are worthy of more developed comment (see below), but as he himself notes, they were not simply representations of status, but active ways in which power was constituted (*ibid.*, 245 n. 4). In a critique of early Bronze Age 'rich' burials, Brück further cautions that we cannot assume personhood was premised purely upon individual qualities or abilities, which can be 'read' from a suite of grave goods that directly reflect the identity of the deceased (2004, 310). She has argued that this draws upon a concept of idealised, often androcentric models of Western personhood which laud the notion of the autonomous 'individual' as a discrete, irreducible locus of identity: acting a free agent, with sovereign control over their 'property'. This has led in some archaeological circles to the preference of the term 'personhood' over identity, to avoid its conceptual associations of innate individuality (e.g. Fowler 2004).

This book suggests a rather different account of the East Yorkshire material to the ones outlined above but not one devoid of power or political strife: it is all too evident that social differentiation *is* being expressed and negotiated through the square barrow burials and the elaborate material culture interred within them. Yet our task is to unpick the complex aspects of identity which such differentiation might represent: age, gender, relations with kin and community, leadership and authority, life-history and achievements, or even the manner of people's death. Osteological evidence must be combined with object analysis, evidence for exchange, and the background of domestic life and agricultural labour, if we are to understand the whole picture. As the starting point for much of our evidence is a burial, we need to investigate the motives of mourners in funerary performances and ask how such ceremonies – rites which created new ancestors – might have benefited the status of the living, both socially and spiritually. For if we really want to understand power within these groups we have to investigate the scale at which it operated, the complex series of attributes or achievements upon which it was based, and the social and material conditions through which it was made possible.

These issues will drive the analysis of burials throughout this book. However, for the purposes of this initial review, it can be said that by the turn of the millennium, the entity previously known as the 'Arras culture' was still frequently cited as the best example of a hierarchical Iron Age society, defined culturally by its common burial rite. Archaeologists acknowledged that whilst the majority of these inhabitants were probably indigenous, specific members or parts of these communities might have originated overseas (Pryor 2003, 344; Bradley 2007, 266).

What's in a name? The Arras culture and the tribe of the Parisi

One of the additional reasons why a Continental origin for at least part of these communities seemed so persuasive is that the area apparently defined by the Arras culture was referred to by Ptolemy as being within the territory of the 'Parisi' (Stead 1979, 93). The culture group is therefore naturalised as the antecedent of the late Iron Age tribe (see Harding 2004, 302). It is then assumed that the Parisi must be directly related to the tribe mentioned by Caesar: the 'Parisii', who gave their name to the city and region of north-eastern France in which they lived, supporting the notion of a migration to the Wolds from this area during the middle Iron Age. Additionally, the Yorkshire square barrow cemeteries, with their occasional chariot burials, have parallels with early–middle Iron Age funerary rites found in the Champagne, Ardennes and Middle Rhine areas (Stead 1965; Anthoons 2011). Isn't even the place-name 'Arras' suggestive of further links, passed down orally through the generations?

The methodical work of Ian Stead has addressed each of these ideas in turn. First, he showed how the type-site name of 'Arras' was in fact a recent derivation of earlier Anglo-Saxon words (1979, 7): 'Erghes', becoming 'Ererhes', 'Arows upon the Wolds' and finally, 'Arras' by the sixteenth century (Smith 1937, 230). It therefore had no connection with the modern town in northern France. Second, Ptolemy's *Geographia* (dating to the 2nd century AD) was composed in Alexandria – far from the shores of Eastern Yorkshire – although it was based on a series of first and secondhand accounts dating to the time of the Conquest of Britain. In it he states 'the territory near to the Good Harbour is related to the Parisi whose town is Petuaria' (Ptolemy ii, 3, 10). Petuaria has been identified as modern day Brough-on-Humber: a connection confirmed by a Roman sculptural inscription at this site (Stead 1979, 93), whilst the 'Safe-Haven Bay' as Ramm translated it, probably relates to Bridlington (1978, 22). Ptolemy describes this important coastal feature itself as the Bay of the Gabrantvices, interpreted by Jackson as meaning the 'horse-riding fighters' or 'the cavalrymen' (1948, 57). For Ramm, this was further evidence of a link with the chariot-traditions of the 'Arras culture' (1978, 24), but he also cites Jackson's note that it might be a diminutive name, referring ironically to the 'colts' or 'kid fighters'. Whatever it's meaning, Ramm still saw this sub-group as part of the larger tribe of the Parisi (*ibid.*, 22).

However, as Stead points out, there is a gap of at least four centuries between the naming of these tribes in the early Roman period, and the posited invasion of the 'Arras culture' *c.* fourth century BC. It is currently not possible to demonstrate whether the two tribes (in France and in Britain) shared a common origin, though future isotope studies may assist in this quest. The sharing of a name may be mere coincidence (James 1993, 102): there are, after all, multiple tribes of the 'Brigantes' recorded in both Britain and Gaul yet no direct link is posited here (J. Koch, pers. comm.) We do not even know if this as a self-ascribed term (and if it was, this would be strong evidence for some kind of cultural link) or one imposed by the Romans. It is therefore elucidating to ask what this name may have *meant*. 'Parisi' can be translated as those 'who command', or who 'get things done' (Koch, pers. comm.) and perhaps this descriptive name reflects the experience of the Romans who first encountered this populace in the 1st century AD. It has also been translated as 'the people of the hill' or even 'the spear people' (see Gohil 2006, 158–9) – a name with particular relevance for East Yorkshire's 'speared burial' rite (Anthoons 2011). If this was not self-ascribed, the Romans may have applied this term to a region they were trying to get to know, inhabited by diverse groups of people whom they could swiftly characterise, and who they recognised as sharing affinities with areas on the Continent. Whatever they found (see Giles 2007a), by the time they crossed the Humber in AD 71, the square barrow burial rite had not been practiced for nearly 100 years (Stead 1991, 184).

Iron Age archaeologists have recently argued that the notion of 'tribes' as regional political entities may also have emerged relatively late, during the first century BC (Hill 1995c; Wells 2001). Their scale and political power can be understood as a product of the peculiar historical circumstances surrounding the threat of the Roman invasion, and the consequences and opportunities which both preceded and followed conquest (*ibid.*, Creighton 2000). Interestingly, these tribal names, and those of the chiefs or kings who represented them, were promoted through media such as coinage and sculpture, yet no inscriptions bearing the name 'Parisi' have so far been discovered. We still do not know if it was one that the inhabitants of Arras would have recognised or used to describe themselves in the middle Iron Age.

As for the much-debated issue of the Continental affinities of the square barrow burial rite, Stead's own excavations in the Great Wold Valley (1991, 184) and in the Champagne region (Stead, Flouest and Rigby 2006), as well as his masterful comparative synthesis (1965; 1979), convinced him that there were many subtle but important distinctions. The design of square barrows and the idea of interring chariots or carts had well-established parallels on the Continent but in the Yorkshire Wolds, the vehicle was commonly dis-assembled before it was placed in the ground. The burials were crouched or flexed in East Yorkshire, contrasting with the extended inhumations on the Continent. As Higham put it, this implies that the inhabitants of the Wolds were 'less than fully conversant' with the burial rites which they were supposedly adopting (1987, 5). The distinctive local ceramics bore no relation with their fine Continental counterparts, and even the decorated metalwork was of local manufacture and design, albeit inspired by Continental Celtic art. There were very few examples of direct imports, and even the small pieces of Mediterranean coral seem to have been traded as substances rather than as part of finished items. In sum, Stead concluded that although there had been a clear exchange of ideas which had a powerful effect upon the 'religious life of a tightly defined community', this might have been introduced by a powerful, wealthy minority, 'adventurers, mercenaries … or a few farmers' (Stead 1979, 93) or even a 'well-connected evangelist' (Stead 1991, 184). They need not have been rulers, he argued, but their ideas were influential (Stead 1979, 93). Harding echoes this interpretation, arguing for 'the adoption by the ruling power of innovative cult practices' introduced by 'missionaries' whose interests lay in the 'ritual disposal of the dead' (2004, 36). Both interpretations arguably owe a debt to Hawkes (1940, 211) and Childe's model of Neolithic 'megalithic missionaries' (1958, 129), in turn inspired by the phenomenon of early Celtic Christian missions.

More recently, Cunliffe has posited an alternative model, in which the local East Yorkshire elite sought to emulate 'exotic' Continental fashions, as a means of distinguishing themselves at home, and enhancing their status (1995b, 48). James saw this association with the Continent (represented by their use of Celtic art) as vital to an emerging social elite who sought to 'join the wider political and cultural circle of their peers, with whom they allied, intermarried and fought', adopting the 'ideology and lifestyle of established aristocracies in neighbouring regions' (1993, 92). The use of Continental style customs and artefacts was a way of promoting their membership of this 'international aristocracy' (*ibid.*, 92–3). Higham argues that the exchange of slaves and raw materials initially secured their access to such exotica, but that it was 'returning mercenaries or warriors' who adopted and brought back novel sepulchral customs, in order to display their foreign contacts and ensure political dominance in the broader region (1987, 5).

Most authors now agree that there was no large-scale invasion into the region (Cunliffe 1995b, 22, though see Pryor 2003, 344). However, the movement of ideas (both funerary and artistic), as well as the exchange of some objects and substances, does imply some contact with the Continent. How frequent this was, who it involved, and what it meant, will be discussed later. What is evident from the above historical review is that the Iron Age of Eastern Yorkshire has played a pivotal role in constructing ideas about prehistoric race, ethnicity, culture and society, throughout the nineteenth and twentieth centuries, precisely because of its curious mix of local and exotic features. The task facing archaeologists today is to ask whether such approaches to identity – with their inherent focus on questions of cultural origin and affiliation, and implicit assumptions about the nature of hierarchical 'Celtic' society – are actually sufficient ways of *understanding* these communities. If not, what might an alternative approach look like?

Relational approaches to identity, landscape and material culture

Critique

In the antiquarian, culture historical and social evolutionary models, identity was conceptualised as something innate: inherited by virtue of bloodline and birthplace. What people did, and how they did it, was an expression of an identity which was already fully formed and fixed: whether through the inheritance of innate racial potential and physical form, conservative cultural practices, prescribed ethnic traits, or even stage of social evolution they had reached. Ingold has called this the 'genealogical' model of identity (2000a, 136). The implication is that the essential components of 'who we are', are handed on from our progenitors, rather than arising from our place in the world (*ibid.*, 135). It is an approach which fosters the idea that people's efforts and actions during their lifetime had little bearing on their identity, the essential aspects of which were already prescribed by the past.

As we have seen, archaeologists have therefore tended to focus on the key attributes which distinguish such groups – a burial rite, a distinctive type of pottery – rather than exploring what binds them in common with other people. Such characteristics assume an exaggerated importance in our accounts, as the defining factor which separates them from others and indicates their 'stage' of social evolution. In the process, we flatten any sense of internal diversity within a region. We forget to ask how similarities and differences were reproduced and what they actually meant, in terms of peoples' day-to-day perception of themselves. The way that archaeologists in the 1930s–50s represented these communities was through the 'culture map': illustrating the distribution of type sites or key object styles. They compared these with natural features or supposed tribal zones to identify the territorial edges of these groups. New discoveries challenged such boundaries, such as the Ferry Fryston chariot burial, found in West Yorkshire in 2003, which had to be presented as a cultural 'outlier' of the Arras tradition (Harding 2004, 36) – related to or associated with the Eastern Yorkshire population (Boyle *et al.* 2007, 154). Do we need to endlessly redraw the maps, or think differently about identity?

Agency and structure: a theory of practice

The key problem with many of the above approaches is that they lack any concept of human agency: a sense that people's identity was affected by what they *did* over the course of their lives, both daily actions and long-term projects (see Barrett 1994). I am therefore arguing against a determinist view of humanity, in which identity is believed to be controlled by external factors such as race or culture, or processes like social evolution. I would argue that identity is not something you simply 'have' or 'are', but is constituted through what you do in the world (Giles 2007c, 105). Identity is a matter of practice: it takes work – the work of living in the world with other human beings, animals, plants, places and objects. Even the body we are born with, and which grows and develops partly according to a genetic inheritance, is framed and understood within this social context.

In place of a determinist view of history and identity, many archaeologists have drawn upon Anthony Giddens' concept of the duality of structure and agency (1984). His theory of structuration has proved attractive because it insists that it is here – within people's ongoing actions – that broader social institutions (political entities, social principles, systems of religious belief etc.) are reproduced: they have no reality outside of human practice. John Barrett in particular (1994; Barrett, Freeman and Woodward 2000; also see Barrett and Fewster 2000) has applied these ideas to prehistoric and Roman case studies. Agency is not the 'free will' of the individual to act in any way they please but rather, it describes an agent's capabilities for action, given the circumstances in which they live (Giddens 1984, 9). Following on from this, a key principle in Barrett's work is the idea that archaeological material culture is not a mere residue of past action but rather represents the very conditions *of* that action: both constraining and enabling human practice (Barrett 1999b). These conditions are historically specific. In this, he follows the important Marxist tenet that people make their own history but not in the circumstances of their own choosing. Importantly, these conditions are not simply material but also social, so we must explore the web of their social relationships, in order to analyse how people acted under both sets of affordances and constraints. Structuration theory is also valued because it has given archaeologists a way of understanding how social transformation might happen, without resorting to explanations of external stimuli. It argues that agents who are struggling to deal with novel situations, unforeseen events or the unintended consequences of previous actions, will 'improvise', based on their knowledge and experience, within a series of cultural rules (Taylor 1993) resulting in unique solutions. This is what might be called a 'generative model' of social life (Fajans 1985, 368, LiPuma 1988, 220).

This brief review of agency thus suggests that if we want to understand how social institutions are reproduced *and* transformed, archaeological analysis should be located in the intimate, micro-scale of social action. The sociologist and anthropologist Pierre Bourdieu's work on practice has been helpful here (1977). He has used the concept of the *habitus* to describe how durable dispositions – ways of acting in the world – and the deeply held principles upon which they are based, are subconsciously embodied as people grow up within particular societies, to re-emerge as people improvise in daily life. He suggests that social action is for the most part carried out in a 'practically conscious' way, emerging from the orientated and skilled body, in a series of habituated dispositions, habits and gestures (bodily *hexis*). Quite simply, people act in certain ways because it feels right or appropriate. When they make a mistake or commit a social *faux pas*, they are corrected or criticised, and the background world of cultural rules or norms is thrown into sharper relief. This world may also be revealed more explicitly in ceremonies or rituals which aim to disclose the way things are. Bourdieu's theory of practice is useful because he directs us towards both the day-to-day conditions and extraordinary events in which certain kinds of identity and knowledge are reproduced, through the lens of interactions with material objects. Like Giddens, he stresses that social institutions do not govern human actions but are reproduced in social practice.

Both of these approaches have proved influential in interpretive or social archaeology: part of the post-processual paradigm in British archaeology (Hodder *et al.* 1995, Thomas 2000). However, there are issues arising from the use of Giddens' structuration theory in prehistoric archaeology. Since it was developed by sociologists examining action within advanced capitalist societies, it has little to say about non-Western or small-scale, prehistoric societies, which are largely set up as a foil to contemporary modernity. Its dominant paradigm is arguably economic, and Giddens' analysis focuses on the control over both authoritative resources (human actors and persons) and allocative resources (material, technological). There are two key problems with this. First, an over-riding concern in Giddens' work is the theme of socio-politics and the conditions in which power is reproduced and transformed. Power as a human motivation also features strongly in the work of those who employ Giddens' theoretical approaches, particularly Barrett. Second, in Giddens' work, human and non-human agents are held apart as conceptually distinct objects of analysis. Using anthropological analogies, I want to question whether such views need to be modified to deal with the analysis of small-scale, prehistoric agricultural communities.

Affective sociality: a relational approach to identity

Archaeologists inevitably use ethnographic analogy to interpret the past, and it is incumbent upon us to be explicit about our sources, selecting those which are similar in some respects (such as social form and organisation) to the example we seek to interpret, whilst not expecting them to map 'like-for-like' in all respects (the difference between formal and relational analogy: Wylie 1985). Whilst Iron Age archaeologists have drawn widely on analogies with African society, or the early medieval Celtic societies of Ireland, recent studies of Amazonian and North American Indian tribes can also be elucidating. In an edited volume, Overing and Passes use this ethnographic material to suggest that for the most part, life in such small-scale communities is focused on learning how to 'live well' with other people (2000, 2), and to 'live right' in the landscape which they inhabit (see Basso 1996). This is the task of affective sociality (Overing and Passes 2000, 2–3): of learning how to belong with others and act as an affective agent in the world. It is a consuming concern because it is ongoing and difficult: the risk of social failure, misunderstanding and loss of face, are high. Other people are not only supportive and generous but capricious, jealous and competitive. Such competition may take many different forms, in diverse arenas: exchange, martial display and combat, conspicuous consumption of resources including labour (see Sharples 2010). Yet through these events, individuals often strive to maintain a tranquil, 'good/beautiful' life, acting appropriately and compassionately towards others (Overing and Passes 2000, 2). This is the all-too neglected 'solidary labour' as Lynch describes it, of pastoral care and love (1989): the labour of creating houses and settlements, tending bodies through feeding or nursing – even the labour of grief – through which people are inculcated into being a proper member of a family or community. It is not an area which receives much attention in Iron Age literature, though Barrett (2000) and Sharples (2010) are notable exceptions. My interest in these social relations undoubtedly relates to the impact of feminist archaeology on what is – and is not – considered a valid topic of discourse, particularly in later prehistory, where themes such as artistic creativity or warfare and violence, traditionally dominate.

Without doubt, as people seek to distinguish themselves within a broader community – defining who is in and who is not, patrolling the boundaries of belonging and behaviour, and competing for power and renown – violence can often arise. Unlike the classical authors keen to legitimise their conquering of a martial race, we need not attribute to this to an innate blood-lust. Bellicosity can be a strategic socio-political trope (Harrell 2009) whilst anger itself can be understood as a corollary of love, where it is necessary to inflict revenge on the behalf of humiliated family or community members (Alès 2000). Yet these actions are framed by social codes – by what it deemed socially acceptable or inappropriate even in moments of violence, and we should be interested in the exact form they take. Amongst the societies they studied, Overing and Passes note that 'hate, greed and jealousy' are often seen as potentially destructive: emotions which must be carefully managed lest they jeopardise the delicate balance of social relations (2000, 3).

I find these ethnographic analogies useful because they address communities of a similar scale to those of later prehistoric East Yorkshire, who also spend a large proportion of their time gardening or cultivating as well as herding and hunting. Such activities inevitably create tensions over relations as well as resources, both within and between communities. The notion of 'conviviality' as a key motivation in social relations therefore provides an important counterbalance to Giddens' focus on power, without diminishing peoples' capacity for acts of negative, as well as positive, reciprocity.

Vitally, this approach presupposes that identity is a relational attribute (Brück 2004), and is irreducibly social and inter-subjective: that people always act *in mind of* others. It contrasts greatly with notions of the 'autonomous, self-animated, and self-enclosed agent' (LiPuma 1998, 54): the individual defined in terms of its relationship with society, which lies at the heart of Western concepts of personhood (Strathern 1988; Brück 2004). As Fowler argues, this rather fictional notion of the individual (which was integral to the successful working of capitalist states) was increasingly fostered in the Historic period through economic and legal structures, and particular 'technologies of the self' (after Foucault and others): portraiture, journals, headstones, private possessions and wills (Fowler 2004, 13). But the discrete 'individual' was itself an *ideological*, even mythologized construct (LiPuma 1998, 54). Sociologists and anthropologists have countered that interpersonal connections provide the basis of personhood in most societies (Busby 1997; Carsten 2000; Fajans 1985; Finch and Mason 2000; Ito 1985; LiPuma 1998; Strathern 1988).

Relational approaches to identity argue instead that personhood unfolds as a process of growth and maturation, within a field of social relations in which the individual is constantly positioned with respect to other beings (Ingold 2000b, 3). These positions are shot through with issues of knowledge, experience and power which must also be negotiated (Barrett 1994), both the hierarchical tensions of rank and status, as well as more horizontal relations of kinship, gender, age-set and skill (Morgan 1996). Relations shape experience and inform encounters, providing a particular perspective on the world (Fowler 2004, 20).

They influence peoples' ability – and propensity – to act towards others in particular ways, giving personhood its particular character or hue (*ibid.*, 9). Identity is therefore comparative: emerging through this constant dialectic of similarity and difference (Jenkins 1996); relatedness and differentiation (Myers 1991).

Models of personhood

There are different models of relational identity, ranging from extreme examples of 'dividual' or 'partible' personhood in Melanesian (e.g. Strathern 1988) to the permeable persons of India (e.g. Busby 1997; see Fowler 2004 for a useful summary of case studies and examples). Dividuals are conceived of as composite and multiply authored beings, who owe parts of themselves to others – these attributes are therefore 'partible' and can be extracted or exchanged. In contrast, permeable people are conceived of as having a stable core of attributes, but are osmotic: able to be permeated by qualities that influence their internal composition, composed of (and in turn, emitting) flows of substances (e.g. Busby 1997).

However, LiPuma has argued that all cultures possess 'both individual and dividual modalities or aspects of personhood' (1998, 56). There is always the bodily locus of action, which inherits certain traits and accrues a personal biography across time, just as there is the common recognition that these bodies, and their histories, are the product of interwoven relations. The important implication of this is that identity can never be reduced *entirely* to someone's relations, since individual intention, memories and desires inevitably shape an agent's actions. Successful relations may require partnerships but they can be both initiated and terminated by the individual. Thus, LiPuma argues *'persons emerge precisely from that tension between dividual and individual aspects/relations'* (1998, 57, original emphasis). Different cultures place different emphasis upon the degree to which aspects of relationality or individuality are expressed and sanctioned.

This relational model of personhood also challenges the notion that people are composed of biogenetic substance (inherited from one's genealogical forebears) overlain by the cultural traits of that community (Ingold 2000a, 133). Instead, the body is itself seen as composed of contributive exchanges of substance, nurture, care and education (Battaglia 1990; Strathern 1988; Barth 2002). From conception, people are literally 'grown' through these material and social transactions (Fowler 2004, 160; Finch and Mason 2000, 164), into particular ways of acting, perceiving, knowing and moving (Ingold 2000a). Categories such as gender are learned *through* the body: there is no other way of experiencing, reproducing and even transforming such attributes but through the repetition of embodied performances (Butler 1993).

Relations with non-humans

Social bonds can be made with animals as well as people, who can be accorded
both personality and agency, and may personify or be associated with spirits or
ancestors (Morris 2000). Differences between domestic and wild species or those
who dwell closely with humans, aspects of behaviour or the affordances they
offer to people, can lead to their categorisation in different ways. Other kinds
of organisms such as plants and trees, even bodies of water or distinctive rock
outcrops may also be perceived as animate: having histories and characters, and
harbouring benign or malevolent intentions towards their human and animal
co-habitants (Bird-David 1999). Some of these beings do not necessarily dwell
in the same world nor even in the same time as people: spirits and ancestors
are also vital to this skein of relations.

In addition, people establish long-term relationships with objects which they
may accord agency due to their complex history or 'biography' (Kopytoff 1986),
the conditions they impose on the user (Gosden 2005) or their perceived force
or powers (Giles 2008b). Objects are never mere symbols of identity but extend
personhood and agency, enabling action and 'making' certain kinds of people
(Scarry 1985). They may embody stories or aspects of the self, and are drawn
upon to 'tell' past events or evidence personal skills (Hoskins 1998). They can
also 'shape' the very body we live in, through our dress and accoutrements;
the handling of certain implements and tools, or even weapons (Gowland and
Knüsel 2006). In contrast to Giddens' analytical separation of human from
material resources, Latour regards this relationship of human and non-human
'hybrids' as a messy, material amalgam through which 'people-things' are made
(1993). More radically, Clark has suggested that the material world is encountered
in such a way that it 'scaffolds' the very development of an embodied mind:
encouraging the making of cognitive connections as it simultaneously engenders
the development of particular muscle groups and gestural skills (1997). Brain,
body and world 'collide' in Clark's vision of 'wetware' cognition, extended
through the 'wideware' of bodily interaction with external media, shaped by
and shaping the context or environment of that action (2008).

The material world is not restricted to portable artefacts however: spaces
become places through their meaningful inhabitation and modification by
social agents (Casey 1996). They, in turn, shape the people who inhabit them,
both psychologically and physically, as the terrain of a place – its topography,
pathways and forms of transport – influence posture, rhythm and gait (Ingold
2000a) whilst the atmosphere and architecture of places colour experiences and
encounters (Bachelard 1994 [1958]). Some cultures believe that this bond with
place is literally ingested through the consumption of food and drink grown in
the landscape, or absorbed through contact with land and its mineral substances
(LiPuma 1988). Other groups place more emphasis upon an intimate knowledge
of place as the means by which these relationships are formed (Layton 1995).
As a result, places gain identities and stories, as memories are attached to the

locales in which meaningful events occur (Basso 1984). Landscapes therefore influence the very web of social ties which are possible at any one time (Barrett 1999a; Edmonds 1999).

These anthropological studies remind us that non-human beings (animals, plants and material objects, even places) are not mere 'resources': anything that can be perceived to grow and develop, and have an affect upon people, can be conceptualised as an active agent (Bird-David 1999, Ingold 2000a and b). It is important for us to realise that ancient people may well have thought in this way too.

The contextual nature of identity

The above analogies provide us with a series of relationships we can explore in the past. However, identities should not be thought of as 'fixed'. As people grow and develop, so too does their sense of personhood (Ingold 2000a, 144). Identity is therefore an ongoing project – multiple and fluid – which shifts according to what one is doing, where and with whom. It is contextual. This provides us with a methodology for examining how senses of identity might have shifted according to place, task and the co-presence of others (Edmonds 1999). Not even death freezes the picture, Jenkins cautions: 'there is always the possibility of a post-mortem revision of identity' (1996, 4).

Bourdieu's theories of practice may suggest that for the most part identity is not the subject of continuous reflection and concern, but there would have been countless instances where it was thrown into sharper relief: a moment of social ineptitude or remembered tensions, the meeting of strangers or distant contacts, and rites of passage where identities were transformed. Bubbling under the surface of everyday life was this continuous struggle to make oneself intelligible to others: to 'fit in' and 'belong' (Cohen 1982). Butler has described this process of identity as a frail and vulnerable business (1999). In these Iron Age communities, the most mundane of acts would have been subject to the sharp scrutiny of other kin and neighbours, who were assessing how you shaped up to who you were supposed to be: whether you lived your life in a 'convivial' manner or could be relied upon to extract a vendetta if the need arose (Overing and Passes 2000). Using Goffman's metaphor of social life as a play or performance, such 'face-work' was risky and had to be carefully stage-managed, as people negotiated their multiple roles in different contexts (1969; 1999). The costs (of doing right by others, giving gifts, hosting events, even taking revenge) were considerable, but as we shall see, the benefits (of gaining security, status and honour) evidently made it worthwhile.

Concepts of identity are not only situationally and culturally specific but also historical. All people are born into specific communities, at a particular time in history, from which they attempt to make sense of the world around them. At any one time, the nature and intensity of relations between neighbouring settlements or valley systems, across regions, or even with distant communities on the Continent, varied considerably. I am therefore interested in the particular temporal character of these relations, since as Ingold suggests: 'there is no way of describing what human beings *are* independently of the manifold historical and environmental circumstances in which they *become* – in which they grow up and live out their lives' (2004, 215). It is thus important to explore how transformations in social relationships were caught up in broader changes of these social, material and environmental conditions.

Summary

In the rest of this book I will explore how people's sense of personhood arises not simply through their own discrete capacities but through the web of social ties and material relations in which they are emplaced. In Brück's eloquent words 'it is people's relationships … that make them what they are' (2004, 311). I will explore the character, composition and scale of these relationships through the coming together of people and materials, in social projects. In other words, any artefact (a linear earthwork or roundhouse, a human body, sword or a chariot) can be seen as the outcome of transactions and exchanges which 'implode' within it. Composite objects, made of a variety of materials and through numerous skilled hands, offer particularly rich insights into this web of relations: both near and far, past and present.

I use the metaphor of a 'web' advisedly, as geographers, sociologists and anthropologists have become increasingly sceptical of the idea of relational 'networks' (Hetherington and Law 2000; Ingold 2008). As used in Actor-Network Theory, relations are envisaged as mere connections – lacking any material presence – in a network in which agency is distributed across human and non-human actants (*ibid.*). In contrast, the description of relational identity as a web stresses how relations are 'spun from' the very substance of agents, providing a set of material conditions under which connections can be established (Ingold 2000a). These knotted threads or 'meshwork' provide a series of material affordances: the very grounds for the possibility of interaction (*ibid.*). As a craft metaphor it also captures the material aspect of making relations, through a technology which was central to identity and appearance amongst these communities.

In order to examine such relational webs, and reveal contrasting aspects of people's sense of identity, we have to analyse different contexts of social life. Put simply, I am interested in where people were working, what task they were engaged in, and with whom. The rest of the book is therefore divided up into a series of chapters, each focused on a particular arena of social life. Chapter 2 examines the way in which the landscape was inhabited and defined, and how potentially contentious transformations were negotiated through relationships with the 'mythical' monuments of the earlier prehistoric past. It focuses on the linear earthworks of the Wolds, and explores what these might tell us about the scale of communities involved in their construction, as well as implications for the organisation of agriculture and pastoralism. Chapter 3 focuses on the making of places: exploring how both settlement and cemetery architecture were used to structure particular scales of domestic residence and concepts of belonging, constituted through memory and genealogy. It also questions what the close spatial relationship between the living and the dead might mean, in terms of the role of an ancestral community.

In Chapter 4, attention turns to the detailed demographic information from the cemeteries, to explore the composition of the community: what did people look like, what kinds of lives did they live, and what threatened their well-being? The skeletal evidence is used to explore aspects of origin, diet, disease and injury, but this is tempered in Chapter 5, by a consideration of patterns of relations between people and grave goods. This part of the book critiques the notion that objects can be used simplistically to 'read' the identity and status of the deceased, exploring instead the complex intersection of meanings which things can represent. Grave goods help negotiate death, as metaphors for relations and aspects of personhood, heirlooms, gifts or powerful equipment for the afterlife. By exploding them outwards into their web of relations, the 'craftscape' of exchange and skilled production is revealed, whilst their biography is also explored through tracing aspects of wear and repair. Patterns of grave goods, as well as the treatment of the body and funerary monuments, are used to explore the subtle differences in practice which distinguished family groups or valley systems, as well as the shared beliefs which bound them into a larger sense of community.

Chapter 6 focuses in detail on social performance: small-scale and daily acts of domestic and agricultural labour, occasional events of craftwork and exchange, as well as more spectacular ceremonies such as funerals. By exploring how settings and objects became partners in performance, it reveals the material and social conditions in which power was reproduced, as well as the multiple aspects of identity and life-history upon which authority was based. Of course, such power was predicated upon access to both knowledge and materials, and in Chapter 7, the notion of journeying is explored through the exchange of substances, ideas and people. It examines what contact with distant places might have meant, and how exotica were used to potent effect amongst these small-scale communities. It also explores the consequences of interactions with others, through the theme of violence. The chapter argues that death itself may have been understood as a journey, structured through the careful location of the dead by trackways and streams. Chapter 8 reflects back on the three themes of the book: landscape, identity and material culture, through the place of the chariot in Iron Age East Yorkshire. It uses this object to pick apart the social web of relations through which these communities were defined, to explain how such vehicles attained their special significance as exemplars of success, honour and prestige.

CHAPTER TWO

History Making: Linear Earthworks in the Landscape

Introduction: beating the bounds

In 1721, a party beating the bounds of the parish of Kilham 'came nigh the Danes Graves in Driffield field' (Kilham Parish Register: 15 May 1721 – cited in Mortimer 1899, 287). This extensive square barrow cemetery – originally numbering over 500 barrows (Greenwell 1865, 108, n. 7) – was located at the junction of the parishes of Driffield, Kilham and Nafferton (Stead 1979, 16). It made an obvious feature for the later medieval villages to utilise as both the edge of their parish boundary, and as a meeting point between groups. For centuries, pathways to the site had been marked from all directions, by long stretches of linear earthworks, coalescing on the cemetery, but by the eighteenth century, at least some of them had been flattened or ploughed out. In this period of agricultural improvement (Harris 1961; 1996) it was provident to check what one's neighbours had been up to: the 'beating of the bounds' (usually conducted around Rogationtide, culminating in Ascension Day – 40 days after Easter Sunday) provided just such an opportunity. Whilst this custom may have had early medieval origins, by the eighteenth century it involved a perambulation of the parish boundaries every few years, by religious and secular leaders (Thompson 1991, 98). The circuit of distinctive features, which might include boundary stones, well-known trees, hedgerows and springs or streams, was often 'beaten out' using long wands, rods or staffs. Its purpose was to remember and re-establish the limits of the parish, and thus the boundaries of its rights and responsibilities. Ale was drunk, cakes were eaten, and hymns or folk songs sung. Such social gatherings helped consolidate community identity and its ties to the land, and prayers were directed towards the fertility of the soil and protection against foes or ills. The group was often accompanied by young children who might be beaten or whipped; 'bumped' against styles and stones; or dunked in a pertinent stream or ditch, so that knowledge of these boundaries was vividly and memorably embodied (Hammerton 1931, 219; Thompson 1991, 98 n. 3). From Kilham that morning, rode out the 'Vicar and twenty horsemen' (Mortimer 1897, 287). What made their perambulation particularly distinctive was their decision not just to circuit the barrow cemetery but 'out of curiosity … [to cause] a man to dig in one of the said graves' (Mortimer 1899, 287), discovering 'a large thigh bone, one leg bone, and one skull of no extraordinary size' (*ibid.*). In the context of this rite, their mere 'curiosity' may have concealed a deeper motive: to exhume and witness one of the ancient forebears of their land.

This is the earliest recorded excavation of an Iron Age square barrow, and the circumstances of their investigation bring together a number of key themes which will be explored in this chapter – the role and purpose of boundaries, the claims they made upon certain ancient or natural features, and the 'stories' or rather 'histories' that were being told about the relationship between people and place. The role of the ancient dead in these narratives (as the Kilham boundary-beaters' own excavation suggests) was key. Boundary beating persisted into the eighteenth and nineteenth century partly due to its vital social function but also due to a lack of accurate maps. Yet as these parishioners knew, maps alone would not suffice: they were two-dimensional, and represented things not as they were seen in everyday life but from an aerial view. In order to verify their nature and upkeep, such boundaries had to be walked, ridden and beaten: felt in the sole of the foot and (for the unfortunate youngsters) the bumps and bruises earned during this rite of passage. In a similar vein, if we are interested in what prehistoric boundaries mean, we should also approach them at the scale at which they were built and inhabited. This is a challenge for archaeologists when they are used to trying to make sense of large-scale earthworks at the landscape scale, as with transcriptions of aerial photographs. In the Yorkshire Wolds, the aerial mapping of these linear features was carried out as part of Cathy Stoertz's survey for the RCHME and published in 1997. Drawing extensively on this seminal work, the challenge of this chapter is to understand what these patterns meant on the ground.

Whilst some features survive as upstanding banks and ditches, many were ploughed out in the nineteenth and early twentieth centuries (as Mortimer noted in a letter dated 1866, cited in Giles 2006, 281). Yet antiquarians such as Maule Cole and Mortimer described, recorded and excavated them, and later research and developer-funded excavations have provided further insights into the methods of construction. This range of sources enable us to investigate their date, character and use, so that we can begin to interpret how the long-term division of the landscape during the first millennium BC reworked social relationships and rights of place.

Constructing relations, making histories

Character

The linear earthworks known locally as 'dykes' include single bank and ditch features, double and triple bank and ditch alignments, and occasionally as at Huggate (on the western side of the Wolds) multiple, parallel series of banks and ditches. Many of these features began life as pit alignments, and in some cases (as near Thwing), these form 'runs' of more permeable boundaries in between lengths of bank and ditch. Many of these dykes are discontinuous, and others have obvious entrances or gaps along their length, as if guiding movement towards particular entries and exits. This led Stoertz to suggest that the linears may be primarily 'boundary markers, rather than … physical barriers' (1997, 62). Some are short in length though others (such as the Great Wold Dyke)

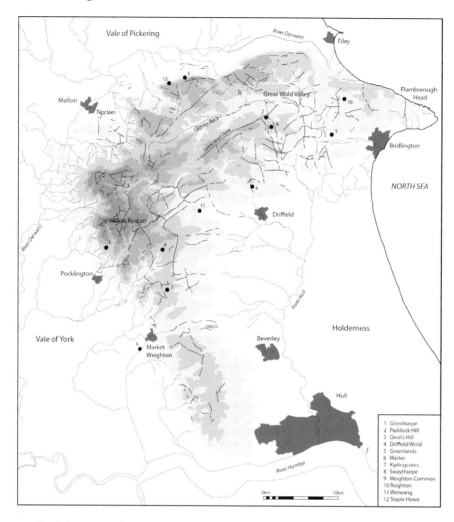

FIGURE 2.1. Linear earthworks and late Bronze Age/early Iron Age enclosed sites on the Yorkshire Wolds. Based on Stoertz 1997, 42, fig. 20 and 1997, 64, fig. 33.

run for kilometres (Figure 2.1). Yet as we shall see, their apparent coherency as organised 'systems' may be deceptive.

Their size and shape, even in Mortimer's lifetime, was impressive. His trench across an earthwork ditch at Fimber found it to be 7 foot (2.13 m) in depth and 'v-shape' in profile: narrowing from 14 foot (4.27 m) wide at the top to a mere 7 inches (178 mm) in diameter at its base. Upstanding lengths of bank preserved in woodland (as at Aldro) reach several metres in height (Stoertz 1997, 40). Yet aerial photographs reveal considerable variety in the scale and complexity of these linear features. At Huggate, the parallel row of six banks and ditches runs across a narrow neck of land between the heads of two deep valleys, marking the watershed. They terminate to the east at a point where a ridge-way track crosses the neck. It is a stunning and impressive location, but the multiplication of monumentality is unnecessary. This is a show: a show of exertion and labour, re-sculpting this key crossing point. At Vicarage Closes, Burton Fleming meanwhile (Figure 2.2), a broad linear earthwork runs across

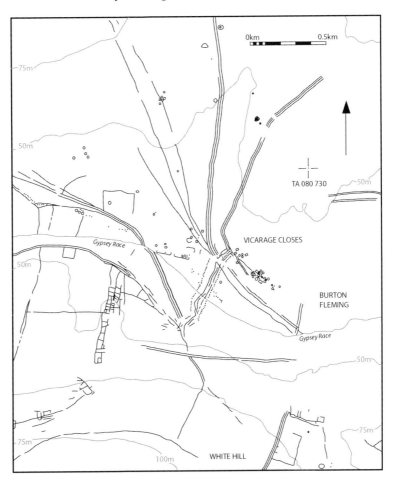

FIGURE 2.2. Linear earthworks at Vicarage Closes. Based on Stoertz 1997, 76, fig. 41.

the base of a valley, and thus across the course of the Gypsey Race stream and its floodzone (Stoertz 1997, fig. 22 and 40, see also chapter 7). It is flanked to the east by two lengths of finer parallel earthworks, and a series of pit alignments. Another pit alignment flanks it to the west. Running down towards this complex, from the north, the north-west, west and south, are a series of medium-sized parallel strands of multiple dykes, as if channelling movement from the higher lands, down into the valley base. Here, the impressiveness derives from the complexity of the different features, spread out across a broad valley to encompass those coming from multiple directions.

As these two sketches indicate, there is considerable variety in the relationship of these dykes to the local topography, not least since the region of Eastern Yorkshire is itself so diverse. In her study, Cathy Stoertz distinguishes between two main zones:

- The High Wolds: characterised by deep, steep 'dry' valleys – here, the linear earthworks tend to cut the chalk plateaus into fairly large zones; the dykes run along the upper edge of valleys and across ridges, with multiple 'runs' of linear earthworks dividing or converging on key points

- The Southern and Eastern Wolds: characterised by more rolling, open 'slacks' – here, the linears are less interrupted by the topography and run for longer lengths (some, for many kilometres)

John Dent further distinguishes between different types of earthwork (2010). Cross-ridge dykes concentrate at the heads of tributary dales (as found in the Great Wold Valley or the Great Slack) and he considers these as both marker points and barriers which restrict movement along the ridge way, which is itself often further marked by another dyke (*ibid.*, 31). Then there are the shorter, simpler lengths of single dykes which he suggests functioned as 'route-way' markers rather than continuous boundaries, and guided people or kept stock from straying into localised areas of cultivation (*ibid.*, 32). Finally, there are the longer range dykes which – he argues – represent a broader vision or sense of design, running parallel to the topography. Dent notes that whilst many of these are punctuated by gaps, their general purpose seems to have been to prevent free movement across the watershed (*ibid.*, 33). To Dent's typology we may add the phenomenon of overlapping or 'braided' earthworks (especially where they run through late Iron Age/early Roman 'ladder' or 'droveway' enclosures) which are probably the result of shifting hollow-ways: trodden, rutted and reworked over many generations (Stoertz 1997). In sum, the exact form and use of these earthworks would vary according to their location and proximity to settlements, fields and routeways.

Date

Our knowledge of when the linear earthworks began to be constructed has grown in recent years, thanks to the impact of developer-funded archaeology, alongside the results of generations of antiquarian and research activity. John Mortimer noted how they respected many round barrows, such as Aldro 88 and 256, which date to the early Bronze Age (1905a). Sherds of re-deposited early Bronze Age pottery have been found incorporated into earthworks at Wharram Percy (Mortimer 1905a, 50) and near the Sykes Monument at Sledmere (Manby 1980, 327). A fingertipped bowl at the latter site could either be late Bronze Age or early Iron Age in date (*ibid.*; Grantham and Grantham 1965). At Lady's Graves, near Fimber, pits containing clay mould debris from bronze-working were cut into the earthwork bank (Manby 1980). The moulds suggested the manufacture of swords, long-tongue chapes, socketed axes and socketed spearheads (Challis and Harding 1975, 15) of 'Wilburton' style, dating to the later Bronze Age (Burgess 1968). A bronze dirk was also found in the gravel hillwash from an earthwork bank at Walkington, and calcite gritted pottery similar to that found in the late Bronze Age 'hillfort' of Thwing, was found in a section cut across an earthwork running north of this enigmatic site (Manby 1980, 328). Slightly off the Wolds, at West Heslerton, a wheel-rutted trackway flanked by a northerly ditch, and series of pit alignments, also yielded pottery of late Bronze Age date (Powlesland 1986, 133–4). Early Iron Age pottery was apparently found in the ditches from Huggate Dykes, when sectioned by W. J. Varley (Challis and Harding 1975, 161, fig. 65). At Caythorpe, work in advance of a gas pipeline investigated an undated multiple ditch and pit alignment which ran east–west along a valley floor for over 2 km (Abramson 1996). A second earthwork to the north was superimposed over an earlier pit alignment, and the intersection of the two yielded later Bronze Age pottery, animal bone and flint (*ibid.*, 13). However, a pit alignment near the Wold summit contained ceramic sherds, flint flakes and animal bone, dating to the middle Iron Age: 400–40 cal. BC (2170± BP) – an alignment which was itself re-cut by a later linear ditch of unknown date (*ibid.*, 20).

A date of construction sometime in the later Bronze Age or early Iron Age seems likely for many of the earthworks, yet several continue to be modified throughout the first millennium BC. For example, pottery dating to the middle–later Iron Age was found underneath a linear earthwork bank at Walkington Wold (Bartlett and Mackey 1972). Meanwhile, at Cowlam the south corner of a square barrow ditch ('D') and the edge of its central platform had been removed by a deep linear earthwork, whilst the centre of this monument was also truncated by a slighter parallel dyke (Stead 1986, 9). John Dent's excavations at Wetwang Slack also demonstrate that linear earthworks which bound this settlement and cemetery were dug and re-dug, well into the late Iron Age (Dent 1984a). One of the western linears running along the side of this valley preceded the square barrows which formed two lines on either side; yet its southern counterpart was overlain by square barrows at several points in its length (Dent 2010, 120). This excavation would suggest a major period of modification before and during the main period of use of the cemetery (*c.* fourth–first centuries BC). Meanwhile, at Easington, a juncture of two track-ways, defined by linear ditches, has been dated to the later Iron Age (Evans 2009, 259). Some of the linear boundaries are not continuous ditches but pit alignments, as at Cat Babbleton. Here, the excavator Cardwell, was able to trace how they were 'dug through' at a latter stage (possibly even during the Roman period), to form a more even, ditched profile (1989). Similar Romano-British modifications were recorded at West Heslerton (Powlesland 1988, 103). Wherever these earthworks form the basis for late Iron Age and Roman trackways, or enclosure boundaries, it is clear they continued to be altered and adapted. However, Roman, Anglo-Saxon and Medieval pottery in the upper ditch fills of many earthworks suggest that their main period of active construction ceased in the later Iron Age or early Roman era. In conclusion, any illusion of a coherent system or ordered design seen from the air has to be unpicked in detail at each site, since the different histories matter. Most sites represent a palimpsest of projects: the work of many generations, if not centuries.

Constructing boundaries, constructing relations

Let us turn, then, to consider the making of the boundaries themselves. A phase of planning or tentative demarcation is suggested by the presence of post and stakeholes under earthwork banks at Fimber (Ehrenberg and Caple 1983; 1985). This may indicate a coming together of groups: a level of assembly and decision making which helped reproduce a broader sense of community (Bradley and Yates 2007). In other places, it was the ditches which were initially laid out as a series of pits, and often later dug through (as discussed above). The earthworks at Vessey Pasture provide further evidence of stake and post-hole 'planning' phases (Buckland *et al.* 1992; 1993). At Lady Graves, Fimber, small pits were separated by small causeways, flanked by parallel banks (Mortimer 1905a). The exact purpose of such pit 'alignments' is much debated. It has been suggested that they form neat 'planting pits' for small trees or shrubs, encouraging the growth of a hedgerow (Haughton and Powlesland 1999, 57). However, there is little evidence in the fills of such pits to suggest tree boles, nor of erosion as might be found under the lip of a hedgerow. Instead, Rylatt and Bevan argue from the permeable nature of these boundaries that they were symbolic rather than practical barriers (2007). In various examples, they point to their frequent association with, or ability to retain, water: creating a mirror-like effect of pooled reflections (*ibid.*). Whilst this is rarely the case on the Wolds, one example of a ditch performing a similar function might be evidenced at Leconfield, in the Hull Valley. Here, an undated linear earthwork (similar in morphology to the first millennium BC examples from the Wolds, and running adjacent to two possible square barrows) proved to be very shallow in depth (Dent 2009). The excavator interpreted this as a response to the high water table in the local landscape, which would quickly have made this a water-bearing feature whose 'depth' was illusory (*ibid.*, 69).

The majority of the dykes on the Wolds were generally much deeper, using height to impress: some of the ditches proving to be over 1.5 m below ground level, flanked by steep banks. Estimates of manual labour suggest that an adult can move 0.8 cubic metres of spoil per hour (Lock, Gosden and Daly 2005, 143) and Shaw noted that earthwork banks can be effectively created through 'back-shovelling' or scraping the soil, complementing basket-work (1970, 380). However, picking through solid chalk to create these ditches would have proved arduous, and even a single dyke running for 100 m or so, would represent the work of around 250 hours, or a month's continuous work for an individual. Just one of the triple-ditched earthworks running down towards the Gypsey Race at Vicarage Closes, Burton Fleming would have taken a team of ten people over two months solid work to complete, and there are four such linears, as well as subsidiary dykes and pit alignments, meeting at this point in the landscape.

Mortimer notes that 'in some places first one side of the rampart and then the other had been cast up' (1905a, 377), suggesting that 'different lengths of ditches were excavated by separate gangs of workmen, in advance of each other' (*ibid.*). Such 'gang-dug' sections have also been identified at Caythorpe (Abramson 1996), West Heslerton (Powlesland 1986) and Cat Babbleton (Cardwell 1989). This tells us something about the composition of labour and the division of responsibility amongst those who made these earthworks.

One interpretation is that this gang-work involved the mutual aggregation of contrasting groups of people to work on the project, at particular times. Perhaps this was seasonal work. Perhaps these were extended family groups or else neighbouring communities who each contributed a section of their population. The truth is we do not know enough about the temporality of these projects, having never bothered to excavate a large section of upstanding bank, where we might gain insights into both working methods and the time over which they were constructed. Whatever the circumstances in which they were dug, the shoulder-to-shoulder work, the back-breaking picking and basket-carrying, the sweat, the cuts and the bruises, would have generated a strong sense of solidarity amongst these teams. Perhaps also, some competitiveness (Giles 2007c, 110). Boston's observation of earthwork building in Nigeria recalls 'the intensive effort on the behalf of the young men … [who worked in] relays, taking it in turns … [with] a great deal of encouragement, shouting and appeal to group pride' from both the younger labourers and the older men 'who were there to supervise' (Shaw 1970, 381). These were the conditions in which ties of kinship and affiliation were cemented (Wigley 2007), and new forms of authority might emerge … probably not of an over-arching elite, dominating the proceedings, but the day-to-day competence and vision of someone able to motivate their team and provide for them during these periods of labour. This is important, and it is something that Niall Sharples has paid attention to in his recent account of hillfort building (2010, 122). He describes such large-scale earthwork building as an expression of 'potlatch': the conspicuous consumption of labour and resources, as a means of defining communities and showing off muscle power as well as wealth (2010, 116). Meat, grain, water and – probably – alcohol, would have had to be provided. Summer may have provided the ideal time for this work, representing a 'lull' in the agricultural calendar.

These times of earthwork construction may have provided opportunities for other relationships to be forged: for stock and people to meet at a larger scale, reproducing a broader sense of community at a time when it was subject to some friction. No doubt partners were found, and a few boasts and blows exchanged. Such projects bound people together in a highly visible work, which could be seen by rivals, who may be on the move through these valleys. Yet every hour spent on these earthworks was labour and time taken away from another activity. Their scale suggests that whilst this was important, vital even, it had of necessity to be accomplished over a long period of time. The dykes demanded inter-generational commitment and pride, with each era adding its own touches: a new pit alignment, an additional parallel bank, a subsidiary ditch sub-dividing what had already been ordained.

Constructing histories

By its very nature, a physical boundary causes bodies to pause, to reflect, respect and re-route their original path of movement. In so doing, it changes the nature of that individual's relationship with place, as well as their relations with the people who have constructed that feature. In other words, a physical boundary is also a social boundary: meant to convey relations of authority and power which relate to the rights someone has in those places. This 'altering of the earth' (to borrow Raymond Williams' phrase, 1989) was no doubt contentious. In formalising rights of way, in specifying points of entry or exit, or demarcating access to particular resources (pasture, woodland, water), at least some of these works were contentious. At the site of Tormarton, Gloucestershire, an early version of a linear ditch was associated with some of the most horrific evidence for interpersonal violence in the British middle Bronze Age (see Osgood 1999). Some families benefited, others lost out. Previously, this had been a matter of mutual negotiation: discussion and argument, reworking rights on an annual or generational basis. This left room for manoeuvre at a later date. The notion of trespass would not have been strongly defined, because of the fluidity of such a system. However, once paths were prescribed, and thresholds framed, they created the conditions for new forms of resistance: occupation, over-stocking and grazing, trampling or poaching of the land or fouling of water sources (Giles 2007c).

The need for the linear earthworks, and the labour invested in them, suggest such rights were under contest, and that there was a desire to place such matters beyond dispute. But how did the linear earthworks achieve this authority? Put simply, their makers laid claim to features in the landscape which were already meaningful: known, named and redolent with stories. Iron Age people dwelt in a 'mythical landscape' that had to be interpreted and retold by each generation (Barrett 1999c). What we recognise as anthropogenic monuments (long and round barrows, the standing stone at Rudston and neighbouring henge and cursus monuments) or materials (flint scatters and polished stone axes, found hoards of metalwork) were only part of a series of remarkable features which distinguished this landscape. The volatile and capricious Gypsey Race streams, with their springs and soak-away holes; the glistening outcrops of chalk breccia known locally as the 'Fairystones'; the still meres of Fimber and Fridaythorpe; all of these had to be explained according to an inherited body of stories, which would have also narrated rights of use. Groups would have navigated their way through the dales and slacks, using these landmarks. Over time, of course, people became attached to them through their own biographies: herding the sheep as a youngster, past the great barrow at Duggleby or winning prized blue-clay for making pots from the spring at Burdale. Such features and the stories attached to them would have been part of how people learned to 'live right' in the land and with other beings (see Basso 1996). They were thus ripe for coercion in these new architectural projects.

Springs form the terminals of a number of earthworks along the scarp edge of the Wolds between Aldro and Birdsall (Giles 2007c, 111). Earthworks also cluster around other examples, as at Tancred Pit Hole (Figure 2.3). The natural meres at Fimber and Fridaythorpe appear to be the focal point of a

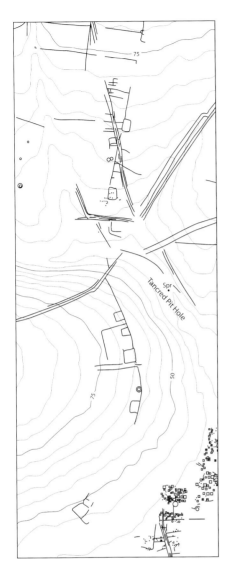

FIGURE 2.3. Linear earthworks at Tancred Pit Hole. Based on Stoertz 1997, map 2.

constellation of earthworks. At one level, such bodies of water represent obvious nodes in the landscape, around which people would gather: as well as human use, water was particularly vital for cattle, which require 12–15 gallons (*c.*54.5–68.2 litres) of fresh water a day (Porter 1991). These meres and springs took on a new importance in the early Iron Age, as many of the smaller, natural ponds formed in sink-holes or dolines, were beginning to dry up (Hayfield, Pouncett and Wagner 1995). From the lithic scatters found around their edges, the dolines appear to have been used from the Mesolithic through to the later Bronze Age, but scenes of confusion and contestation may have arisen as these ancient watering holes dried up, and new sources were sought out. In settlements, as in historic times, water was probably collected in cisterns or tubs, positioned under the eaves of each thatch (draw wells and dew-ponds were part of the improvement movement of the eighteenth to twentieth centuries: Hayfield, Pouncett and Wagner 1995). Yet water would only have been present in the deepest of dales on the High Wolds, as in Waterdale and Burdale, where it penetrated the valley floor as a spring or emerged over perched marl beds, to form small swampy areas (Hayfield and Wagner 1995; Hayfield, Pouncett and Wagner 1995, 393; Aylwin and Ward 1969). Even in the Historic period, 'rake rights' carefully enshrined the ability of a shepherd or stockman to take his flock or herd to water from a village like Birdsall, up onto the Wolds. At Raisthorpe 'spring' (identified by Hayfield and Wagner as Vessey Ponds, 1995), Birdsall beastmen might allow their stock to drink and graze for the time it took 'for a man [to] sole a pair of shoes' (*ibid.*, 58). In the Great Wold Valley, and villages such as Kilham and Garton Station, streams known locally as the 'Gypsey Races' provided more secure sources of fresh water. As at Vicarage Closes (see Figure 2.2) these became the nexus of a series of earthworks and pit alignments, controlling access from different zones down towards the stream. (See Chapter 7 for a further discussion of the seasonal behaviour of 'Gypseys' and their possible symbolism).

The prehistoric prescription of access to water, using the dykes, suggests this could be a source of tension. Even in historic times, this can be seen in events such as the 'Battle of Fimber', fought in the dry summer of 1826, and recounted to the antiquarian, John Mortimer, by one of his uncles. The inhabitants of Fridaythorpe had been granted the privilege of watering themselves and their stock at times of need, at the neighbouring village of Fimber, but when the upper mere (reserved for human use) finally dried up, they were turned away. Men, water carts and cattle marched on Fimber, determined to 'tak[e] by force what had been granted them as a favour' but which they saw 'as a right' (Mortimer, in Hicks 1978, 3). The battle – fought with sticks, stones and, no doubt, a few pieces of agricultural and culinary equipment, wielded by the cottagers' wives who also got involved – resulted in 'several broken heads, duckings in the mere and the final expulsion of the invaders' (*ibid.*, 4). The 'scrimmage' was a source of enduring tension between the villages but it was also 'long afterwards looked upon … with much satisfaction, and a considerable amount of pride' (*ibid.*, 4). Indeed, Mortimer's uncle, Matthew Welburn, used to exhort him to feel the dent in his scalp which was the enduring scar of his part in the set-to (in Hicks 1978, 4)! We must be careful about assuming a direct analogy with prehistory, but these villages were dealing with the same constraint upon resources that Iron Age communities would have faced. The Battle of Fimber tells us this could be a source of potential tension, and that such violent incidents helped define the identity of rival groups, and the stories they told about the places to which they belonged (a theme I will return to in Chapter 7).

It was not just valuable resources which were circumscribed by the linear earthworks but impressive features (Giles 2007c). At the top of Burdale, a pair of earthworks terminate close by the strange pillars of chalk and flint breccia known locally as the 'Fairystones'. The rocks, formed along fault lines where chalk, flint and quartzite were compressed, were more resistant to weathering than the rest of the dale, and were left standing proud of the surrounding turf, as flat-topped outcrops. They are remarkable natural features which, in local folklore, had supernatural power and could be visited at night by men eager to see their future wife (Nicholson 1890 [1998 reprint]). In Back Dale, a set of raised, elongate mounds, the Raisthorpe tumps (which Mortimer found to be natural piles of chalk resulting from faulting and ground mass movement), were built into the 'run' of a linear earthwork, taking the place of a bank at these stages (Mortimer 1905a, 19). These diggers may have felt they were respecting the acts of ancient monumental bank builders: emulating their impressive (but actually, geological in origin) architecture. At Birdsall Dale, meanwhile, an earthwork appears to have been built over the fissure of a natural fault itself. Perhaps it caused vegetation to grow differently or was marked by a change of texture in the chalky soil – either way, the diggers of this ditch exaggerated and monumentalised what was already a cleft in the earth (Buckland *et al.* 1992; P. Wagner, pers. comm.). Finally there are swerves or gaps in some of the earthworks to which we can attribute no obvious cause. It is possible that these represent entrances or gates, but they might also be features which have long-since disappeared such as impressive trees. In a largely cleared landscape, the decision to preserve rather than fell an old tree would have been significant. It would have not only provided important shade and shelter for people, birds and small mammals but also a striking silhouette. The growth and development of a tree (its seasonal budding and shedding of leaves, uprooting of the turf or cracking and falling of old branches) may well have endeared it to human inhabitants as an animate and responsive presence (see Jones and Cloke 2008): a kind of living monument.

However, one of the most common associations of the linear earthworks was with Bronze Age round barrows: sky-lined mounds upon which they set their sights. Sometimes there was a relationship of respect, and the earthworks look as if they were 'set out' or made to terminate at a distinctive barrow, as at Crowsdale. Others meander around the monument, causing a distinct kink or deviation in its route, as can be seen near Thwing or Aldro 88. Sometimes, they made more active use of such features. The large barrow at Aldro, C76, was encircled by a 'double entrenchment' which had pilfered material from the original mound to swell the banks of the enclosing dykes (Mortimer 1905a, 72–3). This habit was also noted at Calais Wold (*ibid.*, 160) though this time, it also marked an apparent entrance through the dykes. At Aldro 256, linear earthworks from three different directions met. Once more, the ditch diggers had robbed spoil from the main barrow to increase the size of the northerly bank, but in doing so, they had disturbed a cremation vessel, and its broken sherds and crazed bone, as well as flints and sheep/goat offerings, were spread across the face of the new earthwork (*ibid.*, 61; Giles 2007c, 113). A similar scenario was inferred from a section of the earthworks near the Tatton Sykes Memorial, where the Granthams recorded scattered remnants of a Food Vessel, Collared Urn, cremated bone and flints, as well as small piece of bronze wire, mixed up in the bank material (1965, 356). However, no trace of the original monument was left: it had been completely subsumed within the new earthwork. We might imagine the puzzlement or shock such discoveries caused: handling substances they would have recognised, intrigued by their strange form. We might expect them to have felt perturbed and awed but in some cases, the archaeology suggests a very deliberate act of despoliation or erasure. This was the case at Wharram Percy 127, where Mortimer demonstrated how the round barrow had been savagely cut through: disturbing an inhumation in the western half but leaving an old cremation intact in the eastern fringe of what was remodelled as the earthwork banks. As Mortimer noted, at times the dykes respected and incorporated these ancient burials but in other cases, they were obliterated:

> destroyed in a ruthless manner, probably by a people having no regard for the monuments so carefully and so laboriously raised, by cutting a trench right through it and squandering the once treasured contents
>
> 1905a, 52.

These dramatic acts suggest the past was powerfully drawn into a new discourse on belonging, and rights to place and resources. Where they were effaced, it suggests the wiping of ancestral anchorage from the face of the land, as if it had never been. Where they were sequestered into new projects, it helped legitimate what were evidently contentious claims. But this was not simply about legitimisation: this was the creation of a new sense of history, in which the ancestors (as a generic body of long-gone forebears) were being drawn into a direct relationship with early Iron Age peoples. It was the telling of a particular narrative of belonging, in which a sense of descent and connectedness to the burial mounds of ancient individuals was being mobilised. Rarely, this connection was being assertively reinforced with the interment of the newly dead, into such ancient burial places. Mimicking the cremation rite they witnessed, two shallow vessel burials were placed at the edge of Riggs barrow 33: one cremation with a small carinated bowl (Mortimer 1905a, 175, fig. 441) and another with a slack-shoulderd jar with bevelled rim (*ibid.*, 176, fig. 442). Another plain urn containing 'burnt wood slightly mixed with a little burnt bone' was placed in an oval hole at Painesthorpe barrow III (*ibid.*, 128, fig. 328). Garrowby Wold C99 ('Kity Hill') may represent a further cremated burial dating to this late Bronze Age/early Iron Age period, interred in an earlier round barrow (Mortimer 1905a, 149, fig. 396). (Mortimer records the presence of an 'Anglo-Saxon' shield and flat piece of iron near the surface of this barrow (1905a, 149), but given the fact that the adjoining barrow 'B' is the famous Grimthorpe warrior burial, used as a frontispiece for his 1905 volume, it is also possible the shield and plaque are middle–late Iron Age in date). Together, these examples represent a rare but identifiable practice of late Bronze Age/early Iron Age cremation in 'secondary situations in barrow mounds' (Manby 1980, 319).

There are examples of other cremated, urned burials dating to this period at Garton Slack (*ibid.*, 351) and Thwing (*ibid.*, 355), though they are not interred within round barrows themselves. There are also a number of crouched inhumations which may be of a similar date: at Towthorpe 43, the body was associated with a plain vessel with internal rim (Mortimer 1905a, fig. 29). Sherds dating to this period have however, been found in the outer ditches of a round barrow at Walkington Wold (Bartlett and Mackey 1972, 8, fig. 14), whilst other early Iron Age style sherds, associated with an antler tine pick, ox bone and charcoal, were reported in the 'cenotaph' round barrow originally recorded by the antiquarian Greenwell: Weaverthorpe barrow XLVII (Greenwell 1877, 201, Challis and Harding 1975, fig. 21, nos 4 and 5). No cremation was noted in the vessel interred into Ganton Wold round barrow XXVII (Greenwell 1877, 174, fig. 92) nor with sherds ploughed out from 'superficial internments' at Barrow II, Langton near the 'Three Dikes' (*ibid.*, 136) but these may represent surrogate offerings rather than the cremated body, made in an appropriate place (Giles 2007c, 114). At Aldro 108, a fascinating collection of cremated bone and fragments of fused bronze weapons (ferrules, sheaths and a dagger or halberd fragment), together with two bronze plaques encircling lenticular pieces of polished glass or crystal, were found in association with a finger-tipped vessel, in a broad but low mound (Mortimer 1905a, 56, fig. 108). Mortimer sent this parcel of objects to Sir John Evans for evaluation but this famous archaeologist was unable to offer a more precise date. However, Challis and Harding argue that the bronze ferrule included in this assemblage is similar to late Hallstatt examples found in wagon burials, dating to the sixth or seventh centuries BC: a fascinating but so far unique Continental connection (1975, 42–3, fig. 20; Harding 2004, 26).

It appears, then, that the later prehistoric inhabitants of the Wolds made no division between what we have come to class as natural versus anthropogenic features: both were apposite sites to lay claim to, add to, and draw upon, in these new works. The long-term consequences of architecture on this scale, was to alter the way in which rights were negotiated: giving them monumental form and beginning to place them beyond annual, verbal negotiation. Through their construction, and the additions each generation made, they themselves became mnemonics of labour and sweat: 'congealed histories' through which people traced their rights of place (Ingold 2000a). Quite simply, it created a different relationship between a generic ancient past, and the recent, generational past: entwining these two different temporalities in a much more specific genealogy of place. In the next chapter, we will explore how this discourse seems to have developed through the new square barrow burial rite.

Inhabiting the land

Territory or tenure?

It has been argued that these linear earthworks go hand-in-hand with the development of territories, whose centres focused around enclosed sites dating to the late Bronze Age and early Iron Age. In plotting the position of Grimthorpe, Paddock Hill, Devil's Hill, Greenlands and Swaythorpe and others, Stoertz illustrated how they apparently lay in the centre of large-scale 'blocks' of land, defined by the dykes (see Figure 2.1, Stoertz 1997, fig. 33). On the basis of these positions and their description as 'hillforts' they have literally been interpreted as the central residences of competitive chiefdoms (Brewster 1963; Powlesland 1986, 156; Bevan 1997). Yet this is a disparate group of sites, which have been poorly investigated (Harding 2004). The relatively small size and cluster of structures and craft debris at Staple Howe (Brewster 1963) contrasts with larger sites such as Devil's Hill or Grimthorpe, where evidence for storage, food and craft production, and the exchange of exotica sits at odds with an apparent lack of domestic residence, such as roundhouses (Stephens 1986; Stead 1968). Paddock Hill, with its hengiform enclosure and central structure is unique, and appears to have a more ceremonial focus (Manby 1985; 1986; 1990) whereas geophysics surveys of enclosures such as Greenlands show few internal features; they may instead have been stock enclosures (T. Pacitto, pers. comm.). Where dates exist, such enclosed sites appear to have gone out of use in the early Iron Age period, well before the beginning of the square barrow burial rite.

These sites are complemented by a range of evidence for more ephemeral domestic activity, discovered as part of the British Museum's Settlement Project (Rigby 2004). A range of pits and small features were excavated, often containing the products of craftwork, food processing and animal tending and butchery, dating mainly to the period 900–600 BC (Rigby 2004). The repeated clustering of dozens of such features at places like Woldgate (Burton Agnes East Field and West Field/Tuft Hill) is truly remarkable (Stoertz 1997, map 2). Rigby's interpretation is equivocal: they could represent permanent occupation in structures which themselves have left no trace, or else they may represent 'seasonal or intermittent' occupation (2004, 125). The high volume of craftwork and evidence for agricultural processing also led her to propose that such seasonal visits might have been orchestrated around 'special regular events like fairs and religious environments' (*ibid*.). In a marvellous piece of insight, she notes that the pits seem to represent a desire to 'tidy up' after such events, cleaning the land and concealing (or offering back to the earth) the remnants of such festivities (for a similar argument relating to examples of Neolithic deposition, see Garrow *et al.* 2005). Notably, this way of life – and the pits which represent it – seems to have ended right at the time when the square barrow tradition began to be practiced, heralding changes not just in where people were buried but where they lived, and the permanence of this occupation (Rigby 2004, 106).

To sum up, in the period in which the linear earthworks began to be constructed, domestic life for at least part if not all of the population, may still have largely been lived in a residentially mobile fashion, with particular seasons of the year marked by residence in certain places. The exact purpose and role of the enclosed sites or pit clusters varied between groups, whose movement back and forth across the Wolds seems less constrained by an exclusive sense of territory (defined by permanent residences and monitored boundaries) than characterised by a sense of tenure. In this alternative view, different groups may have travelled through and made use of the landscape, negotiating presence and absence in particular places at specific times, so as to minimise clashes of interest (see Giles 2007c, 109). Yet as I have argued above, the construction of these linears suggest something about this way of life was under contest … perhaps even under threat. There was a need to monumentalise what had previously been a matter of verbal agreement, suggesting such rites were in dispute. Yet what purpose did the earthworks serve? In order to understand this, we have to know more about the way in which the broader landscape was being managed.

Landscape management

The construction of the dykes would suggest a largely cleared landscape in which these newly dug earthworks (with their banks of freshly turned chalk rubble and silt) were starkly visible. Open grassland is indeed indicated in the molluscs from early–middle Iron Age pits discussed above, as at Hanging Cliff, and some charred weed and grain seeds indicate cultivation and processing in the vicinity of the Pit Site at Burton Agnes (Wagner in Rigby 2004, 84 and 86). In the Great Wold Valley at Willow Garth, near Rudston, there is evidence for clearance of woodland, which Bush and Ellis argue was combined with ploughing, to exacerbate soil erosion in the Iron Age (1987) though the amount of woodland cover on the Wolds may not have been as extensive as was once thought (Neal 2010). However, increased clearance or cultivation has also been blamed for the deposits of colluvium which cover parts of the latest Iron Age site at Melton (Fenton Thomas 2011, 364). Molluscs from the square barrow cemetery excavations at Garton Station and Kirkburn suggest a predominance of dry, short-turf grassland which was being grazed, with little evidence of shade-loving species (Thew and Wagner, in Stead 1991, 150). However, the barrows in which the 'speared' burials were interred (see chapter 1) indicate a much more localised damp and moist environment, with rich grassy vegetation (*ibid*., 151), indicative of the nearby presence of the Gypsey Race. Land which was seasonally flooded in winter may have provided lush pasture in late spring and early summer when other forms of fodder had become scarce. Pollen was remarkably preserved on some of the bronzework from the Kirkburn burials, suggesting a local environment of short-turf grassland (possibly pasture) with both wet and dry elements, as well as broader evidence for cereal cultivation nearby (Greig in Stead 1991, 154). Some of the best direct evidence for cultivation comes from the carbonised plant remains at Garton Slack Area 9, which indicate the growing of six-row hulled barley, contaminated by a few wheat seeds and some wild oat grains (Keepax, in Brewster 1980, 682). Both this deposit and another set of grains from Garton Station 6 had been processed and cleaned before they became deposited (*ibid*.). Historically, the Wold soils require frequent manuring and liming to be productive (Matthew 1993), so it is likely that Iron Age cultivation was shifting, allowing plots to lie fallow and regenerate.

Down in the Hasholme Valley to the south-west and the Humber lowlands to the south-east, peat formation since the Bronze Age created areas of bog, with wet oak-alder carr and a mosaic of other wetland habitats, giving way to grassy conditions on the intervening sandy ridges (Heath and Wagner in Halkon *et al.* 2009). Yet the pollen preserved within such peat also indicates heavy woodland clearance and mixed farming with cereals, at places such as Hornsea Old Mere and Roos Carr (Halkon *et al.* 2009, 24). Indeed, the peat is sealed in various places with colluvial sediments caused by further clearance (Dinnin 1995). This would have meant that lowland areas such as the Foulness Valley became precious sources of developed woodland, providing both rich hunting opportunities and sources of timber for structural projects as well as fuel for iron working (Halkon *et al.* 2009). The amount of deadwood however (represented in the beetle remains), indicates only small-scale management of such woodland (Heath and Wagner in Halkon *et al.* 2009, 37). Marine incursions in the early Iron Age created a broad network of tidal inlets along the River Humber, probably encouraging riverine travel, as evidenced in both the Hasholme and South Carr Farm boats (*ibid*., 27–8). The 600 year old tree felled to make the former craft for example, was probably derived from such woodlands (*ibid*.). Halkon therefore envisages a strong role for the Hasholme valley as a production zone, for both timber and iron, supplying the middle-late Iron Age communities of the Wolds (2008). However, we should not rule out the existence of small stands of mature timber, as well as the ready growth of ash, hazel, fruit and nut species, amongst zones of pasture and arable on the Wolds.

Interpreting the earthworks

What role did the earthworks play in such a landscape? Elswhere in Britain, they have been interpreted as part of an intensification of agriculture, dividing pastoral from arable use, and defining infield from outfield areas (Bradley and Yates 2007). This is the interpretation favoured by Dent for the linear earthworks which broadly enclose the valley side, settlement and cemetery at Wetwang Slack (1982; 1984a). He argues the 'infield' area on the richer valley-side soils may have been used for field plots, with the outer banks used to keep out foraging stock. Thus the banks and ditches of the dykes could at once be boundaries and barriers, tracks and droveways: 'either simultaneously or successively' performing multiple functions (Stoertz 1997, 41). Whilst some marked short-distance movements between valleys, others demarcated broad zones of higher land, as at Aldro Brow, Fimber or Kilham. This circumscribing of areas of the landscape has been interpreted by Chris Fenton Thomas as evidence of the demarcation of 'grazing grounds' or 'pasturing estates' (1999). He argues that these were well-renowned areas of rich grazing to which communities would seasonally bring their stock, from the surrounding Vales and Plains. Certainly, the distinctive flaring entrances or funnelling mouth features of some earthworks strongly suggest the coercive movement not just of people but their flocks and herds, from one zone to another, or between resources such as grass, shelter and water (Stoertz 1997, 43; see also Fenton Thomas 2003; Halkon 2008; Dent 2010). In this, they resemble the so-called 'ranch boundaries' of later prehistoric Wessex, which have been argued to represent territorial land divisions centred on valleys, ensuring access to a range of ecozones: water and riverine pasture, cultivatable valley-side soils and higher land (Bradley *et al.* 1994). This system, Sharples argues, mimics the 'parallel reaves' of Dartmoor (2010, 44–5). Yet the Wolds earthworks do not quite work in this way. Whether we look at the high western 'grazing grounds' or the longer-range dykes of the Great Wold Valley, I would argue that they do neatly circumscribe distinct territories so much as loosely define areas of high pasture, and the access routes up into them (Giles 2007c). Many show an obsession with defining 'means of ingress and egress' as Mortimer puts it (1905a, 369). This suggests many were designed to regulate the to-and-fro movement of people and stock, rather than demarcate permanent residence in one 'block'. In some cases, this may have been (as Fenton Thomas imagines it) a seasonal arrival of shepherds or cowhands from the surrounding low-lying Vales and Plains, with their stock, seeking to share the resources used by those living on the Wolds (2003). In other cases, the earthworks appear to negotiate what were probably diurnal movements, between good grazing land and important sources of water: meres, springs and streams.

Historical documents from the Yorkshire Wolds once more give us an insight into how this use of pasture – and the problems associated with attendant rights or customs – were alive and well in the seventeenth century. The remarkable 'Farming and Memorandum Books of Henry Best of Elmswell' date between 1617 to 1645 (with some later additions – published as Woodward 1984). They record aspects of farming and craftwork practice, productivity of land and stock, details of employees, and debts owed and paid. The Bests lived at the cusp of great changes: improvement and enclosure were on the horizon, and whilst the scale of their farming was different to later prehistory, some of the key constraints they lived with were analogous: soil quality, availability of pasture and water. Their farm at Elmswell was situated on the edge of Driffield, at the mouth of the slack in which both Wetwang and Garton lie; indeed, it was separated from the latter parish by the Garton Balk, 'an ancient trackway' (Woodward 1984, xxiii). Elmswell benefited from a cluster of springs which were invaluable to the neighbouring parishes. In the 1700s, despite Wetwang's mere, Lord Bathurst's agent noted that 'water is much here wanted' and during dry summers, when its pond dried up, its inhabitants were frequently 'obliged to drive their Cattle three miles for water' to the Elmswell springs and brooks (Sykes' Papers and Letters 1770–1782, 38, cited in Harris 1961, 35). Yet though Elmswell had abundant water, it lacked sufficient grazing, and routinely rented 'beast geats'/'gates' higher up on the Wolds (at Burdale, Cottam, Raisthorpe, Seldmere, Fridaythorpe or Huggate), between May Day and Michaelmass (Woodward 1984, 125). Grazing was so wanted that even the informal browsing of the Cottam sheep walks (which the Bests took as a right associated with their land), was 'carped at, and sometimes disputed with my ancestors' though as Charles Best (grandson of Henry) goes on to note with pride, 'they [the Cottam freeholders and farmers] were always worsted' (Woodward 1984, xxxi). This dispute frequently took the form of tit-for-tat wrongdoings. On the 23 June 1625, John Edward allowed his cattle to trespass over Henry Best's oats (Woodward 1984, 203). On July 7 1625, Henry Sloe and others drove John Edward's '*mucke Coopes*' (small, two-wheeled ox-carts) over Best's tenants' oxgangs – and back again! – at their master's command. This resulted in a hearing at the King's Bench and later, the York Assizes. But this did not settle the matter. Two generations later, John Best (Henry's son) records an altercation with men he finds ploughing out the 'Castle-dyke-heads' – an 'aunciant bounder' – with the intent of sequestering this disputed turf. This is noted as being the 'sheepe-walk, West-parte, in Cottam field etc.' (*ibid.*, 220). On Cathy Stoertz's 1997 survey (Map 1: furthest south-east corner), this is transcribed as a single ditched linear earthwork which appears to be of prehistoric date. John Best angrily makes them 'turne over their Harrowes and goe quite of the Lands' (Woodward 1984, appendix I, iii, 220). When John's *neateheard* (cattleherd) finds the men back there again, he threatens them with a beating! John instead threatens them with another trip to the assizes, for the removal of 'bounders, hutts, and land marks' (*ibid.*). He appeals to their father's and grandfather's memories, which he argues, would attest to his own rights, as they had been sealed with a 'solemne procession round about the sayd Sheep walke att my First entrance' (i.e. when he inherited the estate: Woodward 1984, 222–3). At this point, we come full circle on the themes of this chapter … rights of use traced in ancient features, resulting in contest and friction which carries on down the generations … two and half thousand years after some of the earthworks which feature in Best's account were probably constructed.

Following the herd

So far in this chapter, I have tried to situate the appearance of large earthwork boundaries in the late Bronze and early Iron Age, within suggested rhythms of agricultural practice: the diurnal and seasonal movements of stock to and from pasture and water, alongside the tending and growth of arable crops. I have argued that the linears marked a major change in the ways in which customs of use and rights of place were negotiated, and I have pointed to the increasing role in this discourse, first of the ancient dead, but increasingly during the first millennium BC, more recent forebears. Such rights were bedded in and reiterated not merely through further works on the dykes themselves, but through their day-to-day use: following the herd.

Imagine an early morning in late July, on the High Wolds: Vessey Pasture Dale. The cattle are on the move, their breath steaming in the early chill, as they shuffle and rise: snuffling new calves, licking their hides. The dale can hardly be seen because of the heavy mist which has descended: a sea fret, caused by the meeting of cold air from the coast with the warmth of the land. Led by the herd's matriarch: a senior female, the stock begin a slow but steady walk, guided by the snaking passage of a linear dyke along the dale bed, towards water and new pasture. The only sound is the sticky, muffled tramp of hooves, along the trodden earth and cowpats, which line the way. Gradually, the fret burns off: skylarks can be heard, and the broad light blue expanse of the Wolds skies, arches overhead.

Walking with such stock would have been the everyday task of a particular group in the community. It may have been a job for children or young adults, in the company perhaps of a 'neateheard' as Henry Best put it: an adult whose main role was to care for the stock. Alternatively it may have been a more prestigious activity, the risks of which necessitated an older, perhaps even armed, age-set, as is the case in many African societies where cattle are the prize to be gained from raiding (Fukai 1996b). Even in historic times, the skill, hardship and courage demanded of 'drovers' was often seen as directly analogous to those required of a warrior, and stockmen were frequently armed in preparation for trouble (Haldane 1997).

The animals that our Iron Age communities tended 'on the hoof' were sheep and cattle, whose butchered and buried bones are evidenced in the settlements such as Wetwang and Garton Slack. These two species were a key source of milk and other dairy products; hide; fleece; bone; horn; sinew; and occasionally, meat. People were dressed and kept warm by these creatures: sheep wool was woven and embroidered, and pinned by elaborate brooches (see Chapter 5). Dung would have been used to fertilise the fields, and may even have been burnt as fuel. Their horn decorated the hilts of weapons and tools, and hide was used to cover their shields, and make pouches, sheaths and scabbards, as well as the straps, reins and ties which held chariot and horse-team together (Chapters 5 and 6). Lamb and mutton were eaten regularly as part of funerary rites, and more rarely pork. Pigs may have been penned closer to houses to benefit from household scraps or they may have been tended by a swineherd, and allowed to forage more broadly (see Chapter 4). Although some butchered cattle bone has been recovered from the settlement, beef was never eaten as part of a funeral rite, suggesting they may have been seen as a conceptually distinct or different species, whose consumption was rarely appropriate. Hill's study of Wessex faunal remains reminds us that Iron Age communities may have had different ways of dividing up the animal world, privileging some species over others, due to the nature of their symbolic meaning (1995b). Whilst evidence for neonatal sheep and goat at sites like Garton Slack was slight (perhaps suggesting shepherding out on the hills), there was a high proportion of neonatal cattle and young claves which may have been deliberately slaughtered: perhaps suggesting they were corralled closer to the settlement (Noddle in Brewster 1980, 771). Such cattle almost certainly provided the traction for the plough, and may have been seen as partners in the production of both cereals and dairy produce: staples of Iron Age life. Alongside these species were the ponies who drew the chariots, perhaps stabled separately either close to settlements or in ranch-settings.

The so-called 'defended' enclosures such as Greenlands may have had a special role in providing 'stances': overnight or seasonal shelter for stock (Haldane 1997), perhaps at key times of bad weather or lambing. In addition, there is an intriguing set of interlinked earthworks near Weaverthorpe, whose long, parallel enclosures are quite unlike anything else seen on the Wolds (Stoertz 1997). They are unfortunately as yet undated, though at one point, a square barrow cemetery can clearly be seen to intersect with one of the linear ditches. A limited programme of excavation (for a BBC episode of *Timeflyers: Between the Lines* 2002b) did not satisfactorily resolve their origin, though a lack of Roman pottery strongly suggests a prehistoric date. They also appear to relate to a suite of dolines on the valley top which contained scraps of copper alloy, calcite-gritted coarseware sherds and flints but no iron: this might suggest a mid–late Bronze Age date for the 'silting-up' of these water features, in keeping with the dates outlined above. The excavated ditch terminals were themselves sterile, though the funnel entrances, patches of organic-rich clay, and suite of stake and postholes, suggested a special role in stock care. Their scale, appearance and relations with other features tentatively support a date sometime in the late Bronze Age or Iron Age. During the filming of the programme, an elderly relative of one of the farmers told the crew that he was puzzled as to why we were bothering to dig them: he could tell us what they were for. His grandfather had told of a time when these banks still stood, and they were used for 'sorting out the cattle' – separating calves from mothers, selecting which to take to market, and so on. This remarkable piece of oral memory suggests that in the mid-1800s, before they were ploughed out, they were found to work well for such a task. In prehistory, their purpose may well have been similar: cattle ranching on quite a large scale.

Yet working within these landscapes, close by the racing stables of Malton, the similarity of some of the narrowest of these elongate enclosures to the 'gallops' (used to train, exercise and pasture horses) is also apparent. Although purely speculative, another possible use of the Weaverthorpe enclosures may have been the breaking and training of horses, particularly to work in harness. The narrowest of these enclosure runs would have provided clear corridors over gently rolling topography, with which to accustom a team to a vehicle and driver. There has been much speculation in Iron Age literature about the stock management of horses, which may have been bred in fairly small numbers and reared with greater care than some other species (Locker in Lawson 2000). Recent studies from Wessex have suggested that whilst some may have been bred locally, others were captured from wild herds and then broken. Some of these prestigious animals may even have been exchanged as impressive gifts, between communities who were quite far apart (Bendry, Hayes and Palmer 2005).

What were these animals like? All of these species were substantially smaller than their modern equivalents, which have benefited from generations of 'improved breeding'. Ponies stood at around 13–14 hands (13.2–1.42 m) in height (based on a unique find of the horse-team at Arras, and later Iron Age/early Roman horse burials at Kirkburn, Legge in Stead 1991, 144): sturdy and strong, and clearly capable of skilful, paired team-work for vehicles. Traction for ploughing (as has been discussed) may instead have been provided by cattle, for which the nearest contemporary analogy is the diminutive yet beautiful Dexter (an ancient Irish breed). Meanwhile, the delicate and flighty Soay (once more, an ancient breed whose stock was conserved in the Hebrides) are the closest in size and build to Iron Age sheep. Few of the pigs found at Wetwang or Garton Slack were of a size to suggest that they were boar (Noddle in Brewster 1980), and the funerary offerings from the Great Wolds Valley similarly suggest an inclusion of pork or suckling piglet (Stead 1991) yet wild boar was on occasion hunted (see below).

While we will never know the colours of their hide or fleece, or the shape of their horns, we know from anthropological accounts that these are often highly prized aesthetic attributes of what was effectively 'wealth on the hoof' (Fukai 1996a; see interpretation by Sharples 2009, 203). Remains of horns from Garton Slack suggest they were longer and more curved than the classic Celtic shorthorn variety (Noddle in Brewster 1980, 771). The clipping of ears, branding or horn manipulation may have furthered both the distinctiveness and perceived beauty of such beasts (Coote 1992; Grasseni 2004), as well as ownership and relations between herds (Hartley and Ingilby 1990; Osborn 1996). As a medium of exchange, through which debts could be instigated or honoured, bridewealth or dowry paid, and births and deaths commemorated, stock were vital to social relations. They may also have been acquired through raiding: daring feats of theft through which age-sets demonstrated their strength and courage (see summary in McCabe 2004, 96). Such raids often precipitate further feuds (Parker Pearson 1994, 79). Stock would therefore have been important symbolic as well as economic resources: themes that are well rehearsed in the anthropology of cattle (Galaty and Bonte 1991). Such transactions could make individual animals living embodiments of lineages, through which people might trace their connections to other families and groups (see Edmonds 1999, 27–8).

Naming practices are often key here (Ryan *et al.* 1991, 96). They also provided a metaphorical collective – the herd or the flock – analogous to that of the human community. Such animals were vital symbols of prestige, whose hides may have been kept glossy, or horns shaped and polished, by their devoted owners (Fukai 1996a). Eventually of course, such skin or horn would become incorporated into composite objects of exquisite craftsmanship, carrying forward the memory of favoured animals, and also possibly, some of their attributes, into the finished tool or weapon (Giles 2008b, 65).

These ancient breeds also helped connect people to place. Even today, hardy 'hill sheep' are still described as being 'heafed' to the land or 'hefted': they have a special, biographical connection, passed down from ewe to lamb and learned through practice, that amounts to a kind of social geography (Hartley and Ingilby 1990; Hunt 1997). Where to go for the best grazing and shelter, favoured sheep scrapes and places to lamb, which paths to take and the boundaries of familiar pasture: this practical knowledge results in an intense bond between flock and landscape, which is not easily disrupted (Hart 2005; Law and Mol 2008, 70–1). Cattle too, have an intimate bond with the grazing grounds in which they live: the matriarch leads her herd to water and to milking, to grazing or shelter overnight, which results in a rhythm of movement that needs minimal human intervention (Porter 1991). Yet people did accompany their stock, and as they walked with them, they no doubt developed a sense of fellowship with their charges, such that their own identity may have been defined in part by the beasts they cared for and guarded (Chadwick 2007). An 'ambulatory' sense of knowledge about the world and their place in it would have been learned through these repeated rhythms (Ingold 2000b), in which the mutual skill of both animals and herders – knowing where to go and when – was drawn upon to ensure survival and success (Lorimer 2006). It created familiar pasturing grounds – 'stints' – which were special not 'in spite of their likely use for practical activities such as grazing … but precisely because of them' (Roberts 2007, 105). Such 'going around' was not just fundamental to the vitality and growth of the herd but to the bond between people and place, and the rights these rhythms helped reproduce through hoof and foot-marks.

As Chadwick conjures evocatively in his discussion of the cropmark landscapes of the north midlands, the archaeology of these movements and the relationships they fostered is attested in mundane features which are normally dismissed or overlooked: trackways, paths or drove-ways (2007). In East Yorkshire, paths have been found running alongside earthworks, as at Walkington Wold (Bartlett and Mackey 1972) and Riplingham (Wacher 1966). Scuffed entranceways were also found at breaks in banks near Duggleby Lodge (Lawton 1992) and Fimber (Ehrenberg and Caple 1983; 1985). Such marks denote the repeated rhythms of pasturing, watering and shelter, which created a series of connections between places, prescribed by the linear earthworks. This archaeology is vital because *these* are the contexts in which competing groups worked out their tensions, jostling for prestige, power and rights of way, through their herds and flocks. As one elderly Turkana woman put it, when talking to the ethnographer McCabe, pastoralism is both necessary and dangerous, for ultimately it is the 'cattle [who] bring us to our enemies' (2004, 105).

A time and a place – Melton

One new site, excavated under developer-funded conditions, enables us to view this period of landscape and social transformation in detail. This is the site of Melton, lying just inland of the north coast of the River Humber but within easy reach of the foot of the chalk Wolds (Fenton Thomas 2011). By the middle Iron Age (*c*.500 BC), a set of three parallel ditches running north–south had been dug across an area of open grazing (*ibid.*, figs 199 and 200). Two of these earthworks clipped the edge of an ancient round barrow, suggesting it had not just been used as a marker for the alignment (*ibid.*, 359) but that its incorporation into this new project may have been a contentious act of appropriation. Through discussion in this chapter, we have become familiar with the scale and form of these features but we must remember that in each case, their digging was a potential divisive act, with long-lasting consequences. In between these ditches ran a small pit alignment, and traces for post-pipes in some of these suggest they may once have held large wooden stakes: perhaps representing an early stage of the boundary (*ibid.*, 368). Others show evidence of re-cutting, indicating they were cleaned out and re-defined. A slighter ditch was also truncated by the easternmost earthwork, again suggesting phasing to this complex set of features, and their maintenance and care over time.

To the north, this triple linear feature stretched on and away towards the steep foothills of the Wolds (a few hundred metres away) suggesting that this was an important axis of movement. This may have been for taking stock between areas of pasture, or guiding the flow of people from the Wolds to the Humber foreshore and back (Fenton Thomas 2011). Yet it was at this particular juncture that a series of activities began to focus. A further set of earthworks crossed the site east–west, forming a junction with a hollow-way to the east. The east–west trackway became the focus for a number of important features: three 'four-post' structures, probably best interpreted as raised stores or granaries, as well as some pits containing burnt stone, fired clay from an oven and 'lid-seated' cauldron vessels, diagnostic of the fifth–fourth century BC (*ibid.*, 363). There was also a system of linear gullies with postholes which probably represent fence-lines: in one of these was found a fragment of wild boar tusk, pierced for suspension – perhaps a memento of a dangerous and glorious hunt. This 'open' settlement and occupation has the overall feel of something inhabited seasonally or sporadically and may not represent permanent residence (Fenton Thomas 2011). Such a model ties in well with the rhythms of movement discussed above, supporting the notion that at least a section of this population was engaged in pasturing activities which took them away from Melton itself and up onto the Wolds.

Whether people were living here year-round or not, the presence of a unique set of burials indicates this was a significant place for people to be interred. Seven inhumations in small grave pits were found in a small linear cemetery, along the eastern edge of the north–south boundary (Fenton Thomas 2010, 371). The radiocarbon dates suggest a range between the eighth and sixth centuries BC, most likely clustering towards the latter part of the period. As discussed above, burials or cremations dating to the early Iron Age period are extraordinarily rare, and have largely been found as secondary insertions in earlier monuments. At Melton, this connection with an ancient feature may also be present. At the centre of this group of burials lay a primary coffined inhumation of a male, complete with many sherds of Beaker pottery. A later burial – also a coffined male – had cut into this grave, as if recognising and mimicking the earlier rite. Fenton Thomas posits that an early Bronze Age grave may have been marked in such a way that it enabled these much later Iron Age inhabitants to uncover and investigate the grave: interring one of their own dead in a manner in keeping with this ancient forebear (2011, 48, 373). However, it is also possible both interments date to this early Iron Age phase, and that the former was merely associated with residual Bronze Age material, re-deposited in the grave fill. Whatever the case, the latter grave deliberately and strategically sought to associate the newly deceased with the exact place of burial of either a known or presumed ancestor. (This is a theme which can be seen as a growing concern in the square barrow cemeteries – Chapter 3). One of the other graves contained a double burial, pairing the body of an elderly woman with that of a young girl. Indeed, most of the burials were of women, and the osteological report suggests the stresses and strains of agricultural life (including some fractures, evidence for disease and infection, poor nutrition and work-related physiognomic changes to teeth and hands) had taken their toll (Cafell and Holst in Fenton Thomas 2011, 46).

This startling evidence suggests we may well be seeing an emergent inhumation rite, which preceded any Continental contact. A lack of systematic dating of other flat grave crouched inhumations may mask analogous early Iron Age examples (a point made by Brewster in 1980). Alongside the other examples discussed above, Melton suggests that Iron Age people were developing a discourse on place and belonging which involved formal inhumation, close to ancestral mounds and important boundaries. They may thus have been predisposed to the arrival of Continental ideas on burial which elaborated an existing nascent mortuary rite: enhancing the appearance of such graves through the addition of a square barrow monument. This is what happened at Melton itself. Close to the juncture of the earthworks and the early round barrow (as well as the small mounds of the early Iron Age graves), a single square barrow was constructed. It contained an inhumation with an offering of pork, and a Corieltauvian coin dating to the first century BC, suggestive of a late burial towards the end of the fashion for this rite. By this stage, the settlement had grown. The postholes and ring gullies of four roundhouses attest to more permanent residence, associated craft activities such as iron working (indicated by slag, a hearth base and a whetstone) and weaving (loomweights and bone needles), with cereal and weed seeds, hazelnut fragments, and grass and turf debris, suggesting a range of cultivation and resource management activities nearby (Fenton Thomas 2011). Extensive colluvial deposits under these features suggest either woodland clearance or more intensive cultivation had begun to dramatically change both the appearance and use of the land to the north, increasing hillwash, downslope towards the settlement (*ibid.*, 364). By this stage, the north–south linear had become a sunken hollow-way, running north to the Wolds and south to the shores of the Humber. There is a feel of much greater permanence to the site at this point in its history, not least in the presence of the monumentalised burial, and the increasing division of the landscape into demarcated task areas. The settlement has many parallels in other droveway or ladder enclosures on the Wolds, yet at least part of this inhabitation was contemporary with the square barrow and therefore, of interest to this study. After around a century, when the roundhouses were falling into decay, a series of infant and animal burials were interred into the edge of these domestic sites. The silted-up ditches of the trackways indicate yet another shift in the site's use: hereafter, a period of abandonment. Other ladder enclosures developed into later Roman nucleated farmsteads: a pattern repeated elsewhere on the Wolds and in Holderness (Giles 2007a).

Conclusion

The site of Melton captures the broader social and landscape transformations which characterised the first millennium BC in East Yorkshire. In the early Iron Age, a concern with creating boundaries and demarcating routes of movement was accompanied by ephemeral, possibly seasonal settlement but also a rare set of early burials. It began to formalise the relationship between a particular group of hard-living people, and this place between the waters of the Humber and the hillslopes of the Wolds. In the next few hundred years, more permanent settlement, represented by roundhouses and craftworking evidence, cultivation debris and a new, monumentalised burial – a square barrow – suggests an increasing desire for permanence, both of the living and the dead.

Melton thus provides us with a unique insight into the different temporal rhythms which structured people's lives during this era. At an immediate level, the movements of people and stock created a series of interlinked cycles: day-to-day watering and pasturing; the seasonal patterns of lambing, calving or foaling; gathering for shelter, shearing or culling. This annual cycle was of course nested within the sowing and harvesting of crops, and gathering of other resources. Those cyclical rhythms were in turn situated within a generational one: the life-cycle of the family, and the works, events and incidents which marked its history within a broader community. Finally, it has been suggested that an ancestral rhythm was beginning to emerge amongst these communities, in which distant or more recent forebears were used to negotiate access to resources. What the chapter has tried to conjure is the particular kind of history that was becoming important to these communities: one concerned with descent and inheritance, strategically linked to rights of place. This is the context in which the square barrow burial rite was taken up by these communities, and it is to that process that the next chapter now turns.

CHAPTER THREE

Building Biographies:
Houses and Households

Introduction

When the Rev. Maule Cole visited the cemetery at Danes Graves in the late nineteenth century, he described the appearance of the barrows 'as cobbles on a pavement' (1897, 300). What he recognised in the broad, low mounds was that it was not height, nor magnitude that mattered to the Iron Age grave diggers, but the effect of the sheer number of small monuments, and the way they clustered, cheek-by-jowl, alongside each other. Aerial archaeologists often describe their appearance as looking like 'frogspawn': the boundary ditches of each barrow often shared with its neighbour to create an indivisible community of the dead, in which each individual nonetheless has a discrete and notable place … a part within a whole. What did this architectural relationship mean to those who constructed it, time and time again?

This chapter will explore the tension between an apparent emphasis on the community and the consistent demarcation of individuals within it. It will explore this dialectic through both cemetery and settlement, in order to examine the ways in which relations were constituted between people, in both life and death. Within the cemetery, a pattern of internal differentiation can be seen in the clustering of barrows in different regions, which, I will propose, was an expression of relatedness. The chapter will analyse the particular place of the chariot burials within such cemeteries, noting that they were 'set apart' from these family clusters. I will then go on to discuss the lesser known settlements dating to the middle–late Iron Age, apparently characterised by their 'open' organisation. Yet here, too, the chapter will argue, there is a sense of loose clustering into different household 'zones', suggesting a sense of internal division, probably along lines of kinship. In both settlement and cemetery then, I will argue that the use of architecture to express and reproduce social relations (and sometimes, significant distinctions) was key. However, the dominant motif which emerges from these sites is an interest in building a sense of long-lived residence and permanence, grounded either in the life and longevity of the household, or the serried ranks of ancestral dead: anchoring this community to the valley which it inhabited.

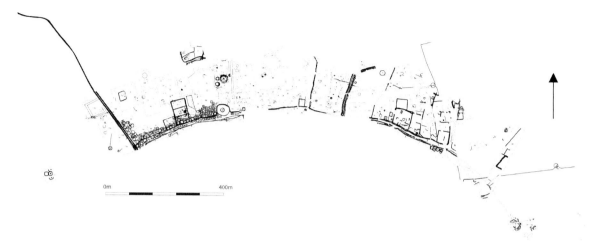

0m   400m

Square barrow cemeteries

Living with the dead

> The dead surround the living. The living are the core of the dead. In this core are
> the dimensions of time and space. What surrounds the core is timelessness.
>
> 1996a, 62.

This the first of John Berger's *Twelve Theses on the Economy of the Dead*. Working
and writing within a small peasant farming community in the Haute-Savoie,
Berger is attuned to the exchanges which happen between the past and the present:
the weight of memory which accrues over time, and the ongoing influence of the
dead amongst the affairs of their descendents. 'Having lived', he argues in the last
of his theses, 'the dead can never be inert' (*ibid.*, 63). For the middle–late Iron
Age inhabitants of Wetwang and Garton Slack, this close affinity with forebears
is made evident in the juxtaposition of the cemetery (running along the lower
edge of the valley side) with the settlement (perched just above it, Figure 3.1).
Excavations by a series of archaeologists … the Granthams from Driffield, T.
C. M. Brewster and John Dent … proved that the places of the living and the
dead were contemporaneous (Dent 1982; 1984a). This cemetery was within close
walking distance, and environmental evidence suggests many were set within turf
downland that was actively grazed (Stead 1991, 179). Here, the living lived close
by the dead. It was arguably the organisation of that cemetery which structured
their sense of time – in terms of a sense of genealogy and descent.

The square barrow

Let us begin by describing the monuments which make up these cemeteries.
Typical barrows in the Makeshift cemetery were between 4.0–5.4 m square, with
smaller examples no more than 3 m across and larger examples reaching 10 m
in diameter (Stead 1991, 7). Chariot burials meanwhile, can range from 12 m
diameter (the largest grave at Wetwang Slack: WS454) to 8 m diameter at Ferry

FIGURE 3.1. Wetwang and
Garton Slack settlement
and cemetery, showing
areas of excavation and
features dating from the
middle to the later Iron
Age. Composite image
based on maps by T. C.
M. Brewster 1975; 1980;
and John Dent 1984a;
1985; 2010.

Fryston (Boyle *et al.* 2007, 131). However, at Danes Graves, the 27 foot (8.2 m) diameter of the chariot burial was exceeded by a 30 foot diameter (9.1 m) mound which contained the remains of five individuals, and a 33 foot diameter (10.1 m) barrow containing a female buried with a beautiful 'wheel-shaped' pin (Mortimer 1897, 3–4). Square barrows up to 12 m in diameter were also found at Garton Station whilst the K5 chariot burial at Kirkburn was 12.5 m across (Stead 1991, 17 and 25). At Scorborough, where the barrows still remain unploughed, the overall diameter of the mounds can reach 15.6 m in diameter (Stead 1979, 18). However, as Dent found in his analysis of Wetwang, there was no simple correlation between barrow size and the relative 'wealth' of the burial interred within it (1984a).

The original depth and width of the surrounding square ditches have, in many cases, been diminished by the erosion of the original ground surface through ploughing. However, in the Great Wold Valley they average 0.85 m deep and 2 m wide (Stead 1991, 7). At Garton Station a 'two-phase' construction is suggested in barrows H and J, where an initial enclosure was dug and rapidly backfilled (there was no silting) before a slightly larger extension was made to three sides (Stead 1991, 21 and fig. 20). This may suggest an initial phase of planning or marking out, replaced by a more monumental final version.

At Danes Graves, Greenwell found that some interments had been made in very shallow grave pits in the subsoil: leaving a slight depression rather than being cut into the bedrock (1906, 260) – a pattern noted also by Stillingfleet at Arras (*ibid.*, n. a). There may well have been a number of true 'flat graves' and their subsequent removal by the plough may explain some of the apparently 'empty' barrows found by Stead in the Great Wold Valley which might otherwise be interpreted as cenotaphs (e.g. Stead 1991, 9 – R113, R149, R198). Most burials however, were interred in sub-rectangular grave pits up to 1.2 m (Stead 1991, 8) or 4½ foot (1.4 m) in depth (Mortimer 1911, 43).

Original heights are also hard to estimate: when the antiquarians recorded them in the late nineteenth century, surviving upstanding mounds at Danes Graves varied between 15–30 inches (38–76 cm) up to 3 feet (91 cm, Mortimer 1897, 2) or even 3½ foot (1.07 m) in height (Greenwell 1906, 260). From the volume of spoil available from the grave ditch of the large Pexton Moor barrow, Greta Anthoons has calculated a maximum original height of 1.35 m (2011). In contrast, at Scorborough in the 1970s, the maximum height of surviving barrows was only 30 cm, resembling a broad, flattened platform (Stead 1979, 18). Inevitably, as the upcast spoil from the mound began to erode, the barrow mounds soon achieve a more rounded profile (Stead 1991, 7), explaining why antiquarians were so late in recognising the dominant 'square ditched' plan (Stead 1979). Excavating on Skipwith Common in 1855, for example, William Proctor realised that although the mounds 'are circular ... [they were each] surrounded by a square fossa' (1855, 187). However, Stead and Dent also found distinctive Iron Age barrows with round encircling ditches within their cemeteries: the former, in isolated cases at Rudston and Burton Fleming, as well as a cluster of 'speared' burials at Garton Station (1991), and the latter particularly in the 'late' phase of use of the Wetwang cemetery (1984a). Sheppard also argued that many of the barrows at Eastburn were in fact circular rather than square, although no detailed plans were made at this airfield salvage excavation on the cusp of the Second World War (Sheppard 1939).

Cemetery location and size

Several of the cemeteries are located in clear reference to 'ancient monuments', most notably at Wetwang Slack where an enormous early Bronze Age barrow, 'D', was encircled by a middle Iron Age linear earthwork (Dent 1979, 27). This linear ran on to the west: forming a discontinuous ditch running along the base of slack which delineated the southern margin of the cemetery (*ibid.*). Examples of smaller square barrow cemeteries built close to round barrows include Craike Hill (near Garton) and Raisthorpe Wold (near Wharram). Meanwhile, the axial alignment of the Burton Fleming–Rudston cemeteries roughly follows that of the cursus monument running along the valley base (Stead 1991, fig. 1). Indeed the dense accumulation of cemeteries in this fault-twisted stretch of the valley may well relate to the presence of particularly impressive ancestral features alongside the cursus routes: Maiden's Grave henge and the Rudston monolith – giving the area a special ancestral cachet or spiritual significance (Dent 2010). As the last chapter discussed, Iron Age people inherited a 'mythical landscape' (Barrett 1999c) full of curious works which they sought to draw into their own projects for a variety of ends: re-negotiating their sense of identity and belonging to place, at a time of significant change.

Many cemeteries are quite small, and were either short-lived or added to only rarely, such as Kirkburn and Garton Station. Some of these are found in elevated topographic positions and are early in date (like Cowlam; Stead 1986). Others are more low-lying and – as a tightly involuted brooch from a burial at Caythorpe indicates – occupy the middle period of the rite (Dent 2010, 22). There are also isolated burials (Grimthorpe, North Grimston) accompanied by swords, which may be distinctively late (Stead 1991, 181). However, the majority of barrows are found in larger cemeteries which accumulated over centuries: in the case of Wetwang Slack, probably 250–300 years. They are usually positioned in or near the base of valleys (Wetwang and Garton Slack, Burton Fleming and Rudston) or else in visually dominant topographic locations, such as Arras. Counted together, the spread of cemeteries running along the north–south 'turn' of the Gypsey race number 279 burials (Stead 1991). At Wetwang Slack, a total of 446 burials were excavated, including some 'double' mother and infant burials, or secondary insertions in the surrounding ditch (Dent 1982, 437). Brewster excavated a further five burials within the parish of Wetwang, and a total of 46 burials at Garton Slack, again including double adult and adult/infant or neonate burials. This remarkable valley complex also included three chariot burials, lying to the west of the main Wetwang cemetery (Dent

1985) and a further chariot burial on a ridge south of this, at Wetwang Village (Hill 2002). At Arras, there were over 100 barrow mounds (Stead 1979, 9; though Greenwell suggests nearer 200, 1906, 255), at Eastburn 50 (*ibid.*, 18) and at Scorborough (one of only two barrow cemeteries where the mounds have not been completely ploughed out) there are at least 120 (*ibid.*, 18). Folklore recalls that the other example of a surviving cemetery – Danes Graves – once contained over 500 barrows, standing proud of the surrounding chalk farmland (Greenwell 1865, 108, note 7).

Rarely, we can glimpse the preparations which led to the digging of these graves. Some burials retain evidence that the land was partially de-turfed, and that sods (or similar organic matter) were placed on the bottom of the grave pit (as suggested at the chariot burial in Garton Slack 11, Barrow 2: Brewster 1980, 387). A chariot burial at Garton Station contained a dark patch of silt rich in molluscan remains which seemed to represent a turf deliberately included in the grave (Thew and Wagner in Stead 1991, 150–1). Grass impressions were also noted just below the sword hilt from R24, suggesting a tussock or sod was present under the burial (Stead 1991, 124).

Burial rites

In his 1991 summary of excavations in the Great Wolds Valley, Stead was able to describe four main variations in burial practice. Burials on both the surface and in grave pits (rite 'A') were commonly crouched or contracted, and many of them were laid on their left-hand side, with the long axis of their body orientated north–south, so that the deceased effectively 'faced' east. Opposing examples, where the body was placed on its right-hand side, facing west, are also common. Most rite A burials are single inhumations of adults but double burials are also known, including paired adults as well as mothers and neonates/infants. (Some have secondary insertions into either the barrow mound or surrounding ditch: characterised as rite 'D' – see below). At Danes Graves, however, grave no. 85 contained five individuals. Elsewhere in this cemetery, there were three rare primary burials of juveniles (Stead 1979, 17). Out of the burials analysed for this study, 60% were interred with some kind of durable object (though of course the other 40% may have been associated with clothing and organic artefacts which have since decayed). As a percentage of the total, this figure was considerably lower in certain cemeteries, such as Wetwang Slack. The most common inclusions were a simple earthernware jar, which often included a joint of mutton or goat (Figure 3.2). Items such as brooches, bracelets, bead necklaces, and rings or pendants are also included, alongside rarer examples of weapons and tools. Evidence for coffins, in the form of soil stains and mineralised wood, are also found in these burials. This form of burial may have begun around the fourth–third centuries BC and continued to be practiced into the last phases of cemetery use. (These grave goods are discussed further in chapter 5).

In contrast, rite 'B' is characterised by flexed or extended burials, often

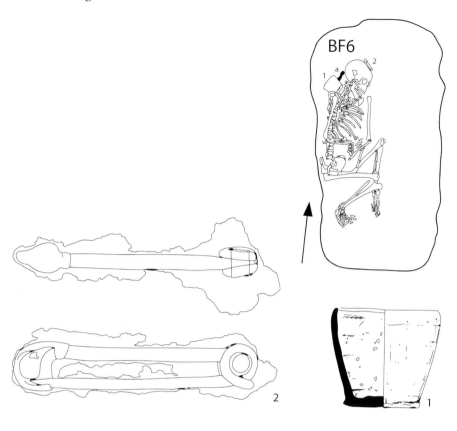

FIGURE 3.2. Iron Age square barrow burial with jar, brooch and joint of lamb. BF6, based on Stead 1991, 213, fig. 116. (N.B. objects not to scale)

orientated with their long axis east–west. Corpses may be laid on their back or sides. Many lack a surrounding enclosure ditch, being interred in the 'interstices' between earlier mounds or were nestled up against earlier features such as linear ditches, suggesting they may not have been covered by a barrow (e.g. R199, R200, R201). Where they include grave goods, these are often characteristic of the latest phases of this burial rite, *c.* first century BC–early first century AD. A higher proportion of these graves contained tools (relating to textiles, carpentry and metalwork) or weapons (spears, swords, shields and knives) than rite A graves. Spindle whorls are only found in rite B burials. Offerings of pork were common, but mutton was rare. Few brooches were found and there is no example of a rite B burial which contains a ceramic vessel. Stead has interpreted this as a 'late' phase of the burial rite, developing from rite 'A', perhaps within the space of a generation (Stead 1991, 181), indicating subtle ideological shifts amongst these communities towards the end of the Iron Age.

Rite 'C' is used by Stead to distinguish burials accompanied by unusual traits: key amongst these is the inclusion of pork (though as we have already seen, this was also found in many rite 'B' burials), but also more complex or composite grave goods such as swords or mirrors as well as the famous chariots and their fittings (1991). Rite C burials often respect the dominant posture and orientation favoured by rite 'A' but often without a coffin: in the chariot burials, the body is instead placed within or covered over by the dis-assembled remains of the cart box. Its pole shaft is usually placed along the long axis of the grave, with the axle below the feet, and the yoke usually along the back, often with the horse-gear still attached. The box is usually placed over the body, or else the body is placed within it. The wheels may be laid on the floor of the grave (as at Arras, Wetwang Slack, Garton Slack, Wetwang Village and Kirkburn) or propped at the side (as at Garton Station). However, examples from both the North Yorkshire Moors (Pexton Moor, Cawthorn Camps) and West Yorkshire (Ferry Fryston) indicate that some vehicles were interred whole, more akin to their Continental counterparts: wheeled into deep grave pits, with their trappings intact (see Chapter 6 for further discussion). All but one of these burials are single inhumations (Danes Graves being a double burial: Mortimer 1897; Greenwell 1906). Rite C burials contain a range of impressive artefacts: weaponry (swords in decorated scabbards, shields and rare spearheads), rare pins, brooches, iron mirrors, bags and boxes.

Rite 'D' describes secondary burials found interred into the top fill of the grave pit, the barrow mound or surrounding enclosure ditch. It was added by John Dent to Stead's typology, to describe large numbers of this sort of burial found at Wetwang Slack (1995, 74). The rite is predominantly used for infants and juveniles, who are usually unaccompanied by grave goods. It appears that the primary purpose was to locate these individuals in relation to an established relative or ancestor. Dent also suggests this rite is characteristic of the latter phases of the cemetery's use (1984a).

Rite A dominates most cemeteries, but rite B is also found particularly in the Argam Lane section of the Rudston cemetery with a couple of examples found also at Burton Fleming, and isolated burials at both Wetwang and Garton Slack. The secondary burials of rite D are also particularly common at Wetwang and Garton Slack. Cart or chariot burials are found in many of the major cemeteries such as Arras, Danes Graves, Garton Station, Kirkburn, Wetwang and Garton Slack, and Beverley Westwood, with apparently 'stand-alone' examples recorded from other sites such as Wetwang Village, Hunmanby, Middleton and Pexton Moor amongst others. Examples of rite C may have been present at the other Great Wolds Valley cemeteries but were simply not discovered in the excavation programme.

Dating burials

There is an inherent problem in the absolute dating of Iron Age burials, arising from the plateau in the radiocarbon calibration curve (Haselgrove *et al.* 2001). The style, form and fashion of artefacts, alongside stratigraphic evidence for depositional sequences, have therefore continued to play an important part in our understanding of the square barrow burial rite. Stead believed that the earliest square barrow burials might be fourth century in origin, continuing up until the early first century BC (1979). Individual cemeteries however, would have had their own distinct history of interment. The four rites overlap in time but there is sufficient stratigraphic and artefactual evidence to suggest rites A and C mainly pre-date rite B, and that rite D also becomes more common in the latter phases of cemetery use (Stead 1991).

It is only recently that a larger suite of radiocarbon dates (undertaken for the 'Technologies of Enchantment' project) have been made available through the Celtic Art Database (Gwilt, Joy and Hunter 2010). These have been added to by dates ascertained as part of isotope analysis in a forthcoming study undertaken by an interdisciplinary team (Jay *et al.* 2012), to try and ascertain a finer understanding of both the main era of square barrow burial and the dating of the chariot burials. The results of the latter group's preliminary analysis for the Wetwang Slack cemetery indicates that burials began here in 420–245 cal BC (at 95% probability) with the last burials ending around 200–130 cal BC (at 66% probability – all dates, Jay *et al.* 2012). This gives a lifespan for the cemetery of around 180–290 years: two or three centuries. Their analysis of a range of chariot burials suggests that these may have begun in 400–300 cal BC (at 65% probability) and could either represent a relatively short-lived 'pulse' of burials, or a more protracted era of one-off interments (*ibid.*). Some chariot burials were no doubt direct contemporaries (Stead 1991, 181). Finer modelling of chariot burials containing short involuted brooches has suggested these might be placed, for example, two generations either side of 200 cal BC (Jay *et al.* 2012). This would suggest the chariot burials are neither diagnostically early nor particularly late.

The above dating programmes situate the chariot burials within the middle part of a much longer period of cemetery usage, usually spanning 200–300 years. During this time, we might anticipate that there were particular 'pulses' or trends in burial style, reflecting shifts in both fashion, cultural preference and underlying ideology. What is clear however, is that this burial rite ended well before Rome crossed the Humber. Indeed, although early Roman imports were reaching the north coast of the estuary in the late first century BC–early first century AD (as at Redcliff: Crowther, Willis and Creighton 1989), none of these products are seen in the late Iron Age burials. It appears that the communities of the Yorkshire Wolds – for whatever reason – were not engaging in sustained exchange with such early ports of trade (see Giles 2007a). Combined with the relative lack of distinctive late Iron Age fibulae from these cemeteries (apart from R175: a 'Nauheim' style brooch and WS117), it appears that the square barrow burial rite had largely disappeared by the first century BC.

Orientation

In his burial rite typology, Stead noted the mourners had arranged the corpse in preferred orientations and postures, with subtle changes over time (1991). What did such choices mean? Three aspects of orientation may have been significant: the long axis of their body (where the head and feet were placed), the side on which they were laid (left or right) and the way in which the corpse was turned to face. These attributes may relate to important cosmological principles: the rising or setting of the sun and moon, or the appearance and passage of various cosmic entities such as key constellations. They may indicate important cardinal orientations (discussed further below), which were thought to be auspicious, or else were related to the time or season of death. Alternatively, cardinal directions may have related to people's sense of kin-based or ancestral/spiritual 'homeland', so that they were faced towards the land to which they were headed in the afterlife. Equally, they might have been used to indicate the clan or kin group from which people hailed: their natal valleys perhaps. Another possibility is that they were 'faced' towards particular architectural or natural features: the run of the valley, down which visitors or strangers might pass, the house they had lived and died in, or the drove-road they had taken each evening with their stock. Finally, the side on which they were laid may have indicated left or right-handedness, or the values and principles these directions embodied for different communities (see Hertz 2004). These meanings may have intermixed in complex and subtle ways, and they are ultimately beyond our understanding, but we can note some interesting trends.

As a relative proportion of the total number of burials, one orientation dominates (Figure 3.3): burial with the head to the north, feet to the south, lying on the left-hand side, facing east. Close behind this is its cardinal opposite: head to the south, feet to the north, lying on the right-hand side, so that the body was still facing east. This may support Parker Pearson's idea of an 'orientated' Iron Age body, for whom the east conjured a series of auspicious meanings (1999a; see also Whimster 1981). In relation to funerary rites, its association with the rising of the sun and the dawning of light might have been used to suggest powers of regeneration and cyclical renewal. In addition, many of the valley systems in which these cemeteries were located opened out towards the east. Ultimately, to the east lay the sea, and the important harbours of Bridlington and the landing point of Flamborough Head. If there was any myth of a distant, Continental 'origin' of the ideology which underpinned this burial rite, east may have been perceived as an ancestral homeland, with which these communities had spiritual (as well economic) ties (see Chapter 7).

However, there are also a considerable number of burials – particularly at Rudston, Burton Fleming, Wetwang and Garton Slack, where people are buried facing the opposite direction – west – through orienting their head to the north or south, and lying the corpse on either left and right-hand sides. The west was the position of the setting sun, as well as the heads of the major valley systems, the origin of many springs and streams (such as the Great Wold Valley Gypsey Race), and the highest point of the Wolds, running along its north-western scarp edge. Again, these associations might be drawn upon in the funeral rite, to conjure metaphors of death (the sinking sun, passing into night) and renewal (the origin point of the main source of fertility in these valleys: water). Parker Pearson has suggested that westerly facing orientations might be a way of marking social difference, of elites or other segregated

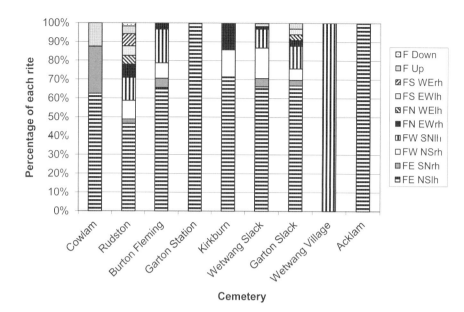

FIGURE 3.3. Orientation of the body in the grave, in different cemeteries. Key: (e.g.) F = facing direction; WE = head to west, feet to east; rh = lain on right-hand side.

groups (1999a, 45) yet there is no simple correlation of this orientation with burial rite or grave goods. To the west of the Wolds lay the iron-bearing region of Hasholme, and ultimately, the Irish and Atlantic seas. Burial facing west may have evoked memories of birth districts (perhaps these individuals had 'married in'), special places (the highest points of the Wolds, studded with earlier prehistoric monuments) or more distant places and communities with which these individuals had strong associations, even trading links.

As noted above, burials facing north or south, with the long axis of their body orientated east–west (or *vice versa*) are characteristic of rite B, and thus cluster in the same cemeteries where this late rite appears: Rudston and Burton Fleming, as well as Wetwang and Garton Slack. It is not clear what this 'reversal' of the major cardinal orientation meant: it might have marked a major ideological shift but continuity in other respects suggests it may simply have been a means of signalling difference from the older tradition.

Single and multiple burials

The majority of burials are single inhumations, the exception being the 'mother and neonate/infant' interments which suggest death in late pregnancy, during childbirth or in the postpartum period. In these examples, the child is sometimes *in situ* in the womb, or between the legs (see Chapters 4 and 5). In a number of cases, the inclusion of two adult burials in the grave may have influenced their position, buried 'top to toe' (e.g. R118 a and b, R51a and b and WS447–448) though others are buried side-by-side (BF61 a and b, WS54–55, WS228–229, GS8/10 burials 3 and 4). Most of these burials contain a mix of adults and genders with no clear cause of death. However, R152a, an adult

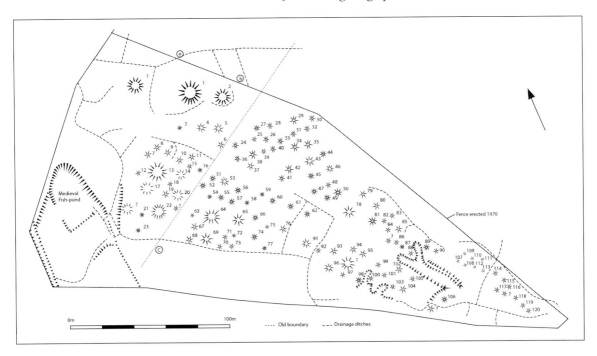

FIGURE 3.4. Scorborough
cemetery. Based on Stead
1979, fig. 4.

male 25–35 years old, probably died from an attack from behind with a spear, which would have penetrated his heart. The shaft has been snapped off, and he has been placed on his back. A second, slightly younger probable adult male, has been placed in the grave alongside him, in the same orientation, but this body is slightly inclined towards or slumped against the first body. There are no obvious injuries on this skeleton, but their contemporaneous death suggests several possibilities. It could be chance coincidence, with two adult men dying around the same time of different causes, who were paired together to have company on the journey into the afterlife. Alternatively, they may well have been killed in the same frenzied attack: a raid or altercation. R152b may even have been the perpetrator of the injury, who has been put the death alongside his victim, as a matter of blood-honour. He could even be a partner, close relative or companion, whose grief may have prompted his accompaniment of the deceased into the next world. The only example of a triple burial comes from Rudston: R185a–c. This adolescent and two juveniles are all buried with their heads to the south and turned inwards towards each other, but the burials were superimposed, suggesting they had died within a short space of time of each other, and were interred in the same plot. The burial of five individuals at Danes Graves is unprecedented (Mortimer 1911a). It included three adults and two juveniles – four of which were laid on their left-hand sides with their heads placed in a variety of different cardinal directions (one of the child burials was too decayed to discern its orientation, Greenwell 1906, 305). This latter child burial, along with two of the adults, appear to represent a primary interment, with another adult interred a foot above the burial pit surface and the final child inserted just under the covering mound. This last child wore an iron armlet, and the two primary adults wore bronze armlets: perhaps suggesting a family tradition or fashion. Unfortunately these remains no longer exist, but death either from a related disease or violent attack may be a strong possibility in this instance.

Cemetery architecture: constructing relationships

Moving beyond the arrangements *within* individual graves, what can the spatial arrangements *between* barrows tell us about these communities?

Maule Cole ventured that the 'peculiar groupings' of the mounds at Danes Graves site respected an 'ancient British way', as has been suggested in the last chapter (1897, 300). (Other cemeteries also share this strong relationship with linear earthworks and the trackways these may represent – for further discussion, see Chapter 7). Aerial photography confirms at least 400 barrow mounds once stood on this site (Stoertz 1997) but the impact of ploughing had reduced the number of barrows to 197 by the time of the first Ordnance Survey map (East Riding Archives and Local Studies, 1855: OS/1/144). The antiquarian Greenwell stated that these barrows were 'not arranged with any regularity' though he did note 'sometimes three or more are placed near to each other' (1906, 259). Yet his fellow excavator Mortimer disagreed: in the western corner of Danes Graves in particular, he argued, they were 'arranged roughly in lines' (1898, 119). This phenomenon of linear arrangements, clustering and grouping, can be seen in many of the larger cemeteries. For example, at Rudston in the Great Wold Valley, an initial row of barrows appear to respect a linear earthwork to the south, with two parallel rows subsequently reflecting this alignment (Stead 1991, fig. 7). Elsewhere in this cemetery, a central square barrow R27 is surrounded by three subsequent barrows which 'share' its original central ditch. Close by, burials R42–43 again share ditches built progressively alongside each other. Another 'row' can be seen between barrows R135–R147 (Stead 1991, fig. 13), whilst a multiple cluster of barrows (both square and rare, round ditches) is represented by R154–R167. Amongst the upstanding barrow mounds at Scorborough, multiple patterns are revealed between the barrows: larger mounds with circling 'satellite' burials, infilling the interstices, or smaller 'rows' and alignments (Figure 3.4). Yet it is the cemetery of Wetwang Slack which allows us to explore these arrangements most fruitfully, through the exemplary work of John Dent (1984a). From the air, the cemetery looks like an impenetrable conglomeration of barrows, many of which share adjacent ditches, producing the 'frogspawn' effect'. Yet by unpicking the stratigraphic relationships recorded in ditch cuts, compared with artefactual evidence such as brooch styles, Dent was able to piece together the history of this cemetery.

The initial burials appear to have been aligned along an existing trackway running west–east, along the base of the valley. A subsidiary track, running at right angles, formed the western edge of the cemetery, and its more diffuse eastern side (as has already been described) was demarcated by an ancient round barrow, enclosed by a large circular ditch. Initially, the barrows were quite well-spaced out within this 'zone' but over time, overlaps reveal how later burials 'filled in the gaps', seeking to associate themselves with earlier monuments (Dent 1982, 437). At some point, a new linear earthwork was cut east–west, bisecting an 'older' phase of the cemetery from a 'newer' one, and all subsequent burials were interred to the north of this. (The ditch around the ancient round barrow marking the eastern edge of the cemetery was also re-cut at this point). Whilst the motive for this remains obscure, it provided a way of marking the passage of time, suggesting a long-lived community of the dead who could be distinguished as more ancient or more recent forebears. Dent argued that earlier burials tended to be laid flat on the surface of the chalk or in shallow graves on quite large barrow platforms, whilst later burials used deeper grave pits and smaller barrow platforms (1982, 446 – a pattern also noted by Greenwell at the early cemetery of Cowlam, 1877 and confirmed by Stead 1986). Many of the smaller and deeper burials can partly be explained by an obsession in the latest phase for an exact *place* of burial: small barrows (some round, rather than square) were squeezed into the interstices between larger, earlier mounds: all the while taking care not to disturb the earlier burial. Dent argued this was an economic principle: making the most use of space during a time of increased population pressure on land (1982, 453) but an alternative interpretation can be made. I would argue that the over-riding concern by the end of this era was *where* one was buried, next to *whom*. It suggests an obsession with relationships, whether these had a genetic basis or not: creating an architecturally self-evident claim of association … in other words, a sense of descent.

In the absence of any genetic analysis or use of close-grained isotope study we rely upon other indicators to test this hypothesis. From the results of her analysis on the Great Wolds Valley cemeteries, the osteologist Sheelagh Stead demonstrated that burials near to each other often shared distinctive non-metric traits (in Stead 1991, 131–4). The small group of burials at Kirkburn is a perfect example of this, where adjacent burials K3, K4 and K5 shared the same parietal foramen non-metric trait (*ibid.*, 135). At Burton Fleming, burials BF24, BF25 and BF27 share the trait of metopism, as do another cluster: BF36, BF37 and BF40 (*ibid.*). She argued that these patterns reflected 'family groupings' within the architecture of the cemetery. At Wetwang Slack too, three adjacent burials (WS215, WS219, WS220) shared a peculiar spine deformity, whilst WS120 and WS134 shared traits of metopism, which Dent also interpreted as an indicators of kinship (1984a, 99 and appendix III). However, as the next chapter will discuss, the interpretation of such non-metric traits is fraught with problems, and cannot be relied on as a good proxy for genetic affinity (Tyrell 2000). More accurately, it can be seen as an indication that these individuals were part of a shared population living in a common environment. Nevertheless, I find the underlying motif convincing: whether these bonds stemmed from real blood-line connections or merely aspirant claims of decent, individuals in the latter part of this cemetery's life were sacrificing the size of their monument for an esteemed place next to a particular forebear with whom they claimed affinity. (As will be seen in Chapter 5, further connections are hinted at through shared orientations, funeral rites and grave goods, in adjacent burials). In other words, people were working to make these relations explicit, in a manner which endured over time: part of how you demonstrated affinity and provided a way of recounting it in the future *was* through the architecture of the cemetery. The barrows thus provided a set of architectural mnemonics which could have been mobilised in genealogical discourse. Inevitably, this provided an opportunity for some people to lay claim to a relationship with a particular ancestor to whom their links were rather distant, or even fictive.

At Wetwang, Dent was able to prove that the cemetery grew first from south to north, before dividing into three broad groupings in its later life: west, central and eastern (1984a). He interpreted this as three broad family or kin groups, beginning to favour discrete 'zones' or plots of burial, by the second–first century BC. However, the fact that they are all part of a broader whole – a combined cemetery – suggests a notion of wider affiliations or neighbourliness: principles which need to be explored further through the ways in which the living dwelt with and farmed alongside each other. Some phasing might be hinted at in burial and object styles: a short-lived 'pulse' of burials consisting of seven interments with La Tène II involute brooches at Makeshift, contrasts with the nearby Argam Lane cemetery where all 15 brooches seem to pre-date this fashion (Stead 1991, 83–92). However, if some of these brooches were curated and handed down as heirlooms, they may not indicate a particular phase so much as a favoured family fashion: meant to distinguish one group from another.

Why was this notion of relatedness so important? Ingold notes that ethnographers often portray agro-pastoralists as obsessed with geneaology (2000a, 133). Probing this trait – which is by no means a universal – he instead suggests that genealogical thinking is actually carried out within the context of a *relational* approach to the generation of knowledge and substance:

> That is to say, it is embedded in life-historical narratives of predecessors, of their movements and emplacements, and of their interventions – oftentimes from beyond the grave – in the lives of the successors
>
> 2000a, 134.

In other words, genealogy becomes a means for both thinking through *and* enacting particular kinds of relations: presenting a 'history of persons in the very peculiar form of a history of relatedness' (Ingold 2000a, 136). Once more, Ingold reminds us, this cannot be taken as a 'given'… even when it is presented as such by virtue of a notion of 'inheritance' … it takes work to perform and recount that lineage. It may have been presented of course, as a matter of bloodline but even this had to be recounted, enacted: describing someone's identity as a position within a *field* of relationships. Yet such relations may not have been restricted by notions of biological descent: in the late Iron Age communities of Gaul as well as early Medieval Ireland, people could become part of a 'family' not merely through direct genetic affinity but also a series of institutions such as fosterage, strategic alliances and marriage, apprenticeship, even hostage taking (Karl 2005; Anthoons 2011). In more recent ethnographic examples, Lambert discusses Rajasthani concepts of identity which not only rest on procreative links or these additional social mechanisms but also 'village kinship' (drawn particularly from the mother's natal village, 2000). 'Consanguinity', as Janet Carsten comments, can thus be based on 'shared qualities and affects transmitted through bodily substances *and* the local microenvironment' (2000, 22, my emphasis). She points in particular to the role of food, and events such as feasts, in creating bonds of affection and attachment that are equally part of what constitutes 'relatedness' ... people are literally 'fed' and 'grown' through these exchanges. When such events extend over significant periods of time, that community also becomes bound together by 'a mesh of stories and incidents if not family relationships' (Thomas 1991 cited in Shanks and Pearson 2001, 139).

We might posit then, that the community of Wetwang and Garton Slack felt itself to belong together, in part through the use of the cemetery to perform and articulate its various lineages and their relations with each other. Why was this important to them? They were trying to establish a sense of belonging. Gabriel Garcia Marquez puts this well in *A Hundred Years of Solitude* when one of his characters declares that it is not enough to have a child born in a particular locale: 'a person does not belong to a place until there is someone dead under the ground' (2000, 14). Time mattered. It gave them a sense of identity which stretched back through their parents, and their parents' parents. At Wetwang Slack, there are a series of female burials with blue glass bead necklaces, which seem to be spaced fairly evenly along the base of the slack, and are fairly early in its sequence of use. Many of these form the 'epicentre' of a cluster of later burials, which cut into or adjoin these 'founder' interments. For example, WS274 with 49 blue glass beads, is cut by WS262, which is in turn cut by WS261. WS236 with 77 blue glass beads, cuts WS235 but is in turn cut by WS241, then WS243 and WS242. WS249 with 75 blue glass beads, is cut by WS252 and then WS250. All three of these women are aged between 35–45 years (minimum estimate) and thus are amongst the more senior female members of the community: women of some eminence – matriarchal figures perhaps – whose graves formed a focus for their descendents.

This vast community of the dead would have confronted visitors, incomers or strangers, with the sheer weight of their numbers. It provided the broader community with an impressive series of lineages: anchoring them in place, through time. This was a distinctive change from the earlier Iron Age period. Such ancestors could now be remembered and named: their relationships rehearsed down the generations through the 'architectural geneaology' of the barrows. And so whilst these are individual inhumations, and people would no doubt have been able to articulate the personal biography and life history of the deceased, the ways in which these barrows were constructed made clear their interconnectedness: the *relational* nature of their identity, and their place within the wider whole (see Brück 2004). Given this, ties of family allegiance must have been held in delicate tension with the broader identity of the community. It took skilled and courageous individuals to hold such a group together, across their differences and divisions … this, it will be argued, was the role fulfilled by those honoured in magnificent funerals, with remarkable grave goods (Chapter 6 and 7). Interestingly then, when we view the location of many such burials … those with chariots, swords or mirrors … we often find that they are strategically 'cut out' from the main cemetery: either isolated as a proximate group within its heart (as at Arras) or located in a separate cluster set aside from other burials (such as Wetwang Slack and Wetwang Village) or even in cemeteries of a mere handful of 'special' burials, as at Kirkburn or Garton Station. It has been suggested that this is because they represent some form of 'royal' dynasty or elite family plot (Dent 1985) yet if this was the case, we might expect to find examples of juveniles, given the same treatment merely by virtue of their bloodline. An alternative interpretation is possible. If the notion of relatedness expressed through architectural affinity holds good, it might alternatively suggest that in death, as perhaps in life, such individuals were seen as 'cut out' from, and standing above, any mundane kin relations: aloof from the pettiness of such ties, able to adjudicate without prejudice, and to stand for the whole.

Arguably, it was the breakdown of that broader sense of community – always under threat from more individualistic interests – which led to the fission of its member households, and the creation of bounded settlements, separated from each other in space: the droveway or ladder enclosures dating to the late first century BC/early first century AD. As Dent describes, the open communities of the middle Iron Age, unified under impressive figures of authority, were replaced by these expanding hamlet-style settlements (2010). This also helps explain the apparently abrupt abandonment of the burial rite, and the disappearance of cemeteries which – as both symbols and celebrations of that larger community – had lost their meaning and relevance (Giles 2007a).

Summary

This section has explored the character of the square barrows, and the location and size of the cemeteries which were built over a course of several centuries. It has pointed to the importance of earlier prehistoric features, and how they sought to incorporate round barrows as well as earthworks and trackways, into these new architectural and mortuary projects. It has argued that the history of these cemeteries show changes in practice, from shallow early burials to deeper, late grave pits. It has also shown how Iron Age barrow ditches could be both square and round in plan, and it has discussed the different types of burials we find in these cemeteries. The overall impression is that whilst impressively large barrows often contain burials marked out as special in some way (by grave goods or number of interments) size was not the dominant issue. Instead, there was a strong preference for *where* people were buried, which strengthened over time. It has been argued that this was an expression of affinity, even descent. This was a palpably different way of being in the world, compared with the early Iron Age; one which has more in common, in fact, with the narratives of affinity and descent suggested in early Bronze Age barrows (Mizoguchi 1992; Barrett 1994). Yet what was different about these communities was the fact that the lineages of the dead were accompanied by settlements in which longevity of occupation was also important. It is to this evidence that the chapter now turns.

Place-making

Middle–late Iron Age settlement

Evidence for settlement which is contemporary with the square barrow rite is rare, and the best excavated example is the extended valley complex of Wetwang and Garton Slack. The apparent uniqueness of this site is likely to be deceptive since it is only here that archaeologists have been able to open-area strip a sufficient zone of the well-drained valley running to reveal the open settlement running alongside its cemetery (cf. Fenton Thomas 2008). Indeed, when the British Museum decided to look for the middle–late Iron Age inhabitants of the Great Wolds Valley in the 'Yorkshire Settlement Project', they mistakenly targeted the extensive pit features around Woldgate, only to discover these were largely early–middle Iron Age in date with little overlap with the square barrow rite (Rigby 2004, 106). As Rigby herself put it 'the scarcity of later pits … [implies] major changes in land use with the development of the Arras culture in the second half of the first millennium' (2004, 106). This change in land use was one of increased permanence, expressed not just in the numerous barrows of the dead, but the more monumental and long-lived houses of the living.

It is at Wetwang Slack that John Dent began to uncover this transformation. Here, a total of 80 round structures were found, spread over two square kilometres (see Figure 3.1; Dent 1982, 449). A substantial proportion of these represent the classic domestic structure of later prehistory: the roundhouse, but these 80 structures date to a broad range of periods (early Iron Age and into the later Roman period) and some represent the 'rebuilds' of houses on an old foundation (a point which will be returned to below). Other round structures may represent tool-stores or stock shelters, and in a rare few cases, funerary structures which Brewster termed 'mortuary houses' (1980). In other words, at any one time at Wetwang there would have been substantially less than 80 roundhouses. Though Dent later criticised his own population estimates, in an early study he argued this might represent a hamlet style community of between 35–84 individuals at any one time (1982, 450, 452). Notably, in the middle–late Iron Age, there are no permanent boundaries in this open settlement: the fence-lines, ditches and elaborate earthworks are a feature of the latest Iron Age period, as the valley was carved up into bounded enclosures. It is possible of course, that the in-between spaces were marked by garden or cultivation plots, which have left little trace (Dent 1984a). Even so, the appearance of this type of settlement is enough to prompt archaeologists like Cunliffe to argue that it represented 'an attitude to the community, and perhaps even to the ownership of land' which had no obvious counterpart in other areas of Britain (1995b, 56). Building on this idea, Sharples argued that status was not being expressed through differentiation in house size or form but rather, portable wealth:

> The Yorkshire elite does not appear to require elaborately bounded settlements or particularly substantial houses to define a status which is so well represented by the elaborate metalwork one finds in these graves

> 2010, 243, n. 3.

However, at both Wetwang and Garton Slack, there were examples of otherwise unremarkable roundhouses, demarcated by rectangular enclosures. At Wetwang Slack 9, a double-ring roundhouse B9:6, facing east, was flanked by a scatter of five shallow pits: accessible through the tight entrance of this enclosure (which appears to have been built over or adjacent to a pair of raised storehouses, Dent 2010, 59). At Garton Slack 14, a small palisaded enclosure which no obvious entrance contained another single roundhouse, from which came a penannular brooch and solitary glass bead, whilst a bronze bracelet had been deposited in a nearby pit. The houses are not particularly grand in size nor differentiated by depositional practice, so they do not appear to have an overtly ceremonial or communal focus. Instead, the act of enclosure may have been a significant way of distinguishing either their occupants or the use of this space: set apart from the rest of the 'open settlement'. Whilst it may have been a way of providing community leaders with a degree of architectural seclusion, emphasising the drama of visiting such individuals, these structures could equally have been used for events such as initiations or even mortuary rites. Further upslope at Wetwang Slack 11, another enclosure defined a pair of roundhouses with internal pits, whilst a small square enclosure in the south-east corner was associated with a nearby hearth, suggesting its possible use as a smithy (Dent 2010, 60). In this case, it may have been control of the craft which was significant, not just to limit danger from fire and fumes to the rest of the settlement, but to protect knowledge of this mystical craft and draw on its powerful associations (see chapter 6 and 7 for further discussion). Hence, within the symbolism of an open settlement, there were certain spaces 'set apart', defined by either the nature of their inhabitants or the activities which were undertaken there.

Alongside the roundhouses were a group of more irregular features: semi-circular slots which may well have been more ephemeral stock shelters or wind breaks (Dent 2010, 53), isolated posts or pairs which may have been hay-ricks or racks, and a variety of post-built structures on a square or rectangular plan, which have traditionally been interpreted as raised stores or granaries. Dent notes that a pair of post structures at Wetwang Slack were associated with evidence of burrowing by small mammals, strengthening this association (*ibid.*). However, some may have been raised platforms or watch-towers to scrutinise the grazing of stock, weather patterns, and the comings and goings of people in the valley (*ibid.*). Finally, there are pits, which may well have been used for storing grain, permitting a significant delay in its use (Reynolds 1979). However, they are generally small.

This valley-based settlement, with its internal 'grouping' or coalescence of residences is impressive, and so far, unique. However, tentative examples of other settlements have been uncovered through a variety of research and developer-funded projects. One of the best examples of Iron Age open settlement was found just to the north of the Wolds, at West Heslerton site 1 (Powlesland 1986). By the late Bronze Age, a pit alignment had been established running east–west, which was later cut-through by a narrow slot ditch (a pattern reminiscent of the sequences discussed in the previous chapter). To the north, a substantial group of roundhouses varied between 7–8 m diameter, and some had ancillary postholes suggesting porch-style entrance features (e.g. Structure 1). One structure had an oven or hearth base and a dense concentration of pottery (Structure 6). Over 20 sub-rectangular structures were also found, some of four-post construction but others with more elaborate six or seven post settings (Powlesland 1986, fig. 56). There were also a small number of pits. Rigby dated the ceramics of this complex firmly to the earlier Iron Age period (Powlesland 1986, 159) though she noted that some of the fabrics and forms have affinities with ceramics from the Burton Fleming cemetery (*ibid.*, 146). It may well represent the kind 'short-lived and intermittent' activity characteristic of the earlier Iron Age transhumant communities (Powlesland 1986, 159) yet its open character and range of features clearly shares much in common with the middle Iron Age settlement at Wetwang and Garton Slack. Interestingly, to the south-east of this site was a small trackway defined by wheel-ruts cut into the soft sand, with an average wheel-base of between 1.0–1.5 m diameter (Powlesland 1986, 134). These are in keeping with the most recent measurement of the internal track of the chariot found at Ferry Fryston (Boyle *et al.* 2007, 127) but may be on the small side compared with chariots at Wetwang and Garton (see chapter 6).

In contrast to the early Iron Age site at West Heslerton, many of the recent discoveries of Iron Age settlement relate to the first century BC: the other end of the period we are interested in. At Rudston, traces of late Iron Age occupation were found underneath the later villa. One eroded ring ditch gully and a more northerly arc of chalk wall (shadowed by an outer clay band) were found under Building 7 (Stead 1980, 19). On the East Site, at least six drainage gullies represented three phases, indicating that at one time, around four roundhouses stood on the site (Stead 1980, 21). The repeated rebuilding of houses on old foundations was a noted feature of this complex but the likely date of these houses places them in the first century BC and thus at the latter end of the square barrow burial era (*ibid.*). Other sites span the second–first century BC period, and thus at least partially overlap with the burial rite. At Creyke Beck, seven roundhouses were found, two of which were particularly well-preserved (Evans and Steedman 2001, 67). Group D included a double-ditched roundhouse with internal post-ring, and Group K contained a structure defined by a circular slot with basal post-settings, and an outer eaves drip gully (*ibid.*). This latter structure enclosed a deep pit containing significant amounts of carbonised cereal grains – chaff and weed seeds with barley, spelt and some emmer (2001, 68). Both sets of features were close to a major east–west linear earthwork and the site continued into the early Roman transition, incorporating a small 'animal' cemetery characteristic of these ladder settlements (Giles 2007a). North Cave is also characterised as an open settlement site, with eleven roundhouses represented by a variety of ring ditches and post-circles (Dent 2010, 60). This site may again begin around the second century BC but continues into the first century AD, with evidence for fence or hedge lines. Iron smelting was also carried out on this site, and the slag had been used as temper for the pottery made nearby.

Off the west side of the Wolds, a site at Carberry Hall Farm also contained two roundhouses, the second rebuilt on the site of the first, set within a ditched enclosure rich in plant and insect remains, suggesting the presence of a nearby pond (Humber Field Archaeology 2000b). This site also yielded iron working slag and hearth bases, as well as a hand-made jar of first century BC or slightly earlier date, but the enclosure ditches, infant and animal burials found here are characteristic of the latest Iron Age and early Roman period. There is an isolated roundhouse at Bempton Lane, near Bridlington, which may be of middle–late rather than later Iron Age date (Evans and Atkinson 2009, 252). Meanwhile, the roundhouses at Easington (Dimlington Road Gas Storage facility) probably date from the first century BC (Evans and Atkinson 2009, 259). They were associated with iron smithing slag, hearth bottoms and tuyère fragments, as well as a copper alloy crucible sherd and a structure tentatively identified as a pottery or salt drying kiln (WYAS 2007). A set of overlapping roundhouse ditches, representing rebuilding on the same foundations, were found at East Garton but the pottery again suggests a latest Iron Age date (*ibid.*, 262). Meanwhile, at Swainescaif, a couple of roundhouses, square post structures (granaries or fodder racks) and shallow slots and post/stake holes representing fencelines, also appear to date to the Iron Age, though whether they are early or late in the period has yet to be established (Evans and Atkinson 2009, 273).

This collection of recently discovered sites, both on and off the Wolds, probably represents a range of both permanent and more seasonally occupied residences, some with extensive agricultural features, others with craftwork evidence. In many cases, only the earliest phases overlap with the square barrow burial rite but there are a small number of more convincing examples. At least one of the roundhouses recently excavated by Network Archaeology at Shepherd Lane, Beverley was associated with a La Tène style brooch, suggesting a middle–late Iron Age date (Evans, pers. comm.).

At Caythorpe, on the summit of the wold, three circles of postholes excavated by NAA were interpreted as roundhouses (one of which was rebuilt, Abramson 1996, 18). One was associated with weathered sherds and a jet fragment suggesting a probable Iron Age date. These houses were importantly associated with two burials: one crouched adult burial and one disturbed infant burial, both apparently interred with Iron Age jars (*ibid.*, 20). Further along this parish, and close to the Gypsey Race stream, a second site has also yielded settlement and funerary evidence which may be contemporary in date. Here at site 3B, a series of seven roundhouses (some rebuilt on the same site) and ancillary structures were located on the north side of the river bank. (J. Fraser, pers. comm., courtesy of Humber Field Archaeology and the developer, *Centrica*). Just opposite, on the south side of the bank, were a set of Iron Age burials. One adult was interred in a square barrow, and clustered around it were four contemporary burials, including an inhumation with a spear, as well as a sword with a campanulate hilt. There were also suggestions of shield fittings laid over the man's lower legs. The discovery of a saddle quern and worked wood in the settlement tentatively supports a middle–late Iron Age. A separate development close to this site undertaken previously by NAA also revealed two square barrow burials: one of a juvenile primary burial, without grave goods, later re-cut by a young adult burial interred into the same grave pit – both orientated north–south (Abramson 1996, 20). The second square barrow burial was an adult orientated east–west, accompanied by a simple flint flake (*ibid.*, 21). The proximity of such inhabitation close to the monuments of the dead is reminiscent of Wetwang and Garton Slack, whilst the affinity between the burials and the Gypsey Race, mimics relationships further upstream at the cemeteries of Rudston and Burton Fleming. In addition, there is the site of Melton, discussed extensively in the last chapter, in which a late Iron Age square barrow burial was associated with a growing number of roundhouses and associated agricultural storage and craftwork, though once again the site's main use dates to the latest Iron Age/early Roman period. In sum, if we are to find the settlement which accompanies our square barrow burials, it suggests that the spaces adjacent to the cemeteries, especially on slighted elevated valley sides, represent the most likely locations. Only close-grained geophysics or open area excavation will help us identify such sites.

Roundhouses and households

From the above examples, it is evident that both post-ring built or ring and groove roundhouses are found on middle–late Iron Age sites in East Yorkshire, relating to different construction methods as well as availability of timber (Dent 2010, 20). Double and single-ring roundhouses are known, with some evidence for a transition towards the latter over time (*ibid.*, 52). Some roundhouses had terminal postholes or porches and quite a number had external drainage gullies (*ibid.*, 48). Most were of wattle-and-daub wall construction, with one example of clay-walls found at Sewerby (Steedman 1991) and small chalk foundation walls found at both Rudston (Stead 1980) and Caythorpe (Fraser, pers. comm.). In the Wetwang-Garton complex, Dent notes that most roundhouses had evidence for internal supports, with external ring grooves, and varied in diameter from 4m to 13m, with most between 6.5–9 m diameter (2010, 50). We might suspect the smallest of these had non-residential functions, as animal shelters, pens or wind-breaks. Some may not have been roofed, whilst those without obvious entrances may be hay-ricks or fodder racks. In contrast, some roundhouses had internal post and stake holes which suggest furniture settings. Most floor surfaces had been removed by the plough, as had any evidence for internal hearths, though pockets of old floor surfaces survive at Garton Slack 10 house 1 and Wetwang Slack house B9:4a. In the case of the latter, two successive compressed chalk floors had subsided into the top of an in-filled pit, both stained and charred with the probable location of an internal hearth (Dent 2010, 52). Dent notes that around 40% of roundhouses at Wetwang contained internal pits, but only in a few cases did these appear to be deliberate 'silos' for grain or other substances to be stored underground. These include a group of rectangular pits which Dent argues may have been lined by wooden bins or chests (*ibid.*, 54). Other household activities are hinted at in the presence of loomweights: a group of these found on the floor of Wetwang Slack 1 house 2 may suggests the original presence of an internal loom (*ibid.*).

The roundhouses were loosely clustered into zones within the open settlement, positioned in groups along the valley floor (Figure 3.5). For example, to the west of the linear earthwork which marks the edge of the cemetery at Wetwang Slack, there are four roundhouses in a row, running south–north: B12:1, B12:3 and B12:4 and B12:6, with a possible fifth house to the rear of B12:1 and B12:3. On the other side of the boundary, B8:4, B9:5 and B9:6 form another cluster. At Garton Slack, GS18 contains House 3, House 2 and House 1, in an almost identical, north–south arrangement. Again, in GS3 and GS 19, there are further clusters of roundhouses grouped together. This is not a universal pattern – there are as many examples of isolated roundhouses, or simple pairs – but it does suggest that rather like the cemetery, there were preferred 'zones' of affiliation between roundhouse groups. What did this mean? First, we have to ask what the roundhouse itself represents.

It has often been assumed that a roundhouse would contain a 'family' group, yet our definitions and representations of this often reflect the values, relations and even class structures appropriate to our own era (see Phillips 2005; Brück and Goodman 1999). Yet late Iron Age societies had a much more flexible definition of kinship than genetic affinity, with established mechanisms such as fosterage or adoption, for expanding the group beyond blood relations (Karl 2005, Parkes 2006 and Anthoons 2011). Can they then be defined by the structure they dwelt within, as a 'household'? Again, this is a loaded and problematic term, which focuses on the architecture as a physical frame of activity, rather than upon the social relations which may cross-cut such structures (Brück and Goodman

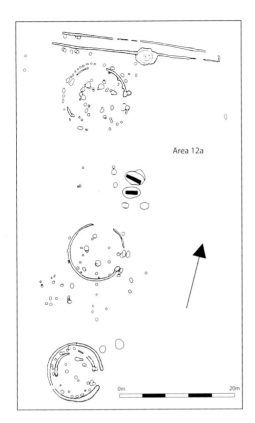

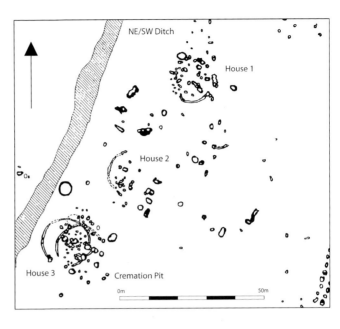

FIGURE 3.5. Clustering of roundhouse groups within Wetwang Slack and Garton Slack settlements. Based on Dent 1984a and Brewster 1980, respectively.

1999, 5; Sharples 2010, 187). Since we know so little about the nature of family make-up, the division of labour and rights amongst gender and age-sets, and the spatial and architectural organisation of tasks, we risk disguising forms of collaboration between households which may have been vital to family or community life. However, in his study of Iron Age Wessex, Sharples continues to use the term 'household' to refer to a 'co-resident' group, whilst noting this did not have any necessary functional significance (*ibid.*, 187).

Nevertheless, these impressive structures did frame daily life for these inhabitants, and were thus a key arena for the sharing of intimate social relations, and the learning of preferred cultural traditions, habits of behaviour as well as ideological principles (Bourdieu 1970; Parker Pearson and Richards 1994; Carsten and Hugh-Jones 1995). As Bachelard once put it, 'they [houses] are in us as much as we are in them' (1994 [1958], xxxiii). Close relationships must have developed between households and the buildings they constructed, dwelt in and finally abandoned (see Sharples 2010). This may have led to a metaphorical bond between the life-cycle of the house and those of its inhabitants (Brück 1999). Whilst Iron Age roundhouses could have lasted for several generations, with occasional repairs (Reynolds cited in Brück 1999, 149), an interesting and recurrent feature of the East Yorkshire roundhouses is the rebuilding of subsequent houses upon the same foundations. As well as the examples mentioned above at Rudston East Site, East Garton, Carberry Hall Farm and Caythorpe (both the NAA and HFA sites), Wetwang and Garton Slack contain numerous examples. At Wetwang, roundhouses B8:4 and B9:5 are completely replaced by later buildings. B7:3 and B7:7 were replaced by B7:4 (and this latter structure itself had two distinct phases of use). Other roundhouses had two distinct stages of use, usually representing a rebuild on the exact foundations of a larger diameter house, as at B9:4, B12:1, B12:4 and B12:5. In Brewster's excavations, he also noted extensive rebuilds at GS18 House 3, GS 5 semi-circular slots/House 1 and GS19 semi-circular slots 1–3: the latter two examples both represent three successive rebuilds of houses on slightly different foundations. It is evident that in many cases, the resulting building was slightly bigger, grander, perhaps representing the burgeoning success and fertility of the household. The complete dismantling of the fabric and structural timbers of the house would have been a challenging endeavour, but the preference for rebuilding on or near the same footings suggests that this consecutive history was vital. In replacing these houses, people re-encountered the traces of previous generations, working through a history of descent, and encasing the 'ghost' of the original house. As Brück and Goodman put it, the 'people that have dwelt there and the actions that unfolded there all impart meanings to a place' (1999, 14). It was this exact plot – redolent with those memories and associations – which rooted the household, giving it a feeling of ancestral anchorage and belonging. This was a sense of being centred on a domain (Barrett 1994, 147).

If we pair together this evidence with the fact that roundhouses often cluster together in small groups, as discussed above, we can begin to interpret some of the significance between these associations since, as Lawson argues, 'geometry organises our relationships' (2001, 100). It suggests that many families chose to associate themselves with specific neighbouring households. This reminds us of the cemeteries in which people chose to be interred in particular locales, creating 'clusters' of burials. Both in life and death, *where* you dwelt was part of how those relationships were constituted, reiterated and remembered.

Orientating life: the house as cosmological arena

The other striking feature of these roundhouses, as with many examples from Iron Age Britain, is their obsession with an easterly or south-easterly orientation. This has been interpreted by some archaeologists as a concern with major cosmological events, specifically, the rising of the sun at the equinox and midwinter (Oswald 1997). The importance of this latter event for farming communities has been poetically evoked by Gabriel Cooney, for this is the moment when 'light returns to the land' – when crops, animals and people begin to 'grow' (pers. comm.) Both practically and symbolically, it is a pivotal moment in the agricultural year. However, the preference for an easterly orientation has been seen more prosaically by others as a concern to avoid westerly winds and maximise sunlight into the roundhouse interior

(Guilbert 1975; Pope 2007). However, Fitzpatrick (1994) and Parker Pearson (1996) suggest that this key orientation reflects two key conceptual cycles in Iron Age life: diurnal and seasonal. They argue that the orientation and internal organisation of the roundhouse (in terms of use and task-zones) reflects the use of the house as a metaphor for intersecting patterns and schedules of agricultural life, pivoted around the rising sun. For example, the light, south side of the house would have been conceptually linked to daytime and domestic tasks, whereas the darker, north side of the house might be reserved for storage and sleeping. In other words, the roundhouse enshrined a prehistoric 'cosmology'. As Sharples points out, it is therefore also likely that the roundhouse enshrined a final temporal cycle: that of its occupants' lives (2010, 201). Whilst there are problems with the evidential basis of this argument (for example, the lack of well-preserved floor surfaces with primary deposits, Pope 2007), there is no need to see a divorce here between the practical and the symbolic. Carrying out craftwork in a well-lit space may have made sense not just because one could see better, but because it 'felt right' in terms of broader cosmological understandings of the pattern of life. Certainly the notion of leaving the house in an auspicious direction – that of the sun-rise – and returning to it as the sun set behind, literally illuminated people's experience of the day: shaping their comings and goings in harmony with the passage of the sun and the seasons.

Whether every roundhouse was internally organised along the lines suggested above is more debateable, and certainly the evidence for this is not currently available from East Yorkshire. However, as Parker Pearson pointed out, the square barrow burials do indicate a strong concern with the way in which the body is 'faced' in death, predominantly preferring an easterly orientation, in keeping with the houses in which these people lived (1999a). Once again, it shows close ideological and symbolic correspondences between the realms of the living and that of the dead.

Conclusion: living with the dead

This chapter began by discussing the burial rite which was used to define the 'Arras' culture, analysing its character, form and date. It has highlighted the peculiar arrangement of burials within the major cemeteries and how these grew over time: suggesting Iron Age people used the architecture of the square barrows to construct and remember relations. The chapter considered what such 'geneaological thinking' might represent: Ingold's 'peculiar … history of relatedness' (2000a, 136). It compared these arrangements with those of the living, noting that here also, the apparently 'open' settlement was internally organised into specific groups or clusters of roundhouses (complementing more isolated households) many of which were repeatedly rebuilt on the same foundations. Residential groups were defined in subtle ways from those of their neighbours, and showed a strong attachment to a particular locale: rooted to the land through a history of occupation. In conclusion, both the open settlement and developed cemetery created a symbolic sense of a greater whole ... a community defined by common residence and customs, in which, nonetheless, families and households maintained a sense of difference. This was expressed strongly through preference for particular places of inhabitation and burial, articulated through a history of connections – of relations – over time. As the following chapters will go on to discuss, it was also reiterated through minor differences in burial rites, orientations and grave goods.

In the realm of both the living and the dead, these practices speak of a developing discourse on place and belonging which was rooted, earthed. This act of 'settling down': of continuing to inhabit the same place over many generations *and* burying their dead very visibly, close-by, were key ways in which these communities established their tenurial rights to the land (Brück and Goodman 1999, 12). Even if diurnal tasks of watering or seasonal rhythms of stock movement took certain sections of the community away from these valleys, the generations of the dead stood as witnesses to this right of place. Ultimately, such rights may have led to the dissolution of this community, under the weight of different interests and claims (Giles 2007a). However, during the middle to late Iron Age, someone leaving their roundhouse in the sharp frost-light of a midwinter morning, would look down to the cemetery of the dead and already know their place within it, and the particular forebears and descendents who would keep them company. As John Berger puts it in the last of his *Theses,* the living awaited the experience of the dead: it was their future, for 'by themselves the living were incomplete. Thus living and dead were inter-dependent. Always.' (1996a, 63).

CHAPTER FOUR

Life and Death
in an Iron Age Community

Introduction

The last chapter reviewed the relationship between the living and the dead, represented in the settlements and cemeteries of the middle–late Iron Age in East Yorkshire. It is the remains of the dead however, which hold the detailed clues as to the quality of those lives, and the many threats they inevitably faced. If they survived birth, and bouts of disease and poor harvests, they still had to face the risks of child-bearing, the effects of a life of physical labour, rare but devastating moments of violence, and – if they were lucky – a slow degeneration into old age. Agricultural communities depend on large, strong families to carry out the day-to-day tasks of arable and pastoral work, so every life would have been valued, but death was not a distant and terrifying spectre. As we shall see, it was a frequent event, experienced in an intimate and immediate way. However, some of our preconceptions about how brutal and short life must have been in prehistory will be overturned by the burial evidence.

This chapter reviews the information that can be gained from human remains in the square barrows, in order to analyse the make-up of these communities (by age and sex), their physical appearance, health and diet, risks of disease and injury, and the evidence for violence amongst these communities. It also reviews evidence for peoples' geographic origins, residence patterns, and relative mobility, from childhood into their adult years. Finally, it addresses a point raised in the last chapter: whether we can use osteological information to investigate aspects of relatedness between the burials. Throughout, it seeks to interpret aspects of life and death in the context of the agricultural landscape and small-scale settlements in which people lived.

Death, loss and memory: the burial of K6

The barrow numbered K6, at the site of Kirkburn (Stead 1991, 93, 224), gives us an intimate insight into the consequences of one untimely death (Figure 4.1). A young woman, 17–25 years old, was laid on her left-hand side, orientated north–south, so that she faced east. Her body was flexed, tilted towards her left-hand side: legs drawn up together, one arm propping her body, the other draped over her chest and belly. The cause of death was undoubtedly linked to the second body in the grave: that of a newborn infant, 9–10 lunar months old (i.e. full-term birth-age). The child's remains were found as if in the position

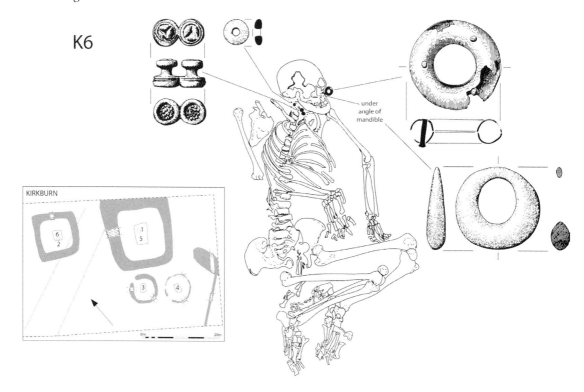

K6

KIRKBURN

FIGURE 4.1. Burial K6.
Based on Stead 1991, 93,
fig. 69.

of birth: head-down, between the mother's legs. The osteologist who examined the burial, Sheelagh Stead, considered that the umbilical cord may well have remained attached, and concluded that this was the evidence of a disastrous still-birth, which took the lives of both mother and infant (in Stead 1991, 136). It is also possible, however, that she died during childbirth, and that the foetus was expelled during post-mortem decay.

The experience of witnessing this traumatic death, and the impact of the loss of not one but two lives, must have been devastating. Death in childbirth during later prehistory – contrary to what we might expect – was rarer than we might think, as I will discuss below. Fear and suspicion may have followed such a 'bad' death, which was not only traumatic but threatened the fertility of the community, through 'the loss of regenerative potential' (Bloch and Parry 1982, 16). Special effort certainly seems to have been put into the commemoration of this woman, who is buried in a large barrow but interestingly, not within one of the major square barrow cemeteries. Instead, Kirkburn marks the position of two square and two small round barrows, apparently separated from other burials nearby (such as Garton Station) by a series of short lengths of linear earthwork (one of which pre-dates K6, Stead 1991, 25). The inauspicious nature of the death suffered by this woman (perhaps seen as spiritually dangerous or potentially polluting), may have meant that she could not be buried amongst her kin group, but required a special location. This is suggested by the remarkable character of other burials in the group: K5 is a cart-burial complete with iron mail shirt, whilst K3 is another example of a 'speared' burial (as at Garton Station, see Chapter 1), this time interred with a marvellously decorated sword and three spearheads: thrust into the grave, point-downwards, perched just above the chest of this adult male. Most of these interments are therefore unusual in the elaborateness of the ceremony and the character of the grave goods concerned.

The previous chapter had an overt interest in landscape context: examining where people were buried and how this might relate to the construction, marking and remembering of kinship and community. The burial of K6 gives us further insight into these issues, for some months or years later, a similar tragic event befell another woman from the area (K2). This time she was a little older, 25–35 years of age, and had almost reached full-term in her pregnancy (8 lunar months), before her untimely death. She was laid on her right-hand side but orientated east–west, facing north; her knees once more drawn up, and arms crossed. The foetus, which had inevitably died with her, was found *in utero*, its tiny bones now scattered within the post-mortem collapse of its mother's pelvis (in Stead 1991, 136). Whether it was something related to the pregnancy itself (a condition such as eclampsia), or a sudden infection or illness, this event again robbed the community of two more lives. The mourners returned to the place of burial of the earlier woman, and interred her in the same mound: digging through the barrow to make a shallow interment in the earlier grave pit. Sheelagh Stead noted in her original report that surely 'K2 was buried with the knowledge of the nature of the death of K6' (*ibid.*, 136). Such secondary burials are rare: there are several in the cluster of barrows at Rudston (R94–114) but these are interred in the barrow ditch surrounding the primary inhumation, and may have been made some time later. In contrast, the re-cut into the primary grave pit of K6 might suggest quite a short interval between the two deaths. What we are seeing here is memory at work: knowledge of a similar death from the past, brought to bear upon a second disaster, to help make sense of it and inter the deceased in an appropriate place.

How did such events affect the families these women left behind? In order to understand this, we must investigate the demography of these communities: exploring who was buried with whom, and who is under-represented or missing from these cemeteries, comparing the archaeological evidence with suitable ethnographic and historic analogies. We must evaluate their average life-expectancy, and the common fears they faced from illness, disease and violence. Only then can such deaths be set in their proper social context.

People in the Iron Age: the skeletal evidence

The analysis conducted below is based upon data gathered from the most recent excavations of Iron Age cemeteries, in order to ensure that the contextual and osteological analyses are reliable. These comprise: Acklam Wold (Dent 1983), Garton Slack and Wetwang Slack 5 (Brewster 1980), Wetwang Slack (Dent 1984a),

Cowlam (Stead 1986), Rudston, Burton Fleming, Garton Station and Kirkburn (Stead 1991), and Wetwang Village (Hill 2001). New analysis of the Wetwang Village burial (Hill 2004) and the Wetwang Slack cemetery is currently ongoing (Jay *et al.* 2008; King 2010) which will slightly revise key data such as gender and age distributions. Where possible, the most up-to-date information (especially on trauma and disease) has been utilised (e.g. King 2010). The population sketch below should therefore be regarded as an interim statement, pending a more up-to-date synthesis. Some case studies consist of hundreds of barrows (Wetwang Slack and Rudston) whilst other examples represent a single inhumation (Acklam Wold and Wetwang Village). The key cemeteries of Arras and Danes Graves are omitted from the detailed statistical analysis due to the antiquarian date of their excavation, but important patterns of evidence from these and other examples are highlighted in the more general discussion.

The total number of available burials from the selected cemeteries is 815. Over and above this can be added the burials collated by Stead (1965) from Arras (over 70 in total but many of which have no human remains recorded) and Danes Graves (106), Eastburn (14), Grimthorpe (5), Scorborough (6) and a variety of isolated examples (Calais Wold, Wharram Percy) including sword inhumations (Bugthorpe, Grimthorpe, North Grimston) and other chariot burials (Cawthorn Camps, Beverley Westwood, Huggate, Hunmanby, Middleton-on-the-Wolds, Pexton Moor). Over 1000 Iron Age burials have therefore been excavated from this region but this represents only a fraction of the total square barrows known from aerial photography: Stoertz estimates at least 3250 are known from her survey of the chalkland alone (1997, 39), and a good proportion of these will have had secondary insertions interred within them at a later date. It is probably futile to estimate how this relates to the original prehistoric population of the Wolds. However, Harding suggests that there is no reason to suppose the whole of the population was buried in the corresponding cemeteries (2004, 7). Only detailed analysis can reveal if there has been some selection on the basis of status or wealth criteria, or even age or gender.

Age

On the basis of the available data, the spread of age at death of the Yorkshire cemeteries is largely in keeping with what would be expected from an agricultural community. (Comparative data are drawn here from the studies presented in Chamberlain 2006). Differences in the age 'brackets' used by individual osteologists have been reconciled by grouping figures together under the title of neonate (under 0 years of age), infant (0–1 years of age), juvenile (2–12 years old), adolescent (12–16 years old) and adults (defined by 10 year age brackets, with a final 45+ years of age category). Importantly, the archaeological ageing of skeletal data leads to a distinctive mortality profile which is not known from real-world case studies (Chamberlain 2006, 90), reasons for which will be discussed below.

In the data analysed (Figure 4.2), there is a classic peak of mortality in the neonate–early infant bracket (under 1 year of age), representing the risks of late miscarriage and still-birth, difficulties during delivery, as well as postnatal infection or other factors (such as nutrition or feeding) due to which an infant may have failed to thrive. The analysis conducted by Jay *et al.* (2008) indicates that some of the un-aged infants also represent late miscarriages (e.g. WS199, WS206, WS267, WS276, WS430, WS434) or death in the first few months of life. However, although some cemeteries have a larger *relative* proportion of neonates and infants to adults (such as Garton Slack and Kirkburn) the overall figures for neonate and infant deaths are not as high as might be expected. When combined with the contextual information, it is evident that infants under 1 year of age rarely received an individual burial of their own: they are usually found as part of a double burial, or as secondary insertions into the barrow mound or ditch. For neonates, this always appears to be the case, although it is possible that some of the 'cenotaph' barrows, where no central burial was found, might have originally held their fragile remains as surface burials. From as young as 2–3 years old however, children were, on occasion, provided with a permanent, individual grave and monument. There is no strict divide then, between a group of children who were classed as not yet fully human (and unworthy of interment) and their adult counterparts, but the youngest members of the community appear to be more frequently buried directly *in relation to* and thus with, an established adult. Adolescents are frequently found interred in their own grave, and Sheelagh Stead suggests that puberty may well have marked their full transition into adulthood (in Stead 1991, 127). However, as will be seen below from the analysis of grave goods, there are differences which suggest that more subtle distinctions may have been drawn between different adult age groups.

As for the low numbers of infants and neonates, it is probable that a large number have been missed due to their burial in a shallow grave or on the surface of the chalk, and subsequent truncation by the plough or other post-depositional disturbance. Others may have been interred as secondary burials which have again been ploughed out. At Garton Slack 7, a remarkable barrow mound (Barrow 3) contained the remains of no fewer than seven infants, along with two adult women: all as secondary burials to a primary adult male extended inhumation (Brewster 1980). Infant remains were also found amongst disarticulated assemblages of animal bone from some settlement areas, suggesting a few may have been buried in non-cemetery features (Dent 1984a). In the Great Wold Valley, infants were only recorded at Kirkburn, suggesting poor preservation conditions also took their toll (in Stead 1991, 126). In addition, inadequate excavation techniques (such as a lack of sieving) or fieldwork methodology might be to blame: square barrow ditches are seldom completely excavated, thus secondary burials of small infants in these contexts may easily have been missed. Alternatively, some infants may have been disposed of in another manner, interred in unidentified locations.

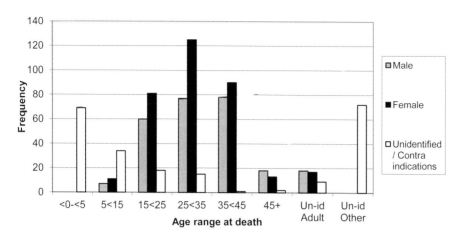

Age at death (all cemeteries)

FIGURE 4.2.
Demographic analyses
of all burials (all
cemeteries).

It is normal to expect a comparative 'drop' in mortality rates between juveniles and adolescents, and this is seen in the relatively high numbers of 2–12 year olds dying young, compared with those reaching their teens (12–15). However, the adolescent age category represents a much shorter span of years, so once more, this is not as marked as might be expected. What is noticeable is the sudden increase in numbers of young adults, dying between the ages of 15 and 25 years, and particularly 25–35 years of age. The majority of these individuals are female, and high rates of mortality in the younger gender group can be attributed to death in childbirth at the peak of fertility (late teens–early 20s), or postpartum-related conditions. However, the relative risks of this condition have probably been slightly over-estimated, since natural childbirth avoided many of the risks associated with medical intervention and disease seen in early industrial societies (Chamberlain, pers. comm.) and it would not explain the highest peak in the late 20s–early 30s age-set, where fertility is likely to have dropped. There are significant numbers of males dying in this age-bracket too, and only a handful of these can be directly attributed to violent trauma (see below) suggesting that disease and the stresses and strains of agricultural life also took their toll.

The significant decrease in deaths in the post-45 years of age category appears, on the surface, to suggest a community in which people rarely lived into their 50s and 60s. In other words, there was reduced longevity in the prehistoric past, due to a mix of health risks. However, Chamberlain notes that the skewed appearance of such archaeological mortality profiles (towards a high peak in mid-adult mortality) can be attributed to preservation issues (which may favour more robust, younger-adult skeletons) and a 'generalised and systematic bias towards under-estimating the age of death of older-adult skeletons' (2006, 90). This is beginning to be addressed through new evaluations of the dataset (e.g. King 2010). Nonetheless, even if their numbers have been under-estimated or ill preserved, those that did live to see a third or even fourth generation of offspring would have been valued as repositories of long-lived knowledge and social history.

Sofaer makes the point that archaeologists are prone to turning a process (of ageing) into a series of social classes or categories (such as adolescents or elders) rather than striving for a more holistic view of the life-cycle as it was lived and experienced (2006). To guard against this, we must look across life histories of particular individuals: gaining an insight into the practices and activities through which people grew and aged, and which shaped their bodies (Gowland and Knüsel 2006). We must also examine the important intersection of age with attributes such as gender and class, and aspects of diet and disease. In addition, we should analyse their bonds with places (where they were born and how far they moved in their lifetime) as well as their relations with things, in order to achieve an understanding of what it meant to be a senior woman or young man in these communities, and how these roles were achieved. This will be a key aim of the following chapter.

Sex

In the analysis of sex, it is vital to avoid biological determinism. The complex mix of biological and cultural criteria through which gender was constituted in prehistory cannot be reduced to its skeletal correlates (Sofaer 2006). In addition, the simple binary opposition of male/female fails to do justice to the range of physiological conditions which exist, nor cultural concepts such as third genders (Gilchrist 1999) or dividual personhood (where differently gendered behaviour may be exhibited in the actions of the same individual, Fowler 2004). Yet for reasons discussed in Chapter 1, the physical attributes of sex inevitably play an important part in the embodiment of identity: as Sofaer puts it, 'sex has a material reality' (2006, 96). Aspects of robustness or femininity, size and strength, and body form and appearance, are caught up in the development of gendered identities. In addition, osteological analysis provides a vital guard against the sexing of bodies on the basis of grave goods – common in the antiquarian period – which simply imposed contemporary stereotypes about gender roles (such as male warriors or female care-givers) onto the prehistoric past.

The osteological analysis of sex is based upon observations of physical characteristics, largely in the shape of the pelvis (related to the functional differences required for childbirth in women) as well as the appearance of the skull, alongside other attributes and conditions (Sofaer 2006, 90). But as Sofaer points out, these criteria are judged on the basis of a sliding scale of 'hyper-maleness' and 'hyper-femaleness'. In between lie a whole series of less evident examples, where sex cannot be easily ascribed, or where there are 'contra-indications' between one set of criteria (e.g. skull form) and another (e.g. pelvic shape). It is important that archaeologists are honest about such cases (as will be seen below). Nevertheless, the combination of analytical criteria tends to cluster in two broad groups, and it is thus possible to assign the majority of an adult population to one or the other end of this spectrum. (For obvious developmental reasons, the sexing of pre-adolescent skeletons is fraught with difficulty but they are a vital group to consider in discussion of gender, since this is a key period of physiological change and the development of adult roles).

A distinction cannot be neatly drawn between sex (as a biological attribute) and gender (as a cultural construction) (see Gilchrist 1999; Sørensen 2000). Sofaer therefore suggests that sex (as a relatively stable physiognomic condition but only one of the potential referent points for gender) can be identified and distinguished from expressed sexuality, which encompasses the social and historical significance of sexual difference (2006). To put this another way, sexuality is a product of gendered discourse and performance: it is potentially unstable and plural, and thus cannot be deduced from skeletal remains alone. The problem is that archaeologists inevitably rely on the sexing of burials to interpret the 'gendering' of grave goods and therefore the ascription of certain life-roles: repeating the essentialist approach that they themselves criticise.

In keeping with the approach followed in this book, Sofaer sees the potential for a much richer relational approach, in which osteological analysis is thoroughly integrated with an analysis of the social practices through which distinctions are structured and reproduced. These can include bodily appearance (female foot binding, or head binding/shaping being extreme examples), posture and deportment (which may be structured through clothing and equipment, and may be depicted on figurines or in paintings) and labour (gendered aspects of tasks such as grinding corn or carrying heavy loads). Sofaer thus locates gender in the temporally and socially specific *relations* which exist between people, using the concept of the 'plasticity' of the body to remind us of the gradual engendering of personhood through repeated practices (*ibid.*, 98, 105). These may have specific health consequences for the individual, leaving identifiable impacts upon the skeleton. However, many of these are slight and require further comparative study (*ibid.*).

The analysis conducted by Sheelagh Stead on the Great Wold Valley cemeteries throws up a number of interesting cases where 'contraindications' require us to think carefully about issues of sex and gender. A tall female with masculine brow ridges and cheek bones was found in burial GS8, but the skull from this inhumation is neat, with 'fine small teeth' and she has all the attributes of a female pelvis (in Stead 1991, 127). There are no grave goods interred with this individual. However, another burial – R163 – whose skull 'lacked male characteristics' was buried with an iron sword and shield (*ibid.*). She was recorded as a 'possible female' (*ibid.*, 127) but the director of the excavation had misgivings: 'not according to the grave goods', he wrote in the burial index (Stead 1991, 205). It is possible that both men and women were trained in martial combat in the Great Wold Valley but the analysis presented below will argue for a strong association between acts of violence, weaponry and male burials. Of course, 'she' may have been regarded by her community as male, or as an honorary male, possessing masculine skills or attitudes in her relations, even if not in aspects of her physiognomy. Alternatively, she may have been equipped with these weapons to carry out a particular task in the afterlife (such as retribution) or decorated with this honour as a symbolic defender of her community. Any one of these interpretations is possible: the challenge for us, as archaeologists, lies in being open to these alternatives. In addition, there are two burials which showed some male skull characteristics, but whose limbs were very slight: R57 (buried with a sword and spearhead) and R148 (buried with a shield decorated with an iron boss, in Stead 1991, 127). Meanwhile, burial R2 was characterised by its large limbs but there were some female characteristics, and s/he was buried with a jet bangle and a glass bead ear-ring or hair decoration, as well as iron brooch. All of these burials are recorded as having 'contraindications', in terms of their sex. This scrupulous analysis may give us a faithful insight into the complexities of physical appearance and social identity, which these communities negotiated through the way in which individuals lived out their lives.

In terms of the rest of the East Yorkshire data, of those burials which were positively sexed (Figure 4.3), there are more female than male burials (337:258 or 57% compared with 43%). In some cemeteries, the proportion is equal or almost, particularly the cemeteries from the Great Wold Valley such as Burton Fleming and Garton Station. In contrast, at Wetwang Slack, 59% of the burials were female, and at Garton Slack, it was 64%, showing more of a marked discrepancy towards female burials. For the Wetwang cemetery, Dent interpreted this as an indication that adult males in their prime might have died 'away from home' in disputes or raids, as part of an age-related war-band, and were buried elsewhere (1982). They may also have been absent as long-distance herders, returning after either of these periods of duty, to marry relatively late, to younger women. Alternatively, higher numbers of female adults might suggest a polygamous society or one where there were female slaves, servants or unmarried relatives (who came from more distant communities) were assisting in the household (I am grateful to Andrew Chamberlain for this observation). However, recent re-analysis of the Wetwang Slack cemetery suggests there is no statistically significant difference between the number of men and women (King 2010), so caution must be used when offering an explanation of these patterns.

In terms of mortality rates, it is obviously difficult to comment on relative risks for male and female juveniles, as the criteria used to distinguish between them were still growing and forming. Amongst the older teen-young adult age bracket (15–25 years), 25% of women died young: a figure mirrored amongst the male burials, where again, 25% of all men died at this age (Figure 4.4). As discussed above, this suggests that there were equally strong risks of mortality for men and women during their late teens and early twenties, and that disease, the stress of agricultural life, birth related trauma, occasional violent incidents and accidents must have been frequent underlying threats.

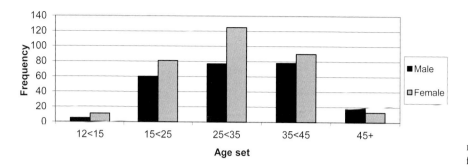

FIGURE 4.3. Male and female burials by age-set.

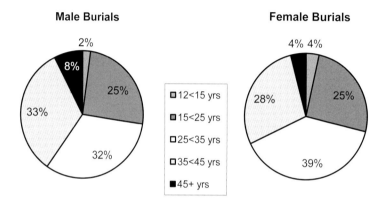

FIGURE 4.4. Comparison of mortality ratios by age-set for men and women.

However, women were evidently assailed by a higher mortality risk than men in their 20s and 30s, perhaps as a result of successive pregnancies or the stress of child-feeding and rearing, coupled with agricultural labour. 40% of all women died in the mid-adult age bracket of 25–35 years old but only 32% of men died in this period. Men were more likely to survive into their late 30s and early 40s than women (33% dying between 35 and 45 years of age), and there were more male survivors reaching the elder age bracket of 45 years and above, than women (8% of all men compared with only 4% of all women). (Again, these observations are made with the proviso that the age at death of many senior individuals may be under-estimated).

Life and death, disease and injury

Appearance

The majority of the people from these cemeteries who survived into adulthood appear to have lived productive lives, and were healthy and well-nourished. (The following synthesis is derived mainly from S. Stead's analysis of the Great Wold Valley cemeteries (in Stead 1991), Jean Dawes' analysis of Wetwang and Garton Slack (in Brewster 1980 and in Dent 1984a) and Sarah King's PhD analysis, 2010). These communities averaged 5 ft 7in (1.7 m) in height for men, and 5 ft 2 in (1.56 m) for women, amongst the Great Wold Valley cemeteries (Leese in Stead

1991, 173): slightly taller than individuals at Wetwang Slack (around 5 ft 6 in for men, 5ft 1 in for women (1.68 m/1.59 m)). These populations were both taller than contemporary inhabitants of the hillfort of Maiden Castle, in Dorset (*ibid.*). Whilst the racial interpretation of skull measurements is problematic (as discussed in Chapter 1), they nonetheless reveal something of the average appearance of these individuals, which Leese recorded from the Great Wold Valley cemeteries as broadly doliocephalic: long heads, and narrow faces (in Stead 1991, 172).

Their teeth occasionally exhibited dental caries and amongst the Great Wolds Valley cemeteries, these were twice as high amongst women as men: possibly as a result of calcium deficiency caused through child-rearing (*ibid.*, 128). Rare abscesses (such as R55) must have been extremely painful, leading this individual to avoid both closing his jaw and eating on the left-hand side. As people aged, periodontal disease and the effects of a gritty diet (grain was processed using querns made from erratic and sandstone sources) took their toll. R107, aged over 45 years old, had three abscess cavities and had lost at least five teeth before his death. Enamel hypoplasia (a non-specific stress indicator) was only noted in a few cases, such as R119, who died young (17–25 years old, *ibid.*, 128). Diet will be further studied in the next section below.

Disease and injuries

Traumatic injuries which left a skeletal trace occurred in 21% of the adult population at Wetwang Slack, and were slightly more common amongst men, but most of these appear to have been sustained through accidental injury (King 2010). Very few traumatic injuries were noted in individuals under the age of 13 (*ibid.*). The most common trauma identified across the cemeteries were fractures, which may have been caused through slips, trips and falls from heights, injuries involving heavy objects or assaults by livestock, or even falls from moving vehicles, as is common in a rural agricultural community (Judd and Roberts 1999). The most frequent fractures include those to the hands and wrists, particularly amongst adult men (e.g. WS106, WS132, WS193), fingers (WS296, WS379), feet and ankles (WS62, WS82). There are also examples of a fractured knee (WS113), ribs (WS120, WS183, WS198), lower arm fractures (radius: WS101, WS318 and ulna: WS358), as well as legs (the tibia, or shinbone: WS92 and GS1/2 Single Grave 2, or femur: WS307 – an injury which led to a bad infection). There are multiple examples of left and right fractures to the shoulder (clavicle or scapula) – most of which had healed – many of them found on older males: R43, R84, R112, R192, BF2, GS4 (one of the 'speared' burials), GS1 4b Single Grave 1, WS90, WS102, WS190 and WS227. Whilst these fractures of the shoulder may easily have been caused by an awkward fall, landing on an outstretched hand or shoulder, direct blows (sustained in contact sports or fights) may also have involved. There was one example of a dislocated wrist (WS101) which may relate to a fracture of the radius (King 2010). A dislocated shoulder (from the female chariot burial, WV1) may have arisen from a fall, fight or a severe wrench of the joint (perhaps, as the local newspapers excitedly reported, when trying to control a runaway team or falling from a chariot driven at speed)! The atrophied upper arm and scapula of R162 may indicate an early fracture which interrupted blood flow to the arm, making it prone to frequent dislocation (S. Stead 1991, 135). Another traumatic shoulder injury may be indicated on WS21 (King 2010). There is one example of a healed cranium fracture of 23.1 mm length on an elderly male (WS221), attributed by King to an accident (*ibid.*). Another older male (around 36–45 years, WS291) had a healed fracture of the jaw bone and a subadult WS336 (13–17 years) had experienced some kind of traumatic blow to the mandible which affected the growth of their molars (King 2010). It is not possible to determine whether these latter injuries were sustained in accidents or disputes.

Soft tissue damage was noted on a variety of limbs, including the upper leg of the female burial R132: an injury which Stead argued might have been caused by trauma such as a kick from a horse (in Stead 1991, 136). R100, another young woman, displayed soft tissue damage of the right collar bone which had led to severe inflammation. Other tissue damage includes GS6 (a male chariot burial, where the tibia was damaged but had healed), R148 (a burial with a shield, where the right radius or lower arm bone had been injured), R164 (damage to the right ulna, one of the lower arm bones) and R107 (a male sword burial, where the right index finger had been subject to severe swelling, causing pathological change in the bone). Osteoarthritis was noted in the knee of GS10 (a male adult sword burial, again associated with the 'spearing' rite) and the ankle and foot of R182 (a sword burial). These pathologies, coupled with the vehicles and weapons found in their graves, suggest a greater incidence of injury and bodily 'wear and tear' amongst those training, practising and carrying out feats of horsemanship and combat.

Work also took its toll. The flattened cervical (neck) vertebrae of GSl 7, Barrow 3, Burial 11 was probably the result of persistent load-carrying, and severe osteoarthritis of the spine in another individual was postulated as the result of carrying something like a yoke over long periods of time (Dawes in Brewster 1980). Osteoarthritis of a finger (K8, elderly female) and a fractured hand (GSl 11, Barrow 2, Burial 1, male) may also have been work-related, and there is one example of a 'septic' finger (R84). These cuts, blows and breaks to fingers are expected in the range of agricultural and craft-work, represented in the settlement evidence. A woman of 26–35 years had evidence of a classic 'shoveler's fracture' of a thoracic vertebrae (WS100, King 2010), and a possible compression fracture of the spine or congenital condition was recorded in a slightly younger woman (R76) which led to severe arthritis in the affected region. Compression fractures in the wrist and ankle bones, or lumbar or thoracic vertebrae were repeatedly noted in the Wetwang Slack population, especially amongst its older inhabitants, and may derive from age-related degeneration or one-off traumatic events (King 2010). In this study, King also noted a high incidence of *Myositis ossificans traumatica* amongst adult women, often on the humerus: muscle inflammation which affects the soft tissue, caused by repeated minor trauma. It is commonly associated with young adults participating in sports (*ibid.*), but may in this case indicate a repeatedly enacted, strenuous domestic or agricultural task (perhaps grinding of grain using a rotary quern?). Similarly, *Spondylolysis* – a condition which may have a genetic basis but also appears to be associated with activity related stress during adolescence/early adulthood, was again noted in several cases, particularly amongst women (King 2010). Odd dental wear patterns may also indicate occupational traits: six women and one man from the Great Wold Valley cemeteries had significant wear on the front teeth (especially the incisors) compared with their back teeth (S. Stead in Stead 1991, 129–130). Three other women had especially worn inner surfaces of their front teeth (*ibid.*).

In the Great Wold Valley cemeteries analysed by Stead (1991, 138), she noted that of the 111 individuals with sufficient preservation to facilitate analysis, 42% of both male and female burials exhibited osteoarthritis of spine. Both genders appear to have been carrying out repetitive tasks (such as ploughing and harvesting) and load-carrying (e.g. grain, water, firewood), stock-tending and food production (such as herding and milking), and – we might posit – the carrying of young infants, which gradually damaged their necks and backs. However, in the 25–35 year age category, only 42% of males were affected, compared with 69% of females. This might suggest older adult women were carrying out specific tasks that led to a higher incidence of the disease in this age-set and gender-group. Three further incidents of spinal osteoarthritis appeared to have arisen after more traumatic events (R76 and K8, female, and R160, male) whose cause is uncertain. Osteoarthritis was also interestingly noted in the hips of older men at Rudston (R164, R144, R43 and R181) but cases involving women were noted at Garton Slack (Dawes in Brewster 1980). One severe case of multiple arthritis (hips, knees, spine and jaw), was found in an adult woman: BF6.

There are also hints of a range of rare afflictions: a possible case of polio (BF17), leading to an atrophied or shortened right lower leg (Stead 1991, 137); a benign tumour on a cranium (BF48, *ibid.*, 137) and a possible malignant tumour on a left arm (R132, *ibid.*, 137). King noted two cases of healed rickets in the Wetwang Slack population (2010). There was also an indication of an infected mouth, causing a pitted palate, from Burton Fleming (BF11). One individual may have suffered a loss of hearing through a build-up of calcareous deposit in the ear-canal (BF20). Possible cases of tuberculosis were tentatively suggested by Dawes from Garton Slack, who also recorded an example of Paget's disease (misgrowth of new bone) in a male burial from Garton Slack (in Brewster 1980). Marked differences between robust and more feeble limbs were interpreted by S. Stead as indications of differential growth but they could also be due to post-depositional affects (R34 and R88). However, Dawes argued that differences in the robusticity of opposite humuri and hands might be indications of 'habitual weight bearing or bracing' with an upper arm on one side, paired with 'fine manipulative function' in the opposing hand (in Brewster 1980, 753).

Alongside this range of conditions and injuries we might expect to find in such communities, is the evidence for more isolated events of trauma. In terms of deaths associated with childbirth, out of all of the cemeteries excavated there are only five examples where a mother and foetus or neonate are interred together, suggesting a direct cause of death for both: K6 and K2 (reviewed above, Figure 4.1), WS156, WS309 and GSl7 (Barrow 4, Burial 1). These poignant tableau represent the horror and grief of a double loss, in late pregnancy or at birth itself. However, there are multiple other examples of infants interred as secondary inhumations in existing barrows, where the mother may have survived despite the loss of the child.

Violent trauma

Other burials suggest more deliberate incidents of inter-personal violence, indicated by sharp or blunt force trauma, penetrating wounds and likely 'parry' fractures or defence wounds. The head in particular, appears to have been a popular target for violent wounding: either to kill, cause debilitating damage or precipitate extensive bleeding. R162 (an adult male) appears to have suffered mild trauma to the back of his head, and WS114 (a young adult male) was cut across the back of his head and had fractures to his ribs: peri-mortem injuries which may have been made using a thin bladed weapon … a dagger or fine sword (King 2010). WS118, a woman in her 20s, had received a cut over the orbit of her eye which had healed. WS119, an older-adult male, also had a cut above his eye, 11.40 mm long, as well as a fracture to his right clavicle, the slashing qualities of which suggest the use of a thin bladed instrument (*ibid.*). Both injuries had healed, and may well have been sustained in the same incident. The older adult male WS94 had received a devastating cut to the right side of his mandible, removing both bone and muscle attachments: an injury commonly associated with attempted decapitation, yet this injury showed evidence of active healing as well as a possible haematoma (*ibid.*). A large penetrating trauma to the front of the skull in WS152 (an elderly adult male) created a wound 19.06 mm long by 7.01 mm wide with an internal hinged fracture caused by a thin blade (perhaps a spearhead, *ibid.*), but again this showed strong evidence for healing. Depressed fractures to the cranium (caused by weapons such as slingshot or other heavy blunt objects) were noted on WS154 and WS129 (in the latter instance, leaving a 14.42 mm oval 'dent' in the skull, King 2010: somewhat reminiscent of the injury to Mortimer's uncle, from the Battle of Fimber)! Meanwhile, the fracture to the ulna and phalanges of WS358 (an older male) may represent a classic set of defensive wounds, gained as he tried to parry a blow with his left arm (*ibid.*).

Perhaps most fascinatingly, the young man buried with a chariot and fine sword in WS453, had a fracture of his right radius, and a substantial sharp force trauma wound to the back of his skull, creating a hole 30.89 mm in length (King 2010). It is not clear if the two wounds were received at the same time but both had healed: in the case of the skull wound, leaving a permanent hole in the cranium, which astoundingly, showed no signs of infection. The blunt trauma around the site of the head wound would suggest a heavy blow, either from a sword or a heftier weapon such as an axe (*ibid.*).

Other skull injuries include the Acklam Wold sword burial (an adult male with sword cuts to the back of the head, Dent 1983: see Chapter 5), and two burials from Danes Graves, where Mortimer noted a healed scar of a cut 2 inches long on the forehead of DG45, and another sharp-edged weapon cut on the left-hand side of the skull, 1.5 in long and 0.5 in deep (38.1 × 12.7 mm), on DG104, perhaps inflicted shortly before death (Mortimer 1897; 1911a). At Garton Slack (GSl 7, Barrow 3, Burial 11) a 6 mm puncture wound which showed signs of healing was interpreted as the result of a direct blow to the top of the head of this elderly male (Dawes in Brewster 1980). Blows to the face are seen in the fractured nose and ribs of WS47 (an elderly man) and another broken nose (WS226, an elderly woman). A traumatic blow to the face was certainly responsible for a cut on the frontal bone and development of a cavity above the molars in R3 (an adult female). These healed injuries might have been sustained during a fall or vigorous event, but we should also be open to the possibility that some of these injuries represent domestic violence or broader neighbourhood disputes, which were not lethal in intent.

The position of weapons within a body suggests a likely cause of death in a number of instances. Spearheads found embedded in the skeleton may have been the direct cause of death in four recorded cases. R94 (a young adult male) had one thrust into his back from behind: it was deflected to the right side of the spine, out towards the front of his body, where the tip snapped off (Stead 1991, 137). R152a (an adult male) was also speared from behind, so that the spear head entered his left-hand side and probably penetrated the heart (*ibid.*; Figure 4.5). In contrast, R140 (also an adult male) appears to have been attacked from the front: the spearhead penetrating his right pubic bone, being twisted into the pelvis from a downwards angle (*ibid.*). (Whilst this could be an example of post-mortem 'spearing rite', the angle involved and the broken socket of the spear suggest that this injury was inflicted before death, possibly as he lay prone before an enemy, and the shaft of the weapon was subsequently snapped off before his burial). An iron spear interred in a female grave from Wetwang Slack (WS211) was described by the excavator as being embedded in the region of her 'stomach' (Dent 1984a) and may represent a cause of death, though this might be instead be a rare instance of a female 'speared' burial. Finally, a spearhead was recorded in a burial from Garton Slack (excavated by the Granthams) embedded in the shoulder of a skeleton (Stead 1979).

These examples suggest that inter-personal violence was infrequent but brutal. Many of the cranial injuries are to the front of the face, suggesting the victim faced their attacker, but others to the back of the skull may indicate that the perpetrator took an opponent by surprise (as might be common in domestic disputes or spur-of-the-moment quarrels) or whilst an enemy attempted to flee

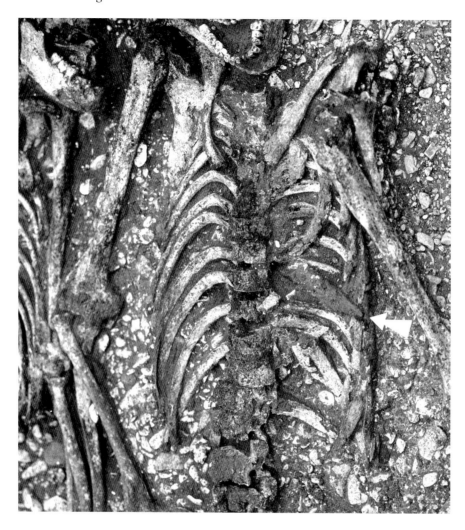

FIGURE 4.5. Burial of R152a showing position of spearhead, indicated by arrow.

or lay incapacitated. Such injuries may of course have been accompanied by other surface wounds not detectable on the skeleton, causing significant pain, blood loss, and even death. It is acknowledged that the figures presented here underestimate the overall incidence rate of violence, as much of this would leave no skeletal trace. However, many of the violent trauma injuries showed signs of healing, suggesting these incidents were seldom fatal. They would still have left their scar – and perhaps, psychological changes – which altered the status and identity of the wounded individual. In her PhD thesis, King discusses an account of sabre-induced skull injuries (the closest historical analogy for Iron Age sword injuries) dating from the American Civil War, written by attendant Surgeon-Generals (2010). They noted that whilst such wounds were rarely fatal, they commonly precipitated the development of a more explosive temper and violent nature. Though these individuals frequently survived, such character changes may have altered their relations with family and community, following inter-personal violence. It is interesting that the majority of these Iron Age wounds, and the most severe ones, are found on adult males. This may suggest that they had a special role in combat (whether or not they were 'full-time' warriors) or were more likely to be drawn into violence on the rare occasion it flared up, in disputes, set-piece duels or during raids.

Summary

At this point it is important to reiterate that all that can be traced of violence within these communities are injuries which leave a skeletal trace (fractures, soft tissue damage and cuts) or where weapons are found *in situ* in the body. Such evidence does not allow us to fully investigate issues such as persistent, small-scale physical abuse or domestic violence, which were no doubt present to some extent. Severe flesh wounds, bruises, burns and scalds, poisoning, hanging and the cutting of the throat, rape and strangulation, would leave no obvious trace on skeletal material whose preservation can, in any case, be variable. The thrusting swords used by these communities may have led to many more deaths than we can identify (Simon James, pers. comm.). Fighting with iron knives (which are also found in graves) may have been culturally significant: causing scars which became embodied mnemonics of prowess (Giles 2008b). Again, this would not be visible in the osteological record.

Nevertheless, this 'sketch' tells us a great deal about our Iron Age communities, not least that whilst accidental injury is quite high, levels of inter-personal violence are surprisingly low, given the fact that this is arguably the most materially impressive 'martial culture' known in Iron Age Britain. We can contrast these communities with a comparable population from Wessex, where Redfern recorded a higher incidence of violence (including injury recidivism: multiple injuries, suggesting a sustained attack or encounter: Redfern 2008; 2009). Interestingly, amongst Wessex women, the majority of injuries were blunt-force trauma or fractures, derived from deliberate violence rather accidental injury. She has interpreted this as evidence that they were 'active participants in episodes or violence, or were members of an 'at-risk' group' as 'victims of aggression' (2008, 149, 153). King also conducted an explicit comparison with sites in Hampshire, confirming that there was a higher rate of fatal wounding in the latter sites (2010). The context from which many of these remains were recovered, such as pit deposits, may be significant: representing a select population whose violent death required their abnormal mortuary treatment (Sharples 2010). Nevertheless, these hillforts and defended enclosures, with their dense concentration of roundhouses, contrast with the open settlement of Wetwang and Garton Slack. It is possible that living in a denser population within Wessex, amongst communities who defined themselves spatially and socially from others, brought new social problems: leading to higher rates of interpersonal violence both within and between households, but also against rival groups or tribes (as suggested in Sharples 2010).

These studies also provide fascinating glimpses into different codes of combat and violence, in contrasting regions of Iron Age Britain. In East Yorkshire, men were more commonly involved in interpersonal violence, and there may well have been specific rules regarding the treatment of women and minors during incidents such as raids. This is not to suggest the Wolds was more 'peaceful' than Wessex nor its people less aggressive (see James 2007) but in an area famed for its weaponry and chariots, it is possible there was an elaborate code of honour which encouraged multiple stages of posturing and martial display, before actual bloodshed occurred, and where it did, this was seldom followed through to the death. These ideas will be discussed further in Chapters 6 and 7.

The 'sinful' couple?

To end this section, I want to discuss a curious burial which brings together many of the above themes: sex, death, disaster and violence. When T. C. M. Brewster began to reveal a large grave pit in Wetwang Slack trench 5 in 1975, great excitement mounted as an elongated slot to the north of the rectangular pit became evident. Brewster expected to find a chariot burial within it: the slot representing the extended cart pole, lying north–south in the grave. But as the infill was gradually scraped away, all that was found was the burial of a couple, laid side-by-side, in a crouched position, orientated north–south, but with their heads facing inwards – towards each other (Figure 4.6). They appeared to have been laid on a bed of turf, represented by a rich lens of loam (Brewster 1980, 672). The burial on the left was identified as a young adult male (17–19 years old): gracile, with 'slightly effeminate features' (*ibid.*, 671). On the right was a slightly older adult female (20–25 years of age). The man was interred in a curious posture: on his back, his arms tightly folded on his chest, wrists crossing just under his chin, as if bound. The skull was turned at an unnaturally sharp angle towards the woman to his right, and below his left ear was found a small assemblage of decorative items: a triangular bronze pendant pierced for suspension, a 'paste' bead (reminiscent of a spindle whorl) and a circular polished jet ring. The woman was, in contrast, unadorned though a sheep's tooth was apparently found clamped within her jaw (*ibid.*, 673). She was slumped against his corpse, lying slightly on her left side, her forehead resting on his shoulder and her right arm reaching across her belly, to lie on his chest. What Brewster recorded next was extraordinary: the shadow of a broad timber stake (3 in (76.2 mm) in diameter and over 1 ft (*c.* 305 mm) long) appeared to have been driven through her right wrist and his left elbow into the bedrock beneath, pinning the couple together in death. It may have been fire-hardened or charred, since Brewster records it as 'carbonised' (1980, 673). For Brewster, the clue to this curious burial lay in the additional discovery of a 6–month old foetus, apparently expelled from the woman's womb, once more found as if *in situ* after a miscarriage or premature stillbirth.

In the publicity associated with this discovery, this double (or rather triple)

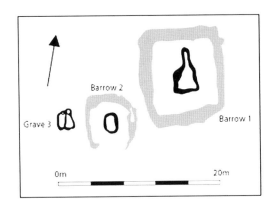

Wetwang Slack 5
Barrow 1, Burials 1&2

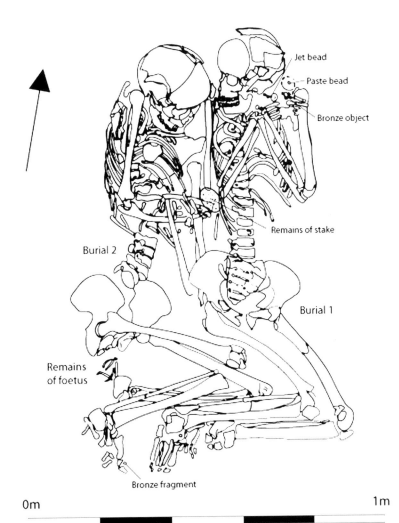

FIGURE 4.6. WS5: The
so-called 'sinful couple.
Based on Brewster 1980,
fig. 501.

burial became known as the 'sinful couple' (Brewster 1975). Brewster posited the idea that the couple had had an illicit affair, resulting in a pregnancy which (at 6 months) could no longer be concealed. He considered that the younger man might have been put to death, and his unnatural posture was the result of *rigor mortis*, whilst his older lover may have been drugged or suffocated, and was either buried alive or soon after the moment of death: miscarrying in the grave as a result of her 'maltreatment' (1975, 114; 1980, 674). Given the focus on family relations, household identity and place identified in Chapter 3, it is probable that there were harsh sanctions against unapproved affairs, as suggested by classical authors such as Tacitus: this is one of favoured interpretations of the 'shaved and shamed' female bog bodies from northern Europe (Giles 2009). Perhaps the sheep's tooth in the mouth was a symbol of an adulterer, and the dressing of the 'effeminate' young man in ear-rings or pendants usually found with women (see Chapter 5) was an act of shaming emasculation. The woman's own corporeal chaos, embodied in her miscarriage, may have been seen as fitting evidence of their moral corruption. Yet as Brewster acknowledged, there were 'no signs of a struggle, or a death spasm' (1980, 674). The expelling of a foetus can be a normal part of bodily decay following death, and since *rigor mortis* is merely a brief phase following death, the difference in their postures did not quite ring true. However, the story caught the attention of an avid 1970s' audience, and a radio play was made based on the discovery, in which a parallel affair between the wife of the site director and a handsome young digger, shadowed the story of the ancient couple, ending this time in a disastrous road crash (J. Dent, pers. comm.). This interpretation may tell us more about attitudes towards sex in the 1970s than in the 2nd century BC!

An alternative interpretation is equally possible. The woman may have died during her pregnancy from various conditions, such as a convulsion caused by pre-eclampsia or other illness. Such deaths may have been rare but devastating. The whole tableau of this burial evokes, as Brewster himself noted, an air of intimacy and tenderness: the woman 'snuggled close to her partner of eternity' (1980, 672), hips and knees pressed together. It is equally possible that following her death, and the untimely loss of their offspring, her partner decided to take his own life, in order to accompany her into the next world. We rarely discuss the possibility of suicide in prehistory but if there was a strong sense of an ancestral community, it would not have had the stigma associated with Christian doctrine. The stake might thus represent an eternal coupling of the pair, but given that both of these deaths may have been especially troubling, it might also have been a symbolic means of keeping their restless or grief-stricken spirits 'in place', as they completed their transformation as members of the dead. Perhaps the intention had been to provide them with a chariot, to speed their journey into the afterlife but for whatever reason, this funeral gift was withdrawn. Alternatively, a 'spiritual' version of this vehicle may have been conjured for them, during the funerary rite, and space was made for it in the grave. We will never know the full story behind this scene, but we can intuit that it was a disturbing and memorable event, which had ruptured not only the bodies of those involved, but also the social fabric of the community itself.

Diet: you are what you eat?

Moving away from dramatic deaths such as the 'sinful couple', the background health of the population was inevitably linked to their diet. In recent years, studies of stable carbon and nitrogen (and also sulphur) isotopes have shed light on the foodways of both people and their herds, alongside the traditional analysis of environmental evidence such as faunal remains and seeds. These isotopes are present in foodstuffs people and animals have eaten whilst their bone was actively forming (Jay *et al.* 2008; Jay and Richards 2006). The recognisable patterns in how these isotopes are processed and ingested allow archaeologists to reflect on both the types of foods eaten as well as the kinds of environments in which plants were grown or animals raised (*ibid.*). Typically, analysis is carried out both on collagen from tooth dentine (reflecting the period from approximately 2½–3 years of age, to the completion of root formation at around 14 years old) and collagen from bone (which relates to longer-term dietary preferences in the last ten years before death: Milner *et al.* 2004; Jay and Richards 2007, 78). These twin sources of evidence can therefore elucidate changes in consumption habits or environmental residence patterns, from someone's childhood into their adult years.

Most of the carbon and nitrogen in human bone originates in the protein aspect of an organism's diet, and these techniques are particularly useful in recognising the degree of animal protein present (not just meat but dairy products) and its origin: whether from a terrestrial or aquatic (freshwater or marine) environment. There are problems: substances which contribute a small (up to 20%) but perhaps, culturally significant, amount to a diet may not be detectable (see Lee-Thorp 2008). Low protein plant food substances may be all but invisible in bone collagen but detected in bone carbonate, requiring the application of different techniques (*ibid.*). Also, our knowledge of natural distributions of stable isotopes in different kinds of ecosystems and under varying conditions requires further regional contextual studies (*ibid.*, 942). The background 'values' used to interpret results are based upon modern observations, after millennia of transformations to the environment. This inhibits our knowledge of ancient ecosystems (*ibid.*) but this is more of an issue for archaeologists investigating hominid diets than later prehistoric communities' foodways.

The analysis of Iron Age diet from isotope evidence has largely been carried out by Mandy Jay, who has contrasted human and animal material from Wetwang Slack cemetery and settlement, with other key sites from Britain (Jay 2008; Jay and Richards 2006; 2007; Jay *et al.* 2008). She has concluded that the diet of the inhabitants of Wetwang was relatively high in animal protein, suggesting the consumption of meat and dairy products on a frequent basis.

Milk and cheese are likely to have been key staples of the Iron Age diet though no residues of these foodstuffs have been positively identified from the East Yorkshire sites. However, the isotope evidence from infants and juveniles at Wetwang Slack suggests that breastfeeding had been somewhat restricted in early infancy, indicating the introduction of supplementary foods at a relatively young age (Jay *et al.* 2008). The analysts compared the infant data with values from adolescent and young adult females in the cemetery (the latter used as 'putative mothers' for comparison, *ibid.*, 330), and compared these values with medieval and historic case studies. They suggested that at Wetwang Slack there was a more restricted intake of human milk (in contrast to the comparative case studies), with the early addition of animal milk and/or plant gruel at some point in the first year of life (*ibid.*, 336). By the age of 2½, the isotopic ratios of children indicate they were sharing a similar diet to that of the adults in their community (*ibid.*). This makes sense within the context of an agricultural community, where infants would have to be weaned between 1 and 2 years of age in order to facilitate the next pregnancy within the fertile 'lifetime' of the mother (Chamberlain, pers. comm.). The availability of dairy substitutes, and a residential lifestyle would also assist this process but there may also have been a strong symbolic importance to the ingestion of dairy products, which might be linked to the special status of cows within these communities (Chapter 3).

From the funerary evidence, sheep appears to be the main source of meat, and occasionally goat, but pig (or more rarely, boar) is also represented in a variety of burials (Legge in Stead 1991). Low numbers of neonatal lambs and piglets in the settlement suggest successful husbandry and an avoidance of butchering animals very young, or 'culling' them before the winter (Noddle in Brewster 1971). However, some very young 'suckling' piglets were sacrificed for funeral ceremonies (see below). The settlement evidence tells a slightly different story, since cattle are evidently being raised and slaughtered at Wetwang and Garton Slack but beef is never included as a portion of meat for the dead, in any Iron Age burial from the East Yorkshire cemeteries. As has been discussed in Chapter 2, it is likely that they were used primarily for dairy produce or blood (as amongst the Nuer) and traction, and were rarely consumed as beef. Relatively high numbers of neonatal cattle at Garton Slack settlement led Noddle to suggest they might either have been killed very early for their supple hides, or else they had failed to thrive and survive the winter (in Brewster 1980). The predominance of discarded 'heads and hooves' at Wetwang might indicate that when a mature cow was killed, the majority of the carcass was taken elsewhere (Scott cited in Dent 1984a), perhaps for consumption of the relatively large quantities of meat, during intra-community events. Wetwang also produced some evidence for the 'jointing' of carcasses into smaller units and a number of cattle long bones had been split to extract the highly nutritional marrow (*ibid.*).

In terms of other sources of meat protein, a cache of slingstones at Wetwang Slack might indicate the main weapon for hunting, alongside the spear (Dent 1984a). However, there is little evidence for this activity: rare remains of red and roe deer were discovered from this site but the majority of the pig bones from both settlements and cemeteries are not large enough to suggest the systematic hunting of boar. The lack of suitable habitats on the cleared landscape of the Wolds may help explain these patterns. Hunting may have been a prime motivation for expeditions off the Wolds, into the heavier woodland and game cover of the vales on either side, where the spoils were also consumed.

A lack of sieving at most sites has precluded the recovery of both bird and fish bones. One limpet shell was found in a middle–late Iron Age context at Wetwang, and the remains of a goose were found at Garton Slack (Dent 1984a; Noddle in Brewster 1980) but there is no evidence of other domestic fowl at these sites, such as chicken. The isotope evidence also suggests a negligible marine food input (though see the proviso explained above) and given that the Wetwang-Garton valley is located 25 km inland, and is distant from major freshwater rivers (Dent 1984a; Jay and Richards 2006, 660), it is unlikely that fish formed a major part of the daily diet.

As has been discussed in Chapters 2 and 3, evidence for agriculture is slight. The grazed open pasture which supported stock is evident from pollen and snail evidence from the Great Wolds Valley (Stead 1991). There are no recognisable 'field systems' but Dent suggests that crops may have been grown on the land between clusters of roundhouses, spaced 50–90 m apart (1982). They would then have been broadly enclosed by the large linear earthworks at the top, bottom and sides of the valley, preventing stock from straying into these 'open fields'. Crops would also have benefited from the deeper build-up of soils on these slopes, from the 'downcreep' of colluvium. Cereal pollen was also noted at Kirkburn indicating the growth of crops in the vicinity, and a carbonised deposit of hulled 6-row barley at Garton Slack (Brewster 1980, 686). Within this 'cleaned' deposit (which was either winnowed or sieved), there are hints of other crops: wheat (possibly emmer and spelt), wild oats and various 'weed' species – some of which may have been edible or used for medicinal purposes. Whilst carbonised plant remains are therefore scant, crops are more broadly suggested by the prodigious quantities of saddle and rotary quern fragments from the Wetwang and Garton settlements (Dent 1984a; Brewster 1980). Supplements to this diet were provided by the pear, apple, and wild cherry or sloe, represented in the charcoal from Garton Slack (Cutler in Brewster 1980, 678). Other wild fruits, vegetables and fungi were no doubt collected seasonally.

The above section has focused on the range of foodstuffs which contributed to the diet of Iron Age people on the Wolds, but one of the most important aspects of food is the way in which it can be used to literally exhibit 'taste': to demonstrate differences in preference, access or cultural sanctions, between different age and gender groups, classes or social sects. This is where the isotope evidence proves invaluable. At Wetwang Slack, Jay detected no significant difference between men and women, or most age groups, in terms of the character and quantity of protein consumed. (One exception was the category of elderly men, who shared a distinctive protein profile, though its exact meaning requires further analysis: Jay and Richards 2006, 657). It is possible that there were differences in the amount of either dairy produce or meat eaten by different genders or age-sets (the technique cannot distinguish between these two food sources) but the overall amount of protein consumed meant that no group appears 'disadvantaged' in dietary terms. However, recent re-analysis of the female chariot burial from Wetwang Slack (WS454) noted an interesting disparity between her apparent age as indicated in the main skeleton, and the low degree of wear exhibited in her teeth. King has suggested this may be the result of a refined diet, certainly through her later years (pers. comm.), which may relate to her special status or position in society, confirmed in the manner of her burial.

The results are important since Mike Parker Pearson has suggested that differences in the inclusion of pig or sheep in graves might be related to different classes (elites and commoners), or else represent the totemic associations of different moieties (1999a). He based this on the evidence that the 'richest' chariot, sword and ornamented artefact burials are associated with pig (or possibly boar), compared with sheep bones found in more simple burials (*ibid.*, 56). He saw this as part of a broader Iron Age cosmology in which pigs were seen as special animals, frequently reserved for high status feasting (*ibid.*). Jay has commented that if the eating of pig was confined to a particular group, this should be detectable (pers. comm.), since it would give rise to a distinct 'omnivore' signature which would be strikingly different from those restricted to herbivores (sheep and cattle). Yet all of the individuals studied so far have a common omnivorous profile (*ibid.*). In addition, pig is also found buried with *unaccompanied* male and female burials (eg R8, R41, R57, R172, BF60, K8, WS53, WS239, WS402, GSl4b SG1, GSl9 Barrow 1) suggesting there is no simple correlation between the 'wealth' of grave goods and the animal that was sacrificed. Pigs may indeed have been thought of as special animals, closely allied to and cared for by a household, and fattened up using remnants from their meals, so pork may well have been considered a special foodstuff. Yet perhaps the rationale behind the slaughter of pigs for a funeral was prompted by more complex factors than the deceased's lineage or status. The manner of an individual's death, the effort and wealth the family decided to expend on the burial, the nature or number of mourners to be fed, or even the time of the year (whether there was a suitable litter of suckling pigs to be drawn upon, for example): all of these factors may have fed into what constituted a suitable sacrifice.

The consistency and similarity in diet as indicated by the isotope evidence (supported by a new radiocarbon dating programme) led Jay to conclude there was little indication of an immigrant population. There were two individuals (WWH 14 and WWH 431), who had a marginally different isotope signature but both were examples of secondary burials, lacking grave goods, and so they do not appear to be obvious candidates for Continental immigrants. Instead, Jay suggests one of these individuals represents an adult female who may have had a more mobile lifestyle than the majority of the inhabitants or else was an 'incomer', compared with the majority of the population who otherwise appeared 'local' to the area (Jay and Richards 2006). One of the young juveniles (WS144: a child of 2.5–3.5 years) also had an elevated nitrogen isotope value, which might similarly be explained by a more distant origin, though it is possible this was the result of an extended period of breastfeeding (Jay *et al.* 2008, 336). However, in general, the isotope values across both the earlier and later phases of the cemetery were thus interpreted by Jay and Richards as evidence of a long-term, stable population, who maintained 'unusually consistent' dietary habits throughout the Iron Age (2006, 660).

Relationships with place: origins, inhabitation and mobility

One of the key issues raised in Chapter 1 was the ongoing debate about the origin of the square barrow burial rite, and its links to Continental Europe. Whilst these arguments have previously been based on an examination of craniology or cultural similarities and differences, isotope analysis also offers the possibility of investigating patterns of origin and subsequent mobility amongst a skeletal population. As discussed above, the principle is based upon the measurement of stable strontium isotopes laid down in tooth enamel as it is mineralizing in childhood, from food and water ingested and imbibed during this period (Pollard 2009). These substances contain geological strontium derived from local parent rocks, entering the food system through soil, water and plants, which may all have been ingested by animals (Montgomery *et al.* 2007). In prehistory, it is assumed that people were primarily consuming locally grown food and water, so that their strontium isotope signature reflects the area in which they grew up in childhood (approximately, between the ages of 2 and 8 years, Montgomery pers. comm.). However, this technique is an exclusive one: it can rule out places where a child has certainly *not* been raised, but the likely result is a series of possible 'homelands' where they might have grown up (*ibid.*). A major risk in the interpretation of these results is the temptation to selectively highlight a point of origin which might 'fit' a previous assumption, without highlighting the great range of other possibilities which might exist. On its own, strontium isotope analysis cannot distinguish between different sources, but used in combination with oxygen isotopes from tooth enamels, some of these other possibilities may be ruled out (Jay and Richards 2007, 77).

There are also other complications. Our knowledge of background isotope variation based on parent geology is still quite coarse when considering aspects of human mobility, especially at the smaller scale. In areas of great geological diversity, it is perfectly possible to exploit a range of foodstuffs with highly variable isotopic signatures, without having to travel very far (Montgomery *et al.* 2007, 65). Fortunately the geology of the Yorkshire Wolds, and the sources of drinking water within it are reasonably homogeneous (*ibid.*). Alternatively, where there is archaeological evidence for the importation of exotic foodstuffs, eaten as a considerable proportion of peoples' diet, this will clearly mask the 'local' signature of where they actually reside. Fortunately, there are no such indications in the food economy of the later prehistoric Yorkshire Wolds, though some variation might be seen if the majority of stock were being grazed at a considerable distance from the Wolds and then consumed. The effect of marine-derived strontium must also be evaluated in relation to the coastal or inland location of the sample. In addition, dietary differences can also impact upon strontium uptake: it is suppressed in protein- or calcium-rich diets and enhanced in vegetarian or high-fibre diets, meaning that most of the skeletal strontium isotope signature in an omnivore (such as humans) is derived from their plant-intake (Montgomery *et al.* 2007, 69).

These aspects have been carefully considered by Montgomery *et al.* (2007), who have used a sample from the Iron Age cemetery at Wetwang Slack as a comparative group, against which to contrast results from the national Beaker People Project. In addition, they have analysed the chariot burial and associated pit burials from Ferry Fryston, located off the Wolds, in West Yorkshire (in Boyle *et al.* 2007). To this group they are now systematically adding all of the other existing chariot burials, to test the 'invasion' hypothesis. Whilst their analysis only represents a small sample of the total population, the results are fascinating.

Amongst eight inhumations from the Wetwang cemetery, only one had an isotope reading which suggested a non-local childhood, perhaps originating in a more northern environment (Montgomery and Jay 2008; Montgomery *pers. comm.*). This tight distribution of the rest of the population suggested a relatively homogeneous, locally resident community, who were born on the Wolds and were buried there. The results complement the evidence for dietary habits discussed above but contrast with examples from both the middle Neolithic population (where either multiple origins or many forms of mobility were indicated) and the early Bronze Age population (where consumption from two distinct sources might indicate a form of fixed transhumance or seasonal visits between the Wolds and another region: Montgomery *et al.* 2007, 71). Meanwhile, the evidence from the chariot burials also shows a predominance of local individuals (such as Wetwang Slack, WS454), with the occasional 'incomer' such as the male burial from Kirkburn: K5. This individual is particularly interesting as he is buried with an iron mail tunic: one of the earliest – and the most complete – known from northern Europe, dating to the La Tène I period (Stead 1991, 56). His isotope signature could indicate a distant childhood origin, but the nearest suitable zone is the North Yorkshire Moors (Montgomery pers. comm.) where other examples of the chariot burial rite are well attested.

Based on current analysis, the above data suggests that the Iron Age inhabitants of Wetwang Slack were mostly 'locals' who were born in, raised on and died within the region. This does not preclude mobility between areas of the Wolds, such as inter-marriage between different valley systems, or individuals moving from the scarp edge of the High Wolds down onto the dipslope around Driffield, for example. Mobility may well have varied between genders: the subtle distinctions between grave goods, mortuary traditions, treatment of the corpse and preferred orientations, may well represent patterns such as virilocal residence, where women came to live with their husband's family, following marriage (see Arnold 2005, 17). Evidently, occasional incomers from further afield were also absorbed into these communities, perhaps through marriage, fosterage or even the taking of high-status captives or slaves in raids or through blood-debts. We should not be surprised by this mixing of people: the presence of chariot burials on the North Yorkshire Moors and the outlier in West Yorkshire, and square barrow cemeteries found as far north-west as the Howardian Hills, suggest considerable communication and sharing of ideas *across* this region, not just within the chalk 'heartland' of the Wolds.

A few of these individuals may have come from further away. The Ferry Fryston chariot burial from West Yorkshire and five pit burials in the near vicinity, share an isotope signature which is currently unique in Britain. Although debate is ongoing, it may indicate an origin in a granitic area such as northern inland Scotland (Montgomery pers. comm.): not from the Edinburgh region, where the most northerly example of the chariot rite has been found (Carter *et al.* 2010). The distinctiveness of this group, with a shared origin in their childhood, may suggest this is one of the few occasions where a small-scale 'folk' movement can be attested in the archaeological record (Montgomery pers. comm.): perhaps an individual of some status, accompanied by a retinue (Chadwick pers. comm.) or else a 'founding father' and associated family. It is still however, very small-scale, and the rite itself suggests that during their adulthood, the group had cultural contact with northern or eastern Yorkshire, before their death and burial in West Yorkshire: absorbing – perhaps disseminating – and adapting ideas, beliefs and material culture traditions.

It would be surprising if – from this small sample – we actually identified individuals who also exhibited a Continental background (though Jay and Montgomery are currently testing whether the 'chalk' signature of the Champagne region can be distinguished from that of the Wolds: pers. comm.). This does not mean they did not exist. It might seem obvious to select the chariot burials as likely candidates, based on James' model of contact and competitive exchange between élites (1999). However, such long-distance travellers are equally likely to have been traders, craftspeople or even (as Stead suggested) religious specialists, journeying for economic or spiritual reasons. Indeed, these roles may well have overlapped in the persona of a voyaging artisan, skilled in the making or exchange of exotica (see Chapter 7). They may seldom have received the most lavish form of burial – even if they spread ideas about this rite – since these were probably the preserve of the indigenous community leaders, who adopted and adapted new means of display to their own benefit. In addition, even second generation incomers would have a distinctly 'local' profile, and it is possible the limited sample has missed a first-generation immigrant group.

At present then, we can state that the isotope analysis has helped investigate the origin, relative mobility, and diet of the inhabitants of *one* of the Iron Age cemeteries in the Yorkshire Wolds. It is important that we do not generalise too much, based on a small sample from one case study, but this material represents the best investigated later prehistoric population from Britain, and so the results are of international importance. With the above provisos, it suggests that the majority of the Iron Age inhabitants of the Wolds were locally born and residentially stable, but that these communities had ties with, and were open to, incoming individuals, from nearby regions with which they had contact. Future analysis may also pinpoint foreigners from much further afield.

Exploring relatedness

One of the other aspects which archaeologists believed could shed light on not only residential patterns but also ethnic identity and family groupings, was the phenomenon of 'non-metric traits': minute variations in skeletal and dental growth that can be observed within a population, thought in some way to be genetic in origin. It offered a promising insight into relationships across a cemetery, especially where an immigrant group was suspected. In the osteoarchaeological reports on Garton and Wetwang Slack, as well as the cemeteries of the Great Wolds Valleys, considerable effort was put into the recording of this data and its interpretation. S. Stead, for example, combined her results with dental patterns, and a contextual analysis of burials, to support the idea that geographically proximate burials represented family groups (such as BF4 and BF6; R97, R104 and R107; and R173, R174, R175 and R181). In other words, people who were related to each other tended to be buried close together. If correct, this observation offered support to Dent's hypothesis that the three 'clusters' of burials which developed over time at Wetwang Slack cemetery might also indicate three separate family groups (1984a).

Unfortunately, there is now an extensive critique of this analysis which casts doubt upon this simple interpretation, since the scientific basis of this approach remains to be properly investigated (see Tyrell 2000). Whatever these traits indicate, the level of heritability they represent still remains to be addressed (*ibid.*, 303): they cannot be simply read as evidence of individual family affinities. Some may arise purely through chance and there may be strong environmental or social factors influencing their occurrence as well. At best, they are indicators of general affinity amongst a population. They will therefore be discussed in the next chapter with this understanding in mind.

The clearest way of studying biological relatedness amongst these communities would be the use of DNA analysis. Unfortunately, the prohibitive cost of this technique and the need to sample material as soon as possible (to avoid contamination) has thus far precluded its use on the square barrow burials. In addition, it is by no means clear that our preoccupation with genetic affinity (as a test of parenthood or descent) was shared by prehistoric people. Karl has pointed out that aspects of fostering or adoption, as well as apprenticeship, may well have been key strategies through people were brought into the 'family': extending its influence and ties (2005). As Chapter 1 discussed, the sharing of many different kinds of substances (besides genetic material) alongside extensive sociality, are often the means through which relations are constituted and understood. Whereas the previous chapter argued that architectural affinity may have been one of the means through which people made claims of relatedness and belonging, and this chapter has reviewed the skeletal evidence behind their lives and deaths, the following chapter now turns to the role of portable material culture in the construction of social identities.

Conclusion

The chapter has reviewed evidence for the Iron Age population in the Yorkshire Wolds, exploring aspects of demography, disease and violence, diet and origin. It suggests they were well-established communities, living and dying in the local region, who were open to the arrival of occasional incomers from more distant places. Their health was generally good although the strains of agricultural life, disease and ill-health, and the risks of childbirth and infancy took their toll, as did incidents of violence. Most wounds had time to heal, suggesting a good level of aftercare. There are subtle indications of differences in age and gender sets relating to work and codes of combat, as well as some individuals who had slightly different or privileged diets, certainly in their later years, as if respecting seniority or status. In addition, the analysis has begun to highlight biographies, where the nature of an individual's life, or the manner of their death, may have prompted mourners to deal with their passing in special or elaborate ways. It is to the broader issue of those burial rites, and the grave goods interred with these individuals, that the next chapter now turns.

CHAPTER FIVE

From Hand-to-Hand: Biographies of Grave Goods

Introduction

The last chapter began with the story of a woman who had died an untimely death, probably from complications associated with the late stages of pregnancy or childbirth. To begin this chapter, I want to return to her burial: K6, to look in more detail at what else was included in the grave (Figure 4.1). On the right-hand side of her mandible, at the woman's neck, was a copper-alloy double stud, decorated with raised 'berried rosettes' of dots on one face, and a tri-lobate motif (an impressed sunken triangle) on the other. Just behind this, below where the ear would have been, was a small yellow bead made of amber (D1, Henderson and Freeman, in Stead 1991, 93). These items could have been attachments for a cap or other garment (*ibid.*). On the left-hand side, just below her cheek bone, were two rings. One was made of polished jet (B4): tapered and thinned at the top for suspension (Stead 1991, 92), probably derived from outcrops at Whitby, lying further north on the east coast. The other (A8) was a hollow ring made from two semi-tubular halves, riveted together (*ibid.*). Unidentified organic material was found on both the inside and outer surfaces of the latter item, suggesting it may have 'crimped' cloth or textile.

The position of the amber bead, as well as the jet and copper-alloy rings suggests several possibilities. They could have been ear-pendants (Stead 1991, 93), decorations for the hair, or a necklace which had slipped to the side of the face, as the body was laid in the grave. The copper alloy ring may even have decorated a hair-net or hat, or item such as a simple purse. Importantly, this ring is of Continental type (with outliers also found in Ireland as at Lisnacrogher), and it may therefore be one of the few true La Tène I imports into the region (Stead 1991, 94). Stead notes that on the Continent, they are mostly found with male burials, often in association with swords, but where they do occur with women, they are usually placed in the area of the pelvis, making the position of the Kirkburn example unusual. Their flimsy, hollow construction means that they serve little practical purpose: some are sewn onto garments, and Continental scholars often describe them as 'amulets' (*ibid.*). Perhaps such objects were considered to be 'apotropaic' (protective of the body: averting evil), and given the position on the body observed in Continental female burials, they may have had a special association for women with fertility and pregnancy. This ring may have been made locally but it is just possible it was exchanged hand-to-hand, across the seas, rumoured to be an exotic and powerful charm for childbirth. But as objects travel, their meanings and uses can change (White 1991). Knowledge about how it was originally worn and where it was usually placed may have been lost or else, it was reworked in favour of local customs of dress and adornment.

The fact that this copper alloy ring was paired with jet on one side, complemented by amber on the other, may also be significant. Both substances have a deep, lustrous quality which can be further polished: a brilliance that is enhanced by their mutual ability to pick up an electrostatic charge when rubbed against textiles, fur or hair. They can be softened by heat, cut and carved. Amber is noted for its warmth of touch which contrasts with the cool of metals such as bronze (Woodward 2000, 109, 111), and warm jet gives off a distinctive oily smell. Pliny the Elder (in his *Natural History*) noted the supposed curative effects of amber, which he described as a particularly effective amulet for children, whereas Hippocrates noted its qualities as a stimulant (Woodward 2000: 109). During the medieval period in Britain, jet was also documented for its healing and protective qualities, and has been found in burials as charms and keepsakes, rosaries and relic caskets (Gilchrist and Sloane 2005, Dean 2007). The two materials were often seen as analogous, with jet often described as 'black amber' (John Harrowing, writing in 1610, cited in Dean 2007, 262). They occur together in particularly lavish burials of the early Bronze Age: an oppositional colour contrast which Woodward suggests might have been used to structure ideas about life and death (2000). From the prehistoric period onwards, jet and amber may therefore have been perceived as having some of these special properties, in addition to their decorative value.

In life, as someone moved, these ear-pendants, hair loops or necklace charms may have clanked softly together: impressive flashes of light reflecting off their polished surfaces in contrasting warm and dark colours. They might have been rubbed to give off a dramatic crackle and spark, as people looked at and touched them. This suite of objects may have been personal possessions of the woman buried in the grave but equally, they might have been given to her as a protective talisman during her ordeal, or were used to decorate her corpse and appease her spirit – to keep it in place – after the trauma of her 'bad' death. From Chapter 4, we know that such 'double' deaths were relatively rare. It clearly made a mark on those who watched, and who handed down the story, so that when a similar grief befell them years later, they knew where to inter the body of the woman we know as K2, and her unborn child.

The burial of K6 once more provides an introduction to the key themes of this chapter. I will start my examination of grave goods by considering the process of dying, and relate this to the architecture which may be associated with mortuary rituals. Then I will consider the ways in which grave goods have been interpreted by archaeologists, before reviewing different categories of artefacts, exploring their appearance, character and position on the body, as well as associations with different age and gender sets. (Detailed discussion of the chariot burials are excluded from this analysis, as they will form the main focus of the following chapter). Throughout, the chapter will critique the simple notion of reading identity and status directly from the tableau of a burial. Instead, it tries to build up a more nuanced understanding of the motivations of mourners, and how they used the ceremonies of death to renegotiate their own identity as well as that of the deceased. The chapter also reflects upon the 'biography' of objects, in order to understand the different lives artefacts may have had before they ended up in the grave, and how this might relate to the identity of the deceased, the circumstances of their death, or the values and intentions of the mourners at the grave-side. Finally, using both osteological and artefactual analysis, it highlights some rare instances of the ways in which the lives of particular things and specific people were enjoined.

Death and Burial: an archaeological approach

Dealing with the dead

Archaeologists cope routinely with the consequences of death but we seldom talk about its corporeal reality. Yet the purpose of funerary rites is to deal both with the creation of a 'corpse' and the sensory, emotional and psychological affects this process has upon the bereaved (Nilsson Stutz 2003). Death is usually a process, not a moment, involving a series of biological changes to the body and the disappearance of the social persona which has animated it (*ibid.*, 142). A series of physiological alterations is then set in motion to produce the 'cadaver': the clearly recognisable yet transformed body of the deceased. It is the multiplication of bacteria within the corpse which speeds decay: the body marbles, gas and body fluids (and even a pregnant uterus) may begin to be expelled (Mant 1984; Clark *et al.* 1997). At this stage, the corpse may appear to have a quite malicious agency: smelling, swelling and leaking. The speed of these processes is affected by temperature and water: cold and dry conditions both inhibit putrefaction (Knight 1991). Clothing can initially delay cooling of the body, encouraging bacterial action but it later hinders the access of flies and maggots. By wrapping the body in a shroud, dressing or binding it in various ways, the body is more likely to remain articulated. Placement in a coffin which is well-sealed will also delay decomposition although a more flimsy construction will speed up the process, by attracting moisture and organisms (Chamberlain and Parker Pearson 2001, 49). Different soil types and ground conditions will also affect the rate and nature of decay, and the exact nature of burial (immediately filled in or protected by the void of a coffin or stone coverings), as well as the action of burrowing or scavenging animals, and the inevitable force of gravity, will influence the way in which the skeletal elements 'settle' in the grave (Nilsson Stutz 2003). Objects may even break or become displaced as all of these forces and agents work upon the burial (*ibid.*, 148, 151).

It is hoped that this rather blunt and lurid description of the process of death conveys three simple points. First, without the benefit of modern technology, it can be difficult to identify a single 'moment' of death; rather, through a series of changes, the dying individual is seen as gradually ceasing to be. Sudden, violent death may contrast greatly with this normative experience. Second, it is a physically dramatic, noisome and potentially disturbing event during which the corpse must be handled and prepared for its funeral rite (Kus 1992). Finally, the deceased may not simply be thought of as 'dead' but rather, transformed into a corpse which develops its own persona and animacy, through these processes of decay. It is perhaps no surprise that this stage of death is characterised in many societies as a liminal phase of transformation, in which the deceased is neither the loved, living person they once were nor the venerated ancestor they might become. Instead, they may be perceived as a potentially threatening spirit, who has issues to resolve and must let go of its ties, before it can safely pass over into the next realm, dissolve and decay, or be regenerated into new life – depending on the community's beliefs. Van Gennep has argued that this intermediate stage is vital to most rites of passage, which classically move from a phase of separation, through liminality, towards societal reincorporation (1960).

In the valley of Wetwang and Garton Slack, a number of structures may have been designed to facilitate this process. Brewster called these 'mortuary houses', characterised by their proximity to square barrows and lack of occupation debris (1980). One example is in GS7, where Barrow 3 overlay two earlier semi-circular ditch gullies, and Barrow 1 overlay another example. A further ring ditch gully was found adjacent to the chariot burial in GS11. If these were indeed houses reserved for the dead, they may have been designed to both physically and spiritually 'distance' the corpse whilst the grave and funeral ceremony were prepared, whilst facilitating the laying out, preparation and viewing of the decaying cadaver by mourners. Caution is needed: it is possible that these were simply earlier roundhouses or animal shelters, subsequently abandoned and then built over by an expanding cemetery. However, if a period of display was a common part of the ceremonies surrounding death, this might also help explain the presence of rodent bones found *inside* the skull of an individual from Wetwang Slack (Chapter 6). Support for the notion that at least some bodies were put on view before burial comes from a new site at Sewerby Cottage Farm, near Bridlington (Fenton Thomas 2009). A square barrow here contained the remains of an adult male of 'prominent build' (2009, 275), laid supine in the grave. He was interred with a long dagger with a campanulate hilt and a small missile or spear head (similar to those from Garton Station), as well as the remains of a piglet (a classic rite 'B' style burial: Stead 1991). Next to the barrow was a square enclosure, interpreted by the excavators as a mortuary platform, surrounded by a ditch which had held lengths of hurdles, composing a screen. Upright posts clustered at the corners and south-west entranceway or façade: some with squared or triangular profiles, finished with flat or pointed tips. Smaller stakes ran in-between these posts at intervals of 2–3 m. The meticulous excavation of these features revealed the screen had been removed around the time that the square barrow to the immediate west was constructed, possibly shortly beforehand. The director of the site posited that the body had been laid in state in the enclosure, before being interred in the adjacent grave. This would have provided a focus for the initial funerary rites, whilst the grave was dug and the mourners assembled.

In terms of how death was interpreted, a protracted decline or period of illness may have led families to perceive their relations gradually loosening their ties with the living. Yet others were dramatically ripped out of the social fabric of their community by sudden death. In either scenario, the funeral itself was designed to mend the rents in this social fabric. Family roles would have changed: an old generation may have died out, leaving its descendents to become elders. A key social role may have become vacant, leading to a jostling for power amongst the likely contenders. If the deceased was particularly skilled or valued for a specialist body of knowledge (craftwork, agricultural lore, midwifery, ancestral or spiritual matters), their apprentices or acolytes may now be drawn upon to fill their place. Death provided a socio-political arena in which all sorts of tensions came to the fore. It was the forum in which the life of the deceased was held up to social – and possibly, divine – scrutiny, but it was not only the deceased who had to be transformed during the funeral; others may have gained a new identity or series of responsibilities.

Funerary rites provided a channel for the often intense emotions of bereavement, which might include disbelief and sorrow, anger, grief, relief, celebration, loss and even fear of the newly deceased. Such emotions often play a vital role in the successful 'spiritual' dimension of funerary rituals (Nilsson Stutz 2003, 61). However, archaeology has been wary of addressing the issue of emotion because cultural responses to death can be so vastly different. Speculation on the part of an archaeologist risks falling into cultural essentialism or personal subjectivism (Parker Pearson 1999b, 104). Yet emotions are deeply 'felt' and embodied in people's mourning practices. They may therefore have an explicit material dimension, especially in iconography or grave goods which may formalise particular emotions or represent grief through socially relevant metaphors (Tarlow 1999). By bearing these strategies in mind, and by considering the broader context of the small-scale agricultural communities in which these people lived, we may at least be able to pinpoint individual cases where something about the identity of the deceased or the manner of their death occasioned a unique response, as in the burial of K6 discussed at the beginning of this chapter. We can then write thoughtfully about the *range* of emotions such a 'bad' death might have occasioned.

Interpreting burials and grave goods

The beginning of this book highlighted the popular 'chiefdom' image of the East Yorkshire Iron Age communities, illustrating how this was largely based on a direct reading of the chariot burials as evidence of an elite. The interpretation of either the amount or quality of grave goods as direct evidence of status is based on processual approaches pioneered by Binford, Saxe and Tainter (see summary in Parker Pearson 1999b, chapter 4). They assumed that vertical ranking or stratification into classes would be evident in unequal access to resources, represented in valuable materials buried with the elite. Importantly, the presence of rich infant or juvenile burials were used to infer the existence of a system of ascribed or inherited status but where these were absent, rich adult burials were taken to indicate an achieved system of power, based on accomplishments in both social and political life. Rank might also be reflected in the cost-effort (in terms of labour and materials) which went into the building of a deep grave, chamber or surrounding monument, compared with the simpler graves of commoners (a theory tested by Dent (1984a) on the size of barrows and relative associated 'wealth' in Wetwang Slack cemetery, with equivocal results).

There are several problems with these approaches. First, they assume the social order is directly replicated in the funerary record, as a faithful depiction of peoples' roles in life. Yet as we have discussed, death is an important arena for social contest, in which idealised 'fictions' can be produced to mask or repudiate inequalities in life. As Chapter 1 outlined, there are multiple roles and aspects of identity which constitute personhood: political status is but one attribute which might be represented at death and even this may be intertwined in complex ways with age, gender and skill. In addition, the dead 'do not bury themselves' (Parker Pearson 1999b, 84): funerals are organised and executed by the mourners, whose collective status and power are also reflected in the burial (Leach 1979). The unfortunate event of a relative's demise may become the arena for a display of *their* wealth or legitimation of *their* authority. Lavish generosity, such as a communal feast, may be a way of gaining further political capital, and subsequent memorials highlighted the ongoing, strategic value of the deceased, drawing them back into current events. In fact, the sudden appearance of particularly impressive funeral customs may be a strong indication of periods of political instability in the surviving community (Childe, cited in Parker Pearson 1999b, 87).

Alongside issues of power, the spiritual dimension of death should not be overlooked, since funeral rites were the main means through which people negotiated ideas about sacredness and pollution. Certain items associated with the preparation of the corpse and its internment may have had to be disposed of, having become 'contaminated'. Other artefacts may have been included as tokens of religiosity (such as crucifixes or rosaries in the Medieval world), sacred protection against malign spirits (amulets and charms) or items which ensured passage into the afterlife (such as the coin to pay the boatman, Charon, across the River Styx, in Greek mythology). Broader cosmological beliefs may be reflected in aspects of orientation and posture, as well as the inclusion of certain materials and objects, and their placement in relation to the body. Yet these attributes might also be used to structure and comment upon aspects of the deceased's relationships, with other people, animals, and the land they have lived in (Brück 2004). The role of metaphor and symbolism is key in such events, allowing mourners to articulate subtle values and key ideals, through the inclusion of specific artefacts and the arrangement of the 'tableau' of the grave.

Such objects may have been personal possessions of the deceased, though 'heirlooms' or hand-me-downs may have had a long biography of associations: multiple connections which they presenced at the moment of burial. However, their burial with a particular individual may mean they have become integral to the deceased's identity or skill: human-object partners whose bond was indissoluble, so that they could not be bequeathed. Artefacts might also be gifts from the mourners, either to close outstanding debts (lest the dead 'came looking' for recompense) or to set up new ones with the deceased. This latter scenario reminds us that dead can be a potentially powerful body, able to intercede with the community of the ancestors or other spiritual forces, on behalf of the living. Lavish gifts may have been a way of ensuring future favours. Artefacts can also be provided as equipment for the afterlife, to fulfil a particular role or carry out a task. Meanwhile, the bestowal of 'adult' grave goods upon juvenile burials can be an indication that they will 'grow into' those roles, in the next world.

By paying close attention to aspects such as the style and date of objects, and evidence for damage, wear and repair, as well as changes in the context of their use, we are able to get at their life-histories, and explore how they relate to the individual they are buried with. The origin and character of materials used in complex or composite objects can help elucidate the broader skein of economic ties and craft skill which have come together in their making. Whether things are made purposefully for the burial, or handed down over generations, they can thus help us to explore the social relations they embody. This section has reviewed the phenomenon of death, and archaeological and ethnographic approaches to the interpretation of burials and grave goods. The next part of this chapter turns to the evidence for the preparation and dressing of the deceased, and the different grave goods which were interred with them.

Dressing and framing the body

Fabrics and wrappings

In preparation for burial, many individuals appear to have been formally dressed in either clothes or strips of cloth. Sometimes these were preserved merely as fibrous stains in blackened soil which in Garton Slack 1/2 Single Grave 2 resembled 'a blanket … folded over the body and partly resting upon the sides' (Brewster 1980, 111). More productively, textiles have also been preserved as mineralised fibres, replaced by the oxides in metal objects which lay against them, or pinned them together. They have been most extensively studied in the burials from the Great Wold cemeteries (Crowfoot in Stead 1991, 119). Whilst some of these showed evidence of animal hides and hair, most were of wool. A variety of spinning techniques were used, including a few examples of mixed 'Z' and 'S' systems which would have produced a thorn-proof and rain-repellent surface when woven (*ibid.*). The resulting yarns may have been coarse and uneven but the four-shed twill weaving produced a dense, warm cloth whilst tabby weaves provided finer and lighter textiles (*ibid.*). Crowfoot argues from the position of the brooches in the upper chest area of the body that they adorned outer garments such as a heavy cloak. The repetitious effort put into alternating 'S' and 'Z' spun yarns may be evidence they were dyed different colours, making a simple but attractive cloth. Three examples had chevron or diamond patterns created by the mixed weave, and five graves showed evidence of decorative borders, three of which may have resulted in a hanging 'fringe', with a further example from Wetwang Slack (WS233, Crowfoot, cited in Dent 1984a). A diamond twill weave was also found preserved in a barrow at Skipwith, by Stillingfleet in 1817 (Henshall 1950, 138). Some examples of finer yarn suggest distinctions in clothing were important, as in the chariot burials from Wetwang Slack, and another inhumation, WS167 (Crowfoot, cited in Dent 1984a). The mirror from the female chariot burial WS454 (placed behind her head), preserved an impression of a tablet-woven border, perhaps part of the woman's clothing, but the tangled threads, wrapped around a piece of bone, suggest it may have been a separate band, a fringe associated with a head-covering (*ibid.*) or part of the mirror's wrapping or decoration. One especially well-preserved example from BF20 (the adult male who may have suffered a loss of hearing in his life) was buried in a cloak decorated with a 5 cm wide border of needle-worked cross-stripes creating a 'chequered' effect (Stead 1991, 120–1, figs 79 and 80): perhaps the earliest known example of British hand-stitched embroidery (*ibid.*).

Flax fabrics have survived in the chariot burials from Wetwang Slack, alongside mixed-spun wool textiles, which were well preserved from their contact with bronze artefacts (Crowfoot in Stead 1991, 120). Flax or hemp was recorded, possibly as an intrusive thread from an undergarment, on the BF20 brooch, and these textiles may also have been present at Rudston and Burton Fleming, but were not generally preserved. Other textiles include those preserved on the mail tunic from K5. A coarse wool shift appears to have been worn next to the body, covered by a finer layer, and the mail itself may have had lined 'shoulder tabs' where it fastened over the front of the body (Crowfoot in Stead 1991, 122). Unfortunately, none of these materials survive in sufficient lengths to indicate whether they were old and worn when placed in the grave (suggested for example, by tears or mends), or made purposefully for the burial.

Not enough remnants of cloth survive to be certain whether there were clear differences in women's dress, compared with men, nor if there were age-appropriate items of clothing such as the cloak. However, the scrap of fabric found in the grave BF20 suggests that colour, patterns and style could have been used to reproduce differences not just between age and gender groups but to reinforce status, community or clan membership. Cloth has considerable power in small-scale communities, as an item of dress used to either distinguish or homogenise. It can be used to transform the body in ceremonial rites of passage (such as investiture), create disguises, or conceal that which should not be seen (Weiner and Schneider 1989). The chalk figurines found in the gullies and ditches of the latest Iron Age settlement at Wetwang and Garton, as well as numerous other sites from East Yorkshire (Stead 1988) support the notion that aspects of design were important. Collars, hems and belts, and sometimes even inscribed 'panels' reminiscent of the sewn embroidery or weave of the cloth, are carved with care onto the bodies of these enigmatic figures (Giles 2007a). Ethnographic case studies also indicate the importance of cloth as bulk fabric or finished items which can be used for exchange or stockpiled as wealth and heirlooms (Weiner and Schneider 1989; Feeley-Harnik 1989). Its hand-made nature makes it a classic 'inalienable' object (Weiner 1989), and its softness and fragility lend to it metaphorical connotations of procreation, degeneration, transience and death (Weiner and Schneider 1989). Its closeness to the body: taking on aspects of form, becoming fitted to someone's habitual gestures, or worn through their everyday tasks, create a close affinity between cloth and its wearer. Even fragments of cloth can be intimately redolent of their being and identity. As a substance which is woven together out of individual threads (which must themselves be spun) it is also used as a common metaphor for kin or community relations: the 'ties that bind' which must be stitched together. These may be 'cut' but also darned, mended. Cloth may therefore be used to evoke a series of meanings about identity and mortality, in the funerary context.

Cord, hide products and matting

Cord was possibly noted in an impression on a brooch from R76 (Stead 1991). Traces of hide products (more inaccurately referred to as 'leather') were present in a number of cases, and whilst these might represent elements of clothing such as jerkins or belts, they also derived from other organic objects such as scabbards, knife sheaths and shield coverings. At Garton Slack, Brewster noted three cases of black staining running the length of the body, which he interpreted as the remains of rotted cloth (1980) but this might well have been a more durable substance such as leather. It is possible that bodies were often lain on a soft surface, either of hides, sods, textiles or – in the case of a burial from Wetwang Slack (WS34) and possibly the Wetwang Village chariot burial – sedge/rush matting (Crowfoot's analysis, cited in Dent 1984a, 26; Havercroft 2002). Lime impressions from a burial at Garton Slack excavated by the Granthams in 1965 suggested the presence of matted grass or straw underneath the body; possibly a mat or lining for a coffin (cited in Dent 1984a, 26) but in the majority of cases, little trace of such furnishing survives. These objects may not have been for mere comfort or decoration: in Samoa, mats are key to life-cycle ceremonies – their age and wear evidences connections with the ancestors, and their fragile matter and weave are drawn upon metaphorically to convey the vulnerability and transience of authority and social relations (Weiner 1989).

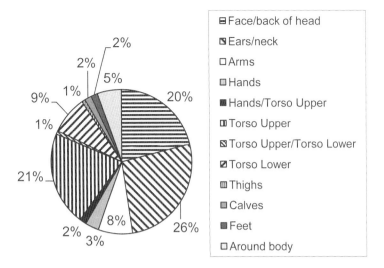

FIGURE 5.1. Position of fastenings upon the body.

Summary

The most common interpretation of the above fabrics is that they represent *in situ* clothing, fastened around the body by a variety of different styles of brooch (made of iron, bronze or composite material) iron staples or pins and bone points/pins, as in life (Stead 1979, Jundi and Hill 1998). Yet the position of some of these objects is curious (Figure 5.1). Items in the vicinity of the ears/neck (26%) and upper torso (21%) may well represent *in situ* pinning of the material around the shoulders or across the chest. However, there are a considerable number of cases where brooches are in front of the face or at the back of the head (e.g. WS34): here, the cloak may have been ceremonially drawn around the upper torso, to conceal the face from view. Brooches found on the lower torso, thighs and calves or feet may be pinning together or decorating separate objects, lain at the side of the body – a bundle of cloth or a bag. But others may be pinning the cloth together tightly around the body: in other words, some of these cloaks may have been 'shrouds', as Dent has suggested (1984a, 28). This is supported by the tightly 'bound' posture of a number of burials, whose lower or upper limbs are so closely pressed together that they must have been held in place by either cord, strips of cloth or a tightly wrapped winding sheet. This is particularly the case in tightly crouched or contracted burials: R60 is a good example, with an iron brooch located in the skull/upper chest area. Meanwhile, BF4, crouched on its back, had its arms folded across the chest, hands up to the face, and ankles tightly pressed against the buttocks. An iron brooch around the knees suggests the cloak or cloth had been used to keep the body tightly bound around the torso, though the feet may have stuck out from beneath the hem of this garment, as with GS10. Garton Slack 1/2 Single Grave 2, is an example of a tightly crouched burial where the black stain of a possible shroud was recorded by Brewster (1980). The male chariot burial WS455 had its arms clamped to the sides of the body, and legs tightly folded, suggesting a slightly more complex binding of the limbs. At Wetwang Village, the woman's calves tightly pressed against her thighs: both drawn up close under her torso, and her left hand appears to have been bent backwards so tightly, it may have fractured the wrist (Hill 2004). There is no simple correlation between these tightly contracted or crouched burials and brooches or pins, so much of this binding must have been effected using strips of cloth which have not survived. Alternately, limbs may have been propped or pressed against grave goods or infill, to keep what we know must have been a rapidly decaying and bloated body, in these compact positions.

These fabrics are important for the light they shed upon the 'taskscape' of these communities (Ingold 1993). These were societies not only involved in cattle pastoralism, but extensive shepherding, and sheep and goats played a vital role not only in the diet of these people, but for by-products such as wool, fleece, hide and horn. The textile remains imply time spent plucking or shearing (probably late spring), carding and cleaning wool, spinning and weaving, even embroidering and stitching: activities which needed good light but may have been carried out throughout the year (see Chapter 3). The suggestion of colour contrasts in some fabrics also implies dying, using plant or mineral extracts. Hides meanwhile, had to be flayed (perhaps following an autumn cull) and soaked, defleshed and dehaired, cured and cut and stitched. Urine, dung, bark and wood ash, may have been used in these processes. Flax meanwhile, had to be grown, harvested and soaked or retted (to remove the fibre from the cellular tissue) and this may have been done in pits or through exposing of the crop to dewfalls and strong daylight, in late summer/early autumn. The making of cord as well as string, rope, basketry and matting (from plant fibres, straw and rushes) would have been important adjuncts to weaving and leather-working. These subsidiary crafts may have been less dictated by the season but the resources may have had to be gathered from watercourses and woodland on and off the Wolds. Although many of these organic materials are not preserved, it is important that we think about the range available to Iron Age people, and consider the timing and landscape organisation related to known crafts, in relation to other tasks (Ingold 1993).

Coffins

The main piece of furniture used to contain the body was a wooden coffin, which survive as discoloured stains in the chalk infill, or as a lime 'crust' (Dent 1984a, 25) or even as mineralised impressions on grave goods. They were recorded most commonly at the cemetery of Wetwang Slack, where a high proportion of crouched and flexed individuals were probably buried in such structures. (Interestingly, there are far fewer brooches from this cemetery, so perhaps the same end of concealing the body was being achieved through different means). They ranged in size from small coffins of 0.95 m by 0.45 m wide to larger versions at 1.20 m long by 0.60 m wide (Stead 1991, 36), though the largest at Wetwang Slack was 1.75 m long (Dent 1984a). This indicates the range of body postures within the coffin: some corpses being tightly bound before being interred (see Chapter 6 for further discussion of an extremely small example at Wetwang Slack). Some of these coffins were portable and probably sealed, where iron clamps or 'dogs' indicate jointed frames (e.g. WS270) but others may have consisted of planking laid around and above the body. It is worth thinking about the sheer volume of wood, carpentry skills and forward planning, involved in this endeavour. Given the largely cleared, open pasture landscape of the Wolds, good timber would have been a valuable substance which required management, and was probably felled in the more wooded environs of the surrounding vales. Dent records that some of these coffin structures were apparently lined with rushes or sedge (1984a, 26: materials which have been fetched from rare spring sites or meres in the Wolds) and the Granthams noted one burial at Garton Slack lined with matted grass or straw (cited in Dent *ibid.*; though these could be further examples of woven mats used to line the coffin).

The upturned box of the chariot or cart, placed over the body of rite C burials, is analogous to these structures, and represents the high end of an ideal about concealing or containing the body: an idea which will be further discussed in the following chapter. Again, the broader taskscape springs into view within the context of such funerals, suggesting that these deaths prompted the bringing together of woodland and wetland organic materials from several kilometres away, to be worked into funeral furniture and furnishings. They may even have been stockpiled well in advance by carpenters, for seasoning and preparation, anticipating such use.

Adorning and provisioning the dead

Range of grave goods and key associations

Most individuals were interred without grave goods (66%) although a significant proportion of these burials were provided with a plain coffin (especially at Wetwang and Garton Slack). We can no longer simply assume these burials represent 'poor' individuals or families, since it is equally possible that their belongings were distributed as heirlooms or that the objects interred were well crafted organic products or impressive clothing, which has long since decayed. The rest (34%) contained some form of more durable belonging or offering, the most common of these being items of bodily decoration (brooches, pins, necklaces, rings, beads and discs, toggles, ties, and bracelets or bangles), more portable items (including weaponry – swords, shields, spears and knives; tools for working metal, wood and textiles; horse-gear; mirrors; containers of various kinds – boxes, bags and ceramic jars) and finally, evidence for food in the forms of joints of meat or whole animals. A variety of substances were used to make these objects: copper alloy (more commonly referred to as bronze), iron, jet and shale, amber, coral, stone, bone and antler, textiles, wood, hide products and fleece. Many of these were joined, glued or stitched together to make 'composite' artefacts, involving the cross-over of skills between different crafts.

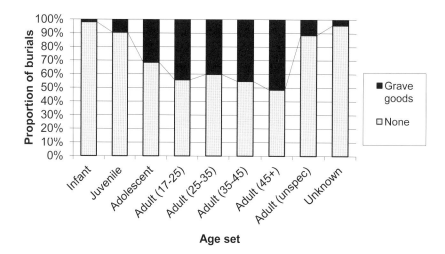

FIGURE 5.2. Provision of grave goods by age and sex.

Age at death has some bearing on the provision of grave goods (Figure 5.2). Infants are normally never interred with grave goods: only one example was buried with scattered fragments of a ceramic jar. Juveniles and adolescents are also rarely buried with artefacts: where present, they are likely to be rings or beads. However, as people gained their adult status, diverse and numerous grave goods became more common, and the highest proportion of people interred with such items (relative to their age-set) are the senior or elderly members of the community. The lack of 'rich' child burials could be interpreted as evidence that there was no hereditary system of wealth: royal or elite bloodlines. Close affiliation with – or possession of – objects may instead have been gradually earned as people passed through life's stages, gained gifts or negotiated exchanges, and evidenced certain skills or abilities. They may have acted as important prompts for memories regarding an individual, and so it should not be surprising if those who had lived longest were honoured with rich possessions, mnemonics or mementos. Those burials with more numerous grave goods may therefore be an indicator of the complexity of the *relations* the deceased held by the end of a long life: in other words, status related to their social interconnectedness (and importance as a soon-to-be ancestor) rather than their inherent, individual 'wealth'.

Ceramics and Food

The most common durable item was a ceramic jar: hand-made, simple earthernware vessels, some with marked shoulders and out-turned rims, others which were more shapeless, upright jars (Figure 5.3). Occasional beaded rims or internal chamfers are also found (perhaps to create a seat for a lid, like the preserved wooden disc complete with finger-hole, found at North Cave, Dent 2010, 39) and there is one example of an erratic tempered vessel with pedestal foot and zones of burnishing (found in grave R143, associated with an involuted brooch of *c.* 2nd century date). Most vessels were simply smoothed on the inside, though a 'slurry' of clay may have been used to create an even exterior, which was sometimes further smoothed or burnished (Rigby in Stead 1991, 104). Interestingly, a narrow range of temper 'recipes' was chosen for interment in the graves, consisting of either erratic (ETW) or calcite (CTW) tempered wares, with a third fabric containing both erratic inclusions and organic temper (1991). (In contrast, a further four fabric types are known from contemporary settlement sites north of the Humber which are not represented in these funerary assemblages, *ibid.*, 95). Rigby considers that at least five different clay sources are indicated from differences in the background matrix (*ibid.*). The large inclusions of erratic-temper were probably added deliberately to the clay, and may originate from glacio-fluvial drifts (Freestone and Middleton in Stead 1991, 163): pebbles and boulders found on the Holderness Plain (especially along its exposed and eroding coastal cliffs), which were heated and quenched to produce large fragments. In contrast, the calcite appears to have been crushed, and probably derives from rare outcrops within the chalk, perhaps exposed during quarrying activities. A rare example of glauconite in one vessel might also derive from the glacial tills but could be from a Speeton Clay deposit outcropping north of Burton Fleming (*ibid.*, 164). There is some indication of valley-based preferences, with ETW fabrics being quite common in the Great Wold Valley cemeteries of Rudston and Burton Fleming (alongside the dominant CTW), but less common from Wetwang and Garton Slack, where calcite tempered wares are the norm. Pots may therefore have been 'readable' in terms of the sources of their clay and temper, and the landscape with which they were associated.

FIGURE 5.3. Examples of ceramic jars from square barrow burials. R186 and BF37. Based on Stead 1991, 115, fig. 77.

R186

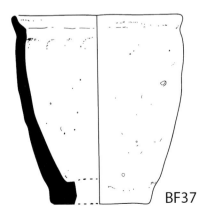

BF37

The level of firing of these vessels was sometimes of such poor quality that the small jars had distorted and fragmented in the grave. The range of colour was also variable, suggesting that neither oxidation (producing red-orange colours) nor reduction or fuming (grey to sooty black) was an explicit intention of the potter. Rigby even suggested that these vessels might have been purpose-made for the funeral (*ibid.*, 105 e.g. R46). However, many had sooted exteriors, suggesting they had been used at least once. In the Great Wold Valley, approximately one third of pots were represented by lower bodies and bases only (*ibid.*). Many of the others lacked all or part of their rims, and even where these were complete they were often cracked or chipped. It is possible that their fragile, ill-fired nature led to frequent breakage in the funeral ceremony or post-depositional environment, but this may also sometimes have been deliberate: a blow to the pot which broke or damaged it, perhaps signalling its end as an affective container. R204 had two clusters of 'token' sherds deposited in the grave from a freshly fractured vessel, suggesting it had been broken elsewhere. In WS154, a handful of sherds had been scattered on the grave floor and the deceased's head was then laid upon them. Further fragments were found in the backfill of the grave. Rigby has suggested that this deliberate 'mutilation or breakage' might be symbolic (in Stead 1991, 108): pots may have had a metonymic relation with human bodies, and had to be ceremonially 'killed' to mark the end of their life.

Only one vessel was ever included in the grave: there were no 'dining sets'. The reconstruction of these vessels indicates some were tall and capacious, suggesting their role as storage jars (capable of holding between 2.5–5 litres of fluid or 1–2 kg of grain). 'Tub' shaped pots were also found at Wetwang Slack (Dent 2010, 39). However, most are smaller and were probably individual cooking or drinking vessels (Rigby in Stead 1991, 107), more suited to holding a portion of stew for one, rather than communal eating or drinking. This is interesting since several of these vessels (not just from the Great Wold Valley cemeteries but Danes Graves and Wetwang and Garton Slack) contained the left humerus of a sheep. These joints frequently showed signs of disarticulation, suggesting a modest portion of a funerary feast which had been set aside for the dead: the rest of the carcase perhaps having been consumed by the mourners or offered as a sacrifice. This joint often stuck out over the top, as if advertising its contents, which may have spilled out in the grave. The front and hind limbs of sheep or goat were also sometimes interred (Legge in Stead 1991). Meanwhile, those burials with pig involved parts of the skull (whole or halved, with or without its mandible, occasionally with one or both front limbs). Again these often show evidence for butchery but the bones may have been de-fleshed before interment (possibly by cooking rather than cutting, *ibid.*). The forelimbs of pig in the Wetwang Village burial, for example, were defleshed before interment. Whereas sheep and goats were killed anywhere between 6 months and 2–3 years old, pigs were often sacrificed at a younger age (12–24 months or younger). Interestingly, meat is never provided for children's burials, suggesting that despite being involved in tending and herding, they were not entitled to such a sacrifice and feast.

Rarely, whole animals were interred: sheep and goats (Calais Wold, Mortimer's barrow C72, Danes Graves 73) and pigs (WS186, and Grindale: a probable rite B burial, Manby 1980). Uniquely, the 'King's barrow' at Arras was recorded as preserving two 'boars' (Greenwell 1906) and two ponies (Stead 1979): one of the latter animals was old, symbolically matching the worn bit with which it was buried. The probable chariot burial at Seamer was also reported to contain a horse (Mortimer 1905a, 358). Cattle have never been recorded in the Eastern Yorkshire burials though they were slaughtered and displayed on the barrow of the chariot at Ferry Fryston, West Yorkshire (Boyle *et al.* 2007). Other food substances will not have survived: libations will have soaked into the porous chalk gravel and cereal products will have rotted away

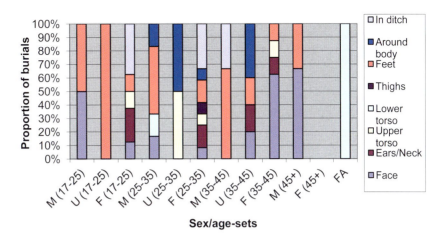

FIGURE 5.4. Position of ceramic vessels in burials, analysed by age and sex.

(unless charred). However, many of the pots had sooty exteriors suggesting they had been used in cooking (e.g. R4).

Parker Pearson, citing Picini, argues that the position of these vessels and food offerings in the grave is significant (1999a, 53). An analysis of the Great Wold Valley cemeteries suggests men were buried with pots 'at their feet' whilst women were interred with them in the area of their 'heads and hands', perhaps portraying a relationship 'between server/provider and served/provided' (*ibid.*). Extending this analysis to all of the cemeteries (Figure 5.4), we can see that of the complete/near complete pots found, 23% were placed in the face/hands area of female burials, compared with only 6% of male burials, whereas 13% were found by the feet of men, and only 6% with women. There does not seem to be any clear pattern related to age, apart from very elderly women, of whom there are few burials but no pots: perhaps they were excused domestic duties! The suggestion of a gendered domestic symbolism is interesting but the picture is confusing, the numbers involved are small, and it may have some meaning other than roles in food production and consumption. Pots are also found scattered around the body and placed in a variety of positions on or near the torso. Interestingly, 13% of pots were found in the surrounding ditch or barrow monument of adult women. This might suggest a secondary funeral rite, which involved the bringing of a pot to the side of the new monument (usually without an offering of meat) and its placement in the surrounding ditch. Given that these ditch fills were seldom fully excavated, this rite may be more common than is currently thought.

Brooches and pins

Brooches are found with both men and women in equal numbers (Stead 1991, 90), and as argued above, may have been used to decorate and secure clothing, as well as pin shrouds around a decaying corpse. They are either made from forged iron or cast copper alloy with elements which were then drawn or hammered out, and some use an admixture of these metals to achieve the finished item. The basic components are a body from which a wire was coiled into a spring on the right (or a 'mock spring' with a rivet), out of which a single pin was drawn (Stead 1996, 38). The brooch was closed by lifting the pin into a catch-plate on the left. This catch-plate extended into a foot, which was often flattened into a platform for some form of applied or incised decoration (*ibid.*). Some forms were only found in the Great Wold Valley, whilst others are unique to Wetwang and Garton Slack. The great variety of types has allowed Dent to construct a detailed chronology, coupled with stratigraphic evidence and radiocarbon dating (1982, 2010). Bayesian statistics have recently been used to refine this chronology, based on all of this associated information (Jay *et al.* 2012), though it should be noted, the analysts have assumed there is no significant curation of these objects, and their depositional sequence more or less faithfully represents change in tastes and styles over time. Table 5.1 summarises the various types and their suggested dates, arranged approximately in order and Figure 5.5 provides illustrations of the main types.

Arched bow and inlaid bow types may have originated in the 4th century BC (La Tène I), with rare examples of early, highly arched Marzabotto types found in graves at Cowlam and Burton Fleming, and from a barrow ditch at Wetwang Slack (Dent 2010, 41). Flat bow types are an insular tradition, emerging from this earlier type in the 3rd century BC and the long flat bow type may be a further variant on this form. However, arched and flat bow types are both found during the middle La Tène period and there is no simple progression from one form to the other (C. Haselgrove, pers. comm.) Short involuted brooches may originate a little later in the late 3rd century BC, continuing into the 2nd century BC (i.e. around 200 BC) alongside other involuted brooches of various types. 'S-shape' brooches also appear around this time. These latter brooches continue in use into the late 2nd or early 1st century BC, when rare La Tène III forms appear (e.g. the high rounded bow and solid catch-plate 'Nauheim' style brooch from R175 or the penannular brooches, examples of which were found at Wetwang Slack and Danes Graves). In general, these are British designs, with only a handful demonstrating distinctly Continental forms: even these, Stead argues, are probably locally made, with hinged rather than true spring mechanisms (1991, 180).

In the Great Wold Valley, arched and flat bow brooches have a strong association with men, whereas long flat bow brooches appear to be preferred for women, as are short involuted types (Figure 5.6). Involuted brooches with applied enamel however, are again strongly associated with men. However, in Wetwang and Garton Slack, the only marked preference appears to be short involuted brooches, which are strongly associated with women, as well as penannular, inlaid bow and S-shape brooches. Dent notes that the 'smaller' types appear to be favoured by women (1982). It is therefore possible that there were gendered preferences for different shapes and styles but given the longevity of the cemetery use, these patterns could relate to other aspects of identity such as kin or peer groups.

Illustration	Description	Type (Stead 1991)	Type (Dent 1984a)	Date
	Arched bow	Type A	Type 1	c.C4th BC+ La Tène I-II
	Flat bow	Type B	Type 2	c.C3rd BC+ La Tène I-II
	Short involuted	Type E	Type 4	c.C3rd BC+ La Tène I-II?
	Long flat bow	Type C	Type 5a	c.C2nd BC+ La Tène I-III
	Long involuted	Type D	Type 3	La Tène II-III
	Involuted: applied enamel and rivulets	Type F	n/a	La Tène II-III
	Involuted: hinged pin mounted in head	Type G	n/a	La Tène II-III
	Involuted: mock spring discs, solid rivulet	Type H	n/a	La Tène II-III
	Short involuted: applied enamel on broad feet	Type J	n/a	La Tène II-III
	Solid foot catch-plate	Type K	n/a	La Tène III
	Penannular	Type L	Type 8	La Tène II-III
	Inlaid bow	n/a	Type 6	c.C4th BC+ La Tène I
	S-Shape	n/a	Type 7	c.C2nd BC

TABLE 5.1. Brooch types.

As mentioned above, though initially influenced by Continental styles, all of these brooches were probably made in Britain, with some distinctly insular styles such as the u-shaped, curved 'involuted' forms (J. Collis, pers. comm.). Some are decorated with coral, such as the elegant splayed rays of the Queen's barrow brooch from Arras and the head, foot and bow of WS155 (Type 6). Others are capped with a large knob or bead of red glass 'enamel' (such as R178, R39, BF10 and the Ferry Fryston short involuted iron brooch), held in place by bronze or iron pins/rivets. One brooch combines both substances in a 'ring' of two coral arcs surmounted by a knob of red glass 'enamel'

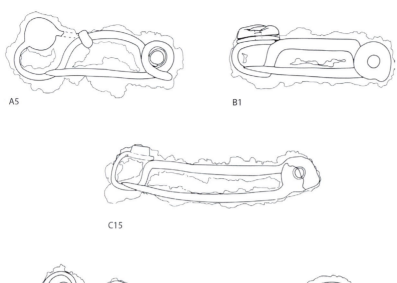

A5

B1

C15

F1

K1

FIGURE 5.5. Brooch types. A= Arched bow, B = Flat bow, C = Long flat bow, F = Involuted, K = La Tène III/Nauheim style. Based on Stead 1991, 81–92.

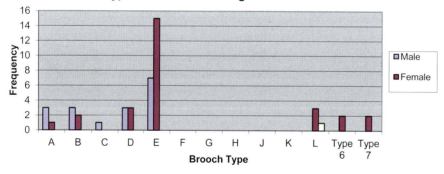

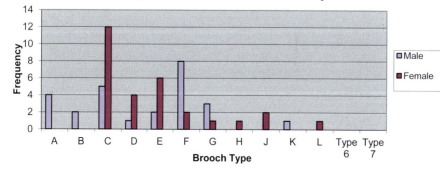

FIGURE 5.6. Brooch styles, analysed by sex, and compared between the Wetwang/Garton Slack cemeteries and Great Wolds Valley cemeteries.

(R22). Some foot plates are formed into a swelling 'globe' (BF56) whilst iron involuted brooches frequently have a bulbous 'humped stop' on the foot. The bronze backs or feet of others are delicately engraved with curvilinear decoration (e.g. WS115 or BF61) or moulded into a triskele design (WS160, Type 1). Other substances such as red and brown carved sandstone, carved into snail-shell like beads, were used to decorate a brooch from Danes Graves, whose pin, catch-plate and back of the bow, are cast and engraved into small swirls, ribs and lips (DG57, Figure 5.7). Beads of fine-grained ferruginous dolomitic clay were used to decorate brooches from Rudston (R102, R39 and possibly R60, R178): fired to bring out the red hue and improve their robustness, whilst a hard, haematite slip also appears to have been used on the bead from R39 (Henderson and Freestone in Stead 1991, 165). A probable amber bead or other red stone was used on the S-shape brooch from WS236. Three beads of red-brown resinous inlay on a striking brooch from Danes Graves (DG95), are also probably amber, combined with a strip of polished light green inlay on the foot and small perforated beads of either shell and/or coral – some still very pink in colour – on the bow-back and head (Stead 1979, 67). The bronze bow is finely ribbed, and the contrasting colours of this brooch are extraordinarily eye-catching (Figure 5.8).

These various beads, strips and plates of adornment may have evoked a series of natural phenomena: berries and leaves, snail shells and stones, and the 'petals' or 'sun-rays' of the Queen's brooch from Arras, sometimes bound in the flowing, chased scrolls, spirals and eyes of curvilinear ornament. They were intimate and tactile objects, worn on the chest or shoulder, which nonetheless embodied a variety of local and distant substances and ideas, in their shape, decoration and embellishment. As they drew together folds of cloth, attention would have been drawn to their striking colours (especially the reds of coral,

FIGURE 5.7. Danes Graves sandstone-bead decorated brooch (YORYM: 1948.930.2)

FIGURE 5.8. Danes Graves brooch DG95.

red glass and sandstone), attractive textures and delicate designs. Yet much of the detail of these objects would have been known only to the wearer, or those in close proximity to them. Many have the appearance of being 'old' objects, with a polished patina on the exposed bronze where it was fingered or rubbed against cloth, and some were clearly repaired during their lives, with replacement pins (Cowlam B/L, BF61a). Others look incomplete, lacking a foot or catch-plate (R118b, BF53, WS180) or spring (BF1). It is possible that they broke in the grave, as the strain of a decomposing body or stress of grave infill damaged these objects. Others may have been deliberately included as old, non-functioning objects – perhaps from expediency – but also as a symbol that their life too was over, their usefulness at an end.

Pins were another form of bodily adornment, more rare than brooches, but found in graves at Danes Graves, Rudston, Wetwang and Garton (Dent 2010, 41). Both straight forms and ring-headed types are known, most of which were made of iron, and they are found with both men and women, in a range of positions: by the face, feet, upper and lower torso, hands and calves. This suggests that, like brooches, they may well have been used to pin clothing or shrouds tightly around the body, or else had a multiplicity of uses. However, two pins – those from Danes Graves and the Garton Slack example from the Granthams collection – were found behind the heads of the deceased (Stead 1979, 77). Stead suggests that they could be hair or even hat-pins (*ibid.*), though again their use on a shroud cannot be precluded.

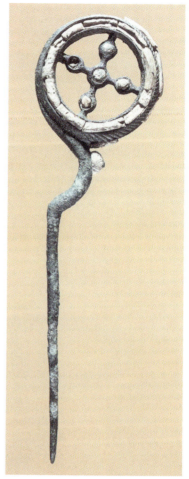

The Danes Graves pin, published by Mortimer as a fine watercolour (1897), is an elegant bronze example, with a long shank, and 'wheel' ring head (Figure 5.9). Its outer circumference is grooved and incised with tiny ribs. A large white bead, attached with a bronze pin, adorns the swan's neck curve. The four inner 'spokes' are decorated with small beads of coral, as is the inner face of the 'wheel' but interestingly, the slender beads used to do this are perforated, suggesting they were originally part of a necklace or bracelet, and have been re-used (Stead 1979, 77). The original artefact may have been traded or exchanged, and was then broken up to decorate a variety of local artefacts, but its previous history would have been visible to the knowing eye. The iron pin from the female chariot burial at Wetwang Slack (WS454) is by contrast small, but its coral inlay is wound round by a thin strip of gold, whose untarnished luminosity would have stood out against the charcoal grey of the iron pin: a remarkable and valuable substance – perhaps recycled from an ancient object, or gleaned from a distant exchange.

FIGURE 5.10. Toe-rings and finger-rings, armlets, bracelets, brooches and necklaces from the square barrow cemeteries.

Items of bodily adornment

Bracelets

A variety of armlets or bracelets were found in the square barrow burials (Figure 5.10). Many were made of bronze, with different closing mechanisms: mortice and tenon types, hook and eyes, overlapping or abutting terminals, or solid rings which were probably seldom removed from the arm. Some had swelled sections which were then decorated (as at Cowlam burial L) or areas of incised ornament around the terminals (BF10). WS60 had eye-like motifs separated by running scroll-work (Dent 2010, 41). Others were delicately ribbed or twisted around their circumference (as in burials from Arras A24 and A4, Stead 1979, 73). One such bracelet, linked to a thick jet ring (found by the Granthams at

Garton Slack), revealed a twisted rope or cord inside, around which the bronze sheeting seemed to have been wrapped and hammered, then punched with decoration (Brewster 1980, 120). This made the bracelet, and others like it, deceptively light (Stead 1979, 75). Made from 'off-white horse hair, linen threads or plant fibres', the material inside unfortunately decayed during inconsiderate conservation (Brewster 1980, 120). Other bracelets were 'knobbed' with ovate sections mimicking the look of beads on a strand (Arras A4, Cowlam LI). A variety of inlays was used to decorate these bronze forms, as with brooches: white inlay/coral (Arras A4), or pink shell/coral (WS160), red glass 'enamel' (Arras W.24), and one with a white-flecked red bead of porphyry (Arras W.24). Iron bracelets were also found, some thin (Danes Graves 45 and 46), others more robust (WS). There are also a series of fine, lustrous jet bracelets (R59, DG2) one a deep bangle with cordons (R59), and others made of shale (R2). In one case, the bronze-smith must have worked carefully with other materials: forging closed the delicately incised bronze bracelet from WS60, which had been looped through a large jet ring (Dent 2010, 41). In contrast, the smith who made the iron bracelet from Middleton-on-the-Wolds merely pressed the two ends close together, after looping onto it two large bone beads (Sheppard 1923).

Only one out of 24 bracelets was buried with a male. In addition, one was found with an un-aged adolescent and one with a burial which showed contra-indications. The rest were buried with females/likely females: four with women aged 17–25, four with women aged 25–35, and eight with women in the older, 35–45, age bracket. This might suggest that bracelets had a strong association with women, and were accrued through their adult lives, being especially common with senior members of the community. They were worn in a variety of positions: on the right and left wrists (in equal numbers) and right and left forearms (though favouring the left, perhaps an indication of handedness). Whilst there do appear to be some preferences (at Wetwang Slack, iron bracelets were especially common on the left wrist), in all probability, the object could have slipped down from forearm to wrist as the body was positioned in the grave, so it is unlikely they represent distinct fashions. In several cases, the corpses wore two bracelets. At Burton Fleming (BF10), two similar bronze bracelets with over-lapping terminals and low relief ornament were found in the same grave: one on each forearm. At Arras (W.24) their positions were unrecorded but both bronze bracelets were decorated with red inlay: one with a bead of red glass 'enamel', the other with the flecked red stone of porphyry. At Wetwang Slack, in one burial (WS155) two bronze bracelets of different styles were found on the left and right wrists, and WS60 had two bracelets of contrasting character (one bronze, one iron with a jet ring) worn on the same left wrist. The antiquarians who excavated Arras even recorded one worn as an anklet (A12). Some of these items may have been deliberate pairs, and might therefore be personal possessions of the deceased. In support of this argument, many were worn (as in one from Eastburn, Stead 1979, 75), or polished and

FIGURE 5.11. Glass bead necklace, Arras (YORYM: 1948.911.1–18, YORYM: 1948.912.1–14, Beads, YORYM: 1948.914.1–4, Beads, YORYM: 1948.917.1–18).

patinated, where the bronzework or ornament may have rubbed against the body or dress (Arras W.24: Stead 1979, 73, Cowlam LI: Greenwell 1877, 210) or were broken and incomplete when placed in the grave (WS349). Others were more pristine (Arras A9: Stead 1979, 75) and may well have been 'new' gifts for the deceased.

Necklaces

The most iconic neck-ornament of the Iron Age – the torc – is ill-represented in the square barrow burials. A bronze torc was found in burial A.5 at Arras, recorded as 14 cm in diameter (Stead 1979, 80) but it is now lost. A beaded neck torc was found at Skerne, near Driffield, but as an isolated surface find (P. Gentil, pers. comm.). Small jet or shale necklaces have also been found: one of nine jet beads from A.5 (Stead 1979, 80) and one with 64 beads at Wetwang Slack (WS336). Wooden and other organic beads would not have survived (Dent 1984a, 171) but other necklaces may be represented by individual artefacts or suites of small objects, discussed below under the category of 'pendants'.

However, the most common necklace from these cemeteries is that composed of glass beads (Figure 5.11). Table 5.2 summarizes the different styles of beads known, synthesising the types or groups from the reports of Stead (1979 and 1991), Dent (1982; 1984a), and Guido (1978). At their most simple, plain beads were formed of a single cobalt blue colour – there is one example of a delicate bead with a brighter turquoise hue (R16), and some from Wetwang which are very similar, but it is not known if this is the result of the original chemical composition or post-depositional weathering effects. One of the most recent finds has been that of a set of miniature plain blue beads, associated with a brooch and mirror at Wetwang Village (Hill 2001). The 'melon' type of bead is also plain blue but moulded into an impressive petalled or lobed form, and this type was interestingly only found in the Wetwang Slack cemetery.

The decorated beads often take the form of an 'eye' design, with a blue background set within a white ring, and a central dot or boss of similar or contrasting colour. The number of 'eyes' varies from three (arranged equidistantly around the waist of the bead) to nine, twelve or fifteen (arranged in diagonal rows of three, which can also be 'read' like the symmetrical pattern of five on a die: two eyes on each side – high and low – flanking one in the centre). Yet this effect was achieved in three different ways (Stead 1979). First, the bead might be impressed with a ring/'annulet' (creating a single but sometimes a double channel) which was infilled with white or whiteish-yellow inlay, creating a simple raised boss out of the bead body: identical in colour and hue. One

Illustration	Bead description	Type/Form	Example
	Plain, rounded: cobalt blue bead	Dent 1982: Type a) Dent unpublished: Type 1 Stead 1991: Type C3 Guido 1978: Group 6iv)	WS139 WS155 WS210 R2 R193
	Plain, rounded: light turquoise blue	Stead 1991: Type C2	R16 WS210? WS376?
	Miniature plain blue (1-2mm)	Hill 2001	WV1
	Blue bead: sub-triangular/globular with 3 *impressed* annulets (equidistant around waist of bead) and white inlay - *blue with single channel inlaid with white, and centre of same colour as bead body* - *as Type i/4a but with double channel* - *as Type i/4b but with small recessed cross inlaid in central boss*	Stead 1979: Type i) Dent 1982: Type d) Guido 1978: Class I/Type I Dent unpublished: 4a) Dent unpublished: 4b) Dent unpublished: 4c)	Arras A.4 WS284 WS236 WS376 WS376
	Blue bead: sub-triangular/globular with 12 or 15 *impressed* annulets (single channel: raised centre of same colour as bead body and white inlay): pattern - diagonal rows of 3 *or* 2:1:2	Stead 1979: Type ii)	Arras A.4 Cowlam B/L
	Blue 'eye' bead: sub-triangular/globular with *impressed* annulets with *applied* centre of contrasting colour to bead body ('framed eyes') - green-blue body with white inlay and brown centre - brown body with white inlay and green-blue centre - green-blue body with dark blue centre - green-blue body with black boss	Dent 1982: Type e) (?Guido 1978: Class 3) Dent unpublished: 5a) Dent unpublished: 5b) Dent unpublished: 5c) Dent unpublished: 5d)	WS249 WS236 WS274 WS284
	Blue bead: layered or stratified 'eye' (dimple inlaid with white then blue lenses), with 9 or 12 eyes	Stead 1979: Type iii) Dent 1982: Type f) Dent unpublished: 6 Guido 1978: Group 5	Arras A.4
	Blue bead with inlaid white scroll/wave or more regular zig-zag	Stead: Type iv) Dent 1982: Type c) Dent unpublished: 3 Guido 1978: Group 5	Arras A.4 R2
	Clear/green translucent bead inlaid with white or yellow scrolls - *clear with multiple waves* - *clear with spirals*	Stead 1979: Type v) Dent 1982: Type g Guido 1978: Class 10/11a Dent unpublished: 7a) Dent unpublished: 7b)	Arras A.4 WS101 WS268
	Melon bead (moulded into 7 lobate sections	Dent 1982: Type b) Dent unpublished: 2	WS209
	Qpaque mustard yellow bead with grooves forming crossed waves	Stead 1991: Type C4	BF19

TABLE 5.2. Synthesis and illustration of glass bead typologies, with examples.

variant even had a tiny cross indented in this boss (WS376). Second, the annulet might still be impressed but the central boss was applied, allowing the artisan to use contrasting colours of glass in the bead and the centre of the eye, ranging from dark blues and greens to brown and blue-black (a 'framed eye'). (The white glass inlaid using the first two methods is very prone to decay and erosion, and is frequently missing). Finally, in the 'stratified' eye beads, a dimple was made in the surface of the bead, and individual lenses of white, then blue inlay, were settled into the dish-shaped depression. This has the effect of creating a more translucent, royal blue centre to the 'eye', where it sits over the white inlay, which – perhaps unsurprisingly – was much more resistant to decay. The 'eye' design is surprisingly common cross-culturally, and is the most prolific form of amuletic bead, designed to avert evil and the jealous or malicious gaze of others (Tomalin 1998). It is impossible to say whether it had this meaning for Iron Age people but the design and the contrasting brilliance of the blue and white colours are certainly eye-catching, if not hypnotic.

The other decorated beads take the form of white wave/scroll or more regular zig-zag patterns inlaid into mid-dark blue beads, and more translucent beads with a greenish hue, inlaid with white or yellow scrolls. One of these kinds of beads has multiple waves in parallel rows (WS102) whilst another has three spirals (WS268). The stratified eye and blue scroll beads are of a similar size but often a little smaller than the impressed annulet beads. The beads with a greenish hue and wave/scroll/spiral decoration are a little smaller again. Finally, there is one example of a fine but broken, opaque mustard yellow bead, with grooves which form crossed waves around the mid-line, from Burton Fleming (BF19).

Unfortunately, the detailed analysis of the majority of these beads awaits publication and this compositional analysis is key to interpreting whether some of the beads derive directly from foreign sources (see Stead 1979; 1991; Dent 1982; Henderson 1991). Whilst glass bead necklaces are uncommon in the Champagne cemeteries, beads do occur on bracelets and pendants (Stead 1979, 81). Some of the East Yorkshire beads are clearly influenced by Continental styles and fashions (especially the blue stratified 'eye' beads and blue beads with white waves/scrolls, Stead 1979, 81) but others appear to be completely insular in style. Henderson has argued that the blue glass which forms the basis of most beads may look similar, but each bead type appears to derive from separate 'batches' of glass with different recipes, suggesting they were made at different times and/or in separate workshops (in Stead 1991, 168). The two blue beads from Rudston (R2 and R16) appear to have been made from the same raw materials and colourant as many from Wetwang, though the plain blue bead from R193 has a different chemical composition, and may derive from another artisan or different period of manufacture (*ibid.*). The translucent-greenish hue beads with white or yellow waves/spirals may come from as far afield as Meare Lake Village, renowned for this type of bead (Henderson in Stead 1991, 168) but there may be other centres of more local production which have yet to be identified. However, the opaque yellow bead from Burton Fleming (BF19) or the glass stock from which it was made, with its high manganese oxide levels, may well be a Continental import which probably dates to the 2nd century BC (Henderson in Stead 1991, 169). Dating the other beads is difficult: Wetwang Slack offers the best opportunity, but all of the bead types represented here seem to have been in use during the two or three hundred years duration of the cemetery (Dent 1984a).

Where excavation has been thorough, beads are usually found around the neck of the deceased, suggesting they were worn in death as in life, in a single strand. There are three exceptions to this: WS155 has a few beads across the chest area, suggesting the main chain may have been disturbed or else a second larger strand threaded with a few beads hung lower on the chest. The beads found in WS209 were scattered across the body, and unless they were actually stitched onto clothing, it suggests the necklace had broken over the corpse, either through natural decay or deliberate action. Finally, the necklace from WS274 was found behind the shoulder, suggesting the beads had either slipped into a cluster as the body was lowered into the grave, or the necklace was placed first into the grave pit and the body lain on top. In many cases, the overall diameter of the necklace suggests a single strand is likely, with the beads either collecting along the lower loop of the thong (e.g. the 34 beads of WS139 which are only 22 cm in total length) or forming a continuous chain, as a tight choker (such as the 52 beads of WS257, 38cm in length) or a longer draped necklace (e.g. the 77 beads of WS236 which are 48 cm long or the 70 beads found in one of the Cowlam burials, Stead 1979). The necklace from Garton Slack was described by Brewster as being 'strung around its neck and across its bosom in an oval loop' (1980, 251). In contrast, the necklace from Arras, which once had over 100 large beads, may have consisted of multiple strands (or a single strand which could be 'looped' twice over) since its overall length would have been over 90 cm. Many beads have abraded and damaged surfaces, suggesting that the adjacent beads knocked against each other, and some must have broken and shattered as these heavy objects swung from side-to-side. It is tempting to think that they were arranged in symmetrical patterns or graduated sets (cf Hughes-Brock 1998), organised either by size or style, perhaps with the most interesting or largest beads forming the centrepiece of the necklace. When finally published, the detailed recording at Wetwang Slack may be able to shed important light on their original arrangement. They are usually found in sets varying from eighteen to over 100 beads, of varying sizes and types (Table 5.3): from small plain examples, 4–9mm in diameter, to large decorated beads of over 15 mm diameter. (NB beads found in ones or twos are listed separately below under the class of earrings or hair locks, Table 5.4).

Three of the twelve necklaces consist just of one type of bead: these are the plain blue glass bead necklaces of Wetwang Slack (e.g. WS139, WS155). Others have a majority of one style with one or two different beads added in (e.g. WS209, WS274) and some are 'composite' necklaces, mixing a variety of styles and colours to elaborate effect (such as the splendid examples of Cowlam B/L and Arras A.4 the 'Queen's barrow', Figure 5.11). By analysing the distribution of each type, it is possible to see distinct preferences for – or contrasting acquisitions of – different bead types. For example, the Wetwang and Garton Slack cemeteries show a preponderance of plain blue glass bead necklaces: even the miniature versions found in the Wetwang Village burial (possibly part of a decorative strand or tie) follow this pattern. However, Wetwang is the only cemetery to also have melon beads present: none has been found in the Great Wold Valley cemeteries, nor are any recorded from the antiquarian

Burial Context	Sex/Age	No. of beads	Bead types	Location on body
Cowlam B (=L)	?F ?adult	70	69 × blue with white scroll 1 × blue, impressed annulets (12), white inlay	On the neck
Arras A.4 'Queen's barrow'	?F ?adult	c.100 (67 survive)	Totals unknown – of existing beads; 19 × blue, impressed annulets (3), white inlay 2 × blue, impressed annulets (15), white inlay 1 × blue, impressed annulets (12), white inlay 14 × stratified blue eye: – *9 with 12 eyes, 5 with 9 eyes* 4 × blue with white scroll 14 × translucent green with white/yellow scroll	Unknown
WS139	F (35–45)	34	34 × plain blue	Under jaw, across neck
WS155	F (25–35)	42	42× plain blue	Around neck and small group on chest?
WS209	F (30–40)	18	16 × blue melon 2 × blue with white scroll	Scattered over body
WS210	F (35–45)	70	70 × plain blue (including some small plain turquoise)	Around neck
WS236	F (35–45)	77	63 × plain blue 14 × eye bead with applied boss: – *13 brown with green-blue boss* – *1 green-blue with brown boss*	Around neck
WS249	F (35–45)	75	59 × plain blue 12 × eye bead with applied boss: – *12 green-blue with brown boss* 4 × stratified blue eye	Around neck
WS257	F (25–25)	52	52 × plain blue	Around neck
WS274	F (35–45)	49 (or 61?)	47 × blue with white scroll 1× blue, impressed annulets (3), white inlay 1 × eye bead with applied boss: – *green-blue with dark blue boss* (fragments of 12 blue with white scroll in box in museum: unrecorded?)	Behind shoulder
WS284	F (35–45)	55	46 × plain blue 2 × blue with white scroll 6 × blue, impressed annulets (3), white inlay 1 × eye bead with applied boss: - *1 green-blue with dark blue boss*	Around neck
WS376	?F (25–35)	76	73 × plain blue (including 1 fine turquoise) 1 × blue, impressed annulets (3) with double channel 1 × blue, impressed annulets (3) with double channel and recessed cross in boss 1 × eye bead with applied boss: – *green-blue with black boss*	Around neck
GSl 8/10 Grave 3 Burial 2	F (25–35)	35	28 × plain blue 7 × blue, impressed annulets (3), white inlay	Around neck, draped over chest
WV1	F (45+)	120	120 × miniature plain blue	Lower legs

TABLE 5.3. Bead types, burial context and position.

Burial	Sex/Age	Item	Position on the body
K6	F (17–25)	Copper alloy stud and amber bead	At back of neck
		Copper alloy ring and jet ring	Under left ear
R2	C (17–25)	Glass bead (blue with white scroll)	Between right shoulder and skull
R54	F (17–25)	Copper alloy ring	Behind the back, just below shoulder
WS363	J (8–10)	3 copper alloy beads	Beneath left shoulder
R193	?F (25–35)	Copper alloy ring	On the neck
		Glass bead (plain blue)	
BF19	C (35–45)	Iron ring	On the neck
		Glass bead (opaque yellow with crossed waves)	
WS73	F (25–35)	Amber bead	At the neck
WS102	F (25–35)	Jet bead	At the neck
		Glass bead (greenish with white/yellow scroll)	
WS312	M (25–35)	Copper alloy ring	At the neck
WS336	?F (15–16)	2 Iron rings	At the neck
WS268	F (25–35)	Glass bead (greenish with white/yellow scroll)	At the shoulder
WS270	F (35–45)	Glass bead (plain blue)	At the shoulder
BF47	U (17–25)	2 Shale rings (identical in diameter)	Side-by-side, in front of face
WS57	F (35–45)	Tweezers (iron)	Behind skull
WS64	F (20–25)	Bronze ring with 3 beads (2 plain blue glass, 1 amber)	Bronze ring and beads – lying on mandible
		Iron tweezers	Tweeezers – by face
WS210	F (35–45)	Bronze ring	At the neck
		Bronze tweezers	
WS245	F (17–25)	Bronze ring, Jet ring, Amber ring	In the neck area

TABLE 5.4. Potential ear-rings, pendants and hair-locks.

excavations at Cowlam and Arras. The unstratified eye beads with an applied boss of contrasting colour are also distinct to Wetwang Slack, and the diverse range of these colours – varying from dark blue to blue-green, brown and black – would have made these necklaces very distinctive. Whilst the blue with white scroll beads are numerous on one strand (WS274), they occur singly or in pairs on other Wetwang examples. At Cowlam, these wave or scroll beads form the majority of the necklace but there are only four of the beads on the object from Arras. Meanwhile, the impressed annulet blue beads (with either three large or 9–15 smaller 'eyes') occur in small numbers within several necklaces at Wetwang but dominate the necklace from Arras. This object also has numerous greenish translucent beads with white or yellow scrolls, which otherwise only occur as singles on ear-rings/hair-braids from Wetwang Slack. Glass beads are generally very rare in the Great Wold Valley cemeteries but one burial includes the striking mustard yellow crossed wave bead, which was apparently broken when deposited (BF19).

How might these distributions be understood? Given the numbers involved and the evidence for their manufacture, it is likely that there were both local and more distant workshops, producing a variety of bead types over a considerable period of time. Some may have been brought back from trading expeditions or were bartered by travelling merchants, from sources as far away as the south-west of Britain or even the Continent. Others may have arrived with incomers: the odd settlers or those marrying-in, who brought an exotic bead or two with them. The rest may have been made as a 'lot' locally, and were then split up over time: changing hands as people moved between families, inherited heirlooms or gave a few as gifts.

Beads are small, tactile and attractive: they can be used as counters (Sciama 1998, 16), or *aides memoire* (Dransart 1998, 140), and their fingered 'telling' could have been used as mnemonics for ritual utterances (as in the case of rosaries) but also geneaological recital, counting heads of stock, or calculating days and seasons. Strings of beads are easily added to or separated, and they thus make excellent exchange items. John Barrett has argued this may have been the case with Bronze Age jet necklaces, which were 'given and then worn, split and subdivided' as gifts which created new kin relations (such as marriage) or in displays of veneration and respect (1994, 122). Ethnographic examples suggest beads have a strong but not exclusive association with women (Sciama and Eicher 1998), and are often used to mark various life-stages (Carey 1998). They may be given at birth or upon puberty, during courtship (Sciama 1998), or upon the entry into a husband's household. They may be used for high status regalia (O'Hear 1998), to adorn a woman as a symbol of her family's wealth, or be used for bridewealth (Eicher 1998). The wearing of ancient 'heirloom' beads may signal both the continuation of a lineage and its prestigious status (Williams 1987; Janowski 1998; Woodward 2002). Different forms, colours and shapes, or ways in which they are worn, can signal kin or ethnic affiliations (Williams 1987; Eicher 1998) and the distinctive forms found at Wetwang Slack (compared with Arras and Cowlam) might support the notion of beads being used to display a valley-based, extended family or clan affiliation. Their natural openings and curvaceous forms often create an explicit and intimate link with female sexuality (Sciama 1998): girls who have begun menstruating or new mothers are often given beads, in which they may dress to parade following their seclusion (Eicher 1998, 107). They may even be a direct indication of the numbers of children women have borne (Williams 1987). Some are used as apotropaic objects, and may have particular importance at times of vulnerability, such as pregnancy or illness (Bradley Foster 1998). They can also be seen as charms for good luck, protecting fertility, ensuring flows of breast milk, or preserving the affections of a partner (Sciama 1998, 16). Mourning may be marked by a lack of decoration and widowhood is often an occasion when beads are passed on (*ibid.*, 26, 30). As aesthetically pleasing items which were no doubt coveted, they might have been used between women to pay small debts or mark and cement bonds (especially in a funerary context). These are interesting possibilities, which may help explain the occurrence of one or two beads of a particular type, cropping up on a necklace otherwise constituted of beads in a different style, or those single or double beads occurring as an ear-ring, hair-loop or pendant. Old beads, with an illustrious history and high value, may have been 'lent out' to suitable relations (Janowski 1998) or bequeathed across generations. There are certainly differences in the relative condition of some beads, as in the Arras necklace, which suggests some might be 'old' and worn, compared with a more pristine set of newer beads. Some necklaces were no doubt 'split' whilst others were 'curated' (Bradley Foster 1998; Hughes-Brock 1998), and some may even have grown through funerary gifts from friends and relatives.

The East Yorkshire beads certainly have strong association with women, especially those of considerable seniority: 35–45 years and older (Table 5.3). In the cemetery at Wetwang Slack, it has been possible to reconstruct the sequence of burials around those interred with blue glass bead necklaces. Whilst these initial burials appear broadly contemporary, what is interesting is that many form the start of a small series of later burials which impinge upon, or cut into the ditches of what we might call these 'founder' female burials, as discussed in chapter 3. In these cases, we might suggest that the bead necklaces represent the accumulated honour of a senior woman who has come through many life-stages: is well-connected and held in high prestige, and whose monument forms a focus for later inhumations.

Finger, toe, ear-rings and pendants

In contrast to bracelets, rings of various types, substances and sizes are found with both men and women (see Figure 5.10). Finger rings are actually rare: one supposedly gold example was found at Arras (A.4: the 'Queen's barrow'), which may be one of the other few true imports into the region (Stead 1979: 86). Two men from Wetwang Slack wore bone finger rings on their right hand (WS114, WS421), whilst two women from this valley wore rings on their left hand: the first made of copper alloy (WS317), the second made of bone (GSl8/10 Grave 2 Burial 2). Toe rings made of copper alloy were predominantly worn by women, with only one male example (GS7). One woman wore iron rings on the first toe of both the left and right foot (WS94). There may also be one example of a shale toe ring, found in the vicinity of the feet of a badly decayed skeleton: BF61a (an unsexed adolescent). A jet ring was also found near the left wrist of WS421, an adult male, but its exact use is uncertain. Other bronze and iron rings of a variety of sizes are known from Arras, but their position on the body was unfortunately not recorded (Stead 1979).

Other rings and beads were found clustered around the head, neck and shoulder regions. Individual blue glass beads around the neck zone are especially common (R2, R16, WS268, WS270, WS277), sometimes found in combination with bronze or iron (BF19, R193) or amber and jet beads (WS64, WS102). Single amber beads (WS73), bronze beads and jet rings (BF61a), bronze and jet rings (WS5 Burial 1) and chalk rings (WS26), are also known. At Danes Graves (DG90) an iron ring was associated with two short tubular bronze beads, and three bronze beads were found behind the shoulder of a juvenile at Wetwang Slack (WS363). Some appear to have been ear-rings (such as the example of K6, discussed in the opening of this chapter) but the odd position of some of them (Table 5.4), beneath the shoulder, at the neck, or even in front of the face, suggest that they may equally have been charms on a necklace, or hair-braid decorations on a plait or dreadlock.

The importance of hair, and its decoration, in the Iron Age world, has been

FIGURE 5.12. Toilet-set (WS210), the 'Arras' ring (Queen's barrow) and the miniature bronze axe on a loop of bronze with blue glass bead (Arras W.57).

highlighted by Miranda Aldhouse-Green (2004). Using ethnographic and classical analogies, she has argued it was an attribute of the body which conveyed important information about the individual's identity (age and gender), status and wealth, virility or fertility. It was the subject of extensive preparation and embellishment (with jewellery, as well as hair treatments, such as Cloneycavan man: the Irish bog body whose 'topknot' was held in place with pine-based resin from France or Spain: Mulhall and Briggs 2007, 74; Mulhall 2010), yet it could also be the focus of humiliation and disfigurement (Aldhouse-Green 2004). Although these beads and rings often occur singly, the shine of the metal, or reflective gloss of amber, jet or blue glass, would have drawn attention to the face, neck and hair, and it is a subtle example of how objects and bodies were entwined in the performance of identity.

A few of the other isolated rings and beads may well be decorations for clothing, or fasteners of some kind: a worked bone toggle was found at the waist of R174 (a young adult male), two bronze tags were found at the feet of WS438 (a female adult) and three copper alloy toggles were found around the knees and feet of K5 (and adult male). A bronze toggle with a bead of inlay, held in place by a small pinnel, was also found in the cemetery at Eastburn, though its exact position was not recorded. Some of these might relate to belts or footwear, and Stead considered the amber bead and copper alloy stud found on the right-hand side of K6 might be a cap or garment fastening (1991). However, there are a number of other objects, found as a suite, which suggest their use as pendants (including small tools from toilet-sets) which might also function as charms. In burial WS64, an adult woman was interred with a copper alloy ring upon which had been strung one amber and two glass beads. The metal had stained her mandible green, suggesting the set may have been suspended on a necklace, and close to this cluster was a pair of iron tweezers, which might have been hung on the same strand. WS210, another adult woman, also had a pair of tweezers, this time made of copper alloy, associated with a ring of the same metal and a small glass bead, found at her neck (Figure 5.12). Iron tweezers were also found behind the head of WS57, and a nail cleaner or scoop was found with a pair of similar bronze tweezers at Arras (A4), suspended on a small bronze ring. Tweezers and cleaners or scoops are important items because they relate to the intimate transformation of the body, as well as having cosmetic and medical applications. They may even have been used in the preparation of the deceased's body for public viewing and burial. Hill has argued they represent a fundamental shift in the way in which the body was conceptualised and performed or presented in the middle–late Iron Age (1997). He argues that in Britain, this was a period in which a more individuated sense of self began to emerge, and that these items were part of a 'technology of the body' through which the modification of personal appearance was a key means of signalling aspects of identity and status (*ibid.*, 103).

There are also other combinations of items. A copper alloy, jet and amber set of rings were found on the neck of WS245 (another adult woman). Whilst these could be hair decorations, the number and character of items involved might also suggest their use as a pendant, whose lustrous or luminous substances may have had the properties of a 'charm'. Other apotropaic pendants may be represented by a four-spoke wheel ornament found at Arras (A5), now sadly lost, but whose symbolism (like the wheel 'hairpin' from Danes Graves) may have evoked some of the complex meanings of movement and power embodied in the chariot. Another item from Arras, the bronze disc pendant found in A4 (the Queen's barrow), was decorated with a sandstone panel (possibly from the Jurassic deposits of North Yorkshire) deliberately smothered in pigment which enhanced its 'redness' (Stead 1965, 64). It was surrounded by three rings of coral beads, evoking connections with more distant places (Stead 1979, 84). The colour red is clearly significant, and may have had important symbolic meanings associated with life and death (Giles 2008b). This pendant appears to have been attached by rivets on the back to a leather strap, which has left its trace in the patina, and has also worn the coral beads, closest to the projecting perforated tag. This suggests the pendant was meant to 'flap' and move, perhaps suspended from a garment or belt, or necklace. Another object from Arras (grave A.17) is less certain as a pendant but it is included here because it was found in association with two small bronze rings (Stead 1979, 86). It consists of a massive bronze rivet, with a slightly domed head upon which traces of hammering can still be seen. Its stem has been punched through a large – and very heavy – piece of fish-shape sheet lead (which may have 'snapped' off a larger piece on the 'tail' edge), and the rivet is flattened on the back into a large circular plate. This curious object may be a fixture or a repair fitting (*ibid.*) for some organic object but the value of this soft, easily worked metal, may have lain in its origins: speaking of contacts perhaps with the Peak District, or further afar.

Finally, a small bronze ring from Arras W.57 was threaded with a diminutive blue glass bead and a miniature copper alloy socketed axe (see Figure 5.12). Although the main period of use for socketed axes was the late Bronze Age, iron versions of these tools were made throughout the Iron Age (Manning and Saunders 1972). Miniature versions of these objects derive mainly from sites

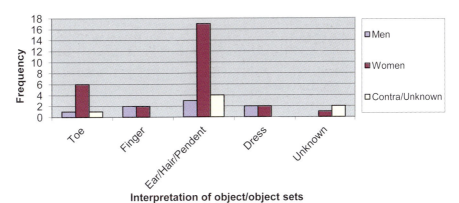

FIGURE 5.13. Body decoration: male and female associations with rings, beads, and pendants/charms.

such as the late Bronze Age-early Iron Age middens (Waddington 2007) or late Iron and early Roman contexts (Robinson 1995). Was this a tiny copy of an object 'out of time': unearthed from an earlier context, or a contemporary miniature? A deliberately antiquated version of a tool or weapon: made to look old. Perhaps the general sense of antiquity about this form was the point: evoking connections with ancient occupants of this landscape or (as a small version of what existed in real life) its' other-wordly or 'impish' inhabitants (Waddington and Sharples 2007, 33). These were things meant to be handled, marvelled at and seen close-to, and it has been argued that the reduction of scale involved in miniaturisation increases the power of these objects (Waddington 2007, 193). The craft skill required also imbues them with exquisite aesthetic qualities that draw attention to the extraordinary workmanship involved in their making (*ibid.*), perhaps lending them talismanic or magical qualities (Mack 2008). Such small versions of the real are key ways in which meaning is compressed, and values are concentrated in a diminutive yet portable form (what Bailey has called the 'plastic power' of the miniature: 2005, 32). Their handling may have created feelings of 'enchantment, play' (Wadddington and Sharples 2007, 33), possession and empowerment (Waddington 2007, 198) evoking associations of the larger version, and magnifying its importance (Bailey 2005). Such items may well have been toys (although their absence from juvenile graves makes this unlikely) or trinkets, amulets and sacred, even ancestral, items (*ibid.*, 32).

Summary

From an analysis of their burial context, it is evident that the items discussed above have a strong, though not exclusive, association with adult women (Figure 5.13). They could therefore be classed as 'jewellery' but if we are to use this term, it must incorporate the idea that these were not only objects of aesthetic pleasure and beauty but crystallizations of age and gender, lineage and wealth, and possibly religious beliefs and sacred power. When grouped together, combinations of items – strings of beads on necklaces, pairs of bracelets, sets of rings or beads, 'toilet' instruments, and decorated plaques – would have shifted and swayed, making a soft clank as someone moved, or chink, as they handled other objects. Even toe-rings would have tapped as people stepped on hard floors or cobbled surfaces. They may have been deliberately audible – certainly to the wearer – accentuating awareness of their movements.

All of these items were extremely tactile, and many show evidence of being repeatedly fingered in their gloss or patina. If some were thought of as charms or protective talismans, this may have had the function of activating the object's power and reassuring the wearer. Their strongly gendered association, size, attractiveness and oral qualities may indicate an additional function, as important distractions for fractious or curious infants to handle and play with around a parent's neck or to grab in their hair. (Today, one can buy deliberately manufactured 'nursing necklaces' precisely for this function). As children grew, they may have been used to teach them about particular values or ideals imbued in the substances and designs employed by the artisan, or stories about the people who had once worn them. The interesting thing about most of these objects is the variety of materials used: iron and bronze, glass, coral, jet, chalk, amber. As composite objects, they crystallised a social geography of relations which stretched across time and space: with people from the past, in the case of heirlooms, or distant exchange partners in other regions and across the sea (Champion 1976). With their traces of wear and repair, patina and abrasion, they would also have become, as Hoskins suggests, starting points for the wearer's story about their own life (1998).

Ear-rings and hair-braids caught the light, and like bangles and bracelets or necklaces, their colour and reflective brilliance exaggerated the gestures of the wearer and caught the eye of those watching. The *weight* of such objects – especially the heavy blue glass bead necklaces – was considerable: in the words of one Ecuadorian woman, 'it used to be a lot of work to wear those things' (in Meisch 1998, 171). They may not have been worn every day but even as part of regalia, costume or for special occasions, the body must have initially been hindered by such objects, until movement with them became habitual. In life, they must have played an important role in gendered performances, and advertised people's sexuality: drawing attention to exposed areas of flesh – necks and wrists, fingers and toes. Beauty, as Mark Doty's poem reminds us, is also a matter of power, and the control of sexuality (both of people's own bodies and the cultural rules which governed access to them) were channelled in part through the objects used to adorn and attract the opposite sex.

In the context of a grave, whether these were personal possessions or generous gifts, the dressing of the dead for a successful afterlife (to rejoin beloved partners or to impress important forebears) was an important – even tender – stage in the mortuary rite. Such a process must have had a special relevance at a time when the corporeal body was beginning to be transformed by processes of decay. This category of grave goods, broadly characterised as items of adornment, therefore evoked a complex series of meanings related to bodily transformation.

FIGURE 5.14. Iron mirrors: left: Garton Slack (GSl 7, Barrow 2, Burial 1); right: Lady's Barrow, Arras. Based on Brewster 1980, fig. 105 and Stead 1979, 81, fig. 32.

Mirrors

The other item which might be considered related to jewellery is the mirror (Figure 5.14). Five examples are known from Eastern Yorkshire: two from Arras (A.3, the 'Lady's Barrow' with chariot, and A.7), one from Garton Slack (GSl 7, Barrow 2, Burial 1), one from Wetwang Slack (WS454) and one from Wetwang Village (WV1). Interestingly, the first Arras example and the latter two from Wetwang are all chariot burials, suggesting that these are prestigious items. All five are made of iron. A.3 has a square-section handle terminating at each end in two moulded bronze fittings, decorated with very subtle punched dots in lines, and an iron ring or 'suspension loop' at the end (Stead 1979, 82). A.7 also had a suspension loop and a further ring where the handle joined the plate (*ibid.*). The Garton Slack mirror was very similar to A.7, but had a bronze moulding in the centre of the handle and at the junction with the suspension loop (Brewster 1980, 245). These gave the mirror an 'impression of strength and symmetery' making it a 'well balanced object, pleasing to the eye in the simplicity of its style … with the silver-like polished iron disc of the mirror and the golden toned ferrules offset against the black iron of the handle' (*ibid.*). The Wetwang Slack mirror has a rounded section handle, with rings at both ends: the upper ring being split to 'grip' the mirror plate. The handle appears to have been shaped into three bulbous sections, with the largest swelling in the centre. Otherwise, it appears undecorated. Finally, the Wetwang Village mirror looks very similar to the one buried just across the valley, with an identical handle, ring and plate arrangement and two smaller, swelled protuberances around the mid-shaft of the handle. The iron plates vary from between 165–198 mm in diameter.

All of the mirrors fall into Fox's 'bar-handled' type (1958, 98), and pre-date the majority of the magnificently decorated bronze examples known from elsewhere in the British Isles (Giles and Joy 2007), being made some time between the late 4th and late 2nd/early 1st centuries BC. Although the Arras burials can no longer be analysed, the other inhumations are exclusively female: WS454 is older than her fine teeth would suggest (King, pers. comm.), whilst the woman at Garton Slack was between 25 and 35 years and the Wetwang Village woman may have been quite senior (over 45 years old). This association with women has often led to the dismissal of these items as mere accoutrements or 'attractive vanities' of high status females (Fox 1958, 84). In both popular accounts and illustrations, they are depicted as a means of beautification or self-admiration. Yet as discussed above, the mirror might have been part of a broader repertoire of objects designed to prepare and present the body during a period of changing concepts of personhood. As 'equivalents' for the weapons which were interred with men in the chariot burials, they may also have had a more powerful role (Giles and Joy 2007). Ethnographic parallels suggest that in small-scale societies, mirrors are used as implements for divination, contact with ancestors and spirits, as well as insights into the past (Tsetan 1995; Smith 2002; Saunders 2001). Their shine, brilliance or luminescence is often seen as a manifestation of spiritual essence or sacred potency, through which a shimmering vision world is experienced by the diviner (Saunders 1998, 226). The iron plate may never have accurately reflected the face held up for scrutiny, but it is possible that its shadowy, broad features were seen by the viewer as an indication of some presence 'beyond' the plate.

Mirrors are held in awe, as objects of intrinsic power, but to be wielded effectively, they must be allied with a skilled seer or ritual specialist capable of interpreting what is seen. The implication of such analogies is that Iron Age mirrors were not only symbols of wealth, made of significant quantities of iron, wrought and polished by skilled craftspeople. They may have been seen as awesome, intimidating artefacts – weapons of a kind – which enabled particular women to wield both aesthetic power and perhaps spiritual authority, in life and death (Giles and Joy 2007). The importance of such an object, especially when allied with a chariot burial as at Arras (the 'Lady's barrow'), was noted by Greenwell in 1906. He noted this 'woman occupied an important place in their polity … [perhaps] even in the position of the ruling power' (1906, 293–4).

Iron mirrors certainly made demands upon their users, requiring particular care to avoid tarnish from grease and rust, as well as polishing on a regular basis. Brewster noted that there were traces of mineralised wood adhering to the Garton Slack mirror plate, which might suggest it had been placed in a casket (1980, 245). The textile band found against the Wetwang Slack burial has been discussed above. Preliminary analysis of the Wetwang Village burial suggest it may have been contained in a bag made of otter fur (Hill, pers. comm.) Next to this mirror was a short involuted brooch, and a long strand of tiny blue glass beads wrapped around itself (perhaps forming a decorative tassel or tie for the bag). In mirror burials and finds from the late Iron Age, Joy has argued that there is often a parallel treatment of human body and artefact (in Giles and Joy 2007, 22). It is possible that like its human counterpart, these mirrors had been placed in a 'coffin' like box (in the case of Garton), or at Wetwang Slack, dressed

FIGURE 5.15. Wetwang Slack (WS454) sealed bronze box with red glass stud and Scabbard style decoration.

or 'wrapped' with decorative textiles. The Wetwang Village mirror may have been interred with the equivalent of a shroud, brooch and miniature necklace. Mirrors may thus have been one of the special objects which were perceived as having an identity and biography of their own.

Containers

Apart from the box and bag discussed above in connection with mirrors, there are two other objects which fall under the broad category of 'container', which I have distinguished from the broader artefact class of ceramic vessels. The box from WS454 (a chariot burial) was found behind the shoulder of the young woman, in a small cluster of grave goods which includes the iron mirror discussed above, an iron pin and two horse-bits (Figure 5.15; Dent 1985). It is a canister made of sheets of copper alloy, forming a circular 'tin' which could never be opened, having been 'crimped' around its rim and base. (A small iron clamp on the lower binding might be evidence of a repair). It was suspended from a small, delicate chain attached first through a loop on the lid and second, to a small riveted handle on the side of the box. It is decorated around its sides and both ends with curvilinear ornament – similar in style to that on the scabbards from the neighbouring male graves (Jope 2000, 249) – and in the centre of each end piece is a roundel inset with red glass 'enamel' (*ibid.*). The overall effect is intriguing, hinting at what might be contained within – yet it is, as far as we know from X-ray analysis – empty (Dent 1985, 11). Jope suggested that it might once have held something organic, and that 'beans or knobs of wood' might have provided a 'modest rattle' (2000, 249). If it had been beaten like a drum, its hollow cavity would certainly have sounded a resonant note, though there is no sign of differential wear suggesting this was the case. Whilst it may not have been a deliberate rhythmic instrument, the 'chink' of the chain would certainly have drawn attention to it swinging at someone's side, and this is in keeping with the aural effect of some items of bodily adornment discussed above. However, it is also possible that its sealing was designed to keep something in – to house some essence or force – a spiritual rather than material entity.

The second box or bag is from Kirkburn, K5 (Figure 5.16): a male chariot burial, and it was placed behind the head, probably by the end of the yoke. It is represented by a series of copper alloy fittings which must have been attached to a lid: 'D' shaped and approximately 5 mm thick, judging by the tubular bronze frame or rim (Stead 1991, 56). In the centre were three semi-tubular rings: reminiscent of the 'ear-ring' found in burial K6 but thinner and finer, split in half and riveted to the box lid. Six dome-headed studs were nailed around the edges of the lid, and there were three small bronze 'eyelets': one at the front (a closure or fastening) and two at the back (probable hinges). The lid may have closed a basket or a fabric or leather pouch: no impressions survive to reveal what material was used, nor what was 'contained' within, but it may have been food or – as above – something less tangible. Boxes and bags are found with both men and women, and whilst some were designed to contain specific objects, others had no surviving or detectable contents. They were nevertheless intriguing objects, lavished with decoration which drew attention to the item's ability to conceal or contain.

Tools

Tools of various kinds and materials were found in the square barrow burials, representing a range of craftwork from the working of bone and antler, metal and wood to textiles and crop processing. At first glance, bone points (which might be seen as a generic tool) appear to occur with both men and women (Figure 5.17), but those in the male graves are interpreted as 'lance-heads' due to their sharpened points (often broken) and rivet holes, suggesting they were mounted on a shaft (Stead 1991, 78). Whilst they may have had other uses than this (Stead 1968), their occurrence in the 'speared' burials suggests that the

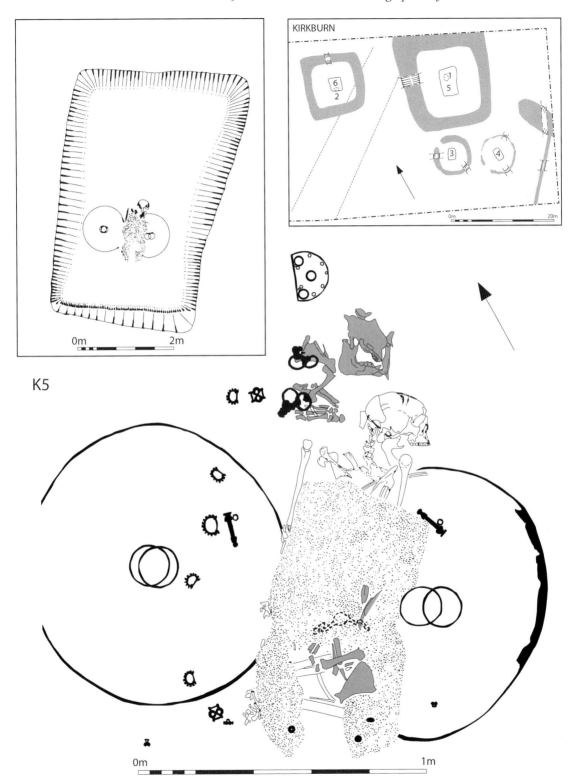

KIRKBURN

K5

FIGURE 5.16. Kirkburn burial (K5): chariot burial with chainmail shirt and bronze 'box lid'. Based on Stead 1991, 227, fig. 127.

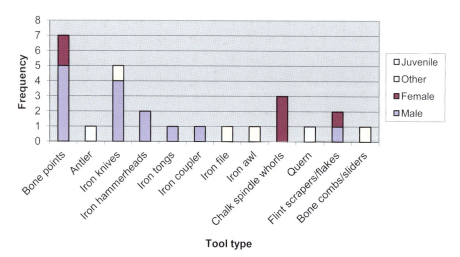

FIGURE 5.17. Associations with tools, analysed by age and sex.

majority of the East Yorkshire ones were indeed forms of weapons, so they are discounted here as tools. The bone points in female graves could be awls but their position around the body suggests they were probably used as shroud pins. Meanwhile, although it is likely flint continued to be used as a handy cutting edge (Humphrey 2003), the only evidence of this is a few flakes and scrapers from the barrows at Cowlam, and these may be residual.

Interestingly, most of the rest of the tools come from the cemeteries in the Great Wold Valley: they are noticeably absent from burials at Wetwang and Garton Slack. Iron knives have an exclusive association with men (and rite B graves), and could be considered as both tools and weapons. Three of them were found on the right side of the body, around the right lower arm, as if 'ready to hand'. The blade of R45 was broken at both ends, but mineralised impressions of willow or poplar suggest it may have been placed in a case. Unidentifiable wood was also noted on the tang of the knife from R50 but the example from R141 had an ash handle and horn collar, and was protected in a leather sheath, which left traces on the hilt and blade (Stead 1991, 79). The knife from BF63 may have had a horn handle and its tang may have been broken before deposition. Two iron hammerheads were found, both from male graves. The example from R87 had a box wood handle, and its tip was damaged or fractured, and the worn but slender hammer from R154 (which could only have been used for delicate work) had a handle of apple, pear or hawthorn (Fell in Stead 1991, 80). A set of tools was found alongside the iron knife in R141, including an iron awl (with a handle of alder, hazel, poplar or willow) found with an iron file of fairly coarse graded teeth: probably for the working of wood or horn. They were placed together with an antler tine (possibly a burnisher) behind the back of the adult whose sex could not be determined (Figure 5.18), possibly representing a work-kit packed carefully together. In grave R154, a possible hammerhead was found with an iron pair of tongs (associated with a coupler, Figure 5.19). This latter object may have been wrapped in textiles but appeared fresh from the forge: a lump of slag lying

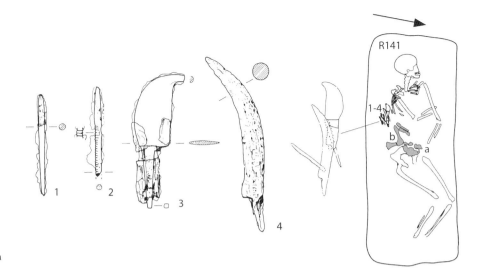

FIGURE 5.18. Burial with
tools from Rudston
(R141). Based on Stead
1991, 203, fig. 110.

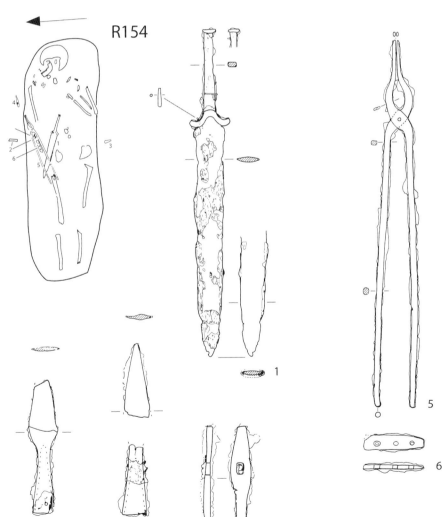

FIGURE 5.19. Burial with
tools from Rudston
(R154). Based on Stead
1991, 206, fig. 112.

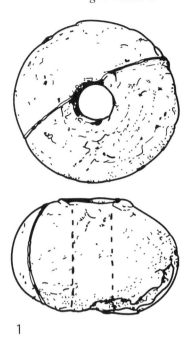

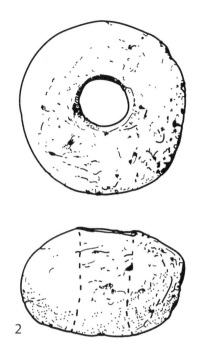

1

2

FIGURE 5.20. Chalk spindle whorls from R92 and R145. Based on Stead 1991, 94, fig. 70.

close by (*ibid.*, 79). These tools were crossed over a sword blade, and there were also two spearheads in the grave. The other tools consist of chalk spindle whorls (Figure 5.20), found exclusively with women. In both R92 and R183, they occurred behind the right shoulder, and in R145, the object was placed near the waist. They may therefore have been worn as 'pendant tools' suspended from a necklace or belt. It is unclear whether the bone combs and sliders found in Garton Slack 11, Barrow 2, were actually associated with a 'cenotaph' grave, or if this feature is merely a pit (Brewster 1980) but these items may have been used for human hair preparation/decoration as much as the combing or carding of wool. Finally, the upper half of a beehive quern was found in WS177, under the head of a young child (8–10 years old). As a symbolic 'pillow' it may have evoked associations with food production, nurture or regeneration which were appropriate for this untimely death.

Whilst the number of examples is slight, and the individual with contraindications from R141 reminds us not to make simple sex distinctions on the basis of skeletal criteria alone, this cemetery suggests tools had gendered associations (see Figure 5.17): men with iron implements for working metal, wood and bone, and women with tools which handled softer materials like textiles. Whilst these may represent real gender differences in craftwork, and such items could be read as the personal possessions of the 'smith' or 'spinner', they also evoked a series of qualities which helped construct gender relations. To use an ethnographic example: in the words of the Kodi, cloth is to metal 'as women are to men' (Schneider and Weiner 1989, 22). Men may have been associated with qualities of deft but strong work: hammering, hitting, cutting, piercing and forging, more forceful in its nature than spinning, sewing and weaving, which relied on dextrous patience. These implements all allude to the metaphor of transformation: of bringing together substances to make new things, but they achieve this end in different and complementary ways. These values can be drawn on to speak about other areas of life: sexual behaviour, kinship, politics (Hoskins 1988). Such tools may have been included in funerary rituals to structure ideas about death, identity and transformation: the making of new persons as ancestors – but they drew upon the model of power which was appropriate to each sex.

It is interesting that many of the tools were worn or damaged in some way before they were placed in the grave. As effective implements, with a long life-use, it may have been an appropriate time to end their lives but we could also see these mortuary tableau as reflecting the human-object amalgam of which Latour (1993) and Clark (1997) spoke: effective agency represented in the pairing of people with things.

Weapons

The most common form of weapon found in the square barrow burials was the iron spear, hafted to form a short-bladed thrusting weapon. The blades were between 60–140 mm long and were riveted onto coppiced poles of willow (or poplar) and hazel (Stead 1991). Their lack of a mid-rib may have made them liable to bend and break, and many have snapped or become damaged after penetrating shields or piercing the body after being thrust into the grave (as in R174 or GS4). Stead suggests that some may have been purpose made for this 'spearing' ceremony rather then representing actual hunting or fighting weapons (1991, 75). Whilst such 'spearing' rites account for five or six of the cases where spearheads were recorded in graves, at least three of the spearheads listed here are considered by the osteologists to be the likely cause of death: R140, R152a and WS211, and the other ten appear to be personal weapons placed in the grave. Iron knives (of which there are four examples) must also have been common due to their multiple uses, but few have been found. Apart from the new long dagger at Sewerby, there are only two daggers from the square barrow burials (R87 and R153) though interestingly, the former may have been protected by a leather sheath.

Shields may have been up to 1.12 m long, ovate in shape, with iron or copper alloy bindings, bosses and mid-ribs. They were made of a variety of wood species: maple, cherry or lime (R148), willow or poplar (R154), birch (R163), alder or willow/poplar (R174, GS4). Maple is renowned for its fine grain and ease of working, and it also creates an attractive veneer which is easily polished (Thompson 2005). The pinkish-brown wood of the wild cherry or whiteness of the willow may have been deliberately selected for their colours, and poplar wood is particularly good at absorbing shock and resisting splintering: vital qualities for a shield (*ibid.*). Alder and ash are also shock resistant, and whilst the former is lightweight, ash has an innate strength and flexibility (*ibid.*). The strategic and informed choice of wood used tells us of their considerable carpentry skills, as well as the aesthetic concerns which might have influenced the making of these objects. Apart from ash, many of these trees were probably found off the Wolds, and once more, the broader taskscape opens to view, of people cultivating and managing wood, collecting, seasoning and preparing it for use. Some shields were up to 15 mm thick but others were thinner (only 5–6 mm) yet the covering of front and back with hide products (as in the case of GS10) or fleece (such as R174) may have hardened the surface and helped prevent splitting, whilst also creating an attractive finish. It is also possible that the colour and pattern of the hide or fleece was used to evoke the character of certain animals, and related the warrior to particular kin groups.

A number of shields were also decorated with iron and bronze fittings. The shield from Grimthorpe, which formed the watercolour frontispiece for Mortimer's 1905 monograph (Figure 5.21), is the most elaborate, with an oval bronze cap (punched and engraved with a quartered circle design) flanked by two crescent shaped plates of copper alloy, also punched into a 'stepped' motif around their edges. These plates had cracked from use and new nail holes show where they were reattached to the shield (Stead 1979, 55). There were also two lengths of u-shape spine bindings, which probably ran up and down the length of the shield, and a repoussé copper alloy disc whose function was unclear (*ibid.*). Similar spine bindings were found in a burial from Eastburn, and iron spine bindings were found at Wetwang in burials WS98, and WS453 and WS455 (the two male chariot burials). Bronze edge bindings were found in the North Grimston sword burial, associated with a fragment of spine binding decorated with repoussé ornament. A wooden shield with bronze binding was reported in the Hunmanby chariot burial (Sheppard 1907, 483) but Stead argues that the curve of this piece may instead suggest it came from an object such as a helmet (1979, 57). In addition to these examples, there are two beautiful copper alloy discs from Bugthorpe, whose rims are decorated with a 'ribbed' channel in-filled with red glass 'enamel', inset with eight or 12 small red glass studs, surrounding a larger central domed stud: all riveted with small pins. They resemble hips or haws, and would have been eye-catching ornaments, which have been interpreted by Stead as shield decorations (1979).

However, the most impressive martial objects from these graves are the iron swords with elaborate hilts and tapering blades (see Stead 1991, 64). They were almost always sheathed in organic or metal scabbards (*ibid.*, 74): R24 had a willow or poplar wooden scabbard covered in leather, and R144 was made of alder with a leather back and fleece-covered front. R57's scabbard was made of ash, also decorated with a fleece front with a further piece of decorative wood attached to it, and fur on the interior (close to the blade). Others may have been made completely of leather (R107) or wood (ash, in the case of R146) and one had an oak strip which may have strengthened a very thin and fine maple, lime or cherry wood scabbard, R163). The most elaborate chapes come from Grimthorpe and Bugthorpe: stylised 'fish' faces, with pouting lips: the former decorated with six small studs of coral (Stead 1979, 61). Pairs of copper alloy 'belt' discs, one set decorated with coral bead inlaid bosses, were found in both male chariot burials from Wetwang Slack (Dent 1985). However, riveted fixtures on the back-plate of several swords indicate they were suspended at the mid-point along the scabbard back – in the case of K3, by a fur or hide thong (Stead 1991, 68). Two iron rings from North Grimston may have been part of such a sword-chain (Stead 1979, 62). It is likely that this weapon was worn across the back, as depicted in the slightly later chalk figurines (Stead 1988), an argument supported by the position in which many swords are found in the grave: running along the body's spine (Stead 1991).

Stead has argued for a gradual chronological development (*ibid.*) between swords with campanulate mouths, open chape ends and decorated front plates (such as Kirkburn K3, and the swords from Wetwang Slack: WS453 and WS455, possibly dating to the 3rd or early 2nd century BC), to those with lipped chapes and more pointed mouths (such as Bugthorpe and Grimthorpe, possibly of a 1st century BC date). The remarkable 'anthropoid hilt' from North Grimston (Figure 5.22), with its grim face, down-turned mouth and dreadlocked or combed hair drawn into the nape of the neck, may be late 2nd or 1st century BC and an import from the Continent (Jope 2000: 100). By the late 1st century BC/early 1st century AD, inhumations are accompanied by swords with straighter ended hilts such as those from Rudston and Garton Station, in rite 'B' burials. Hilts were made of a variety of substances: metal and glass (such as the remarkable red, yellow and blue glass inlay, set below a bone handle on the Thorpe sword from Rudston, Stead 1979, 62) horn (R24, R154), antler (R139, R182) and wood (R107, WS98). Looking at such objects, we can see how the so-called 'by-products' of both animal rearing and hunting became valuable and attractive components of composite artefacts.

In sum, these implements were decorated in a variety of ways: colours and textures of hide, wood, iron and bronze, antler, horn and bone, as well as inlays (coral and hot glasswork or 'enamel') and cast or inscribed motifs. It was not only the sharpness of the blade that mattered: the appearance of weapons was vital to their affect upon an opponent, and the offensive or protective properties believed to reside in the object (an idea which will be further developed in the next chapter). The most elaborate sword, K3 (Figure 5.23), had an iron framework cut-out and inset with red enamel, in patterns of dots and crescents and running arcades, and horizontal ribs on the back. Both K3 and the swords from WS453 and WS455 had impressive iron discs on their pommels and hilts, cross-filed and inset with red enamel. All three had iron back-plates, overlapping and clasping the bronze front plate which was decorated with inscribed La Tène art: stylised vine scrolls, varying in form but based on a common theme. Stead considers the affinities between the three swords to be so strong that they must have been made within a generation of each other (2006, 118), perhaps in the same workshop or even finished by the same artisan. However, the sword

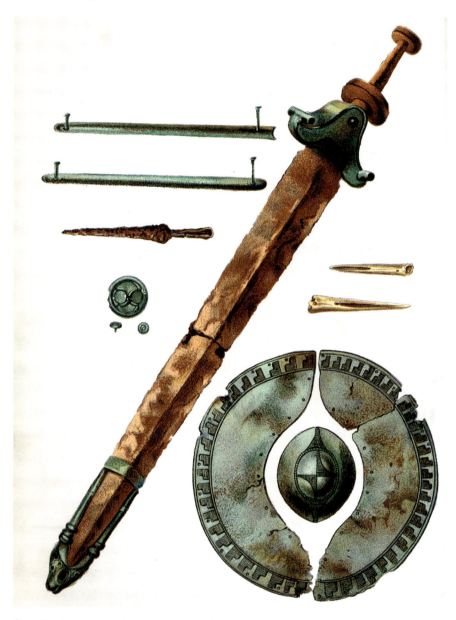

FIGURE 5.21. The grave goods from the Grimthorpe burial. Mortimer 1905a frontispiece.

from K3 has a split front plate, mended with iron fixtures and rivets, whilst the decoration on the front of both Wetwang swords is worn, suggesting all three swords were old: used and passed on, before they ended up in the graves of these three young men – all between 17 and 25 years old.

The age and gender association of weaponry (Figure 5.24) is as marked as the provision of tools, or wearing of certain kinds of personal ornament discussed above. Only one woman is supplied with weaponry (R163), and – as discussed in Chapter 4 – her robustness and strength may have enabled her to fulfil a role normally reserved for young men, whether she was classed as 'male' or not. There

FIGURE 5.22. The North Grimston anthropoid hilt.

FIGURE 5.23. The Kirkburn sword, K3.

FIGURE 5.24. Association of weaponry with sex/age.

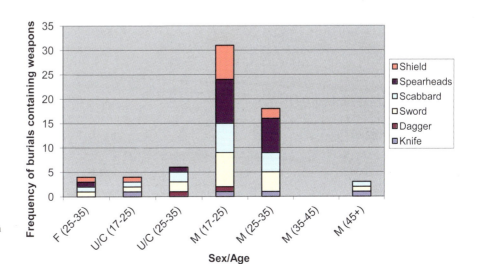

is a strong focus of weaponry in the 17–35 age bracket with only one example of a senior man equipped with sword, scabbard and knife (R45). Though the age of some of these armed men may be underestimated (see Chapter 4), more are found with the younger group (17–25 years) and ethnographic analogies with groups such as the Masai might suggest that this virile and eager age-set has a particular role in active fighting or defense, even if objects like the spear were wielded by adult men of all ages (see Larick 1986 for subtle discussions of identity and weaponry). As Chapter 4 has revealed, violence was rare within these communities but swift, pre-meditated raids may have made the most of the spear as a weapon, whilst staged inter-personal duels might have occasioned the use of the sword. Inauspicious death during this martially-active period of men's lives may have been seen as especially worrying: possibly attributed to witchcraft or sorcery. Perhaps this occasioned the elaborate 'send-off' of the spearing ritual, to ward off the unrest of a frustrated spirit, and ensure their honourable entrance into the afterlife.

Like the tools discussed above, in a funerary setting weapons evoked qualities of power related to brute strength as well as martial skill: the cutting, splitting, stabbing and slicing actions of blades inflicting wounds, the strength required to withstand or deflect blows, the judgement of an opponent's moves and orchestration of a fight. They spoke of ideals related to masculine power, to both attack and defend, which may have been vital to the reproduction of the community's honour and the creation of a prestigious, armed ancestry.

It has been noted that three of the swords had long and – we might suspect – illustrious lives before their burial. Other weapons, such as the shields, also show signs of being passed down, hand-to-hand: damaged and sometimes mended along the way – the repaired scabbard covers from R24 and R139, the fractured hilt of R144, broken tangs of R24 and R146, and damaged or blunted blades (R45, R87, R153). Like the tools, some of these may have been deliberately damaged before their interment, but others spoke of the roll-call of men who had kept and cared for them, as well as those who died or were injured, at their hands. Their perceived power may have bloomed as they accrued violent histories: enhancing the renown of the favoured inheritors with whom they were finally interred. Many of these weapons bear evidence of textile impressions suggesting they were either in close proximity to clothing or were individually wrapped before burial (e.g. R24, R154, WS543, WS545). Such weapons may have had impressive biographies, even names (as in the Anglo-Saxon sagas), and were perhaps entitled to a ceremonial death and funerary rite of their own.

The most obvious example where the biography of an individual and an object were entwined is the burial from Acklam Wold (Figure 5.25; Dent 1983). On the crest of the north-west corner of the High Wolds, overlooking the Vales of York and Pickering, a young man in his thirties was buried in a grave pit cut into the soft, weathered chalk. He lay in a crouched position, on his left-hand side (head to the north-west, facing north-east) and appears to have died a very violent death. He is an impressive individual, with square jaw, and strong

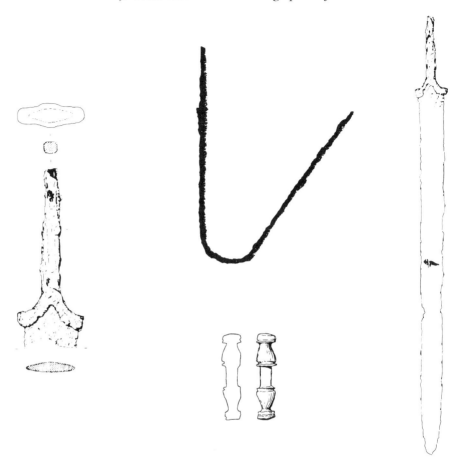

FIGURE 5.25. The Acklam sword burial. Based on Dent 1983, fig. 1.

limbs, yet his body was apparently riven with some form of chronic pulmonary infection (such as brucellosis or even tuberculosis) which has caused extensive damage and bone deformation to the chest region (King, pers. comm.). In addition, a series of sharp-force wounds have left a skeletal trace: none have penetrated the skull but three are deep – biting 6 mm into the bone, and they are between 32 mm and 55 mm long. It is likely they were inflicted with a sword blade or another heavy, long-bladed implement such as an axe. They are all at the top and back of the head: three on the parietal bone, but a possible fourth appears as a sweeping cut to the occipital bone, slightly lower down. A further smaller cut was found over his left eye. There are no signs of healing, so it must be assumed these are perimortem injuries, occurring around the time of death. His body tells a story of an impressive man, brought low by disease, before a violent death.

He was buried with an iron sword, lain just in front of his knees, and a worn and waisted bone toggle with shaped terminals, which could have been a decorative fitting associated with the scabbard. The sword blade is 604 mm long, with a campanulate hilt: the tang of which has lost its tip but bears traces of mineralised wood which may represent the handle. The appearance of this weapon is remarkable. Shortly before it was interred, it was bent through 150°: folding the weapon in two. Traces of mineralised wood remain on the inside of the bend, suggesting it was still sheathed inside its wooden scabbard when the bending took place (Dent 1983, 122), perhaps under the areas where the hands were clasped. The scabbard may well have cracked and splintered under this pressure, producing an awe-inspiring sight. It was a remarkable feat: to bend but not break the blade. Peter Northover has argued that the skill involved in such 'ritual killings' may imply that a smith was responsible (pers. comm.): a convincing idea which would also have been fitting – that the person who brought these objects into being was also responsible for their end.

We will never know the full story behind this burial: perhaps the man had died in a violent duel, and his sword was 'killed' and buried with him. Perhaps his own diseased body was the source of such fear and dismay, that he was set upon deliberately. The sword may have been perceived as 'failing' in its ability to protect its warrior; tainted with such martial ruin, it could not be bequeathed, and so it was vividly sacrificed and buried. Alternatively, this may have been the very weapon responsible for his death: its bloodied blade sheathed, then damaged beyond use, to prevent further feud. Whatever the tale, it not only reminds us that violence was occasionally very real, with horrific consequences, but also that the biographies and identities of people and objects were intimately intertwined.

Summary

This section has analysed in detail the various types of grave goods found in square barrow burials (apart from chariot burials: the subject of the next chapter). It is clear from the most intimate and small-scale item to the most complex object, that highly portable, personal objects were the focus of skilled labour and resources, highlighting the role and importance of craft specialists (Henderson 1991; Sharples 2010). It has described the materials and methods of manufacture they used and aspects of chronological development and dating. It has also tried to reveal something of the 'taskscape' behind the making of these objects: the social and economic webs of relations that implode within Iron Age artefacts. Some were handed down across generations; some were purpose-made for the funeral ceremony. Others were destroyed with the deceased as a mutual ending of their lives, suggesting some of the 'human-object' partnerships discussed in Chapter 1, through which personhood is thoroughly enmeshed in the material world. Through these biographies, this section has also explored connections with the past or even other-worldly inhabitants of this landscape, which heirlooms and amulets may have embodied. The burial of antique or prestigious objects is important, because it allows us to follow the efforts of mourners deliberately 'consuming' wealth in conspicuous funeral displays, as a means of establishing their own position, rather than inheriting or bequeathing them (Sharples 2010, 245, n. 4).

This chapter has focused in detail on aspects of identity such as age, gender and kinship. Detailed analysis suggests that forms of bodily adornment, tools and weapons were used in the constitution and performance of gender roles and distinctions between different age-sets: whilst weapons were appropriate to younger adult men, blue glass bead necklaces were hung round the necks of senior women. This returns to some of the themes discussed by Butler (1990) and Sofaer (2006), raised in Chapter 4: identities were composed through the reiterated amalgams of particular categories of person and artefact classes: not simply in terms of how things were worn or wielded but through the metaphorical connotations they evoked. These related to contrasting models of transformative ability or power – the weaving, binding and stringing together, seen in bodily adornment and textile-work, compared with the forging, riveting, thrusting and wounding of smithing and warfare. The ethnographic examples drawn upon in this chapter suggest that these metaphors of craft skill relate not simply to masculine or feminine ideals and notions of fertility, reproductive power and sexual relations, but they may also underpin other social arenas: politics, kinship and religion. Such meanings may also have been drawn upon in the funerary context to articulate issues to do with life, death and transformation.

Status and power have been explored but not through the number or 'wealth' of grave goods: this will always be a partial and subjective estimate on our behalf, lacking the full panoply of organic materials which may also have played a vital role. Instead, what has been emphasised is the social interconnectedness embodied in particularly complex, exotic or powerful possessions of the deceased, or the offerings made to them. The emphasis placed on 'body' focused adornment suggests *this* was the key realm in which individuated identity and power was expressed, through material culture. It resembles what Sharples has described as an ego-based society, in which individual achievements, skills, life-events or even the manner of death, are of key importance (2010). Such groups celebrate and elevate figures of authority, compared with those where the individual is rigorously suppressed and subsumed within the larger whole of the community. Whilst we need to know more about how power and authority was reproduced, to close this chapter we must step back to consider what these funerary beliefs reveal about that broader community.

General patterns: local traditions, regional trends

It is evident that the square barrow burial rite was practiced across the region of East Yorkshire, in ways which would have enabled people to recognise common beliefs and ideals shared between different communities. Some individuals from the North Yorkshire moors would have recognised the ideology behind the Wetwang chariot burials even if they thought they were doing it 'all wrong'. A herdsman from Holderness would have recognised the barrows along the trackway at Slingsby, as representing a shared world-view and appreciation of ancestry, even if he was not related to these families. Longer-distance travellers venturing to the Continent may even have recognised affinities with such distant groups, as Chapter 7 will discuss. Yet within this broad tradition, individual valley systems had preferred 'ways of doing things' or localised traits in terms of orientation, funerary furniture or preference for certain types of grave goods: the preference for weapons and tools burials in the Great Wold Valleys, the prevalence of blue glass beads at Wetwang Slack, the dominance of 'speared' burials at Garton Station. When we delve in detail into individual cemeteries, even smaller-scale traditions can be seen.

For example, at Rudston, two nearly identical burials were placed side-by-side, parallel to an earlier linear earthwork. R18 and R20 were both buried orientated north–south (facing east), with a calcite tempered vessel, both of which held the left humerus of a sheep. R20 was distinguished by an iron brooch. Flanking these burials is a small row of three, south–north orientated (west facing) burials, one of whom is again distinguished by a brooch (R11, R17, R19). To their west, two north–south orientated (east-facing) inhumations (R2 and R4) were interred with identical iron brooches, though R2 also had a shale bracelet and blue glass bead pendant/hair braid. To the east, two north–south orientated (east-facing) burials were buried with involuted brooches (R22, R25) and to the north, three burials with the same orientation were interred with erratic-tempered pots again containing the left forelimbs of sheep. Finally, scattered amongst these monuments are a series of rite B burials (east–west orientated, facing a variety of directions) without surrounding enclosure ditches.

What is seen at Rudston is a series of localised traditions: one or two burials, placed near each other, which are very similar or identical, including aspects of orientation and grave goods. This is by no means unique. R38 and R39, adjacent burials, are both interred with iron pins, contrasting with a group of burials close by, all interred with involuted brooches (R27, R35, R36, R37, R40). R61–R64 all share a south–north orientated (west facing) disposition, whereas burials to the north of this group favour the most common north–south (east facing) orientation. R76 and R77 share similar grave goods: pots with left sheep forelimbs and involuted brooches, though the temper of their vessels is different, and the latter burial is distinguished by a coffin. Either side of the Gypsey Race stream, one cluster of burials (BF1–22) are exclusively associated with long, flat-bow brooches, but the burials opposite (R190–208) only contain involuted forms. Three adjacent female burials from the former cluster are all interred wearing bracelets but of different substances: bronze and shale (BF9, BF10 and BF11). Patterns such as common brooch styles might suggest that burials happened close together in time, reflecting particular styles which were common or popular at the time. However, at Wetwang Slack, the interconnecting stratigraphy reveals that there is no simple chronological shift from one brooch style to another. Whilst the burials may still happen close together in time, it suggests that there were strong individual preferences for particular fashions of body adornment and funerary rites which might instead relate to family or peer-group traditions, that are expressed through being buried close together in space (as discussed in Chapter 3). For example, burials WS132 and WS133 are both adult females of the same age which were secondary insertions within the same burial mound but at different times, sharing identical orientations, with iron bracelets on their wrists. The young male 'speared burials' at Garton Station (GS4, GS5, GS7 and GS10) are a further example; sharing not only orientation but the distinctive monument of a small round barrow, and the placing of shields over their body before the 'spearing' ritual took place.

In other words, within each cemetery there are multiple 'micro-traditions' where things were done in similar ways, suggesting common affinities between the people concerned – whether this represents actual 'relatedness' through kinship (as S. Stead believed, on the basis of the non-metric traits: in Stead 1991) or the death and burial of peer-group or community members around the same time. (It does not, interestingly, seem to relate to what could be regarded as cross-cutting categories such as 'class'). Either individual families had their own 'traditions' and family grave areas (a model which would support the arguments made in Chapter 3), or the community used particular areas of the cemetery for a time, before shifting to a new zone and slightly changing its rites. Thus whilst common ideals were clearly shared across the region, detailed analysis reveals how they were locally deployed. This observation is in keeping with Barth's notion that individual interpretation, expertise and skill are brought to bear upon ritual matters by sacred specialists (1987). In his study of the Mountain Ok of New Guinea, he argued that even within a tradition of unchanging sacred knowledge, thought to be handed down faithfully between ritual specialists, novel circumstances demanded a degree of improvisation and the exercise of personal judgement. He described this as a generative model of cosmology (*ibid.*): a notion which accords well with the local variation seen in the cemeteries, as families struggled with the exact circumstances and timing of death: disease, violence and accidents forced people to deviate from the 'script' of these performances. They improvised strategically with what they remembered had been done before, what was to hand in the here and now, and in mind of their hopes and aspirations for the future.

Conclusion

This chapter began by discussing the process of death: its physiological affects upon the body, and emotional and social consequences for the bereaved. It has summarised evidence for the preparation of the body and its provisioning with different kinds of personal objects or funerary gifts. A key point of this chapter has been to criticise how archaeologists used to interpret burials and grave goods. Status and identity cannot be read directly from the tableau of a mortuary scene, since this was carefully orchestrated by mourners who had their own agendas, as well as debts and obligations to fulfil.

The careful analysis of different categories of objects and aspects of age and gender have hopefully conjured some of the ways in which young adult men or senior women (for example) were constituted through an amalgam of fleshy bodies and material substances: performances of personhood which were always under scrutiny and revision, even in the event of death. It has highlighted the metaphorical qualities of artefacts alongside their practical use, and discussed how these may have been used to evoke particular meanings or associations in the funerary context. These sections have also hopefully provided a useful review of the wealth of Iron Age material culture available to these East Yorkshire communities, their approximate dates of use and some of the specialist terms used to describe them. The chapter has also used individual objects to reveal the broader taskscape of craftwork through which they came into being, as well as the generation of 'hands' through which some of them passed – their geneaologies – before ending up in the grave.

Finally, it has discussed how apparently common traditions at the regional level were actually executed in slightly different ways, and how even these 'valley' or 'community' level trends are further distinguished by small patterns of similar burials, which may reflect family, peer-group or generational mortuary preferences. It has also suggested that these subtle differences are, in part, the result of people strategically improvising within a body of ritual knowledge and sacred tradition, responding to the exact nature and circumstances of individual deaths in the best way they knew how, given the resources they had to hand. The funeral was thus a dramatic performance – but it was only one of many social occasions, in which people drew upon spectacular objects to help reproduce their authority or jostle for positions of status and influence. It is to this central issue of performance and power that the book now turns.

CHAPTER SIX

Actors and Props:
the Theatre of Life and Death

Introduction

The burial of the person in grave WS209 was a difficult affair. The grave diggers must have balanced precariously on the edge of neighbouring barrow ditches, in the narrow confines of the gap left between three earlier graves, to dig the mortuary pit over a metre deep into the chalk gravel. The slight ditch clipped the margins of these adjacent monuments (WS230, WS242 and WS208), resulting in a barrow that was far from neat: a rather small, elliptical mound. Clearly in this case, as in others (see Chapter 3), it was the exact *place* of burial which was important, located in reference to specific forebears or neighbours. The narrow coffin stain which framed the remains was scarcely large enough to contain a body. When fully excavated, it became clear why. The tightly contracted skeletal remains were folded almost double: the limbs pressed tightly against each other, whilst the head was strangely rotated away from the vertebral column. Inside the skull was a small collection of rodent bones: an infestation which (alongside the tightly bound body) might suggest that a considerable period of time had elapsed between death and final interment (J. Dent, pers. comm.). It is possible that she was brought back to Wetwang Slack from a more distant location – a journey which took time – and that the dessicated and tightly bound corpse had been subject to post-mortem curation practices (see Parker Pearson *et al.* 2005). These may have enabled the 'return' of this individual from a place of adult residence to a location of importance in their life: the place of birth, perhaps. This delay in burial may have been more common than we have thought and may indicate a liminal period in which the deceased was still perceived to have social agency, or a continued role in the community (see Lally 2008, 123). We might imagine a series of stages in this process: primary events of mourning, followed by secondary rites of wrapping, binding and boxing the body for its journey. Finally, the diminutive coffin with its light contents, were placed reverently in the grave, so that the body faced west, lying on its left-hand side.

Everything about this final burial event suggests a restriction of movement, both of the corpse itself and the grave diggers and mourners' bodies, jostling around the lip of the grave as chalk and soil tumbled in. Yet at some point in the funeral ceremony there had been a moment of sudden release: a necklace of blue glass beads (16 bulbous 'melon' beads and two blue beads with white scrolls or waves) had broken asunder, to lie scattered over the corpse. Perhaps the bloating of the body through post-mortem decay had rotted the thread or else it had decayed or become disturbed during the final wrapping process. Another possibility however, is that this was a deliberate and dramatic gesture, by a mourner. There may have been a sudden snap of thread: a 'pop' as the beads spilled over the body, to fall across the chest and belly. Or perhaps a knot was reverently untied, and the beads were poured out of a cupped palm: slipping through the fingers of a close relative or friend. If so, the funeral audience at Wetwang Slack may have been surprised or even shocked by the act: most of these objects (which as the previous chapter argued, appear to have had a strong association with senior women) were tied around the neck of the deceased, as if in life. The skeletal remains were fragmentary and showed indeterminate traits (King, pers. comm.), meaning we are still unclear as to his/her gender. Perhaps she was a robust woman, or else the necklace may even have been a gift from a partner to her husband, rather than the personal possession of the deceased. We might guess at some of the metaphors underlying the theatricality of this final gesture: the marking of an end to things, the unthreading of ties, the loosening of relations …

This is a small example from the Iron Age cemeteries of East Yorkshire of a broader theme I intend to develop in this chapter: the performative character of later prehistoric life and death. By this I mean (in its most basic definition) the deliberate organisation of behaviour in front of witnesses (after Schechner, cited in Shanks and Pearson 2001, xiii). It is a theme which archaeologists have found increasingly useful in their struggle to interpret the ways in which architectural space and portable material culture were used to orchestrate movement or gesture, co-ordinate participants and present bodies (see Barrett 1994; Williams 2006). The above example encourages us to think about not just the staging but the timing of such events. The notion of performance provides a way of thinking through these settings of settlements, cemeteries and earthworks, and amongst this particular world of objects – exploring the ways in which they *might* have been used to dramatic effect.

Archaeologists have drawn in particular, on two different theories of performance: first, Erving Goffman's body of work on the performative quality of social interaction (1969). Goffman suggested that social life could be thought of as a performance or drama, in which social 'actors' stage-managed their different roles through a series of demanding scenes, each of which required improvisation around an agreed series of behavioural norms or expectations (a loose 'script', if you like). Goffman used the concept of 'face-work' to describe the close-up, inter-personal and embodied performance of identity – the way it is marked and remarked upon – through the actor's stance, voice and tone, turns of the shoulder or gestures of the hand (1999). Competent or successful performances are well-received by an audience, but slips, blunders and mistakes can result in stigmatisation: a failure to be intelligible – to be understood. Goffman identified certain practices in social performance: the creation of a 'front' region of more public display, and a 'back' stage region where such impressions lapse, and where behaviour might be contradictory or of a more informal or intimate nature. In his studies, he followed people through changes in 'scene', and analysed the management of their performances as they moved between different social groups. This has much in common with the shifting, contextual nature of identity discussed in Chapter 1, and Goffman's key concept can also help us think through how people 'arrange' private and mundane as well as public and ceremonial events. However, there are problems with his underlying metaphor. Goffman's work can be criticised for its assumption that social actors are their own directors, when in fact our agency is constrained by the actions of others and their expectations; in many social encounters, we enter stages which are already 'set' rather than orchestrating these events ourselves. Indeed, the theatrical motif which underpins Goffman's work might be regarded as disingenuous towards social life, and people's understanding of their identities not as a mere *portmanteau* of roles and costumes which are deliberately 'put on', but a continuously lived reality in which different aspects of personhood come to the fore unbidden (see papers in Lemert and Branaman 1997). Yet there is no doubt that social interaction has a performative dimension, and that one of the purposes of material culture is to frame and enhance the affect people's presence and actions have on those around them. This is the use to which Goffman's ideas will be put in this chapter.

The second major source of influence from performance theory has already been briefly touched on in Chapter 1: this is the work of Judith Butler, particularly her idea that categories of identity such as gender are reproduced through their repeated performance (1990; 1993). What it was to be an elderly woman in these later prehistoric societies relied upon how elderly women behaved. In what Butler calls the 'illocutionary' effect, they enacted that to which their performance referred … their understanding and negotiation of the class of senior womanhood. Of course, their actions were subject to the scrutiny of others, and their approval or vilification, but the key point, as stressed in Chapter 1, is that identity was a matter of practice. Herein lay peoples' ability to resist cultural categories and transform identities over time (1993), though such acts of subversion were of course constrained by the norms of the day. The chapter will therefore argue that performances were central to the reproduction of categories of identity, particular those associated with power and authority, and their intersection with age, gender, kinship and community.

A focus upon performance does not have to refer solely to the large-scale or ceremonial event, though there are clear instances where the orchestration of people, props and settings might have been more pre-meditated and elaborate. The chapter will move between the small-scale, intimate gesture and these larger, more public moments of performance, and it will discuss the different architectural frames, material paraphernalia and dress and adornment, which enhanced these events. In so doing, it will follow the 'lives' of some of the most impressive objects (particularly jewellery, weaponry and vehicles) before they were placed in the ground, as well as the drama surrounding their final burial. This chapter is interested in what this tells us about Iron Age: the social and convivial side of hosting events and meeting with relatives and neighbours, the responsibilities and risks of officiating at rights of passage, and the dangers of meeting with strangers or facing an enemy. In considering some of these possible scenarios, the chapter's aim is to reveal the visual, aural and tactile effects of objects upon people, and consider how they extended the agency of their users, by being wielded skilfully or effectively. At its heart is an interest in the way in which power and authority was constituted within these communities, not just through the charisma of the individuals buried in these graves but also through the spectacular material culture which accompanied them.

Performing life

Pasturing out and herding home

One of the most impressive sights and sounds witnessed in this landscape was not focused on the bodies of people, but their stock: the large-scale movements of sheep and cattle. Chapter 2 discussed the relationship between rhythms of pasturing and the linear earthworks which increasingly marked and divided the landscape: demarcating rights of way and access to the key resources of pasture and water. The hoofprints of these stock, their browsing and cropping, and brushing up against trees and bushes, created day-to-day paths through vegetation which 'showed the way' and eased the passage of those that followed (see Lorimer 2006). Likewise, their favoured spots for scratching, resting or sheltering, left traces of wool, worn turf and bared bark, which evidenced the presence of animals in the 'in-between' places which separated the settlements of their herders. As extensions of the human community, they helped negotiate and reproduce those ties to land: ties which were marked daily, seasonally and annually. Such stock gave shape to the year through agricultural events which would have brought people together: periods of lambing and calving, of gathering for plucking wool, branding and nicking, castrating or culling. Whilst we do not often reflect on the performance associated with stock, in agriculturally based communities, they form the centre of such social gatherings which pulse with festivity. Even routine acts of corralling, herding home to shelter, or turning them out to pasture were occasions for display of human prowess, command and understanding of such animals … to see such a group on the move must have been a truly impressive sight. The colours of their fleeces or hides, the curved and possibly shaped or polished horns, their lowing and bleeting: this was the sound and sight of wealth on the hoof. Those responsible for their protection and wellbeing would have derived pride and status from such animals, and would have been clothed or even armed with shields and swords, decorated with the very bodies of animals they had cared for and respected. It is this synergy between people and animals which would have made such events both impressive and memorable.

The roundhouse

In contrast to the trackways and boundaries which framed the wider landscape, everyday domestic life in the Iron Age took place as a series of movements in and out of the roundhouse: a to-and-fro of people and resources. The small clusters of their pointed roofs (thatched no doubt, with care and pride) influenced pathways between groups of neighbours, trodden into the chalky turf. At Wetwang and Garton Slack, we can see how the broad zone of settlement was defined by large linears to the north, south and west, but what is remarkable within this area is a lack of subsidiary, formalised fences (Chapter 3). Only the ditch which bisects the 'old' and 'new' cemetery at Wetwang, and an enclosed area of craft production (WS11) on the valley side, date to this period. In such an 'open' settlement, the encircled frame of the roundhouses not only provided vital points of orientation, but important stations for encounters.

How did their architecture frame such meetings? Fortunately, we have a plethora of contemporary reconstructions of Iron Age roundhouses (from centres such as the Butser Ancient Farm Project, the Cranborne Ancient Technology Centre, Castell Henllys Visitor Centre and Flag Fen), to aid our interpretation of the archaeological evidence. From the outside, they are testaments to thatching skill and pride. Entering one of these buildings is to be surprised by the space within them: the impressive height of the roof, the contrast between the central area and darker zones around the perimeter – the encompassing feeling of living 'in the round'. Fragments of detail from excavations suggest care was lavished on their internal appearance and finish, such as the burned clay and charcoal, orange-flecked floors from Castell Henllys, which were swept clean and burnished with wear (H. Mytum, pers. comm.).

What is evident from Wetwang and Garton is the frequent orientation of the doorways to the east or south-east. In Chapter 3 this was discussed from the integrated perspective of a practically informed cosmology: facing south-east maximised light, provided some shelter from northerly gales or fierce east winds, whilst providing its inhabitants with an open view down the snaking corridor of the valley. But it also drew upon auspicious associations with sun-rise, particularly at key moments in the agricultural year, and evoked the symbolism of renewal or regeneration. These were the doorways through which the households' members departed and returned, perhaps imparting a sense of 'luck' to their inhabitants' journeys and endeavours. They also framed the entrance of visitors who had been welcomed from the open spaces of the settlement, into a more intimate setting for discussion and exchange. Many of the doorways suggest particularly large and impressive timbers were used to monumentalise these thresholds, as at Wetwang, B12:6, B12:4, B12:3 or B8:4 (Dent 1995) and in Garton Slack Area 18 (Brewster 1980). In some cases at Wetwang, a double set of posts suggest an external porch (B7:11, B9:6, B12:3), providing a further frame for reception, and marking people's entrance into a different kind of space.

Occasionally, pits in the south or west of these structures, suggest areas of storage (Dent 1995) and these have also preserved traces of floor surfaces which give a rare insight into their interior organisation. Beaten earth floors were preserved in B6:6 and B9:5 (Wetwang Slack) but two successive layers of trampled chalk floors were suggested by layers which had subsided into the top of a pit in B9:4 (*ibid.*, 58). Here, patches of burning in the same area suggested a hearth had been repeatedly sited in the same area of the house: on the immediate right-hand side of anyone entering this dwelling (if structure and pit are contemporary). It is often assumed that fires would have been central to these spaces, but it is evident from examples in the south, that by the late Iron Age/early Roman period, people had developed portable cooking facilities (Cunliffe 2003, 83). This might have made such spaces eminently flexible. Internal fixtures and fittings may be represented by scattered post and stake holes, and more major pieces of 'furniture' are suggested by the arrangements of post pairs and arcs of flanking posts in B8:4 (Dent 1995). This might be a frame for a loom, or the footings for a cupboard. Household crafts represented by bone tools and weights were found in several structures. Other areas may have been temporarily screened off through moveable panels or textile hangings. Whilst Dent does not discuss the possibility of a second storey in these wall-slot constructed buildings, internal arcs of posts may suggest either supporting timbers for the roof and/or frames for internal platforms or storage facilities.

Even from this scant evidence, it is clear that any visitor would have glimpsed the 'wealth' of the household as represented by its stored foodstuffs, vessels and tools, evidence for craft skill (both in the very frame and appearance of the house, and its furnishings), as well as the number, appearance and adornment of its members. Closed chests or cupboards, wrapped objects or items on display, may have hinted at the lineage of these families, and their status in the community. Yet importantly, there are no indications (as discussed in Chapter 3) of significantly larger 'high status' dwellings, where the size and architecture of these buildings were used to distinguish the authority of the residents from that of their neighbours. These are not monumental buildings but they were nonetheless key frames of day-to-day experience.

To enter one of these spaces was to be assailed by its smells, textures and noises. Light from the outside penetrated in a broad arc through the door, but once shut, sounds and sights from the outside world were muffled. Smoke filtered through the thatch, leaving a slight haze at the upper levels. Depending on the weather, time of night or day, inhabitants and occasion, these could have been calm places of domestic work and chatter, or vibrant and raucous settings for meals and story-telling. Whilst subtle aspects of seniority or class might have been structured through seating arrangements (such as whom one faced, upon entering), their circularity was key: symbolically bringing people together. Whilst their traces are ephemeral, and further evidence for the organisation of internal activities has been removed by centuries of ploughing, they must have provided the impressive setting for a host of day-to-day activities as well as rarer, more formalised encounters with trusted or respected visitors. This is what

Barrett and Fewster allude to when they urge us to consider how different spaces and times coalesced in the frame of the roundhouse: journeying from nearby fields and pasture, or from more foreign places, bringing material manifestations of the local and the distant, into the same field of experience (2000, 31). The routine rhythm of the agricultural cycle intersected with individual biographies or the life of the household, orientated towards different future projects and goals. It is at this scale of the intimate – they argue – that the sequential practice of its inhabitants held together those larger social structures which we seek to apprehend. This is why the roundhouse, even with its ephemeral remains, is such an important locale in Iron Age life.

Food, drink and entertainment

In order to envisage the character of such events, we can turn to the evidence for their provision, in terms of the food, drink and entertainment which might have accompanied them. It is here that East Yorkshire forms a great contrast with other areas of Iron Age Britain. The earthernware vessels found as sherds in the buildings, and as whole pots in pits or grave contexts, suggest a principle of individual or small-scale consumption, of both food and drink. As discussed in Chapter 4, their distinctive temper may have carried important messages about where someone felt they 'belonged', and with whom: these were not highly decorated, communal vessels. Nor were they particularly well-made or fired (Rigby, in Stead 1991). Whilst there may have been impressive wooden or basketry vessels complementing these pots, they have left no trace. In addition, there is no evidence thus far for metal cauldrons, tankards, fire-dogs, pans or troughs, nor serving vessels, large bowls or dishes: popular items of middle–late Iron Age material culture which might suggest formalised, 'diacritical' feasting (Dietler 1996; Dietler and Hayden 2001). Dietler defines this as a process whereby status is distinguished in part through exclusive dining paraphernalia, to which people had restricted access, alongside exotic foodstuffs which suggest distinctions on the basis of style or 'taste' (after Bourdieu 2002).

Yet the burial evidence clearly indicates that large-scale consumption of meat was occurring on occasions: predominantly of mutton, and more rarely of pork (see Chapter 5). In addition, the settlement evidence suggests that beef was occasionally, if rarely, enjoyed by the community, but never in the context of a funeral. In each case the carcases have been jointed and divided up, and the presence of a 'portion for the dead' might suggest that other body parts were similarly circumscribed by cultural traditions: defined either by closeness of relations with the deceased, role in a ceremony and/or status within the community (cf Parker Pearson 1999a). Some portions bear traces of singeing or burning, and this may have occurred communally (such as an open air spit-roast), with cooked portions 'divvied' out for everyone to see, or else the raw butchered joints may have been given to people to cook on a household basis.

What kind of feasting does this represent? Much depends on who was donating the animal for the feast (and presumably, the liquid refreshment which probably accompanied it)! According to Michael Dietler, 'empowering feasts' are used to enhance the prestige of the donor, where people may be competing for honour and authority (1990). They can be important means of obliquely challenging a rival, or usurping their authority through conspicuous generosity. 'Patron-role' feasts, in contrast, are designed to legitimise and reinforce existing relations of power (*ibid.*). In Iron Age East Yorkshire, both may have been occurring. Providing a sheep for the wake might suggest death was a context for the display of lavish generosity, aimed at enhancing the prestige and standing of the family. However, the choice use of pork for the chariot and sword burials might indicate more 'patron-role' type feasts where existing authority was being underlined by the provision of a special, prized foodstuff. In the famous cinematic account of a Papua New Guinean 'big man' society – *Ongka's Big Moka* – Ongka, the 'big man' spends much of his time negotiating exchanges of pigs and fodder, in order to host an extravagant 'moka' – a one-off feasting and exchange event which will trump his rivals' generosity, create future social debts and seal his renown (Nairn 1974). In this scenario, his wife plays a key role in the feeding and nurturing of these animals: an exacting task which confirms her authority in what might otherwise be perceived as a male sphere of power (see Strathern 1988). However, we are not dealing with an analogous scale of events in Iron Age East Yorkshire to the 'moka', nor do we know whether pigs were the property of specific individuals or households, or whether they were owned more communally. If it was the broader neighbourhood who raised, cared for and sanctioned their sacrifice, this would put a very different complexion upon the event. In more egalitarian communities, such feasts serve the important function of redistributing surplus, whose plenty might otherwise become a source of contention, suspicion and even accusations of sorcery or witchcraft. In this setting, communal cooking and eating deliberately suppresses social difference – feasting can therefore be an important strategy to deter jealous raids or forced requisitioning.

Whatever model we opt for, Dietler's important point is that feasting concerns 'commensal' politics: the negotiation of aspects of identity (such as power but also gender and age), relative to others. Feasts 'unite and divide' at the same time (1996): their festive atmosphere both binding people together *and* differentiating guests from hosts – the servers from the served. They set up a good social ambiance, which may predispose people to the host's moral authority in other settings. Feasts also promote solidarity and community, and cement new bonds, creating a network of indebtedness that may be drawn upon in times of need. In the case of later prehistoric East Yorkshire, it has been suggested that there is little evidence for the kind of high status diacritical feasting in the settings of elite residences, which is typical of many stereotypical images of the Iron Age. Yet the communal eating of meat, particularly at events such as the funeral served to bind the community together – defining internal roles and relations, and allowing some of its members to jostle for power – whilst enhancing the general prestige of the family concerned.

Craftwork

One of the other arenas in which skill was demonstrated, alongside agricultural and domestic work, was the production of artefacts. In a settlement such as Wetwang Slack, it is possible to see an extraordinary array of crafts undertaken by its inhabitants. Worked jet, including a rough-out piece, were found in roundhouse contexts (Dent 1984a). A fascinating chalk plaque, carved with rows of lines, triangles and concentric crescents, was found at Garton Slack (Brewster 1980). This is an example of a larger repertoire of carved chalk discs, weights and spindle whorls, which by the latest Iron Age, is complemented by characterful chalk figurines (Stead 1988). These geometric designs may have mimicked (or even provided the template for) the woven textiles represented in stone loomweights, spindle whorls and a range of bone points and needles. The evidence for embroidery at Burton Fleming (discussed in the last chapter), alongside small bronze buttons or loop ties and scabbard belt fittings, suggests the making of dress accoutrements – male and female – was an arena of particular pride and skill.

Many of these raw materials were obtained locally, and both the ceramics and worked stone assemblages (such as quernstones) speak of contacts between the Wolds and the coast, including the obtaining of jet from Whitby. Even the iron may have come from ore-picking over the local chalk soils, supplemented by sources from the Foulness Valley (Halkon and Millett 1999), though copper and tin must have had a more distant or ancient origin. At their furthest reach, Yorkshire craftspeople were manipulating Mediterranean coral or Baltic amber into local designs which managed to evoke that broader world of Celtic art yet in their own distinct style (Stead 1996 – for further discussion, see Chapter 7).

There were particular crafts which stand apart in terms of their dramatic potential, due to the transformative role of heat and the pressure of time, which demanded controlled speed welded with inspiration. The working of glass is one example, as in the rapid construction of a stratified eye bead; equally, the multiplication of deft and delicate skill involved in the making of the Kirkburn chainmail shirt. Smithing is evidenced at Wetwang Slack, where copper alloy crucible and mould fragments were found in association with ash and broken ceramics in Area 6, in pits 6:530 and 6:534, as well as from a ditch in Area 11. Where identifiable, these represented a lynch pin terminal and terret (Dent 1984a). Smithing slag was also found at this latter site. What is interesting is the location of Area 11: removed from the main open settlement and set within its own enclosure on the north side of the valley. It suggests this might not just be for practical reasons (to avoid noxious fumes and the risk of fire) but perhaps to keep this work out of open view. This may relate to notions of craft mystery or lore, since metalworking in the Iron Age was a craft charged with powerful meanings (Hingley 1997). As in many other small-scale communities, it was likely to be suffused with symbolism and subscribed with ritual (see Giles

2007b). Interestingly, copper alloy working has also been found in a middle–late Iron Age enclosure at Kelk-6, located on a bend in the Gransmoor drain, by the Humber Wetlands Project (van der Noort and Ellis 2000). Dating to the 2nd–1st century BC, sprue cups and mould fragments were found in ditches and pits which also contained fuel-ash slag. Again, this suggests the setting-aside of special areas in which the performance of smelting and smithing was witnessed by a select few.

This may have helped preserve the awe that surrounded the most complex objects which often fused together multiple substances into one exemplary piece: they appeared as remarkable pieces of divinely inspired and assisted crafting (see Helms 1988). Some of these artefacts still cause museum visitors to draw breath in front of the display case: the Kirkburn sword or the Wetwang Slack box. Many are diminutive: the Wetwang Slack pin with its iron core, coral head and shining slip of gold, or the Danes Graves hair pin with its slender bronze swan-neck and concentric rings of coral. Yet the fine manipulation that it took to craft such delicate objects brought with it a certain power of its own (see Mack 2008, 59). One of the key substances which literally 'held things together' has recently been identified as a glue made from birch-bark tar and conifer or pine resin, as found under the terret studs from Wetwang Village (Stacey 2004, 1–2). The making of things was thus a vital performative arena in which knowledge of and skill with materials was demonstrated, but also connections with other people and even the favour of spirits or gods, could be evidenced (Helms 1988). Even by wearing or wielding such objects, others spoke of their access to this vein of power.

Embellishing the human body

Human bodies were decorated and embellished with material culture in different ways, using a variety of substances, textures and colours (as discussed in Chapter 5). We can now go on to consider some of the different social *contexts* in which particular suites of objects may have been used to dramatic effect. For example, the use of finger and toe-rings, bracelets on bare forearms, necklaces, pendants or hair-beads, may have been part of the way in which young adults solicited the attention of future partners. The 'clank' of paired bracelets, or the weighted sway of a decorated braid, would have drawn the ears and eyes of the opposite sex. At social gatherings, meetings or judicial events, the stillness of an elderly woman, weighed down by her blue-glass bead necklace, may have helped lend her an aura of calm seniority. In contrast, ranks of younger men, propped against their elegant spears, would have made an impression of upright strength and readiness. Meanwhile, the rigid back of a man would allude to his bearing of a sheathed sword, which might have been carefully untied with much fussing over straps and rings or chains, for all to see its decorated scabbard plate. The very concealment of the sword in its scabbard alluded to the potential power of the blade, drawing the curious or jealous gaze. Many of the tools (hammers, awls, gouges) and small knives found in the graves were contained within sheaths or pouches. Their wrapping conjured a sense of their latent, potential power, and the skill of the hands, perhaps resting lightly on them at the belt. Such objects did not work in isolation to intrigue or intimidate the onlooker: their impact came from the ways in which their wearers' bodies moved with them, melding together, to impressive effect. Three 'sketches', drawn from burial assemblages, conjure the potential of such amalgams of people and artefacts.

Wetwang Slack 454

The black-and-white line drawing of the woman buried with a chariot at Wetwang Slack (WS454) illustrating a popular pamphlet from the Hull and East Riding Museum, is somewhat romanticised (Humber Field Archaeology 2000a, 28). Dressed in long, sweeping skirts and cloak, she inspects her appearance in her mirror, whilst from her waist hangs the sealed bronze box (the 'bean tin') on its chain. She looks as if she is geared up for a night out in Bridlington, complete with handbag and pocket mirror! The objects are seen as items of female vanity: superficial, decorative embellishments. Yet the context of their burial, alongside a chariot, suggests they were central props to the authority of the deceased (Dent 1984b; 1985).

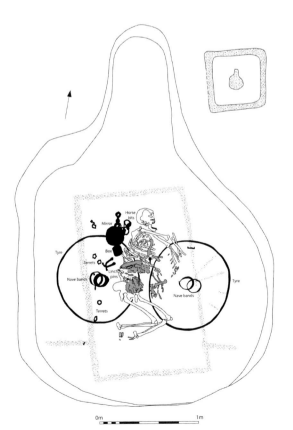

FIGURE 6.1. Female chariot burial (WS454) from Wetwang Slack, containing sealed bronze container and iron mirror. Based on Dent 1985, 89, fig. 3.

As the previous chapter argued, the canister is decorated with the same kind of incised curvilinear Celtic art and knobs of rich, red enamel, found on scabbards in the neighbouring male graves (Figure 6.1 and Figure 5.15). What did it contain? Nothing. Yet what people *thought* it might contain is a different matter … an ancestral spirit or cosmological entity perhaps … the casket would have been a source of both intrigue and fear. As for the mirror, its bulbous-handled form alluded to other craft objects such as tool or weapon grips, and horse-bits or linch-pins (see Giles and Joy 2007), which evoked the control of power. It may well have been decorated in some way: the impressions of a tablet-woven border and fringe, wrapped around a fragment of bone, may have been part of a bag's tie or tassel. If, like the Wetwang Village mirror, this artefact was also concealed from view, wrapped and hung from a peg or stored within a chest, the moment of revelation would have both powerful and intimidating. It would have been impressive at a distance: catching and reflecting the light, but it was meant to work most powerfully on the viewer 'close-up'. These are heavy objects which required two hands to hold them, possibly suggesting an attendant or specialist held them up for 'seeing into'. But what was seen in the polished iron plate was not an accurate reflection … it was a shadowy world of glimpsed movement: a play of light and dark.

James and Rigby note that mirrors both transpose left and right, and permit the viewer to see both ahead of, and behind themselves, at the same time (1997, 39). This may be the source of the mirror's supposed power to look into the future (a special form of divination known as 'catoptromancy'), or interrogate the past: properties that are well attested in the ethnography of mirrors (and mirror-like substances such as pools) amongst small-scale societies (see Giles and Joy 2007). They can also be used to bind oaths, cast spells or effect curses. Such luminous, reflective surfaces work at the boundaries between states of being, and are often seen as thresholds between worlds. Mirrors often play a key role in rites of passage involving self-reflection, or the revelation of change, as well as being instruments for contacting powerful spirits or ancestors (Saunders 1998). Given the quality of the burnished iron plate, perhaps it is not surprising that it might be the generic features of the 'family face' which were glimpsed in such reflections.

As dangerous implements of considerable power, their 'wrapping' and concealment may have had a protective function for the viewer, as well as enhancing the moment of their unveiling. Whilst mirrors may have been communally owned – part of a kin groups' arsenal of powerful ritual objects – the ambiguity involved in what was 'seen' in its surface, and how this might be interpreted, may explain why certain individuals developed a special skill for divination and a close bond with these implements (B. Sitch, pers. comm.). In untutored hands, such visions may have been dangerously misinterpreted – it may therefore have been unthinkable that they were handed on or bequeathed. We know that she was an elderly woman, with worn joints, but her teeth suggest a privileged diet at least in her latter years, if not throughout her lifetime. Whether we read this as evidence that she was from a wealthy or influential family, or was treated to refined foods in recognition of her ritual skill and/or elder status, she was distinguished from others in both life and death. Pork was placed in her grave, to sustain her on her journey into the afterlife: two forequarters of a pig were laid between her outstretched arms and thighs.

By equipping her with the mirror, it is possible that the community was 'keeping the lines of communication open' with the ancestral world: sealing her renown as an ancestor empowered to make future intercessions from the spirit world. The horse-gear provided for this burial is also impressive: rein rings decorated with bulbous Celtic art on the outside of the 'stops' which would have been seen by the viewer, and delicate hatching on the glossy heads of the 'J-shape' linchpins. Yet it is the smallest item in the grave which seals her reputation as a woman of importance. An iron pin, decorated with a knob of coral and finished with a studded and ribbed slip of gold, represents the only surviving example of this element found in the East Yorkshire graves (Dent 2010, 41). Today, it is still untarnished in colour and finish, so that this diminutive pin glows and catches the eye. Whilst it would only have been seen once you were within the orbit of this woman, its combination of substances exuded distant relations with foreign places: another important aspect of her identity.

Wetwang Slack 453

One of the other major events which involved skilled and daring performances with highly charged objects, was of course, warfare. It is the chariot burial of one of the men at Wetwang Slack, which best illustrates the panoply of accoutrements out of which arose a spectacle of intimidating martial prowess. Quite apart from the chariot (which will be discussed below), the man buried in grave WS453 was adorned with a suite of weapons (Figure 6.2). An iron sword was laid over his body, sheathed in a scabbard made from a bronze front plate and rounded, pierced iron chape and back plate (Dent 1985, 88). It was decorated on the grip and pommel with domed metal roundels, keyed for red enamel (Stead 2006, 185). The front plate was embellished with further roundels near the top and where it begins to taper towards the chape (Stead 2006, fig. 88). This plate was incised with a wave-tendril design, spiralling alternately to the left then right, with infilled designs of hatched lobes or triangles (*ibid.*), and it has become worn and faded where it might have been repeatedly gripped to draw the blade. There was an iron loop on the back around the mid-point of the scabbard, and this was associated with a pair of bronze discs, underneath the sword, on either side: the remains of the suspension fittings. These fragile, sheet bronze discs were 'capped by knobs of coral' (*ibid.*, 185). A forequarter of pork had once more been laid upon his chest. A wooden shield was represented by two iron spine covers, and had been laid boss downwards in the grave, whilst over the man's body were a set of seven spearheads, lying at a variety of angles.

The excavator thought that this might imply the spear shafts had been broken before they were placed in the grave (Dent 1985, 88), but they closely resemble the 'casting in' of spears found in the Garton Station burials. If so, the corpse may have been laid within the chariot box 'coffin' (rather than this being placed *over* the corpse), permitting the gathered audience of companions to gaze upon it and throw in their spears, as part of an impressive martial departure into the next realm.

Whilst these may not seem impressive weapons, the only completely preserved example of a hafted spearhead from Iron Age Britain challenges our view of such objects. The Fiskerton spear is a slender, coppiced wand: an aerodynamic javelin 0.01m in diameter and 2m long (Field *et al.* 2003, 25 and fig. 8). Friction from the hand of the thrower was reduced by

FIGURE 6.2. Male chariot burial from Wetwang Slack (WS453) containing sword in decorated scabbard and iron spearheads. Based on Dent 1985, 87, fig. 2.

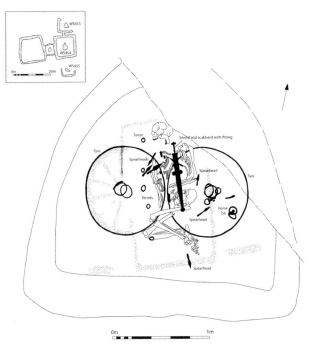

a thin layer of beeswax which coated the shaft (Rylatt, pers. comm.). Skill with this weapon was no doubt honed through hours of target-practice and hunting – spearing fleeing or cornered prey. The lack of evidence for archery in Britain is intriguing, and it suggests that by this stage, both hunting and warfare involved encounters at close-quarters, where quarry or foe could be brought down within an arm's throw. The evidence for violence (people speared in the back or shoulder, or slashed across forehead, forearms or the back of the skull) tells us about the character and rules of martial combat amongst these communities: how and where to wound an enemy. The man buried in WS453 had a severe head wound caused by a sword blow, which had healed without infection but left a permanent hole in the skull (King 2010, for further discussion, see Chapter 7). The martial culture buried with him and other individuals, enables us to augment our appreciation of these bloody performances, which as Harrell argues in her study of Mycenean weaponry, were an important 'part of dialogues of political power, reflecting and shaping cultural and local concepts of identity' (2009, 13).

How did this occur? By training with distinct forms of weaponry, the bodies of combatants had become shaped by them: the development of musculature, balance and rhythm; speed, reflex and stamina (Harrell 2009; forthcoming). Initiates would have begun to see the world differently (Târlea 2004), reacting to stimuli, responding with gestures that marked them apart from other gender groups and age-sets. They may even have seen their identity as 'socially constructed in part from violent acts' (Harrell 2009, 13), accruing respect or reputation from such incidents, embodied in scars or deformities. Theories of performance stress how the body can literally appear to 'dilate' in all-absorbing physical endeavour: transforming appearance through an explosion of energy to transfix audience or enemy. This is most memorably captured in the Irish folk epic *The Tain*, in CuCulainn's 'warp-spasm' (Kinsella 1970, 150). Eyes bulge, muscles flex, limbs distort: the body bellows and blows rain down. If we now add in the dramaturgical effects of these weapons – flashes of colour following the flesh-piercing blade – we gain a sense of how Iron Age bodies and objects melded into an enraged entity to devastating effect.

It is inevitable that the memories of such incidents were impressed upon those who witnessed the incident, or those who lived to tell the tale! Any weapon possesses symbolic capital (due to its potential power to threaten, maim and kill) but the violent biographies of these swords and spears would have enhanced their status. The worn decoration of the Wetwang sword, like that from Kirkburn, suggests that the youth in this grave had inherited an heirloom handed-down with its own powerful reputation. Like its 'brother' in the neighbouring grave and Kirkburn 'cousin' (if we can speak of relations between objects in this manner), it was also invested with other meanings: the exotic connections and craft skill exuded by their inscribed scabbards and decorated grips and pommels. In life, both the front of this man's body (protected by the shield and supported by the spear) and back (hung with an impressively decorated scabbard and sword) presented the viewer with array of exquisite weaponry. The use of contrastive colour and decorative motifs dazzled the eye, inspiring awe, perhaps even terror, at the potential for violence. Part of the purpose of such weapons was to create an atmosphere of charged menace, not only at the moment of violent confrontation, but in other settings – first encounters, judicial proceedings, disputes, and finally, the theatre of death itself – where it could be used to important social effect.

Kirkburn Burial 5

In contrast, no 'weapons' as such were found in the grave of the 'incomer' (perhaps from the North Yorkshire Moors or even further afield, see Chapter 4) buried at Kirkburn in grave 5 (Figure 5.16). Yet this is the grave in which was found the earliest evidence from Britain for a chainmail 'shirt'. We might imagine the dressing of this man in life: a coarse woollen shift was put on first, then a layer of finer fabric. Over this, the mail tunic – a smith's masterpiece – would have been tabbed into place: its breast fastener hooked over twinned studs on the shoulders. The mail would have been transparent – a single layer of interlocking rings: each less than a centimetre in diameter, made from iron wire, locked into four adjacent rings and butt-jointed (Stead 1991, 54). Its weight would have been considerable, influencing the posture of the wearer: a visual token of their strength and stamina. Yet this iron shirt was supple and fluid: tactile, eye-catching.

The lack of weapons in the grave may simply mean that they were bequeathed to someone else, but alternatively, the main function of this tunic might have been to protect an important body against attack (whether from an actual blade or more supernatural forces). The only other object found within the burial (alongside the chariot) was a 'box' or pouch, represented by a 'D-shape' lid (see Chapter 5) apparently lashed tightly shut, using a system of eyelets and ties. Again, a viewer's eye would have been drawn to this object, curious as to its contents: what it concealed within – perhaps organic materials, long-since decayed. The theme of mystery and containment evoked in the box (as with the female burial from Wetwang Slack) alluded to the bearer's ability to possess and control the unseen.

Summary

These three case studies point to the importance of adorned bodies: how they were protected and equipped, for a variety of events … social, martial, ceremonial and judicial. It is likely that there were other performances which we cannot discern archaeologically, which would have been equally important arenas for display … rites of passage such as initiations or marriages, the symbolic combat of competitive sport, feats of daring or dancing, oration and story-telling. This section has tried to conjure some of the sensory qualities of material culture – the way in which they augmented movement and enriched touch and sound, making performances dramatically memorable. It has argued that the individual's adornment with a variety of impressively crafted objects was not simply a symbol of their status. It was the *affect* of wearing them, and the wider associations they brought to the moment (their potential for

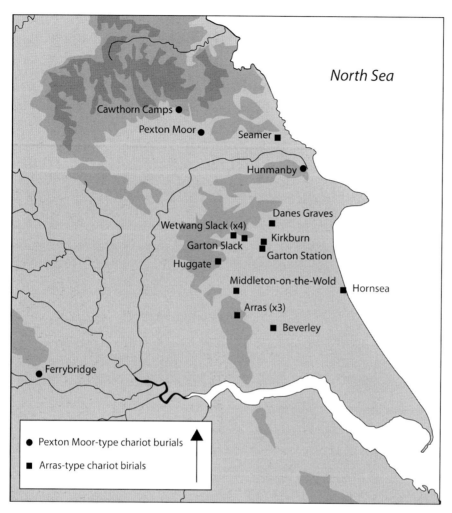

FIGURE 6.3. Distribution of chariot burials in North, East and West Yorkshire. Based on Boyle *et al.* 2007, 158, fig. 107,

violence, to look into the past or future, or conceal dangerous or secretive things) which gave social power its particular character and resonance amongst these communities.

Framing bodies and encounters: the Iron Age chariot

It was not only humans who were framed and decorated in later prehistoric East Yorkshire, using elaborate material culture: considerable attention was paid to horses and vehicles, in the ensemble of the chariot. This section will review the various elements which constituted this most complex of Iron Age objects, considering them both from a technological perspective as well as their sensory or aesthetic effects. I am interested not only in their multiple roles but how the overall impact of this vehicle was successfully achieved, through the union of driver, ponies, horse-gear and vehicle.

In total, 21 chariot burials are known in Britain: all but two of them in East and North Yorkshire (Figure 6.3). Most of these were excavated during

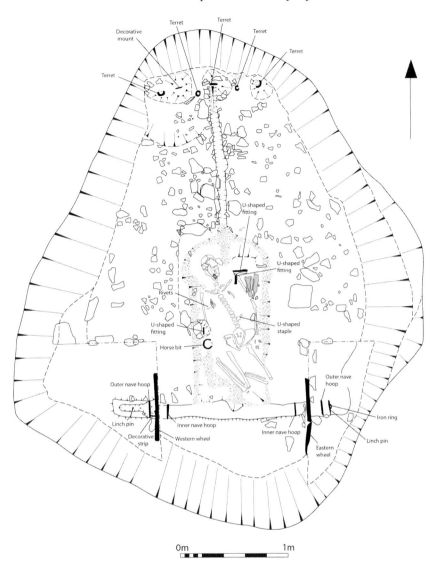

FIGURE 6.4. The Ferry
Fryston chariot burial.
Based on Boyle *et al.*
2007, 126, fig. 86.

the nineteenth century (including the three chariots from Arras) or exist as
tantalising records reported to antiquarians after the burial itself had been
demolished (such as Haywold/Huggate and possibly Hornsea). Four were found
during gravel extraction in the 1970s–80s, one at Garton Slack and three in
a cluster at Wetwang Slack. Another two were discovered during the research
excavations undertaken by the British Museum, at Kirkburn and Garton
Station. Three have been discovered in the current century during more recent
developer-funded work, in Wetwang Village but also at Ferry Fryston (West
Yorkshire) and Newbridge (near Edinburgh, Scotland). A possible chariot burial
was also identified at Slingsby, North Yorkshire but remains unexcavated (Stead
1991, 159, fig. 93). A basic distinction can be drawn between those where the
chariot is buried whole (including both of the North Yorkshire examples: Pexton
Moor and Cawthorn Camps, as well as Ferry Fryston; Figure 6.4) and those

where the chariot is disassembled before it is placed in the grave. Where buried intact, some of these appear to have been laid on the original ground surface and were covered by a mound (Pexton Moor and Cawthorn Camps) whereas Ferry Fryston and Newbridge were interred in grave pits. The 'upright' wheels of the Hunmanby burial may represent another example, or else an interment similar to Garton Station, where the wheels were stacked in the corner, against the side of the grave pit (Stead 1991, 221). In other words, the dismantling of the chariot may well be confined to the heartland of the Wolds.

Archaeologists have long debated the correct term to describe these vehicles. Antiquarians confidently used the word 'chariot', evoking the highly mobile two-wheeled war vehicle – the *essedum* – described by Caesar in *The Conquest of Gaul*, though in *The Agricola*, Tacitus also describes carts and wagons used on the edge of the battlefield. Ian Stead argued that the boxy vehicles found in East Yorkshire were better described as carts than chariots (1965, 259), since at this date, none had been found associated with weaponry. He suggested that they were primarily a funerary vehicle, designed to convey the corpse to the graveside (*ibid.*), an interpretation also favoured most recently by Sharples, in addition to their use for 'short ceremonial journeys' (2008, 211). However, in the summer of 1984, Dent recorded the presence of swords, spears and shield fittings in two new chariot burials at Wetwang Slack (1985). Stead himself discovered chain mail in the Kirkburn burial (1991) but continued to describe these vehicles as carts. Whilst not *exclusively* a vehicle of war, they may have been used in multiple ways in martial events – as the classical authors intimated – to convey combatants to the battlefield, create a platform for feats of skill, make a din and noise which intimidated their opponents, provide a platform for onlookers or even a swift means of retreat (Caesar – *The Conquest of Gaul*, book iv, 33; Tacitus – *The Agricola*, chapter 35 and *The Annals of Imperial Rome*, book xiv, chapter 34). More recently, J. D. Hill hedged his bets, whilst reporting on the 'cart/chariot' burial from Wetwang Village (e.g. 2001) but Boyle *et al.* have resurrected the term chariot, arguing that it captures more appropriately the notion of vehicles of prestige and display, suggested by their elaborate decoration (2007).

This is in keeping with Piggott's archaeological review of wheeled transport, in which he also uses the term chariot to allude to high status vehicles of worth, defined in contrast to carts as horse-drawn 'tension-structures of light bent wood with spoked wheels' (1992, 40). Piggott emphasised their role as 'parade cars', though he recognised the enhanced speed of a more lightly built vehicle held considerable potential for both martial use and display (*ibid.*). If we were to look for an historical equivalent, the light-weight gig or horse-buggy (used as both an elegant mode of transport in difficult terrain as well as in equestrian display) provides an alternative analogy for the East Yorkshire vehicles. However, the term 'buggy burial' lacks the prestigious connotations of the Continental 'chariot burial' and is thus unlikely to catch on! For this reason, the term chariot is used within this volume, to draw attention to its prestigious role in a variety of encounters whilst not ruling out its *potential* use in martial events. The date

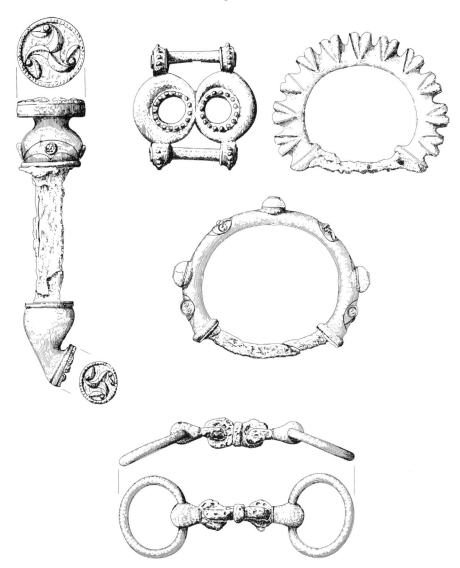

FIGURE 6.5. Horse-gear: vase-headed linch-pin (K5); strap union (K5); lipped terret (K5); knobbed terret (GS6); three-link or loop link snaffle bit/rein ring (K5). Stead 1991, figs 39, 40, 41, 44. *NB objects not illustrated to same scale.*

of these vehicle burials is much debated, partly due to the thorny question of whether some of the distinctive artefacts and art styles in the burials represent 'curated' objects. However, a recent programme of radiocarbon dating as part of the *Technologies of Enchantment: Early Celtic Art in Britain* project, suggests quite a tight range around the 2nd century BC (British Museum 2010).

Horse-gear

The horse equipment used in East Yorkshire comprised bits linked to the head harness, onto which the reins were attached (Figure 6.5). The reins passed from this harness through four rings on the yoke known as terrets, into the hands of the driver. A 5th terret (set in the centre of the yoke) was used to lash this beam tightly onto the pole shaft (Stead 1991, 58), providing some rotational flexibility 'to allow for the horses' gait' (Boyle *et al.* 2007, 143). At Ferry Fryston in West Yorkshire, an additional oval iron ring near this central terret may have provided an 'eyelet' through which the reins passed (*ibid.*, 144), and a similar additional iron ring was found near the yoke at Wetwang Slack 2 (WS454, Dent 1985, 90). Metal strap unions were sometimes present, suggesting their use as yoke attachments (Stead 1991, 47–52), connected to chest and belly bands which have themselves long-since decayed. The pole was probably pegged and braced in a 'T-shape' frame to the axle: a substantial joint which often remains rigid in the grave, whilst the rest of the cart's elements are dismantled (Stead 1991, 59). The wheels were held in place on the axle using different forms of linch pins, and the naves of the wheels were often finished with metal bands. The body of the cart – its box or platform – survives only as a stain in the soil, but clearly rested on the pole shaft, over the axle (*ibid.*, 60), though its exact means of suspension is a matter of debate (see Loades 2005).

Snaffle-bits or rein rings

The majority of the horse-bits are 'three-link' types (Stead 1979, 50) described in Palk's study as 'loop-link snaffles' (1984): two rein rings with side-loops conjoined by a central double-link ring. However, both the Wetwang Slack male burial (WS453, Dent 1985, 88) and the Wetwang Village examples are two-linked bits or single-jointed snaffles (Hill 2004). Sometimes the rings were bimetallic (Cunliffe 1995b): made of iron covered in sheet bronze, with solid copper alloy links (as in the King's and Lady's barrows at Arras). In both of these examples, knobbed 'stops' either side of the side-links were designed to prevent movement and wear (Stead 1965, 37). This was ironic, given that one of the rein rings in the King's Barrow had been miscast at the wrong angle, and could never have been used as a working piece of harness (Stead 1979, 49)! In contrast, the bit from the Lady's Barrow was appreciably worn (*ibid.*). The cast bronze stop on the Wetwang Village bit was decorated with a red glass stud, cross-quartered in a dazzling design and raised on an impressive 'bridge' (Hill 2004) paralleled in the decoration on the Battersea shield (Hill 2002). Solid iron bits are known from the Beverley Westwood, Garton Slack, Wetwang Slack (WS453) and Pexton Moor chariot burials, and a solid bronze example was found at Hunmanby. The fragmentary remains of the iron bit(s) from Ferry Fryston comprised two rings and two links, which may have been conjoined by an organic element (Boyle *et al.* 2007, 141). Corrosion products associated with these elements bore the impression of a flat sheet of horn, attached to a crescent-shape object which was riveted to a thin iron sheet – but it was not clear how this functioned in relation to the bit (*ibid.*). The Pexton Moor bit had a simple 'O' ring as a central loop, with large iron side-links, one of which retains fragments of its bronze case (Stead 1979, 47–8). The side-links are often cast at a set angle from the rein rings (usually around 152°–145°, though it can be more acute; *ibid.*, 49), to fit around the horse's mouth and cheeks. Interestingly, the Wetwang Slack female chariot burial bits are decorated only on the outer bulbous terminal of each set (Dent 1985, 90): suggesting a deliberate elaboration of the side seen by a viewer, with the undecorated terminals on the 'inner' cheeks of the ponies, as they jostled side-by-side.

Snaffle-bits are designed to exert pressure on the corners of the horses' mouth (Littauer and Crouwel 2001, 334) and if used forcefully or fitted incorrectly, can cause significant mouth injuries (Scoggins 1989). Stillingfleet described the Arras bits as 'harsh': similar to 'our own horse-breakers' (1847): a sentiment echoed by Brewster who described the three-link bit type as 'fierce', necessary for driving a team in 'hilly country' (1971, 291). Yet their simple form and lack of subsidiary control features such as spikes, suggests they are actually quite 'soft': designed for communicating intention – persuasive co-operation rather than breaking, training or aggressive coercion (Argent pers. comm.). Whilst dating to the later Iron Age, one of the horses buried at Kirkburn site 2 (not far from Garton Station) may have worn a similar design of harness. It bore 'champing' bit-wear patterns on the anterior surfaces of the upper and lower permanent second premolar teeth (Legge in Stead 1991, 144), suggesting it had also been able to lift the bit onto its teeth, preventing it from 'biting' into the flesh of the mouth (Anthony and Brown 1989, cited by Legge, *ibid.*). The bits suggest drivers were able to convey their desires to a well-attuned and obedient team rather than exerting will through force or pain.

Ironically, there is scant evidence of the ponies themselves: only in two cases do they seem to have been sacrificed and interred with the chariot … Seamer and the King's Barrow at Arras: 'the head of each being placed not far from that of the man' (Greenwell 1906, 280). Stillingfleet records them as being around 13 hands in height (1846, 29), an estimation agreed with by Stead, on the basis of the late Iron Age/early Roman double horse burial near Rudston (1991, 59). A slightly smaller animal is described by Boyle *et al.* on the basis of the Ferry Fryston chariot remains, around 11–12 hands (1.12–1.22 m) in height (2007, 145). We are dealing here with small but sturdy animals, whose pairing and training demanded such an investment that they were spared their driver and vehicle's fate on almost every occasion (as depicted in Peter Connolly's famous reconstruction illustration). Instead, the pair of bits deposited in all but three graves (Pexton Moor, Hunmanby and Ferry Fryston) may have metaphorically represented the team in the afterlife.

Terrets and Yoke

Of the reins which once linked to these bits, nothing remains but stains which suggest they were made of 'leather' – more correctly skin or hide products. They would have passed from the rein rings through the four terrets (normally found *in situ* along the line of the yoke) to prevent the reins from tangling. Yokes varied slightly in length, averaging just over a metre (Stead 1991) and where measurable, were at least 30mm in diameter (Boyle *et al.* 2007, 143). Soil stains under the Ferry Fryston yoke suggested possible decayed 'padding' to ease the weight borne by the horses (Boyle *et al.* 2007, fig. 89).

The terrets were placed with surprisingly regularity at 0cm, 30cm, 50cm, 70cm and 100cm along the yoke (see Stead 1991, fig. 42). They are usually 'D' shaped: their straight bars bound to the flat surface of the yoke (which may have been slightly morticed to receive them) as evidenced in organic staining of 'rawhide' binding at Ferry Fryston (Boyle *et al.* 2007: 138), mineralised skin/leather thongs at Garton Station (Stead 1991, 47) and mineralised impressions of wood or leather at Garton Slack (Brewster 1971, 291). At many burials like Ferry Fryston and Wetwang Slack 2 (WS454), a deliberate aesthetic 'pairing' effect can be noted, graduating from the largest central terret to smaller middle terrets, and medium-sized outer terrets. At Wetwang Village, this graduation was reversed so that the terrets descended in size from the central example to the smallest outer terrets (Hill 2004). The pivotal role of the central terret (lashing the yoke to the pole) was marked by its size, and provided an important flexible joint, responsive both to the movement of the team and the impact of terrain.

Some of the terrets are plain, rounded 'D-shape' bars made of solid copper alloy but others are again bimetallic, with iron cores/bars and bronze sheeting wrapped around the main body (as in the Wetwang Slack chariot burials). Iron bars with pouting bronze 'lip-mouldings' were found in several burials, including the Lady and King's barrows from Arras. At Kirkburn (K5) the smaller terrets had eight and nine 'lips', the medium terrets had ten 'lips' and the central large terret had eleven 'lips' (Stead 1991, fig. 40). Whilst this could represent simple craft expediency or the fact that these were not an original set of matching terrets, Spratling sees such variation as part of the aesthetics of Celtic art, in which uniqueness and even deliberate asymmetry was key (2008, 198, also Jope 2000). The main four terrets at Garton Station were cast entirely in copper alloy with both low-relief ring-and-dot mouldings and incised decoration, but the largest terret had an iron bar (Stead 1991, 47). This terret was marvellously decorated with three settings holding domed discs of bone, secured by copper alloy rivets whose heads bore a moulded 'berried rosette' design. Cast relief ornament on the main body of dot, lobe and trumpet-motifs, further drew the eye. Meanwhile, the Garton Slack terrets were decorated with coral studs, riveted in place with copper alloy pins, though one stud had been lost (Brewster 1975, 111). At Wetwang Slack 2 (WS454) three impressive terrets were decorated with seven coral beads, as well as engraved and cast moulded designs, and two smaller terrets (flanking the central massive example) bore three coral beads apiece. Three coral beads also decorated the set of terrets from Wetwang Village (Hill 2004). Several terrets show signs of wear (such as Garton Slack, GS11: Barrow 2) and a stud from a terret at Wetwang Village was replaced with cut slivers of red glass 'enamel' (Hill 2001). At Wetwang Slack 454, strips of copper alloy may have been nailed to the yoke: interpreted by the excavator as 'repair patches' or decorative fittings (J. Dent, pers. comm.) they are described below as the possible remains of a whip or stock.

Some of these objects evidently had long histories indicated by wear or repair but metallurgical analysis of the terrets from the Ferry Fryston burial revealed them to be a 'sham': leaded copper alloy sheaths, containing a clay/silt core (Swiss and McDonnall 2007a; 2007b). The excavators suggested that if this vehicle had done more than trundle to the graveside, these bronze fittings would have quickly shattered, suggesting these elements of the chariot were purpose-made for the funeral (Boyle *et al.* 2007).

Strap unions

Of the strap unions used to tie other harness elements together, two main forms have been found. The 'figure of eight' form with straight side-bars, cast in copper alloy has been found at Kirkburn K5: decorated with moulded raised dots and concentric rings on their terminals (Stead 1991, 49). Slightly smaller examples were found at Garton Slack (Brewster 1980). Their position in the grave suggests they were attached to the ends of the yoke and were used to adjust the girth, taking straps around 20mm in breadth (Stead 1991, 49). In contrast, the slender open-work strap unions from Wetwang Village could only have taken narrow straps (Hill 2004).

The vehicle

Wheels

The wheels of the chariots from East Yorkshire vary between 70 cm (Cawthorn Camps) to 90 cm diameter (Hunmanby, Garton Station, Kirkburn and the Wetwang Slack burials: Stead 1991, 42). The broad rims of Garton Slack (44 mm) contrast with the narrower widths of Cawthorn Camps (35 mm) and Kirkburn (34 mm). The profile of these rims was often flat or slightly dished and sometimes 'flanged', downturned at the edges, or thickened, either purposefully (to grip the inner wooden wheel) or as a result of use and wear (Stead 1991, 40–2; Boyle *et al.* 2007, 133). The lack of nails suggests that all of the rims were 'heat-shrunk' onto wooden tyres in a dramatic 'tyring' performance: a moment of great risk when the difference of half an inch could spoil the work of both carpenter and smith (Sturt 1923, 119). Expanded by intense heat, the rim would have been thrown over the wheel and hammered into place: the wood quickly doused where it began to smoke and flame from the blistering grip of the iron (*ibid.*, 126). This process contracted all the joints of the felloes (the inner wooden rim), spokes and hub or stock: pulling them tightly into place with a great cracking sound. Where identifiable, these inner parts were usually made of ash (*Fraxinus*) or at Ferry Fryston, ash or oak (*Quercus*). Where they could be discerned from stains in the soil and chalk gravel, as at Wetwang chariot burial 1 and 2 (WS453, WS454), Garton Station and Garton Slack, there were 12 spokes on each wheel, though Kirkburn may have had 13-spoke wheels. These were inserted into sockets in the felloes and did not penetrate all the way through to the wheel rim. This is usually an indication that the felloes were made of a single piece of wood bent into a hoop: its ends butt- or scarf-jointed together, as indicated in the single impression on the iron rims at Wetwang 2 (WS454), Garton Station and Kirkburn (Stead 1991, fig. 34). However, the Ferry Fryston wheel retained the impression of at least three lines or joints, which might indicate it was unusually made of quartered segments dowelled together (unless these were cracks in the timber, Boyle *et al.* 2007, 133) and the Charioteer's barrow at Arras may also have had a multiple felloe construction (Stead 1979, 44). In the former method of construction, the single join was sometimes strengthened or repaired with an iron 'dog', cleet or clamp, as at Danes Graves (DG43/Mortimer 1898 no. 13), and all three Wetwang Slack chariots (Dent 1985).

Craft accounts of cart-making tell us that such wood was carefully selected by carpenters who had sized up its potential as the trees grew (Rose 1937, chapter iii) and were also knowledgeable about how local soils affected the growth of the grain (Sturt 1923, 26). They also designed their vehicles to fit the landscape in which they would travel, knowing the character of the tracks and the effect of weather upon them (*ibid.*, 66). The most detailed analysis of their metallurgical components has been carried out on the Ferry Fryston chariot, and whilst it falls outside of the main distribution of the Arras burials, it throws interesting light upon both the biography of these vehicles and craft organisation in the Iron Age. The iron tyres suggest these wheels were not a matching pair: with different diameters (85 cm and 87 cm) they would have created a slightly lop-sided vehicle. The west wheel was decorated with unique open-work decorative strips, nailed to its outer nave hoop. The iron tyre of this wheel appeared to derive from a single source, with little evidence of intermediary working before it was forged into the final product (Swiss and McDonnall 2007a). However, the east wheel appeared to be forged from many different bars of iron, derived from different stocks or workshops, which had been forged together – creating a streaky banding effect, when viewed microscopically (*ibid.*). Both showed evidence of cold-working, which the metallurgists interpreted as evidence of use and wear, impacting on the micro-structure and hardness of the tyres. In other words, contrary to the terrets from the same vehicle, these wheels had been extensively used before they were donated or recycled from other chariots (one perhaps a little more grand than the other) for the funeral ceremony. Interestingly, at Newbridge, one of the wheels is believed to represent a replacement (Carter *et al.* 2010, 52). On the Wolds, Brewster argued that the Garton Slack chariot had one new and one worn wheel tyre (1975, 111) and Mortimer also recorded that the Danes Graves tyres were of different dimensions (78 cm and 74 cm): a difference too great to attribute solely to distortion in the grave. Finally, it is worth reiterating Peter Halkon's estimates that to make one such iron wheel (weighing an average of 4 kg) would have taken 700 kg of charcoal, representing 5 tonnes of wood and approximately 130 person days of labour (2008, 172). These objects represent substantial investments of resources, time and skill, and may have been re-used or handed down as heirlooms in their own right.

Nave bands

The central piece of the wheel: its nave, hub, or stock, was finished and secured by a series of nave bands on both the exterior and interior faces. These varied between 125–300 mm in diameter and between the fine 7 mm bands from the Lady's Barrow at Arras, to 14 mm wide (at Garton Station) and 50 mm wide (Kirkburn), and were made either in a rectangular or more 'D' shape cross-section profile (Stead 1991, 41–2). Some bands were made of solid iron, as at Wetwang Slack 3 (WS455) or iron cores decorated in copper alloy sheaths, as at Wetwang Slack (WS454), where mineralised impressions also suggested strips of hide had been used on the underside edge of the bands (Dent 1984a). In the case of the King's Barrow at Arras, the bronze case was folded over and tucked under the iron rim, but in the Lady's Barrow from the same site, it was left projecting as a wide flange (Stead 1979, 44). The same effect was noted at Ferry Fryston, but as discussed above, two open-work decorative strips adorned the west wheel. Nailed between the outer nave band and the inner face of the tyre by the spokes, they were delicately shaped to fit the swell of the hub (Boyle *et al.* 2007, 134). The nave bands themselves were low in arsenic but had a significant lead content: a recipe which the metallurgical analysts suggested might be designed to produce a particular colour and sheen (Swiss and McDonnall 2007b). Pure copper alloy nave-hoops were found at Garton Slack and Kirkburn, and a crack in the latter had been repaired with a small iron patch (Stead 1991, fig. 43:4). Interestingly, at Garton Slack, there were three nave-hoops of bronze and one of iron (Brewster 1971), suggesting one had been replaced. The Kirkburn nave bands had a decorative central cordon (*ibid.*), and the nail-heads from the Lady's Barrow at Arras were punched with concentric-ring decoration (Stead 1979, 40, fig. 11).

Pole shaft and axle

Of the pole shaft and axle, jointed to form the main frame of the chariot, nothing remains except slight stains in the soil. At Garton Station, the replacement of a section of the wood by clay-rich infill indicated the pole was at least 1.25 m long. The differential height of these clay lenses gave the excavator to believe the pole had a curve or double-bend along its length, which may have 'arced' over the body interred underneath (Stead 1991, 59, fig. 48). Its probable overall length has been estimated as at least 3m, projecting forward from the axle to the point where it was lashed to the yoke at the front (*ibid.*). The end of the pole sometimes appears to have been finished or decorated by a pole-sheath or cap-end, such as the slightly curved copper alloy sheath from the Charioteer's Barrow at Arras (Fox 1949; Stead 1965, 35).

The axle to which the pole was presumably pegged and braced, varies in its preserved stain between 2.2 m (Garton Station), 2.0 m (Garton Slack) and slightly less in the Wetwang Slack chariot burials (Stead 1991, 59). However, it is difficult to determine the actual wheel-track of the vehicle, since the width of the nave and distance between the linch-pin and end of the axle can seldom be estimated. Whilst beyond these immediate case studies, voids recorded at Ferry Fryston suggested the axle was largely square or rectangular in cross-section, with an axle projection of over 30 cm outside of the wheels' outer rims, and an internal track of 1.37 m (Boyle *et al.* 2007, 127). In the Garton Slack burial, an iron case or cylinder interpreted by Brewster as a pole-cap actually appears to have been part of a binding on the eastern end of the axle (Brewster 1971, 290; Stead 1991, 59) but its twin (if there was one) had either been lost or removed before burial. At Wetwang Village, plastercast evidence suggested the axle had been tapered, with circular swellings inside the wheels to act as 'stops' (Hill 2002, 411).

Linch pins

The ensemble of wheel, nave and nave bands, and axle, were held in place through the linch-pin: a metaphorically rich object still used to describe people or objects that hold things together. As with many other elements of horse-gear, some were composites of iron and bronze, perhaps the most dazzling of which are the Kirkburn 'vase-headed' linchpins (see Stead 1991, fig. 38). Each has an iron stem or shank, with a perforated copper alloy head. These consist of a moulded roundel decorated with 'a relief triskele motif, terminating in 'bird heads', surrounded by a raised beaded border' (*ibid.*, 44). The perforation is also decorated by a raised arch, and between the opposing holes a pelta-like motif encloses a seven-berried rosette design. The upturned foot, resembling a raised horse's hoof, contains a miniature version of the design on the head. At Kirkburn, these objects were corroded together with two 'miniature' terrets (flat on one side, rounded on the other), designed to 'tie off' or secure the strap (approx. 7 mm wide) which once threaded through the perforation (*ibid.*). One of the linchpins had wear facets where the strap bar of its miniature terret had knocked against the metal. Mineralised impressions suggest the thong was made of fur or hide which had not been scraped clean of its fibres.

Parallels for the Kirkburn linchpins exist in the corroded examples from the King's Barrow at Arras, but ring-headed forms are also known, as in the worn example from the Middleton chariot burial. Here, the head-ring is circumscribed by an incised zig-zag ornament, and near the perforation, it is decorated by a roundel inset with red glass 'enamel'. The delicate punched decoration on the iron and copper alloy linchpin from Wetwang Slack chariot burial 2 (WS454) was also worn through polishing and rubbing (Dent 1985, 90). Pure iron 'J' shape linchpins were found at Garton Station, their ring-heads associated with smaller iron rings which presumably performed the same role as the miniature terrets. The same form of linchpin was also used in the Wetwang Village chariot burial whilst simple straight bar 'J' shape iron linchpins, with perforations in their shank and associated miniature iron rings, were recovered from Ferry Fryston (Boyle *et al.* 2007, 136). A square-headed iron linchpin was found at Danes Graves (Stead 1979, 41). In contrast, two well-polished pieces of curved antler from the Charioteer's Barrow at Arras are also assumed to be linchpins: perforated just below a head 'zone' carved with lattice ornament. Again these are appreciably worn. These are paralleled by a pair of deer antler linchpins from Wetwang Slack 1 (WS453), which utilised the natural curve of the tine for strength (Dent 1984a). Brewster even commented that the apparent lack of linchpins at Garton Slack might suggest they were made of hardened wood (1971, 291).

Box/platform and possible decorative elements
The general lack of metal fittings suggest that the superstructure of the chariot was a lightweight platform. It is generally (though not universally) assumed that the soil stains around the body represent the 'box' of the chariot: used like a coffin (Dent 1985; Stead 1991; Hill 2002, though see Anthoons 2011). If so, evidence from Wetwang Slack and Kirkburn would suggest these were straight-sided, solid structures, with some slight evidence for 'planking' noted at the former site (Dent 1985, 48). Though many assume it was inverted to cover the corpse, Mackey notes that the 'shadow' of the soil stain at Wetwang Village became more solid towards the base, suggesting it was laid flat: containing and framing the body (cited in Anthoons 2011). At Garton Station, the hint of an open front end was suggested by such impressions (Stead 1991, 61), an arrangement also suggested by the soil stains at Wetwang Village (Hill 2002), whilst Ferry Fryston had a slightly bow-shaped or open end (Boyle *et al.* 2007). As Anthoons notes, the box may not have been a solid timber frame but could have incorporated wickerwork, hide or textile elements (2011). These 'boxes' varied from around 1.8–1.9 m long, by 1.2 m wide to 1.5–1.65 m long by 0.95–1.0 m wide (Stead 1991, 60). Their size may indicate that there was a single driver whose skill rested in their individual ability to harness the power of vehicle and horse-team. However, being 'driven' by another would have created its own mystique: a motionless body on the move, conveyed through the landscape by the effort of driver and team (Giles 2008, 70).

Most of these vehicles appear to have been made solely of organic components but at Garton Slack, fragments of wood attached to small pieces of sheet bronze were interpreted as part of a collapsed, decorated canopy (Brewster 1971, 291). However, such elements may have been part of the sides or base. Decorative ornaments which might have adorned the vehicle include a bronze disc from the Charioteer's barrow at Arras: dished in the centre with a raised cordon, and pierced through by an iron nail (Stead 1979, 53). Its bronze binding was still attached to a round circle of wood when excavated, and although it could be a shield boss, it might also be part of a cart ornament analogous to historic 'horse brasses' (*ibid.*). In the same burial, a smaller bronze disc with cut-out ornament, delicate iron rings and a nailed strip of iron may represent vehicle or shield fittings. At Danes Graves, another small bronze disc, iron ring and button-shaped plates of thin copper alloy (one faintly engraved with a 4-spoke 'wheel' design) might similarly represent cart ornaments or decorative elements attached to an unknown organic object (Mortimer 1897, 9–10).

Radically different designs for 'chariot' platforms include the webbed, interlaced hide base (Hurford n.d.) and 'Y' frame sides used on the recent

Wetwang Village 'reconstruction' (Loades 2005) but this latter project drew upon multiple sources of evidence such as inscriptions on Gaulish coins, which are anachronistic for the East Yorkshire examples. The easy removal of the box during the funeral ceremony might suggest some underlying suspension system, which could have been easily converted for use at faster speeds in military escapades or show-piece displays (Stead 1991, 61) but at present, no trace of this survives in the Arras style burials.

Driver's accoutrements

A small number of other accoutrements represent the final elements which conjoined driver, vehicle and horse-team. These are the bronze cap, reminiscent of a box-lid (25 mm in diameter) found in the Lady's Barrow at Arras: its two long pins originally fastened to wood, which led Greenwell to interpret it as a whip-end (1877, 456). At Garton Slack, two copper alloy ferrules, arranged in a line, were also interpreted as the far end of a whip or goad: its pommel decorated with a stumpy 'T' shaped case, formed of discs and strips hammered onto the stock end with 19 small bronze nails (Brewster 1971, 290; 1980, 405–6, figs 241–4). Brewster tentatively identified the mineralised wood impressions inside this case as cherry (1980, 385). Two slightly deformed, semi-circular pieces of copper alloy sheeting with punched-dot edging, from the northern end of the yoke at Wetwang Slack 2 (the female chariot burial) may also derive from a flaring whip-stock. Although outside of the key study area, a strange decorative mount from Ferry Fryston, made of copper alloy, may be a unique example of a 'rein connector' (Boyle *et al.* 2007, 141), and its five perforated holes would fit either the strands of hide or fingertips of a slender hand. It was associated with a blackish substance which may indicate it was padded with now-decayed skin products (*ibid.*).

The chariot: interpreting biography and use

The above summary reveals the subtle variation in style and form, around a set of strikingly similar chariot fittings. The notion of such a vehicle may have had its design-origin on the Continent in the 4th century BC (Cunliffe 1995b) though its nearest comparisons in terms of funerary rites appear broadly contemporary from the Champagne region (Anthoons 2011). Soon after, it was being made and deposited in an idiosyncratic manner in Yorkshire. As discussed earlier, new analysis suggests a broad range of possible dates, from the 4th–3rd centuries BC, into the 3rd–2nd centuries BC, with a strong possibility that they cluster around 200 BC: neither particularly early or notably late in the rite (C. Haselgrove, pers. comm.). Some may represent a particular pulse of burials: a trend, within the broader history of these cemeteries. Clearly, more vehicles were in circulation than ended up in graves since elements of these chariots were matched up with other sets: repaired and recycled, when parts broke or wore out. Other pieces (a cherished set of horse-gear, a particularly elaborate wheel) seem to have been bequeathed, gifted or donated, as social occasion demanded. They may even have been circulated as separate, venerated elements as Sharples suggests (2008, 211).

Although it lies outside of the Wolds, the Ferry Fryston chariot has been discussed as a remarkable composite object, with 'sham' terrets freshly made for the funeral, combined with old, distinguished wheels from different workshops and vehicles. The Kirkburn chariot may provide another example. One wheel was slightly more worn, and had a more flanged profile than the other (Stead 1991, 42). Its grazed linchpins (like those of Wetwang Slack 2) also suggest a significant history of use, whilst the non-matching terrets might have been composed from a series of original sets. Whilst one of the Arras horse-bits from the King's Barrow could never have been worn, the bits from the neighbouring Lady's Barrow were well-used. Alongside other evidence for non-matching sets or pairings of old and new objects, these richly varied biographies suggest that the chariot was not simply an elaborate hearse or vehicle for the afterlife – many had long histories of use before they were interred in the grave. But what was the chariot used for?

In a world delineated by linear earthworks and trackways – by the surveillance and scrutiny of people's comings and goings – the chariot enhanced both the drama and 'hitherto unfulfilled psychological excitement of speed in motion' (Piggott 1992, 42). Piggott famously described the Celtic chariot as part of a techno-complex: a 'package deal' of horses, horse-breakers and trainers, harness- and vehicle-makers (craftspeople able to work with composite materials), resources of fodder and stabling, trained drivers and their accoutrements (1992, 45), as well as appropriate settings and occasions for their display. Clearly, the taking-up of such a package had both considerable costs and consequences, so why did the East Yorkshire communities embrace it? If its origins were exotic, its very novelty helped create a sense of difference which helped establish people's authority. The chariot can be thought of as a special technology of power, which literally compressed time and space, and this quality may help us to understand one of its symbolic roles in the funerary context: negotiating the journey into the afterlife (see Chapter 7). Whilst it may never have travelled particularly far or fast (Sharples 2008, 211), it would have provided an 'ostentatious' mode of transport (Coles 2002, 239). Such vehicles framed and raised their occupants above the bodies of others: using physical elevation and distance, to reproduce social standing and difference. Those who rode in these chariots looked down upon people forced to straighten their backs to see it pass (see Kerr 1968, 11). This would not only have helped reassert authority in one's own community but also provided their drivers with a psychological advantage in meetings with other groups, visits to neighbouring valleys, competitive exchange events or displays of strength or prowess. It might also have enhanced authority during disputes: a form of 'visual weaponry' as Coles describes it (2002, 239).

The beautiful workmanship, colour and noise of the horse-gear, the tossed manes and thudding hooves of the horses, as well as the gestures and orders of the driver would have created a memorable performance of arrivals and departures. Sound may have been cupped and channelled down the narrow dales and open slacks of the Wolds, as it approached. Like the horse-brasses of the 19th century (Vince 2010), the auditory and visual effect of this jangling set of shining objects, coupled with kicked-up dust, announced the chariot's approach (Smith 1979, 81). Speaking of the experience of travelling in the creaking, groaning woodwork of a contemporary reconstruction, Mike Loades described it as like being in a wood in a storm (2005). It is easy to see how this assemblage of people, animals and things could create a truly intimidating, even terrifying sight.

Whilst it may have occasionally been used in a vengeful raid, on a field of conflict or even to meet out judicial punishment, it was not simply a weapon of warfare. It would have enhanced all kinds of processions and ceremonies, both religious and social, making an excellent platform for oration and debate, as well as a providing a stage for feats of dexterity and prowess (Pare 1989). The worn, scuffed linchpins, the flattened and hardened wheels, and repaired terrets tell us of multiple events and journeys, empowered by these vehicles. Its final journey was of course, to the graveside: first as a bier or hearse, before it became part of the burial architecture, conveying its occupant on into the afterlife. Either as an individual or family possession, or a communally-owned vehicle harnessed to a variety of needs and purposes, I would argue its importance derived from this flexibility. Wherever it went the chariot 'showcased' wealth and authority: craft skill, the command of animals, the dextrous control of speed and movement … or its corollaries: embarrassing failures to control a run-away team, in-elegant dismounting, unexpected jolts or falls. Driving these vehicles was impressive *because* it was risky: fraught with potential mishap or danger.

The chariot: a technology of enchantment?

The care taken in the making and decoration of its multiple components suggests drivers took great pride in these vehicles: a joy captured in the poem from *The Book of Songs* (a Chinese masterpiece, dating to 800–600 BC) quoted by Piggott in *Wagons, Chariot and Carriages* (1992, 68). The poem begins with a litany of chariot-gear: numbers of artefacts and materials described in loving detail, before the strength and beauty of the reined horses are also conjured for the listener. From the above descriptions, it is evident that many of the decorative touches – delicate punched arcading on a linch-pin, a red glass stud on a terret – would seldom have been seen close-to. Whilst they added to the splash of colour and blurred dazzle of this vehicle in motion, their embellishment suggests it was just as important to 'know' these decorative touches were there. As part of a status set of objects, it no doubt delighted those who prepared this elegant team: fitting and securing the gear and flicking the whip-stock to set them off. Yet were such objects simply decorative? An analogy could be sought with the horse-brasses of the 19th and 20th centuries, which were not only pleasing to the eye but also used 'lucky symbols' (horse-shoes, clover leafs, sun-wheels) to bring good fortune (Smith 1979) and protect vulnerable parts of the horse's body (Hartfield 1965). The motifs on the Iron Age chariot gear may never have been intended to be 'read' like these symbols, but it is worth considering how they were decorated and what affect this had.

The anthropologist Alfred Gell saw complex and intricate art as a special form of technology, designed to catch the eye of an audience: securing them in a network of relations and intentions (1998). He called this a 'technology of enchantment' (1992). Gell used Celtic designs as a key example of artwork which exuded a 'halo effect' of power, derived from its extraordinary complexity and maze of interwoven motifs (see Giles 2008). Allusions to avian and faunal elements, parts of human faces, flows of water or the intertwined growth of vegetation: the deliberately phantasmagoric effects of Celtic art design may allude to ideas about transmutation between states of being or shape-shifting powers, as various authors have suggested (e.g. Green 1996, 137; Stevens 2007). However, it also achieved another important affect. Interlocking patterns, raised or embossed zones which cast other areas into sharp relief, contrastive swirls of hatched decoration and voids, made what Gell has described as a complex 'mind trap' for the viewer (1996; 1998, 80). Its deliberate asymmetry drew the eye, creating a swaying, confusing impression in the observer (Jope 2000). Such art was 'barely comprehensible in its virtuosity' (Thomas 1998, viii) and Gell argued that this was often attributed to magical involvement in the craft process: spiritual or ancestral favour which permitted the human artisan to achieve other-wordly effects. As a result, such objects were often perceived to have innate powers: an agency which could intimidate, awe and disarm (1998). Thomas uses this concept to explain the decoration of both Papua New Guinean war clubs and Trobriand Islanders' canoes, deployed respectively in contexts of war and exchange to demoralise and 'win over' opponents, before the first blows or negotiations had even begun (1995). He describes this as an effective kind of psychological warfare: a 'highly aetheticised terrorism' (1995, 97). The other function of such art however, was to trap non-human forces – malign spirits or supernatural entities – acting as a kind of 'demonic flypaper' in which evil became ensnared (Gell 1998, 84). (A similar idea was discussed long before Gell, in the work of both Lenerz-de Wilde (1977), who commented on the 'potency' of highly complex, geometric Celtic art, and Pauli (1975) who noted its apotropaic potential – V. Megaw, pers. comm.). Highly decorated Celtic art objects may thus have had a dual purpose: simultaneously *protective* of the body whilst *projective* of its strength, power and skill. These ideas add another dimension to the decorated objects of power discussed above, such as containers, mirrors and scabbards (see Giles 2008). Importantly, the chariot gear suggests that in East Yorkshire, it was not simply human bodies which were protected in this fashion, but also horses and vehicles.

In sum, the ensemble of the chariot achieved its power through its technological affects: the visual impact of its appearance as well as the skilled harnessing of humans, animals, objects and vehicle in impressive performances. Even sedate arrivals and departures (such as the tricky manoeuvring around a graveside) exhibited the trusting union born of long-term practice between driver, chariot and team. Such an intimate relationship would have been all the more important if in the Wolds, horsemen and women engaged in the feats of dexterity witnessed by Caesar in Book IV: chapter 33 of *The Conquest of Gaul*. During the invasion of Briton, he describes how the Britons could 'control the horses at full gallop [and] … check and turn them in a moment', or 'run along the chariot pole, stand on the yoke, and get back into the chariot as quick as lightening' (*ibid.*). Like Thomas' Trobriand canoeists, the sheer finery of the chariots accoutrements may have 'thrilled and invigorated' the drivers (1995, 103), but its apotropaic qualities may also have strengthened the resolve of those attempting more risky performances.

Staging death

In *A Man Holding Up A Horse's Bridle*, the author John Berger recalls a local farmer holding out the halter belonging to his aged, white mare, Biche. It is 'encrusted with white from the salt of her sweat and the foam of her mouth' (1996b, 103). '*Do you know what that means?*' the man asks quietly. '*Yes*' the author responds '*it means she has been taken away.*' The farmer continues to brandish the object. '*Fifteen years working together is a long time.*' Finally, he hangs the bridle on its wooden peg behind the stable door. '*Everything has its end*' he says. It was, Berger recalls, 'the only time I ever saw him make a theatrical gesture' (*ibid.*).

This passage perfectly encapsulates the themes discussed so far in this chapter, of performances with objects which bring to light the social relations which underpin their own identity. It also moves us into the final arena of performance I want to discuss: that of death. Berger's story reminds us that even small-scale bits of 'theatre' like this – the hanging of a bridle on a peg, just like the placing of snaffle bits in a grave – can be pivotal ways in which people marked and worked through the loss of close human *and* non-human partners, with whom they have laboured, sweated, even fought. Such objects do not merely represent the conditions of those lives, but the condensations of those identities and relationships. The rest of the chapter explores the performative dimensions of funerary rituals, where they can be glimpsed in the archaeological evidence.

Tableau, poem or play? Performing death

Gazing at the dramatic black-and-white image of the chariot burials from Wetwang Slack, it is easy for a moment to be over-awed by the tableau (Figure 6.6). Take the female burial from Wetwang Slack for example (WS452), discussed above: her arms stretched out in front of the body, as if shaking the reins of her ponies, the cluster of impressive artefacts behind her head and back,

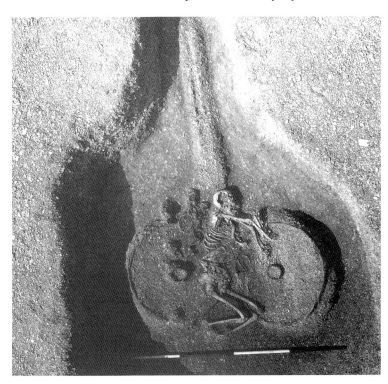

FIGURE 6.6. The dramatic
tableau of the Wetwang
Slack (WS454) female
chariot burial.
COURTESY OF JOHN DENT AND HUMBER FIELD
ARCHAEOLOGY

the structure of the cart arranged under and around her corpse. It successfully
captures the contextual relationship between body, grave goods and funerary
architecture. Yet this frozen moment is an illusion. Burial was a performance:
choreographed in time and space, by the mourners (see Williams 2006). In this
sense, we can think of it as a visual poem: rich in metaphor and symbolism
(Carver 2000), or a play, set within the stage of the grave. There were, no doubt,
speeches or songs to be uttered, roles to perform, but the event (as we shall
see) was improvised in real time. Thus the image we commonly represent in
archaeological publications: the aerial view of the plan or photograph, would
never have been seen by these participants. If we want to understand how
these burials structured peoples' identities, we must be interested in unpicking
the order and character of events: the way funerary architecture structured
relationships between bodies (the proxemics of burial), and affected the sensual
experiences of the audience.

Wrapping and concealment

There is some evidence that the dead were not always immediately interred,
and that some were placed on view (as at Sewerby Farm Cottage and possibly,
Garton Slack), or were curated for a while (as with WS209, whose story opened
this chapter). Primary rites of mourning might have marked the moment of
death, precipitating the gathering of mourners and resources (grave goods, food

and drink) and the preparation of the burial mound. The second stage involved the assembling of corpse and grave furniture. In the case of several of the chariot burials, this took time to organise: gathering elements from different donors, or even manufacturing new items for inclusion, as in the case of the terrets at Ferry Fryston. A more mundane example is suggested in the poorly made ceramic vessels and even some of the spearheads of the Great Wold Valley (Stead 1991). In various cases, there is evidence that during this phase the corpse was gradually concealed, usually within a shroud: closed with pins or brooches. Additionally or alternatively, some were placed in a 'coffin', consisting of planking or a box frame which helped contain the corpse and whose stain survives in the soil. The higher proportion of brooches in cemeteries like Rudston may indicate a preference for the former, whereas coffin stains were more common at Wetwang Slack. In the chariot burials, the box of the vehicles formed the most elaborate kind of coffin, whether it covered or contained the body. In the weapons burials which feature in the next chapter, an additional object helped conceal the body: literally 'shielding' it from open view. The bindings, bosses and mineralised wood impressions of these defensive objects suggest they were commonly laid over the stomach and chest region of the corpse. There was thus a hierarchy of choices resulting in the same effect: the framing and gradual concealment of the corpse from open view. Even the mortuary enclosure at Sewerby, with its hurdle screen, suggests a degree of controlled visual and physical access before interment. Many of the most impressive objects were accorded the same treatment: contained within bags or boxes (such as the mirrors), sheaths or pouches (knives and tools), or – in the case of food offerings – the ceramic jar. Swords of course, were commonly contained within their decorated metal or wooden scabbards. Why this elaborate play of concealment?

Wrapping draws attention to the thing that is being hidden (Hendry 1995): it alludes to what is no longer to be seen. As an act, it thus 'discloses as it can conceal' (Weiner and Schneider 1989, 1). Those who knew what was wrapped – who had seen the final dressing of the dead, the polishing of a mirror, the sharpening of the sheathed sword – were privileged in their understanding of what was hidden. Wrapping thus resonates with what Taussig calls the 'the pulsating magical power of the play of presence and absence' (1999, 175). Power is the right word here: it created a hierarchy of audiences, between those who were intimately involved in the proceedings, and those more distant from the event. It may have been a way in which age and gender or ritual skill, were drawn into sharp distinction, as well as relatedness to the deceased. The act of wrapping allowed a last moment of intimate touch, reverent care: the artistry involved helped make 'special' what was being contained within (Weiner and Schneider 1989), whilst each layer added to its growing mystery and aura. There may have been other reasons for concealing bodies or objects now considered sacred, dangerous or polluting. Jealous or malignant gazes might be considered damaging: wrapping can thus be a protective act (Weiner 1989), or people may themselves become harmed by the sight of something now dedicated to the afterlife (see Brück 2004). In the case of the corpse, this closure from view also helped mark the transformation of the deceased, and the end of contact with the living. It may have been a heart-rending or appalling moment for close relatives. Yet it may also have been the start of the important process of 'forgetting': the corollary of remembrance (Jackson 1996; Mines and Weiss 1993). Concealment thus helped create a tempo of growing finality, and added to the drama of proceedings.

Choreographing death

The final journey of all of these elements may have involved a procession from the mortuary enclosure or house of the deceased, to the cemetery. In the case of the chariot burials, this must have been particularly dramatic – the vehicle being used as a hearse to carry the body of the dead to the grave. However, at Ferry Fryston, the fragile 'sham' terrrets, purpose-made for the funeral, would not have withstood rigorous use, and the excavators suggested that instead, people may have wheeled this chariot gently into the grave pit (Boyle *et al.* 2007, 145). This puts quite a different perspective on the drama of the event, with human surrogates acting as the chariot 'team'. Meanwhile, at the King's Barrow at Arras, the mis-cast horse-bit suggests that the ponies who were evidently present, were either poorly harnessed or did not lead the chariot to the grave-side. This may have made their slaughter all the more memorable and dramatic: their heads laid 'not far from that of the man' (Greenwell 1906, 230).

There is a strong sense in many examples of careful choreography, and the deliberate arrangement of both corpse and grave goods. In the chariot burials, the various elements of the vehicle had to be taken apart, suggesting the presence of the same craftspeople that had made these complex objects. Carpenters and smiths may have co-operated to loosen the linch-pin, remove the wheels and place them on the floor of the grave or at the side of the pit. What happened next varied slightly from burial to burial. The body may have been framed within the box of the chariot (as at Ferry Fryston) or was laid directly over the top of these objects: resting on their iron tyres and spokes. The axle was then placed below the feet: its pole shaft rising over the corpse, to run the length of the grave. Meanwhile, the yoke (often with its terrets still attached) was placed to the side of these crouched inhumations, running along the back of the corpse. Finally, in the case of some burials, the box was lowered over the corpse. Despite a common pattern however, each event was unique, and there is good evidence that it did not always go to plan. In the case of Wetwang Village, when the axle was laid in the grave it was evident that the pole shaft attached to it would have laid directly across the deceased's face (Hill 2004). This led to some furious digging out of a niche at the south-west corner, under-cutting the pit edge and resulting in two piles of spoil which served to support each end of the axle: lifting it above the deceased's head (*ibid.*). Slight anomalies in the northern end of the pit at Ferry Fryston may tell a similar tale of improvised excavation to accommodate the whole chariot ensemble, when it was finally wheeled into the pit (Boyle *et al.* 2007, 125). At Wetwang Slack, the laying of the axle in the elderly woman's grave appears to have shoved the toe bones of one foot away from the ankle joint (Dent 1985, 88): possibly suggesting an advanced state of decomposition. Meanwhile, the woman buried on the opposite side of the valley at Wetwang Village, had her hand so tightly bound, it appears to have fractured her wrist post-mortem (Hill 2004). There is a sense in these cases, of grave attendants trying to improvise within a given timeframe and set of conditions.

Even if there was an idea that funerals were faithful repetitions of prescribed rites, no event was the same: each performance was unique (Barth 1987). This intense 'here-and-now' quality of these rites enfolded the audience, creating a 'time of enchantment' cut out from everyday life (Thrift and Dewsbury 2000, 421). The affect of such rituals was to conjure a sense of the eternal: revealing the cosmological or sacred order of the world (Barrett 1994). As people witnessed funeral after funeral (some as close mourners, some as distant viewers) this repetitiveness was reassuring but it was always held in tension with the immediacy and fragility of the event itself. From this volatile scenario emerged the shared understanding that such ritual performances were highly risky (Howe 2000), requiring skill to 'pull them off' successfully. Whether things were properly and competently done involved an interaction between performers and audience (Schiefflin 1996, 60): their interpretation of the event would not only determine the renown of the deceased but also those officiating over the ceremony (Schiefflin 1985). Such risks were especially acute when dealing with the dead, as inappropriate or incomplete rites might lead to their return with malign intent to the world of the living. Strategies may have included the skilful use of timing, building dramatic tension and punctuating it, to impress the sights, sounds and even smells of the funeral, upon the audience's memory. For example, in the case of R148, the iron cover for the boss and spine of a shield were found face upwards over the corpse, where the shield was originally laid. Yet fragments of the shield's edge bindings were found scattered across the corpse 'for reasons unknown' (Stead 1991, 61). It is hard to explain this patterning through taphonomic processes alone. Instead, as part of a ritual act of 'object killing' the shield may have been split and shattered, creating a noisy and dramatic spectacle, as splinters of wood and fragments of metal flew in the air. Watching the 'death' of such an object may have helped the audience cathartically re-live the fact of the deceased's own demise.

Rites of reversal

Other rites emphasised this finality by the deliberate inversion of norms, or rites of reversal (Norbeck 1971). As both Stead and Parker Pearson have pointed out, the most famous Iron Age example of this is the Kirkburn chariot burial (K5, Figure 5.16), where the corpse was not dressed in the chainmail shirt:

rather, it was placed upside-down, and back-to-front over the body of the deceased (Stead 1991, 54; Parker Pearson 1999a). In the male chariot burials from Wetwang Slack discussed above (WS453 and WS455), the iron spines of the shield cover were similarly found face-downwards in the grave, suggesting they had been inverted (Dent 1985). Spears were commonly laid in the grave with their tips down, towards the left foot of the individual (R24, R57, BF63). The famous sword in the Kirkburn warrior's grave was also placed with its hilt-end at his feet, rather than near to his hand (Stead 1991). One of the most interesting martial interments is that of R144: laid prone in the grave: his sword still apparently strapped to his back, with a spearhead at such an odd angle in the grave, it possibly represents another 'spearing' rite. This manner of burial may well reflect a concern over his death: placing him face-down to prevent his rising again. Sometimes, it was objects which were damaged or inverted: one of the horse-bits at Garton Slack was deliberately cleft in two and placed between the severed parts of a pig's head (Brewster 1971, 290). Returning to the disturbed blue glass bead necklace of WS209 which opened this chapter, if it was not disturbed through decay or re-wrapping, its breakage and scattering over the corpse also marked this death as different from others – possibly marking the end of a long period of liminality, and the deceased's final re-incorporation into the ancestors. Such reversals were not only dramatic but helped express the finality of the funeral proceedings, and like the disassembling of the chariot, may have handed objects over into the next realm by rendering them symbolically 'beyond use'. These rites also have the function of turning the world 'upside down', momentarily exposing, even challenging, the correct or expected order of things.

Representing death

The above discussion has contrasted the notion of a 'tableau' of death with the temporal and spatial dynamics of funerary performance. It has discussed the strategies and effects which people used to negotiate the risky and dangerous nature of such events: transforming the deceased into a successful member of the ancestry and renegotiating their own place and status in the community. Yet inevitably, when we seek to conjure this in an archaeological text or talk, we still rely on static images such as the 'reconstruction'.

For the chariot burials, the most famous of these is Peter Connolly's evocative reconstruction, which forms the centrepiece of the Hull and East Riding 'Celtic World' exhibition. The image has its strengths (the strong sense of movement, representations of grief, debate and disagreement amongst the mourners) as well as some weaknesses (stereotypes of tartan clothing and limed hair, with women and children kept at a suitable distance from male-dominated proceedings). It has become an iconic image for texts on the Iron Age. With the ideas of the above chapter in mind, Figure 6.7 presents a new representation of a chariot burial, by the archaeological illustrator and performer, Aaron Watson. For a

start, it places a woman 'centre-stage': the chariot burial WS453, sketched in detail above. Around her grave are assembled a more varied set of mourners, with both men and women, young and old, negotiating the event together. In our collaboration, we have tried to use hints from the evidence of dress, decoration and hair design, to undermine some of the stereotypes of Iron Age life. It is inevitably an image of our own time with an aesthetic inspired by graphic novel art but informed by the evidence and ideas represented in this book. The two-fold image tries to capture something of the staggered timing and different views afforded to individual participants. It also seeks to capture the organised chaos of such a complex burial: the chariot parts being laid in the grave, the decorated canister being held out for all to see, the mirror catching and reflecting light. In the background, people jostle for a view. We have opted for a more diverse population, representing different age and gender sets. There are more children and infants present, and both men and women are depicted in roles of authority, though the spear and sword bearing warriors are particularly striking. Balancing this, a woman holds the mirror for a last view: some appear captivated by it whilst others shy away. Up close, a senior female elder helps a young mourner negotiate the ceremony, whilst at her side, a pregnant woman symbolises the cycle of life and death, hinting at the rites of fertility which often permeate funerals (Parker Pearson 1999b). The second 'privileged' perspective draws us in: transforming us from distant viewer into a captivated participant.

FIGURE 6.7. Chariot burial reconstruction by Aaron Watson: burial WS454, Wetwang Slack.

Conclusion: performance, risk and reputation

This chapter has discussed the performative character of life and death in the Iron Age settlements and cemeteries of East Yorkshire. It has argued that Iron Age people were skilled at orchestrating the tempo or rhythm of events, using different spatial and material aspects of their environment – houses, barrows, objects, human and animal bodies – to memorable effect. It has focused in detail on the technology, use and meaning of the key artefact used to characterise these communities: the chariot, and explored its use in different social contexts, including the funeral.

Many of the performances I have described relied upon face-to-face encounter and intimate insight into the proceedings to fully comprehend their importance or meaning. Both the scale of these events and their intended audience tells us something important about these societies. By and large, these were not broad gestures in large arenas: they were close-up, intense encounters or ceremonies. Yet they would still have created a distinction in knowledge and insight, between those in the immediate audience and those at a greater distance, whether in the setting of the roundhouse or around the grave. Whilst a larger community may have been present, such events may have relied upon the dramatic mastery and oratorial skill of impressive figures, adept in the use of such settings and empowered with objects such as the mirror, sword or chariot.

Ultimately, these performances concerned power. People's renown or ruin was at risk (Howe 2000). What is frequently overlooked (especially in the analysis of rituals) argue Metcalf and Huntingdon 'is the uncertainty of the outcomes. Rituals may make a show of power, but they run the same risk as other shows: They may fail' (1991, 6). In the funeral context, this was especially important: the afterlife and identity of the deceased (and their goodwill towards the living) was in jeopardy. This brings us back to Richard Jenkins' point that even death did not seal the picture: all was still … quite literally … to play for (1996, 4). The next chapter therefore follows the dead, exploring the notion that the East Yorkshire communities may have perceived death as a journey to be undertaken. It examines the evidence for this by re-considering some of the associations between the burials of the dead and other landscape phenomenon, and it explores the broader cultural meaning of 'journeying' through evidence for travel, exchange and violence between communities.

CHAPTER SEVEN

Making Tracks:
Journeying with the Dead

Introduction

It comes as a surprise, the rising of the water. A spell of heavy rainfall, a sudden thunderstorm or the melting of winter snow… any one of these might act as a trigger. Yet as Daniel Defoe noted, writing in 1724–6, 'none knows when it will happen' (cited in Woodward 1985, 58). Rainfall percolates through the permeable chalk into the underground aquifers, which take time to fill (Knapp 1979) creating a delay before the strange rivers of the area – the Gypsey Races – began to run. Seen today, these clear-running, gravel-based streams are deceptive … shallow trickles, threading through the base of the Great Wold Valley. In other dales they are long dried-up, existing as mere lines or place names on First Edition Ordnance Survey maps, as at Kilham (Allison 1974, 250). Yet in the past, their power was devastating. In 1327, nine tofts in Boynton were flooded by the Gypsey Race, and further flooding in 1352 forced the re-orientation of the village at right-angles to the stream (Cal. Inq. p.m. vii: 14, cited in Allison 1974, 22). In 1809, many of the cottages at Rudston were also inundated (Allison 1974, 316; Royston 1873) whilst at Kilham in the same year springs that were seen 'bursting forth' ran for 20 days (Smith 1937, 97, note 1; ERRO, PR. 2017, cited in Allison 1974, 250) flooding a village which was normally 'dryly seated on the Woulds' (Richard Blome, 1673; cited in Woodward 1985, 29). At Henpit Hole they spouted from the earth 'with such force that a man on horseback can ride under the arch formed without getting wet' (Nicholson 1998, 53). In 1903, during the last severe flood of the Fimber Gypsey, the water stood 5 ft (c.1.5 m) deep in Wetwang Slack (Brewster 1980, 84). Even by 1910 when agricultural drainage in the Great Wold Valley had lowered the water level, an early postcard shows the high 'tide-mark' of flood water, just below the window-sills of cottages at Weaverthorpe (Wagner, personal collection). In 2007–8, periods of heavy rain once again caused flash-floods in this village and neighbouring West Lutton, when the Gypsey Race, which was 'dry one minute' suddenly became 'full to the top' (Beach 2008).

It was into the bed of one of these streams – the Gypsey Race at Garton Station – that the 'speared burials' of several young men (discussed in Chapter 1: Figure 1.1; Figure 7.1 and Figure 7.4) were placed – but why? What did these bodies of water mean to people? This chapter will argue that there was a close association between the dead and not only the water courses but the trackways

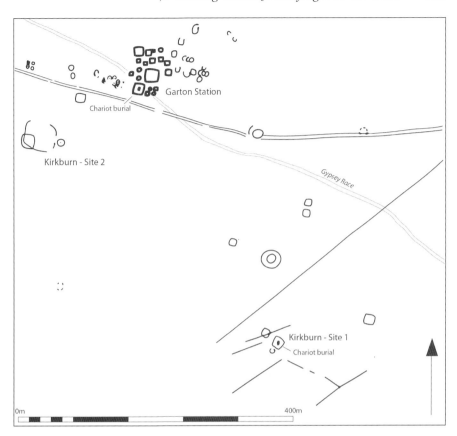

Garton Station

Chariot burial

Kirkburn - Site 2

Gypsey Race

Kirkburn - Site 1

Chariot burial

0m   400m

FIGURE 7.1. The landscape location of the Garton Station 'speared' burials. Based on Stead 1991, 21, fig. 19.

which ran through these valleys (Bevan 1997; 1999a; 1999b). By locating graves next to these phenomena, it will be suggested that death was perceived as a journey to be undertaken, along paths or route-ways which the living also traversed. The chapter will explore the occasionally violent and powerful character of these streams, alongside the opportunities and risks faced along the 'track': building an understanding of what journeying may have meant to people in these communities ... including the travels of the dead. It will explore how interactions between groups ... what went on at their boundaries, the in-between places at which they congregated or meetings with strangers ... may well have provided the flash-points for confrontation. By exploring what came from, or happened at a distance, the chapter will examine how those who mediated with this broader world and its dangers may have earned a special reputation. It will examine the importance of materials obtained through exchange, and how these were frequently incorporated into martial objects. As the last chapter argued, these were deployed in a range of events and encounters between communities, as well as moments of actual conflict. This chapter will conclude by returning to the Garton burials to explore the symbolic synergy between the corpses of young men who died in the prime of their life, and the fertile but potentially violent stream into which these bodies were speared.

Placing the dead

Square barrows, trackways and water courses

In the 1990s, an archaeologist called Bill Bevan became curious about the relationship between the square barrow cemeteries and other features in the landscape (1994). He wondered whether the extensive earlier prehistoric landscape had a significant affect on where Iron Age people chose to bury their dead. Were they, for instance, intrigued by the massive round barrow cemeteries which scattered the Wolds, or the unique standing stone at Rudston? Or were there other features or landscape settings which the square barrow cemeteries favoured? As Chapter 3 has argued, the relationship between ancient monuments and Iron Age barrows is undoubtedly strong in several locations … the 'ancestral' mound at Wetwang Slack being a good example. Also, since the linear earthworks make extensive use of this earlier monumental landscape, there are strong relationships between some round barrows, the routeways constructed by the linears, and the square barrow cemeteries which cluster around key junctions or along their tracks (Chapter 2). In fact, Bevan argued, cemeteries containing over 10 barrows had the strongest statistical correlation with trackways, as opposed to any other feature (over 70%, 1999b).

However, the other significant feature he noted was the presence of water. His analysis suggested nearly half of the cemeteries he looked at were within 50 m of an 'actual or potential watercourse' (1994, 39). Caution is need here, since Bevan assumed that drained hollows and low-lying areas were once meres or marshes, and that all dales and slacks would have had a watercourse running along their base: this is not the case, as many are true 'dry dales', filled with free-draining chalk gravels which would not support a stream. Whilst sub-surface fissures can create streams running along the dale bed, these do not coincide neatly with the underground streams of the chalk (Lewin 1969, 3, 61). It is more accurate then, to state that cemeteries often cluster along the side of dale beds, which in later prehistory, would have provided a natural corridor for movement (see Giles 2000). Despite these quibbles, it is evident that Bevan had revealed an important pattern, further observing that 60% of these cemeteries had an axial alignment in the same direction as the valley bases and watercourses. Whilst Garton Station may be the most dramatic example excavated thus far, there are numerous other cases of close relationships between the square barrows and springs or streams … Rudston and Burton Fleming along the Gypsey Race in the Great Wold Valley; a large cemetery in the Kilham parish along the 'Old Gypsey' and the 'Mineral Spring' (Ordnance Survey map for 1855; OS/11/145); Scorborough which would have been almost permanently wet from the nearby spring and its associated beck (Stead 1979); the cemetery at Eastburn, near to both another old 'Gipsey' as well the springs and becks south of Elmswell (Sheppard 1939); even the isolated Iron Age crouched inhumation found near the spring and stream at Wharram Percy (Mays *et al.* 2007, 60). Whereas other cemeteries like Arras are high and dry, on dramatically elevated land with impressive views, water seems to play a significant part in the 'place' of many of the Iron Age dead. Why might this be the case?

Water in the Wolds

Let us think for a moment about the meaning of water in this region. On the higher lands of the Wolds – the areas which appear to have been carved up for grazing grounds in later prehistory – it would have been scarce. As Chapter 2 noted, it was the ancient dolines, naturally lined with clay, which were vital sources of refreshment for stock and people in earlier prehistory (Hayfield *et al.* 1995). As these began to disappear, further pressure was put upon the larger 'meres' at Fimber, Sledmere, Fridaythorpe, Burdale and possibly also Wetwang. Springs around the Wold edge were vital, such as Leavening Wold, whose spring was 'never known to fail' (Mortimer in Hicks 1978, 21). Villages in this district dreaded drought, and the carefully prescribed 'rake rights' and customs of use mentioned in Chapter 2, helped avoid conflict over this valuable resource, though as the 'Battle of Fimber' illustrated, even in historic times, this occasionally flared up into violence.

The meres were rather different in character to the Gypseys (pronounced with a hard 'g') found in valleys along the eastern arm and dipslope of the Wolds. The etymology of their name is very telling … it is often assumed that it refers to their itinerancy, for they 'come and go' in the landscape, as will be seen. In fact, Smith argues, it derives from the Old English word *gips* – to yawn, gasp or gape (1937, 5), and thus describes the character of the holes through which the streams emerged or disappeared. These were no doubt, sources of great curiosity. For example, the main Gypsey in the Great Wold Valley, rises from a spring at Wharram le Street: now considerably displaced downslope from its prehistoric counterpart. It progresses down the Great Wold Valley, through the Luttons and into Weaverthorpe. Here, the geologist George Young wrote in 1828, part of the current 'sinks down', the rest continuing through Helperthorpe and Butterwick, to disappear completely at Boythorpe Cottages, in Foxholes (1828, 28). It re-emerged at Wold Newton, and the flow became more marked as the stream turned at right-angles, between Burton Fleming and Rudston. In Boynton, Young noted, a series of subsidiary 'gipsies' emerged from chalk gravel, which were usually so covered in soil and grass that a stranger 'could not suppose them to be the source of copious streams' (*ibid.*, 29). It was only when the races were in spate that the water burst forth from its underground course, flooding the area and spilling into the larger channels. Young noted that a mile west of Wold Newton was one impressive spring called the 'Gipsies Head'. Where it emerged, a circular basin of chalk could be seen – several yards in diameter – that never grassed over (*ibid.*). These points of emergence, and the soak-aways down through which the waters descended, must have been sites of awe and fascination. They were also places of danger. One of the long-lived farming families of this valley, the Whittys, have in their possession a delicately stitched sampler, which records the tragic death of a young child: drowned in one such 'Roaring Hole', as they were named, sometime in the 19th century (Whitty, pers. comm.). As in Waterdale's 'Ludhill' ('loud hill') spring (Smith 1937, 172), the name vividly conjures the terrifying vigour and noise of these seemingly animate – even capricious – bodies of water.

As we might expect, there are various folk tales concerning them. As far back as the reign of King Stephen (*c.* 1198), the chronicle of William of Newburgh mentions the 'Vipsies' as a portent of famine (*Chronicles of the Reign of Stephen*, Rolls, i:85, cited in Smith, 1937, 5). By Defoe's time, it was also seen as a herald of plague (cited in Woodward 1985, 58), and even in 1920, Cooper described it as a 'prophet of woe' whilst Smith calls them the 'Waters-of-Woe' (1923, 73). What is clear is that whilst a gentler stream ran for most of the year (Dakyns and Fox-Strangways 1886, 2), strong enough to provide for domestic needs and support several medieval and post-medieval mills along its course (Allison 1974) particular events prompted more cataclysmic, and unpredictable, flows. Even in the early 1880s, when drainage of the surrounding land was already having an effect Young noted that the Gypsey could create a channel 6 ft (*c.*1.8 m) wide by 3 ft (*c.*0.9 m) deep, causing general flooding of the low parts of the valley (1828, 29). This generally happened in late winter or early spring (Nicholson 1998, 53). It is not surprising then, that there is a trail of correspondence recording the fears of the villagers. In 1669 the residents of Boythorpe wrote urgently to the lord of Butterwick manor that this 'little brook' which was 'of great use to all was 'all grown up and the current stopped to the great damage of your petitioners' (ERRO CSR/4/37; Allison 1974, 190). Downstream, the villagers of Rudston were reminded of their duty to 'cleanse' the race, and despite an exhortation from Hudson in 1740 that this 'scouring … only makes the water sink into the ground' the villagers respond that the rite must continue 'otherwise Rudston will suffer damage from flooding' (cited in Allison 1974, 316). The seasonal risk to life and property was clear, and such cleansing or scouring rites were often stipulated in Enclosure Awards (*ibid.*, 191). The villagers may have feared the floods, yet they needed its mineral-rich waters to rejuvenate their pasture land, and provide year-round drinking and washing water. They also seemed to value its medicinal properties. In 1856, Sheahan and Whellan noted that the 'good mineral spring [near Rudston]' which was said to be 'efficacious in curing various disorders' was sadly 'entirely neglected' (1856, 481). The square barrow cemetery at Conygarth in Kilham was also described as being next to a 'Mineral Spring' on the Ordnance Survey Map of 1855 (Sheet 145), corresponding to the 'Old Gypsey'. Such springs and streams were often venerated … near Beverley, part of the beck which flowed into the River Hull was known as the 'Ragbrook' suggesting the presence of fragments of cloth tied to trees around a sacred stream, either by 'lovers … or the diseased for the healing of their sickness' (Smith 1923, 148). We do not know if the Gypsey Races were also decorated in this fashion, but it supports the notion that some local streams were seen as having curative or regenerative powers. Yet they were also, as we have seen, destructive. Perhaps this explains the final rite concerning the races, recorded in local folklore. There was a custom at Burton Fleming that 'when word came that the Gypsey had begun to flow the young people went out to meet it' (Cooper 1920, 80, recounting Hone's *Book of Table Talk*). By greeting it formally and perhaps making appropriate offerings or gestures, Cooper surmised, they hoped to avert ill-fortune, but – he also noted – it gave young men and women licensed occasion to meet each other at a key time in the year (*ibid.*). In 1923, Smith noted, 'children keep up the custom today' (1923, 73). The emphasis upon 'young people' may be an echo of fertility or propitiatory rites which villagers had used for generations to deal with the vital but violent waters of race.

A confluence of topography and weather systems could also cause devastating meteorological events in more elevated villages such as Langtoft. In 1853, forked lightning killed plough horses and severely damaged surrounding farm land (Wright 2000, 126). In 1888, a dense column of water from a storm cloud tore down Round Hill, ripping open fissures and deep holes, and causing a slide of chalk, flint and boulder clay, moved by a body of floodwater over 40 ft (*c.*12 m) wide (Hood 1892). In July of 1892 another large 'water spout' descended over Cottam, Cowlam and finally, Langtoft, once more gouging out deep rents in Round Hill (Hood 1892, plate facing 37). This event caused a flood over 8 ft (*c.*2.4 m) in height, which once more inundated and demolished properties, destroyed possessions and crops, ruining farmland and killing livestock. The waters also revealed an earlier date-stone commemorating a similar flood in 1657. No human lives were lost though there were a few narrow escapes (see Wright 2000). At Wold Newton, meanwhile, in 1795, a storm and the rising of the Gypsey Race reputedly heralded the fall of a 56 lb (25.4 kg) meteorite, which was seen and heard whistling through the air before it landed explosively in a nearby field (Fletcher 1900, 129–30).

We might imagine that dry valleys on the lower slopes of the Wolds avoided such dangers, but Brewster records a Gypsey which used to flow through the slack bottom 'at rare intervals in the past' (1980, 114), as well as the effect of the neighbouring Fimber Gypsey, overflowing into Wetwang in 1903 (1980, 84). He also witnessed the valley flooding during a particularly hard winter … the melting snow cascaded off the frozen soil, filling the valley from 'side to side' with water (1980, 5). Kendall, the geologist, described the damage that such spring floods could wreak, descending 'the frozen floor of a chalk valley and [doing] some tearing up of the turf' (in Page 1907, 83). Either one of these phenomena might have been the origin of the cluster of small 'sinkholes' Brewster identified near to a group of square barrows, in Garton Slack 1 (1980, 114–5). Fascinatingly, in his 1905 monograph, John Mortimer also recalls a conversation with a tenant farmer from Garton Slack, whose father related that 'at times he had to ride in a cart drawn by a horse to enable him to pick up and remove the stakes of the sheep nets out of the water, most of the ground being submerged for a time' (1905, 233). What is immediately striking in this account is the role of a raised, wheeled vehicle which enabled travel along the valley base at a time when it was otherwise impassable. It also suggests the square barrow cemetery here was occasionally lapped by such floodwaters. This may shed further light on the importance of the Iron Age chariot as both a practical and symbolically powerful means of travel at dangerous times of the year.

Travelling with the dead

Bill Bevan argued that many of the Iron Age barrows ran alongside watercourses or trackways: both of which could be seen as channels of movement through the valleys. In the case of the water, he focused on its liminal status: since it did not hold a 'permanent place in the world' he argued, it may have been conceived as 'being between two worlds, appearing in the above ground world of the living for part of the year and disappearing into an underground world for the other part' (1999a, 141). Springs such as the 'Roaring Hole' or Gipsies Head, may well have been thought of as portals, through which the dead were swallowed, and out of which the fertile, replenishing but violent waters of the race, reappeared – perhaps accompanied by the newly transformed spirits of the ancestors. He argued that the 'strikingly cyclical nature' of this disappearance and re-emergence structured ideas about the regeneration of life: both of the agricultural cycle and the ancestral realm. It therefore provided a key temporal rhythm through which Iron Age people framed their world (1999a, 142). As the above section has noted, there is no doubt that there was a seasonal flow to the Gypsey Races, which would have been swelled by the winter rains. The dormancy of the land would have been mirrored in the over-wintering of seed grain and the gestation of animals: the sudden breaking into life – flowering, flowing or flooding – would have been seen as a period of rebirth. Yet the more cataclysmic flooding caused by races in spate, sheet-water off frozen valley-sides or cloudbursts from waterspouts, was an unpredictable and potentially devastating affair. Perhaps by positioning the dead close to the course of such streams or spring-heads, they hoped to control these other-worldly phenomena through spiritual power and intercession. In turn, the streams helped ensure the symbolic departure and return of the deceased: rejuvenated into an ancestral community.

This notion of the dead disappearing and re-emerging as ancestors, could also be structured through the architecture of the trackway, along which they may have been urged to 'depart'. In order to explore this, we need to return to some of the features discussed in Chapter 2. For example, the cemetery at Wetwang Slack seems to have been framed by an earlier track (represented by fragments of ditch D, E and F) running west–east, just above the base of the valley (J. Dent, pers. comm.). On its western edge, it appears to have been delineated by another trackway or slight earthwork, completely erased by later re-cuts of a much more monumental ditch and bank (Dent 1982). As Chapter 3 discussed, at some point in the life of the cemetery, a new linear earthwork was dug to the north of the earlier track, with a bank up-cast on its northern side, effectively

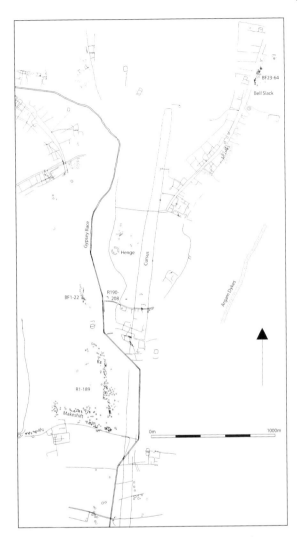

FIGURE 7.2. Burials in
the Great Wold Valley,
showing the cemeteries
of Rudston and Burton
Fleming. Based on Stead
1991, 2, fig. 1.

cutting the area in half: defining an 'older' cemetery from the newer plots. A second ditch dug parallel to this, later became an established track (linear feature group 1.2), suggesting the shifting over time of a path which ran along the edge of the cemetery. Other square barrow cemeteries which are defined or respected by linear earthworks include Foxholes, a small group of barrows just north of the main village at Wetwang, and a larger cemetery within Kilham parish, near Creyke farm (Stoertz 1997, 36). At Melton, a square barrow was located adjacent to a series of parallel linear earthworks and a pit or post alignment interpreted as land boundaries running up towards the step slopes of the Wold edge (Evans 2009, 266). This boundary cut through an earlier round barrow which lay just to the west of the square barrow. This site also marked the junction of the north–south linears with a ditched east–west trackway, and a further holloway which also had Iron Age origins (*ibid.*, 267).

At Buckton Holms, next to the Settrington Beck, three strands of ditched trackway come together, as if designed to funnel stock towards the watercourse. Right in the 'mouth' of this junction is a small cemetery of square (and possibly some round) barrows. At Raisthorpe (near Wold House), the head of a side-dale which leads to a narrow neck of high land (a natural crossing place) is monumentalised by earthworks with segments up to four ditches wide. This junction is once again elaborated by a small cluster of square barrows. The importance of such meeting points is also seen at Vicarage Closes, just north-west of the village of Burton Fleming, where the confluence of multiple earthworks discussed in Chapter 2 is also marked by a small square barrow cemetery on its northern side. Scattered individual mounds are positioned in between the dykes which narrow to a 'neck' that spans the valley base and the course of the Gypsey Race. If we remember Young's account of the floods mentioned above (1828), this is the base of the valley filled by floodwaters in bad years. We are probably looking at a system which was used to bring stock down to water and graze what would have normally been lush summer river pasture. Over all of these meetings points – confluences of different groups and herds, possibly competing for water – the dead kept a watchful eye.

At the edge of Burton Fleming, the Gypsey turns sharply south towards Rudston, and along its course is another cemetery, near Little Argham (burials R190–R208: Stead 1991; Figure 7.2). Here, a series of barrows was bounded on its southern side by 'a droveway running alongside Argam Lane' (Stead 1991, 16). Though the more northerly line of this may be slightly later than the cemetery (possibly removing traces of some of the barrows), the southern line kinks slightly, either around the original mounds or shallow graves now lost (*ibid.*). This droveway sweeps up to the north-east, crossing the cursus monument, and running north towards Maiden's Grave and the Bell Slack cemetery, (burials BF23–64). Whilst these latter two groups of barrows were overlain by the enclosures and trackways of a late Iron Age–Roman ladder settlement, Stead noted that the barrow mounds were 'aligned with the droveway (which in turn followed the alignment of the valley)' (1991, 17). In other words, it suggests the existence of a routeway running down from the northern head of the valley at Bartindale, into the basin of the Burton Fleming-Rudston valley system, along which – of course – flowed the Gypsey Race.

Further down this valley was the Makeshift cemetery at Rudston (burials R1–R189): a reverse 'L' shaped group of barrows which was bounded on its southern side by a pair of ditches. One of these was quite substantial, the other a slight flanking ditch, leading towards the north-western head of a valley at Springdale (Stead 1991, 6). It is likely that this represented a trackway, leading up to a slightly kinked, funnel-shaped entrance where another earthwork from the north makes a junction. Together the two would have diverted stock either into some small 'pen'-like paddocks or out along a ditch-flanked track running west to higher pasture at Greenlands. Another group of square barrow monuments was located at this junction, meaning that people and animals would have driven past the dead, on their way into and out of the earthwork complex, heading east to water or west to grazing grounds. The eastern edge of the Makeshift cemetery meanwhile, was probably bounded by the original course of the Gypsey Race (before it was canalised, *ibid.*), as well as the southern arm of a Neolithic cursus monument, which subtly alters its course to 'run with the race' at this point. The architecture within the cemeteries respects the flow of both channels of movement, running along the dale beds.

Whimster argued that the loose chalk gravel and subsoils of the bases of such valleys may have encouraged the extension of the cemeteries along these lines of least resistance (1981, 114). This may well have been a factor in creating easily shovelled spoil for a barrow mound. Yet it is notable that both colluvium and alluvial deposits from the race would have made these some of the richer soils (P. Buckland, pers. comm.) which as the environmental evidence suggests were situated within well-grazed, short-turf grassland (Thew and Wagner in Stead 1991, 150). In many cases, we can see the confluence of tracks, often defined by linear earthworks and square barrow monuments, channelling movement along natural routeways which led between water and what would have been more open areas of pasture. In other locales, it is the junctions of different land boundaries which are marked by the burials of the Iron Age dead.

At one level, we could argue that this was a political strategy to demarcate rights of use, through ancestral ties. Anyone entering or exiting through such junctions, or taking the easy route down a valley base, would have had to pass by the serried ranks of the ancestors. It was a strong effect of the architecture of these cemeteries that as you moved along the trackways which shadowed them, the sheer number of the dead was gradually revealed. It was a phenomenon which worked most impressively at a walking pace. If they belonged to this community, they would no doubt have felt a sense of deep belonging, as they surveyed their forebears. Memories of recent funerals – the taste of that joint of mutton, the sight of that marvellous sword – may have come to mind. It established the communities' ties with specific locales, making tenurial claims to these places (Bevan 1999b, 140). If passing through from neighbouring areas, journeying between settlements or moving with stock to prized watering places, other travellers would have been awed – even intimidated – by the long-lived lineages suggested in the clusters of barrows.

However, as Bevan suggests, there may have been a deeper symbolic purpose to this relationship between the dead and paths or routeways (1999b). Like watercourses, trackways have a liminal status due to their communal use, by members of local groups as well as strangers (*ibid.*, 141). They 'pass through', conjuring a sense of connection with the place they have come from, as well as the destination towards which they are headed. Perhaps this is why the transitional phase of death is often described metaphorically as a 'journey', evoking the spiritual transformation of the deceased, and their passage into a community of ancestors (see Huntington and Metcalf 1991, 32). Indeed, there is often a coincidence between the 'spiritual journey of the soul from life to death and the physical journey of the corpse' (Downes 1997, 23). This not only provides a temporal structure to the three-fold stages of this rite of passage (separation, transformation and re-incorporation: van Gennep 1960), but can convey the very real belief that the spirit or soul of the ancestor may have literally travelled to a new realm, in space or time. Our dessicated and tightly bound corpse from Wetwang Slack burial WS209, may have physically and spiritually returned 'home' along the track in the bottom of the valley. Such a journey may also mark the transformational period when the 'departed soul is potentially malevolent and socially uncontrolled' (Bloch and Parry 1982; *ibid.*, 4). Ensuring the safe passage of the deceased was the task of the mourners: it is what made funeral rites so important yet fraught with risk. If, as Bevan suggests, the communities of East Yorkshire conceived of death as a journey, then by locating them close to such trackways, repeatedly worn by feet and hooves, or the scouring flow of watercourses, they were helping to 'speed' them on their way. This would of course make the inclusion of a vehicle – the chariot – in a burial, an extremely effective and impressive way of aiding passage into the afterlife. In order to evaluate this idea further, we must explore what journeying meant to people in these communities… how far did they travel and what did they think of distant places? What came from these other worlds, and how were such substances, people or even knowledge, regarded? This is something we can only explore through the process of exchange.

Journeying in the Iron Age

Modelling movement

The importance of seasonal and diurnal journeys in the local landscape was sketched in Chapter 2, as a vital round of movement, fundamental to the negotiation of rights and community identity. As Roberts points out, such journeys are often under-valued compared with longer-distance journeying (2007). Whilst this is true, the ideas, materials, skills and people who came from a greater distance also require investigation. As Chapters 5 and 6 suggest, the Iron Age material culture suggests much of this exchange was quite localised, with objects passing down-the-line between kin groups or from generation to generation. In this instance, the worth of such a piece might be heavily influenced by the history of hands through which it has passed. This method need not involve great distances: the circulation of local valuables, as in the famous Kula cycle of Papua New Guinea, provides a good ethnographic example which elucidates the aim of such regional exchange: to gain personal fame and political renown (Munn 1986). This is achieved by successful voyaging, creating multiple 'paths' of exchange between men, which operate above and beyond the kinship system (Weiner 1988). This supra-local arena complements the wealth and status that might be accrued through direct kinship exchange (*ibid.*).

In contrast, longer-distance exchange can involve the more rapid passage of objects, people and ideas between regions, resulting in the swift arrival of exotica, valued for its strangeness and difference, or distant origin. This form of exchange usually necessitates specialists in travel: intermediaries who voyage long-distance. Whilst they are often cast in the archaeological literature in an economic light (as merchants or traders) both the risks involved and the goals of such exchange, may suggest socio-political or even spiritual motives for such travel. Missionaries and pilgrims for example, seek religious fulfilment through journeying, whilst mercenaries or hero-voyagers, use the dangerous conquests and knowledge gained on their voyage to enhance personal status upon their return.

This theme of distance as not simply spatial but also spiritual is captured in Mary Helms' influential thesis, *Ulysses' Sail* (1988). Through an impressive cross-cultural study, she demonstrates how the exotic can be used as political and ideological capital in small-scale communities. Frequently, she notes, spatial distance from a cultural heartland corresponds with cosmological distance: movement away from one's own '*axis mundi*' involves journeying towards 'places and people that are increasingly different … regarded as increasingly supernatural, mythical and powerful' (*ibid.*, 4). Distant lands are often seen as celestial locales … the origin points of ancestors, spirits or gods. Knowledge of such places – and acquaintance with them (either direct, through travel, or indirect, through possession of ideas or substances from them) – is seen as the purview of 'political-religious specialists' (1988, 5). They alone possess the wisdom and skill to voyage successfully, or mediate with the powerful beings and materials that emanate from such places. Dealing with distance then, becomes part of the repertoire of esoteric knowledge which underpins status, power and authority amongst such communities. Such groups are distinguished by the use of esoteric knowledge or exotica as a means of discrimination, yet part of the art of such power lies in its concealment: hinting or alluding to the mysteries gained from such exchanges (Helms 1988, 15–16).

Travel in Iron Age East Yorkshire

How do these ideas square with evidence for travel in Iron Age East Yorkshire? We must not forget that this could be radically affected by weather. As the example of the tenant farmer illustrates, riding in his cart along the base of the flooded valley of Garton Slack, there were times when certain paths were impassable. This is not to say that alternative directions or routes could not be taken … but the closure of a sanctioned track may have nevertheless been significant. There must have been other times of the year however, when any movement was difficult. Flooding may have rendered marshy areas of the surrounding Vales unrecognisable, swelling rivers, creeks and channels. Heavy snowfall, especially combined with drifting, still frequently cuts off the dales of the High Wolds during late winter. A piece of graffiti found in a 19th century barn at Foxhouse, near Birdsall, recalls the efforts of a team of men who 'walked ten miles to cut you buggers out' (see Giles and Giles 2007, 346): referring to the hand-cutting through snow drifts, which was the only means of getting supplies through to isolated farms and settlements. We should not, therefore, take travel to and from the Wolds for granted. There may have been favoured seasons for journeying over greater distances, which took into account the weather and ease of travel, as well as schedules of agricultural and domestic work.

In terms of water-based travel, from the number of Iron Age vessels found in the region, like the Hasholme boat (MacGrail 1990; Halkon and Millett 1999), the Fiskerton log boats from Lincolnshire (Field *et al.* 2003), or models such as that found with the Roos Carr figures (Coles 1990), it is evident that later prehistoric travel along the creeks, rivers and tidal waters was feasible. Elsewhere in Britain and Ireland, there is evidence for longer-distance water-borne journeys during the Iron Age: the boat with oars and mast, modelled in gold from the Broighter hoard (Raftery 1994), and harbour and port features along the south coast at Hengistbury Head (Cunliffe 1978a) and Poole Harbour (Markey *et al.* 2002). Promontory forts are often closely linked to the sea, by navigable shores and inlets or dramatic cliff-top settings. In North Yorkshire, an early Iron Age coastal settlement was uncovered at Castle Hill, Scarborough (Smith 1927) and given the later positioning of a Roman signal station here, this may well have also been occupied in the later Iron Age. Such features have yet to be identified on the East Yorkshire coastline, though there is evidence for late Iron Age–early Roman trading at sites along the Humber, including Redcliff, Brantingham, North Ferriby and Melton (Challis and Harding 1975).

Material relations

There are very few true Continental imports into the East Yorkshire district, dating to the period in which the cemeteries were used: the gold Arras finger-ring (which has parallels from both Münsingen-Rain in Switzerland and Saint-Memmie, Marne: Jope 1995), the North Grimston anthropoid hilted sword (with a strong parallel in the Haute Marne: Stead 1979, 60–4), some of the glass beads (such as the opaque yellow example from Burton Fleming) and possibly the bronze ring from the Kirkburn mother and infant burial. Rarely, we can posit the movement of British objects travelling back along these routes, such as the vase-headed linchpin found in a sanctuary at Blicquy (Demarez and Leman-Delerive 2001). Substances rather than finished objects were also exchanged: amber for beads (which occurs more commonly on the eastern side of the North Sea but could conceivably have also come from the Baltic region), gold for the finger ring as well as the strip wrapped around the Wetwang woman's pin, and of course coral: most probably from the Mediterranean region (see Skeates 1993 for a discussion of potential sources). Some of the coral beads (such as those on the Danes Graves 'wheel' pin) have perforations which do not relate to the item on which they were found, and these may have originally travelled in strands or as part of another object, before they were shaped into a finished item by a local craftsperson. Both amber and coral stand out as imports in a period otherwise characterised by its 'low ebb tide' of trade (Collis 2001, 3). However, whilst we have a tendency to see 'overseas' materials as exotic, the length of time it would have taken to cross land may also have made some of the 'British' materials equally hard to obtain and therefore special in value … jet from Whitby or the drift deposits on the east coast of Yorkshire, tin from the south-west, copper from unknown sources but potentially Cheshire or north Wales (or travelling as ready-mixed bronze ingots through intermediary sources) and some individual glass beads from the Somerset Levels. The origin of the deep-red opaque glass containing cuprous oxide (often referred to as enamel) may well be local, but like the more copious plain blue beads, no production sites have so far been identified. Rarely, materials might have been recycled from discoveries of earlier prehistoric grave goods or hoards (as the style of the miniature axe discussed in Chapter 5 might suggest). Such exotic substances complemented more local materials: timber and iron (some of which may have derived from the large-scale production sites in the Foulness Valley to the south-west of the Wolds: Halkon and Millett 1999, 225), hide and textile products, bone and antler.

Iron Age perceptions of distance were in part constituted through this world of materials. The rhythms of stock and woodland management as well as kinship exchange must have produced a dense web of connections which wove across the valley systems, connecting the Wolds to the surrounding Vales and Plains. Along these tracks flowed the products of these socially intense and intimate relations, from the bodies of people, animals and the land. These were complemented by rare and colourful substances which were harder to come by, and which spoke of exotic, dangerous, perhaps even spiritual realms. Materials that did not tarnish, or which sparked or held an electric charge (such as jet and amber) may have been seen as especially potent or animate. As has been suggested, this may have made them appropriate choices for the decoration of personal protective objects: charms and amulets, or scabbards, hilts and shield-fittings.

What about the way in which such materials were wrought? What does this tell us about the transfer of craft knowledge, as well as raw materials, into East Yorkshire? The Celtic art used on these artefacts has origins in the Continental La Tène tradition, yet it is clearly part of the Insular Style (Stead 1996). The Yorkshire 'Scabbard Style' (fitting into Stage IV of the Insular scheme, added by J. M. de Navarro to Paul Jacobsthal's classic typology), dates to around the 3rd century BC. Key parts of this style include S-motifs and wave-tendrils, with various filler-motifs (triangles, lobes, tightly coiled spirals, hatching and stippling: *ibid.*, 31). The trumpet-void motif, derived possibly from the Continental half-palmette design (Stead 1996, fig. 34), is found on Stage IV objects such as the Wetwang and Kirkburn scabbards (Figure 7.3). Together

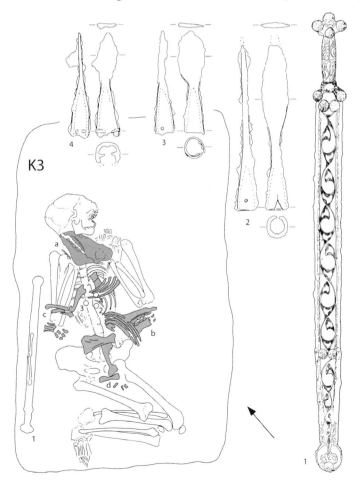

FIGURE 7.3. The Kirkburn sword burial (K3). Based on Stead 1991, 225, fig. 125.

they create panels of incised decoration which – whilst often symmetrical – have a rolling wave which draws the eye down through the design. Stage V ornamentation, using lost-wax casting to create areas of raised relief and depression, or three-dimensional effects, can be seen in examples such as the Bugthorpe scabbard (*ibid.*, 35). Interestingly, there are a number of parallels between this Yorkshire art and that of the Irish Scabbard Style, found on a number of objects from Lisnacrogher (a possible wetland votive site) and discoveries along the River Bann. As well as individual motifs, they may share the practice of central suspension loops, as noted at Lisnacrogher 4 (1996, 32; Raftery 1994, 482). For Piggott, writing in the context of a recent colonial history, this was evidence of the 'plantation of Ulster by Yorkshire charioteers' (1950, 16) yet as both Raftery (1994) and Harding (2007) wryly point out, this model fails to explain the conspicuous absence of the distinctive square barrow burial rite in Ireland which should also have accompanied such colonisation. Writing from a rather different cultural perspective, Barry Raftery simply noted that whilst this did indeed suggest 'close connections between the scabbard makers of north-east Ireland and Yorkshire' (1994, 482), it was not evidence of either an invasion or artistic imposition from one region to another. Both were independently inspired by the Continent but in different ways, and whilst there was evidence for a shared discourse in martial art between the two areas, this was executed according to local taste and skill. For example, the La Tène I style chape-ends of the Yorkshire examples (influenced by Continental designs dating before the 3rd century BC: Stead 1996, 32) are distinctly different to those of the Irish scabbards, as are their iron back-plates. Meanwhile, the triple-dot motifs found on several Irish scabbards, as well as the more delicate bronze scabbard ring chapes, have close Continental parallels not shared by the Yorkshire examples. Despite these differences, the material still suggests some cultural contact (at least in the arena of art, smithing and glasswork) between the two regions. The bronze canister from Wetwang Slack has a close partner found associated with a cremation burial in a ring-ditch at Ballydavis I. Similar in size, it lacks the Scabbard style incised decoration and is instead finished with a central dome on the lid, embossed with concentric raised rings and a small roundel with dot motif, as well as a handle-mount and small iron rivets at the 'lid' (Keeley 1996 cited and discussed in McGarry 2008, volume iii). The miniature blue glass beads found at Wetwang Village have (as far as I am aware) no Iron Age parallel in Britain yet a number of examples are known from inhumation and cremation burials in Ireland, again at Ballydavis (along with a variety of other glass and stone beads, including Oldbury/Meare types), as well as Ferns, Knowth, Oran Beg and Loughey (McGarry 2008, 87–8). Since no analysis has been undertaken, it is impossible to say if their composition is similar. Yet these limited insights into artistic affinities suggest there is further mileage in considering the 'Irish connection'.

The outcome of this study of Celtic art and exotic substances is revealing. It accords well with Sharples description of these communities 'investing resources in the acquisition of rare and precious materials that can only be manipulated by specialist craftsmen and which can only be used by individuals set apart from the community' (2010, 312). In other words, the goal of such exchange and acquisition was to create objects which helped distinguish individuals: in Sharples' terms, an 'elite'. Yet from the burial evidence, it is clear that one did not simply enter this powerful elect through birthright alone: aspects of age, skill and life-history, were part of how leadership was earned, maintained and finally, celebrated at death. In Chapter 3, their relative 'isolation' and special treatment in death was suggested as evidence that they had been 'cut out' from kin relations: symbolised as leaders for the wider community. The evidence suggests such individuals were skilled negotiators, utilising their ideological or political authority to maintain a nested series of relations, spun out from the valleys, through local bonds of kinship and alliance, to more distant regions and even to Ireland to the west, and the Continent to the south-east, where contact was more sporadic. Were these elite themselves travellers from overseas? The current isotope evidence suggests not, but we await more detailed comparisons between the Wolds and Continental burials to be sure (Chapter 4). We certainly need not posit a major invasion to suggest that the notion of building square barrows and interring chariots, as well as some of the core skills and motifs of Celtic art, may have derived from the latter source, but why? What were the motivations for such travel and what made ideas and substances from far away so attractive?

Journeying: renewing relations, gaining prestige

Journeying was itself significant. As Cummings and Johnston note, 'the time that passes in between departure and arrival is frequently no less important or memorable than experiences at the destination (2007, 1). Travelling provided an opportunity to socialise with a small group: forming close bonds, perhaps as a rite of passage associated with age or gender (Helms 1988, 69). At the local level, 'going around' as Roberts has described it, was an important part of movement with stock, revisiting less frequented areas of territory to negotiate aspects of ownership or tenurial rights (2007, 106). These are the kind of journeys envisaged by Fenton Thomas to the grazing grounds on and off the Wolds (2003), facilitated by the trackways which ran long-distance through others' territory (Bevan 1999b, 88). Acquaintances might be renewed, new alliances formed – perhaps with other powerful elites utilising the same suite of weapons of power (James 1999). And along these paths would have flowed exchanges of stock, people, things, gossip.

Anthoons has recently argued that the similarities in chariot burial rites between different regions on the Continent can be explained through elite exchange networks, facilitated by social mechanisms such as strategic marriage, fosterage, clientship or even hostage-taking (2011). This produced a network of connections, resulting in some similarities but also important contrasts in burial rites, art styles and technological knowledge. She underpins her argument with accounts of such practices attested in the writings of the classical authors – particularly Julius Caesar – relating to Iron Age Gaul (*ibid.*). As for the connection between areas such as the Paris basin and East Yorkshire, she raises the possibility that in addition to elite alliances, ideas were brought across to Britain by those being schooled in religious or spiritual matters on an island renowned by the 1st century BC as a centre of 'druidry' (*ibid.*).

Such longer distance voyages to and from wider districts may have been more risky: operating outside the bonds of debt and affiliation, and people known by name or reputation, into the lands of strangers. The material evidence suggests the most distant of these may have involved contact with, or even journeys to and from, Ireland and the Continent. The esoteric knowledge or fabulous experiences gained along the way may have been life-changing both for the individuals concerned and the communities to which they returned (Cummings and Johnston 2007; Tullett 2010). They were the source of fame, prestige and renown (see Munn 1986): stories which would pass down the generations. Yet 'taking the path' (and moving outside of one's own kinship system) was risky. Working on trackways in the Highlands of Papua New Guinea, O'Hanlon and Frankland note the ambiguity of journeying; in local discourse, paths must be blazed, cleared, kept open and re-trodden. Those who 'warm the road' skilfully through exchange and negotiation, are highly valued (2003).

Archaeologists have tended to ascribe such travellers a single motive or purpose, usually related to personal gain or wealth … Stead's list for East Yorkshire included merchants, adventurers, mercenaries or missionaries (1991). Anthoons' study picks up on and develops this religious motive, alongside her broader argument for elite alliances (2011). Yet Helms' study argues persuasively that such journeys combine a number of motives, which intertwine in complex ways to produce influential figureheads: social and political, religious and artisanal (1988). From her cross-cultural studies she argues that success in travel and exchange can be seen as an indication of other-worldly favour: spiritually empowering such individuals. Such reputations are also enhanced by those able to evidence 'control with the metaphor of speed and … superiority with exceptional speed' (Helms 1988, 63). I want to suggest that the role of both the chariot and the boat in the East Yorkshire landscape would have been part of such a repertoire of power. And if, as I have argued above, the ancestors too were thought to undertake such journeys, perhaps they also helped 'warm the roads' to ease the travels of their descendents.

Skilled crafting, knowledge and power

The charm of the exotic: weapons of exclusion?

Contact with the Continent itself might have been rare, sporadic and unpredictable but it was a source of wondrous designs, marvellous skills and beautiful substances. Combined on objects of power like the scabbard, shield, mirror or box, they exuded the power of the distant. And if these distant places were thought of as ancestral locales (to which a handful of people had once travelled or from which impressive figures had once arrived), they charged those objects with supernatural authority. Helms noted that the ability to mediate with such worlds is frequently linked with that of 'skilled crafting': the knowledge of how to make marvellous, other-worldly objects (1988). Like Gell's work on the technology of enchantment, Helms argued that the extraordinary skill associated with such crafting demonstrated 'expertise in manipulating some element or manifestation of universal energy' which ultimately referred to 'understanding of the meaning and operation of the cosmos and its dynamic and animating powers' (1988, 116). Indeed, the knowledge of how to make exotic-looking objects, using new substances or technologies, is often described as being learned from, or bestowed upon people, through their dealings with ancestral or spiritual guides (*ibid.*).

From Richard White's work on the indigenous communities of the Great Lakes region during the 17th and 18th centuries, we know that this process of encounter with new techniques or materials through exchange is never simply one of imposition or acculturation (1991). In what he calls the 'middle ground', things changed their meaning as they moved between arenas of value, being refigured in relation to existing categories, in a search for congruence and understanding. European glass beads were equated with native crystal, metal blades with other sharp tools, and mirrors (likened to bodies of water) became tools for divination. The Indians, White argues, were initially 'trading in metaphor' with people they saw as equivalents of sacred *manitous* since they too (like the spirits) were bearers of other-worldly gifts: used in turn to foster relations with new kin, ancestors, sacred beings or the Europeans themselves. The arrival of La Tène art discussed above is therefore likely to have been initially understood within existing frames of reference. Whilst common motifs or styles may have enabled people to recognised 'a unity at some level' (Megaw and Megaw 1996, 177, citing Spriggs 1990), it was skilfully interpreted and improvised upon by indigenous specialists. The shape-shifting nature of its motifs implies (as the Megaws themselves acknowledge) a multivalent and ambiguous range of meanings which may have changed with both viewer and context (1994; 2001, 22).

As previous chapters have argued, it is evident that this art and the exotic substances which embellished it were deployed on a selective range of objects. Why might this be the case? James and Cunliffe have interpreted this as the result of elite discourse: cultural exchange between powerful polities competing with prestige goods (James 1993; Cunliffe 1995b). In this model, Celtic art is seen as a symbol of status, wealth and power (James 1999, 92): a powerful politico-ideological package which related to codes of warfare, feasting and religious rites. Through such exchange, James argued, elites 'sought to join the wider political and cultural circle of their peers, with whom they allied, intermarried and fought' (*ibid.*, 92). Such 'weapons of exclusion' would have helped create a group distinguished by their paraphernalia: as Weiner notes, the 'regalia of rank is underwritten by the exercise of authority that controls the seemingly uncontrollable' (1988, 108). Although the character and quantity of such objects is relatively small, we must remember that the objects which were interred with the dead represent only a fraction of those in circulation. Complex objects like the chariot may well have circulated as individual prestige elements, as Sharples suggests (2008). It is likely then, that groups were exchanging gifts with each other, to forge alliances and make reparations. We are looking at a group of impressive figures ... community leaders, certainly, if not a traditional Celtic elite ... whose power was underlined by their skilful acquisition and wielding of marvellous objects. What this also meant is that failure for a leader in another arena of power ... a bad harvest, unexpected deaths, inauspicious events ... could be compensated for, or at least negotiated, with powerful objects which outlasted short-term setbacks. Against a background of fluctuating failure and success, they endured as symbols of power which could be drawn on as the need arose, and eventually, buried with that individual, bequeathed to a favoured successor or even seized by a rival.

Making and breaking – the symbolism of skilled crafting

Helms' work has one more lesson for us here. When the skills of exchange and crafting combine in the making of objects used in arenas of authority, the craftsperson is often found at the heart of social power. They may themselves become political leaders, or else their craft may lend others a metaphorical repertoire which evoked power, as in the persona of the 'smith-king' attested in many West African Iron Age communities (Helms 1988). This example challenges our traditional models of Iron Age society, in which the craft specialist is represented as merely supporting figures of authority through the commissioning of prestige gifts (James 1993, 53; Cunliffe 2003, 167, fig. 108). Instead, power may be vested in those who are able to shape and maintain local and distant relations, *as well as* the very objects that evidenced those connections. What symbolically bound these spheres of life in common was the underlying motif of fertility and reproduction, involved in the processes of crafting as well as in social life.

It is smithing in particular, which draws these themes together (Herbert 1993). For example, the processes of gathering and processing ore and grain are directly analogous: gleaning or delving and cutting, picking or winnowing, crushing or grinding, roasting or parching (Hingley 1997). The raw materials of ore and charcoal must be 'cooked', and the eventual 'bloom' (like a loaf) is 'delivered' from the furnace: a process which ethnographic analogy suggests is also suffused with reproductive metaphors and fertility rites (Herbert 1993). Like procreation, and like agricultural reproduction, to make metal was to make life (*ibid.*, 117). And of course, the tools and weapons produced through smithing became the implements of both cultivation and warfare: a twinned symbolism of life-making and life-taking which Hingley suggests underpins the ritual power of such implements (1997). Their use in ceremonial contexts could thus evoke a world of meanings associated with both reproduction and violence, which enabled them to speak to Iron Age people about life and death (Giles 2007b).

In East Yorkshire (as in other areas of later prehistoric Britain: Hingley 1997) they were used evocatively and powerfully in such ceremonies. Two contrasting examples will suffice. In the settlement at Garton Slack, Brewster excavated a fairly shallow pit which he assumed (on the basis of Reynolds (1979) re-interpretations of these features) had once been used as a subterranean granary. On its base, he came across two curious deposits. One was a cache of carbonised grain, representing over 630 g of threshed and winnowed barley (1980, 686). Underneath this was a suite of blacksmiths's tools, carefully packed in straw: a pair of tongs, a paddle and a poker (see Giles 2007b). If we accept this was a deliberate 'thanksgiving' or propitiatory offering, as Cunliffe has suggested was common in backfilled storage pits (1992), then the above discussion helps us to unpick something of its meaning. The deliberate association of the product of a successful harvest with the powerful tools of the smith would have evoked notions of fertility and transformative power: the ability to make things grow, to shape and harvest them. This act of deposition welded together spheres of agricultural and craft life, drawing direct parallels between these areas of power, to a privileged few onlookers.

The second example is from Rudston cemetery (Figure 5.19; R154: Stead 1991, 79–80, 205 and fig. 112). Here, a young adult male (17–20 years old) was buried in a 'spearing' ceremony similar to the Garton Station burials which opened this book. A sword had been placed over the man's chest, and lying crosswise over this was a cache of tools: a delicate hammerhead (once hafted with a handle of apple, pear or hawthorn), a slender pair of tongs, and a bracing 'coupler' which had been removed and laid between the arms of this latter item. The tongs had been wrapped in cloth, which meant that the other item in the bundle – a lump of slag – had corroded onto the handles of the tongs, near the rivet. This set of tools appears fresh from the hearth, complete with the by-product of smithing: slag ... a potent material, redolent with fertility (Hingley 1997, 15; Brück 2001, 157). At this point, two spears were cast into the grave, jammed between the arms of the tongs (Stead 1991, 33). Their sockets were found scattered on either side of the grave, as if they had been violently broken: perhaps by penetrating and shattering a willow or poplar wooden shield, whose traces survive as mineralised stains on the blades (*ibid.*, 63). We can imagine the drama of this moment ... the tongs brought to the graveside with the bubbled and crazed crust from the smelt: wrapped and laid beside the body, before a shield covered it from view, then the final splintering act of spearing, which drove the martial products of smithing back into the arms of the tools which may have made them. Was this individual a craftsman, buried with both the tools of his trade, and masterful exemplars of his skill: the spears and sword? Was he instead a warrior? Perhaps both? Alternatively, rather than being direct indicators of his role, we could also suggest that they were used in this occasion of untimely death, to negotiate passage into the afterlife. Both suites of implements evoked the transformative twinned symbolism of martial and craft power: speaking of aptitudes and qualities such as virility or strength that the mourners felt this individual embodied.

In an era marked by a shift in power from control of exchange to control over agricultural production (stock, tools, land and people), Barrett has argued that political authority became explicitly associated with reproductive power, and control over aspects of fertility such as the agricultural cycle (1989). We could also consider craftwork a vital part of this discourse on reproduction. When such symbols were deployed in moments of ritual, they had power over an audience because they purported to reveal fundamental truths about the world, drawn from a timeless or metaphysical realm: truths which the audience were primed to accept, because they were actually skilfully drawn from real-life experiences by ritual specialists (Barrett 1994, 133–4). In the above two examples, materials associated with the power of transformation (to grow and to fashion, to wound or to kill) were used to deal with aspects of both life (in the case of the propitiatory offering) and death (in the case of the burial). Their success relied upon an understanding amongst Iron Age audiences that these realms really were intimately related, and this once more suggests to us that power amongst these communities may not simply have been a matter of blood-line or elite ancestry. Personal success evidenced in fertility (of families, stock and the land), martial might or skill (craftwork, spiritual or cosmological power) might coalesce, and become the grounds through which people demonstrated and laid claim to positions of authority.

Summary

So far, this chapter has discussed the notion that Iron Age people in East Yorkshire may have conceptualised death as a journey. It has reviewed the evidence for travel and exchange amongst these communities and evaluated how journeying – and the ideas and things which came from distant places – may have been used to underwrite concepts of power. Finally, it has explored how aspects of life and death were negotiated using the symbols drawn from key arenas of Iron Age life: skilled crafting, agricultural reproduction and warfare. It is the latter arena to which the chapter finally turns.

Taking the path – martial culture and violent encounter

In this final section, it will be argued that violence – the capacity to intimidate or terrify, maim, wound or kill – was also a key arena in which authority was demonstrated and contested. Care is needed here, if we are to avoid the stereotypes of the 'war obsessed' Celts who feature in more traditional accounts of Iron Age life, drawn directly from the propaganda of the classical authors.

Unlike those authors, this book avoids assumptions that these people were either an innately 'martial race' or that warfare is an inherent feature of particular kinds of society such as chiefdoms (see also extensive discussion in Whitehead 2004; Parker Pearson and Thorpe 2005). We need to investigate the social and historical context of violence, if we want to understand Iron Age martial culture, and how and why bellicosity (a hostile or warlike temperament) may have been a key feature of these communities' sense of identity – particularly for specific age-sets and gender groups.

Motivations for violence

First, what may have motivated the infliction of physical or psychological harm amongst such small-scale communities? This need not have arisen from any endemic rivalry between tribes: Harrison's study of the Sepik of Papua New Guinea (1995) discusses how the same people may be sociable or violent to each other, in different contexts. Instead, ethnographic studies of violence suggest it often flares around various forms of social or moral transgression. Amongst agriculturalists who were increasingly defining access to grazing land and water, this might be theft or damage to stock and crops; raiding not just of moveable property but people; trespass or the occupation and seizing of resources which must usually be shared and negotiated (Ferguson 1990); intimidation or insult; desecration of sacred areas, objects or beliefs; and of course, physical wounding or injury (Maschner and Reedy Maschner 1998). (Interestingly, raids can be both a means of levelling perceived inequalities as well as a way of procuring wealth: Fukai 1996b). To this must be added the host of fears associated with illness and disease, ill-fortune or disaster, often attributed to malign practices such as sorcery or witchcraft. Kin relations can also be a source of tension (Thomas 1995): preference of fostering or marriage partners; relationships which have soured, proved unfruitful or unfaithful; issues of respect or allegiance between different kin groups. Running through all of this would have been the everyday politics of gender and age relations (Arnold 1995), and contests for prestige amongst age-sets. This latter group may have used forms of ritualised violence such as duelling, which was not intended to be fatal (Abbink 1999). Above these conflicts were the contests for authority between community leaders. Their power (as has been discussed) seems to rest less on bloodline and class, and more on personal skill, reputation and life-history – all of which, of course, had to be perpetually renegotiated and sanctioned (see Clay 1992). Whilst it was a prestigious activity, long-distance journeying was a dangerous undertaking. Those who 'took to the path' risked moving out of the web of relations which assured one's place and status in the local community. In crossing others' lands, negotiating use of their resources, attempting to initiate exchange, or merely passing through, tensions, misunderstandings and frictions might arise.

In such contexts, violence could be a powerful means of consolidating group identity... defining others and outsiders (see Sharples 2010 for a convincing argument for such group definition through violence and abnormal mortuary practice, in Wessex). As the introductory chapter to this book argued, amongst tightly-knit groups, revenge can be understood as a necessary corollary to love (Alès 2000) as well as a vital means of maintaining honour and gaining renown. Both aggressor and victim come to see their identity as partly defined by these events; a painful exchange through which the creation of embodied subjects vividly and memorably takes place (Whitehead 2004, 64). Because it leaves scars in the mind as well as on the body, violent events also provide a means of timekeeping and memory-making, which may become powerful elements of a community's story about itself (Harrell 2009). Placing his fingers in the 'dent' on his uncle's skull, the antiquarian John Mortimer would have appreciated this.

It is the pervasive psychological threat of violence – its 'eruptive possibility' (Whitehead 2004, 18) – as much as the dramatic performance of wounding, which makes it a vital part of the dialogues of political power (Harrell 2009). Yet where bellicosity develops as a trope of such authority (*ibid.*), it usually takes the form of a variety of graded forms of expression. Weapons need to be seen in non-martial contexts as accoutrements of power, and events such as seasonal social gatherings or rites of passage provided arenas for symbolic confrontation in which to show off strength, agility, skill and armament. From these kinds of symbolic confrontations however, disagreement might escalate from 'the violence of verbal or gestural expression through to the violence of armed bodily assault' (Whitehead 2004, 61).

The poetics and practice of violence

When we study violence, we need to analyse what Whitehead has called its 'poetics', by which he means the particular form it takes, and the discourse that serves to amplify the force of violent acts (2004, 6). For of course like sociality, violence is a key aspect of multiple social relations: between elites, geneaological units or even partners (*ibid.*). As an expression of power in multiple contexts (from the household to the field of contest) it can reveal much about the society in question (*ibid.*, 4–5). What does Iron Age material culture tell us about martial poetics? In a study of the image of the warrior from coins, hoards and burials, Hunter argues that there was a hierarchy of weaponry, linked to status: from the common (and multi-purpose) spear to the rarer sword, reserved for an elite (Hunter 2005). As the only weapon designed solely to kill (which embodied both lavish investment of resources and craft skill), the sword was a pure martial symbol (Târlea 2004, 17). Hunter argues this made it the choice weapon for an elite who were constructing a notion of status linked to heroic combat between individuals (rather than large-scale warfare; 2005). It was this symbol, he argues, that they 'took to the grave', whether or not they actually bore these arms in life (2005, 50). In sum, such 'warrior burials' were one of a series of 'projections of a desired image' whose 'actors, props and storylines' varied according to the audience concerned (*ibid.*, 43).

In Hunter's study, over 50% of the British martial burials come from East Yorkshire, so how do the patterns of armament in these graves relate to his model? Spears are a common weapon, in three cases found singly, once occurring as a pair (R154). As relatively short-bladed implements without mid-ribs, they appear to be close-to thrusting weapons, with an equally strong use in both inter-personal combat and hunting. Yet the range of sizes in the male WS453 burial alone suggest they could encompass 'a range of throwing spears or javelins as well as lances or stabbing spears' (Dent 2010, 43). As the probable cause of death in four cases, they entered the body at close range from the front into the pelvis (R140, possibly aimed at the femoral artery), into the back of R94 (lodged between the 12th thoracic and 1st lumbar vertebrae: its snapped tip later found dislodged), in the stomach (WS211, perhaps aimed at vital organs) and through the back (R152a, piercing the heart). Alongside iron spearheads are the bone points which may also have served as sharpened tips to a projectile, found in multiples within burials such as GS5, WS269 and WS346. Sixteen of them were found at Grimthorpe, though as they lay under and over the body, Stead argued they could either be shroud pins or small lance-heads (1968). All three burials of iron spearheads with shields are definite examples of the elaborate post-mortem 'spearing' rite, where the shield had been laid protectively over the corpse beforehand ... so these may not reflect a real-life weapons pairing. Indeed, close-combat with such thrusting spears may have necessitated the holding of the shaft with both hands (rather than launching it single-handed, like a javelin: Fontijn 2005), preventing the use of the shield. In five cases, burials with spears are also found with a sword, suggesting this was a common weapons-set: perhaps using the spear first before the sword was deployed for the final, finishing blows, as in prehistoric Mediterranean epics such as the *Iliad* (Târlea 2005). In that epic, combatants frequently employed rocks or stones during the contest, to batter their opponent's bodies (particularly the head – perhaps to stun or bring them momentarily to their knees) and there are a number of depressed fractures which would fit well with this more improvised use of blunt objects, alongside smaller wounds which might arise from slingshots (as found in a cache at Wetwang Slack), domestic objects or even the fist (in the case of the broken noses).

Meanwhile, the swords suggest they were made for slashing blows from a variety of angles or deep thrusting wounds (though they lack the precision of a smaller, rapier-style weapon). This fits well with the osteological evidence for a variety of fine slashing blows to the back of the head, the front of the face, and rarer wounds to the shoulder, ribs and hands, as well as classic 'parry' fractures to the arm (as discussed in Chapter 4). (Only WS453's head wound provides an example of a deep slicing cut which might be attributable to an axe). The organic components of both the sword grips (bone, antler, wood) and the shield elements (wood and hide products) would have helped absorb the shock of such blows with an efficient 'damping' effect (Târlea 2005). Interestingly, the whole 'sword, shield and spear' panoply is found only twice as a weapons-set (one of these being the new burial from Caythorpe) but occurs in three more cases of the dramatic spearing rite. Lone swords are found in four burials, lone knives in another four, and shields and swords in another two. There is one burial with a shield but no offensive weapon (R148), and the chainmail burial at K5 is otherwise without any martial accoutrements.

What does this tell us? There are more burials with a lone sword than a spear, and spears were more often paired with a sword than a shield, with only a very few examples where all three implements were found together. Even here, the presence of the spear relates more to the martial 'send-off' than equipping the deceased with the full panoply of items. The patterns would suggest that the shield was used in sword combat, to parry, inflict and deflect blows. The spear may have been a more common weapon at the time and this is reflected in the conspicuous consumption of numerous examples in the 'spearing' rite. Yet the sword may be a more common formal funerary gift precisely because of its pure martial symbolism as well as the histories of use which had accrued around it. Hunter's model may still be largely valid, but the five cases of spears and sword found in tandem suggest the former was by no means an inferior instrument: it was part of a suite of weapons selected according to the nature of the confrontation, or the stage the combatants had reached within the fight. The spear was equally responsible for fatalities: three spear-related deaths equalling the number of bodies with sword/knife cuts which show no signs of healing (WS114, Acklam Wold, DG104).

This evidence allows us to identify the zones of the body commonly targeted for injury. The front-facing nature of many of these wounds, and the character of the weaponry used, suggests a formalised set of tactics or rules of combat learned through training. It would have created a certain kind of body, a way of moving and even perceiving the world (Harrell 2009, 13): a martial disposition, as much as musculature, which would have been read in other contexts. The majority of the wounds suggest face-to-face combat: 'duels' orchestrated between two 'champions' (there are no mass graves or extensive recidivism, suggestive of larger scale or more indiscriminate conflict). Cuts from swords or knives contrast with the depressed fractures to the head or face and split noses, which may relate to more 'spur of the moment' altercations. The targeting of the most personable aspect of the body might tie in with Sharples' assessment of these communities as focused on the individual: celebrating or denigrating their personhood (2010). Yet the high rate of healing amongst all of these injuries, suggests such dramatic altercations were seldom fatal: perhaps in part, because of the risks of vendetta, amongst the close-knit households of what we must remember was a fairly small and open community (see, for example, Abbink 1999). There may well have been punitive measures taken against those who took life outside of this code: R152 (discussed in Chapter 5, Figure 4.5) may represent one such scenario. Here, the man fatally stabbed with a spear through the back, lies extended in the grave. At his side, lent against him, is a second male: cause of death unknown. Several alternative interpretations for this burial have already been discussed: perhaps the two men died in the same raid, or this may have been a suicide, prompted by grief from a partner, relative or peer? However, an interesting alternative is that this may be the murderer, who was put to death for attacking his opponent from behind (in a cowardly fashion) in a moment of rage. Perhaps they were sent into the next life together as a way of evening the score, and preventing this incident reverberating down the generations in a blood-feud. In terms of the cemetery evidence, it suggests that it was more strategically effective to have 'walking wounded' – scarred with your wrath – as living testimony to your power, rather than lying cold and dead in the grave. This refers to yet another aspect of power exercised through violence: that of humiliation.

However, we must always be wary of the archaeological conundrum that an 'absence of evidence is not necessarily evidence of absence'. Devastating flesh wounds or fatal organ damage are not detectable from the skeletal remains. As Dent suggested some time ago, a slight under-representation of men in the cemeteries may also indicate some adults died in raiding or combat away from home (1982; see Chapter 4). Some of our most traumatic killings may not be represented in formal burials, as their remains may have been left where they fell or were gathered as trophies by enemies. Some of the apparently 'empty' square barrows may indeed represent cenotaphs for such lost individuals, enabling a commemoration of their bravery and role within the community, in the absence of a body.

Warfare, hunting and travel

It has already been acknowledged that the spear had multiple symbolism, derived from its use in hunting as well as warfare. The two are related, in that hunting can be seen as a quasi-martial activity involving the skills to snare an impressive or ferocious animal, the wit to avoid personal injury, and the final, fatal mastery of another being's body. Success in hunting (which involves journeying between the familiar, domestic realm and distant, wild or unknown regions) is also seen as directly analogous to other prestige-conferring activities, including long-distance travel, exchange or skilled crafting (Helms 1993). All of these involve difficult journeys to distant realms, evidencing that individual's exceptional qualities (*ibid.*). It is obviously an arena in which to practice and hone skill with weapons such as the spear and knife, and is frequently used in initiation rites for age-sets or class groups (Morris 1990). Its spoils confer prestige, accrued from prowess in the hunt, and the taste of different meat would have created a powerful set of communal memories, cementing group identity. Yet as Chapters 4 and 5 noted, evidence for hunting in these communities is slight. Many of the recent chariot burial excavations have confirmed the joints of special meat in these burials as domestic pig, but some of the antiquarian reports describe carcases of wild boar, as in the King's Grave, Arras (Greenwell 1906, 279). Stillingfleet's bronze-encased 'boar tusks' in the Charioteer's barrow at Arras were reinterpreted by Stead as antler tine linch-pins (1979, 90) but antler, nonetheless, does suggest hunting of deer, and red and roe faunal remains were discovered at Wetwang Slack in small amounts. Both boar and deer are, of course, despoilers of crops, which may have led to their classification as 'stealers' or 'thieves' amongst an agricultural community (Hamilakis 2003). Yet the rarity of such hunts, and the limited choice of quarry, may actually point to its significance, as a dramatic 'power-generating strategy' which further reinforced the authority of a martial group and their defence of the community's resources (*ibid.*). It also provided a symbolic contest in which to practice killing with the spear. The wearing of by-products from the hunt (boar tusks, antler tines, hide products or bristles) were not just practically useful for absorbing shock in a shield, hilt or linch pin. They may also have been believed to confer some of the beast's qualities upon the bearer or the vehicle: the ferocity of the boar, the agility and speed of the stag (Fitzpatrick 2008; Giles 2008b). This discussion of substances and their meaning brings us onto the final aspect of martiality – the aesthetics of violence.

The aesthetics of violence: 'seeing red'

The equipment used to wield this power was skilfully made and often elaborately decorated … colours and patterns on shields, conjured from the practised choice of wood and hide, embellished with bronze and iron fittings; wooden, iron and bronze scabbards, lined with fleece or fur, with front plates covered in hide or incised with entrancing Celtic art; iron swords decorated with hilts made of horn and antler, their pommels and tips cut back and in-filled with red glass or decorated with coral studs. In the last chapter, this complex art was discussed as part of a 'technology of enchantment' through which an opponent with malign intent (human or spiritual) might be ensnared (after Gell 1998). In the case of martial objects, Thomas' ideas were used to draw out the psychological terror and awe which might be instilled in an enemy through viewing such weapons (1995). It was argued that this was a vital part of the gradation of violent dispute (as well as achieving dominance in other social settings like exchange) designed to deter actual bloodshed. Such decoration suggests an elaborate 'aesthetics' of violence which we also need to consider in our account, particularly the use of the colour red. Whether achieved through glass or coral, and sometimes red chalk, sandstone or other ferruginous pastes, its selective use on Iron Age artefacts from East Yorkshire is telling (Henderson and Freestone in Stead 1991). A broader palette was available to these craftspeople: as Skeates notes, coral comes in many colours: the deliberate selection of red is significant (1993, 288), likewise the preference of red glass over the blue used in bead necklaces or the yellow rarely evidenced in the hilt of the Thorpe Hall sword (Stead 2006, 196). Red glass, coral and stone features on a range from weapons like the sword, to chariot fittings, pendants and plaques, bracelets and brooches (see Giles 2008b). The colour has obvious symbolic associations with blood, and could therefore conjure both life-giving and life-taking properties. Redolent of fertility, it is also a colour used to evoke more vigorous states of being, such as anger. An analogy between coral and skin or blood may have been the source of its use as an apotropaic and curative substance: worn as an amulet or ingested to protect and heal the flesh, as recorded amongst the Gauls by Pliny the Elder, in his *Natural History* (chapter 11, book 32). As an exotic substance, it also alluded to the skill and power needed to acquire it from a distant realm. In short, the colours, substances and techniques used on such weapons magnified their perceived potency and effectiveness: protecting the wearer's body as well as enhancing its martial aura.

The Kirkburn 'Warrior'

Bearing these themes of the poetics and aesthetics of violence in mind, I want to end this section by looking in detail at one of the most well-known martial burials – the Kirkburn warrior (Figure 7.3). He is a young adult male, who died around 17–25 years old (Stead 1991, 224–5). There is no evidence of disease or injury on the skeleton but that does not preclude a violent death. The important thing, perhaps, is that he died in the prime of his life. He was dressed in a tunic or gown, and then probably wrapped in a cloak, before being laid on his back, slightly flexed: his arms folded upwards so that his hands rested on his chest, right below the chin. On his breast were placed the front portions and skull of a pig, split in two – butchered and apparently defleshed: an offering, or merely the remnants, from a lavish funeral feast. At his side was a magnificent sword, its bronze scabbard decorated with elaborately incised Celtic art and inlaid with blood-red glass at its hilt and tip. It has been suggested that it was made to look as if both its handle and blade-end were dripping from a fight (S. James, pers. comm.): stained with the life-blood of an enemy. The sword appears older than the man: it is battered and repaired several times, suggesting it was well-used and handed down as an heirloom. Yet its design suggests it was a close craft 'cousin' of the swords buried with chariots at Wetwang Slack: 'produced using very localised skills, possibly in the same workshop and within a generation, if not by the same hand' (Stead 2006, 118). This man must have been a well-connected or skilled individual to inherit such a gift, whose power derived both from its impressive crafting and the stories of the hands it had passed through and the fights in which it had been wielded. But this time, the sword would not outlive its master: he was equipped for the journey into death by this weapon. Interestingly, the sword itself was carefully placed with its hilt towards his feet, not his hands. This might be part of a 'rite of reversal': a way of burying the weapon which made it clear that its life in this world was over, or ensuring it could not be wielded by an uneasy revenant: a spirit who 'rose again' to harry the living.

The grave began to be backfilled, but at some point, a vivid and violent performance was enacted over the corpse. Three spearheads were found point-down in the soil: perched just above the chest of the Kirkburn man, possibly piercing the body (J. Joy, pers. comm.). They must have been driven into the soil by a small group: thrust hard into the newly shovelled chalky spoil of the burial mound, so that their tips broke off. In each case, the shaft was intact (Stead 1991, 77–8), suggesting that the wooden haft of the spear stuck out of the mound … like a cluster of bristles or spines on the barrow. These spearheads were not particularly strong, and it has been suggested that they were freshly smithed for the burial (*ibid.*, 79). This does not seem to be the grave of an enemy taken in battle … perhaps the men were his companions in arms, and the spearing of the burial was a vivid act of shared remembrance: a martial send-off … the equivalent of a gun-salute. Perhaps they were his relatives, symbolically marking the untimely death of a beloved husband or son, as well as a vigorous defender of his community. It is even possible that his death was somehow considered ignoble: amongst the Dinka, the 'proper' death of the Spearmaster is one over which the individual himself presides (Lienhardt 1961), since famine and infertility results if 'he is taken by death rather than his taking it' (Bloch and Parry 1982, 16). However, his second symbolic death at the end of a spear may have given him an appropriately martial end, and addressed fears similar to the Dinkas, that the strength and prosperity of the community was jeopardised by his demise. Yet the nature of this rite – spearing the body into the earth – also suggests an underlying fear … a concern that this man might not lie quietly in his grave. Perhaps he was still hungry for life, or looking for revenge. This secondary mortuary rite, a cathartic 'ghost' killing by the group (Aldhouse-Green 2001, 35, 55), might be part of how they contained his spirit: pinning him into the landscape in which he was to become a respected ancestor. Whatever the motives of the mourners, they ensured that his barrow was marked for years to come with the impressive shafts of the spears, projecting from the soil. Even at a distance, silhouetted against a skyline, these poles would have been prompts for his family or brothers-in-arms to remember his life, and the send-off he was given. Such well-coppiced wood would have lasted long enough for one generation to tell the next about both his deeds and his death, so that his fame – and that of his marvellous sword – lived on.

Summary

Finally, we must consider whether the East Yorkshire sword, shield and spear burials represent a permanent warrior elite? Not necessarily. As Fontijn notes, 'warriors' in a small-scale society may be called upon to fight for particular occasions, as part of 'a temporary, context-dependent identity' (2005, 151). We must also remember we are interpreting this evidence from the arena of death and burial: a sword in a burial does not make someone a warrior, even though a warrior may need a sword (see Härke 1990)! At this point it is salient to remember Hunter's point about the projected image of the warrior. Yet this image was increasingly reiterated over the latter phases of these cemeteries use.

Greater numbers of weapons-burials, distinguished by different orientation (east–west) and their small, round monuments, become increasingly common in the latest Iron Age (Stead 1991). We also have iconic, isolated sword burials (North Grimston, Grimthorpe, Thorpe, Acklam) and small cemeteries with a strong martial or violent focus (Kirkburn, Garton Station), suggesting a defined distinction between these men and the rest of their community. The close relationship forged between individuals and their elaborate weapons, or the 'martial send-off' of the spearing rite, suggests a key age-set and gender group, for whom this was an all-defining aspect of their identity. Rather than only representing an elite, it suggests a martial code was woven into the very fabric of life for young and adult men, with both expenditure lavished upon its material accoutrements (into which many levels of the community were drawn), and codes of fighting and honour, instilled through explicit training regimes during early youth.

Conclusion – those that 'warm the road'

This chapter has argued that death was conceived of as a journey, represented in the close relationship between square barrows and routes of movement such as trackways or streams. It went on to explore what journeying may have meant to these communities, and why it was a motif for structuring the regeneration of the ancestors, by exploring what came from distant places. Since the majority of the population were born, raised and died in these valleys, such travellers and the exotic ideas and substances they returned with (or, in terms of foreigners, brought with them) had a special cachet. This idea was followed with a discussion of the role of skilled crafting, employing distant materials and designs in discourses of power. Finally, the chapter brought these themes together in a consideration of martial culture ... objects made from exotic materials used as social 'weapons of exclusion', and as implements of both psychological and physical intimidation, in a political trope of bellicosity.

I want to return now to the curious case study with which I began this book: the four 'speared burials' of Garton Station, clustered around the chariot burial of a senior male (see Figures 1.1, 7.1 and 7.4). We can appreciate the martial symbolism which underpinned their mortuary rite, and acknowledge they were part of an adult male group who probably defined themselves in part, through their combat training and prowess. As such, they set themselves apart from the broader community, forming a small cohort of burials, distinguished in their memorable appearance. Whether they were actual warriors or not, the image projected by their retinue of mourners was of an exclusive funerary arena, bristling with intimidation: encircling the body with martial symbolism. Finally, we are in a position to finally understand why they were buried where they were ... speared into the fine chalk gravel of the bed of a Gypsey Race. As a body of water associated with fertility, which could itself be dangerous and violent, but which was an important medium through which the dead departed this life,

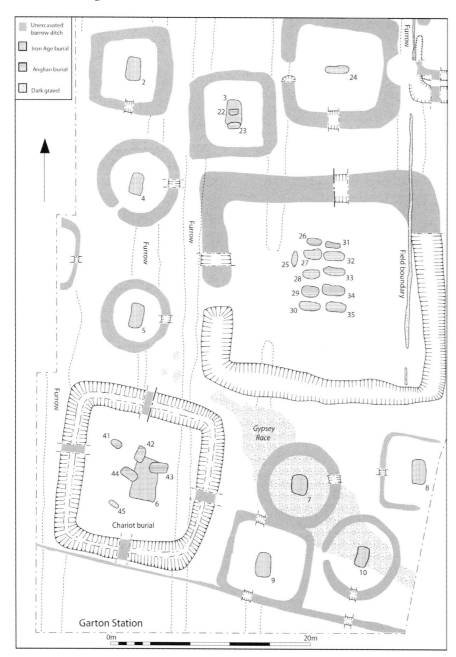

FIGURE 7.4. Garton Station 'speared' burials, located in the base of the Gypsey Race – GS4, GS5, GS7 and GS10. Based on Stead 1991, 22, fig. 20.

the waters sped the passage of the ancestors on their journey, whilst the spears impaled their feared corpses firmly in place. The final chapter returns to these themes of landscape, material culture and identity, through the lens of the most iconic object found in these Iron Age burials … the chariot.

CHAPTER EIGHT

Conclusion

....

The Wetwang Village chariot burial

Bronze terrets, decorated with studs of coral: one lost and replaced with slivers of red glass. A set of horse-bits, wrapped in their reins: their bridges decorated with red glass studs, cross-quartered by decorative bronze designs. Simple yet elegant open-work strap unions: their near-perfect symmetry broken by a reverse 's' drawing the eye to a central stud of coral or red chalk. 'J' shaped iron linch-pins, whose head-rings and upper shanks has been dipped in copper alloy; shadowing the inner and outer nave bands of two iron rimmed wheels. An involuted brooch, decorated with three long coral beads. A delicate strand of dozens of tiny blue-glass beads, arranged near the edge of a plate of iron … a magnificent mirror, joined by an open ring to the swelled bulbous designs of its decorative handle.

This litany of the horse-gear, complemented by the classic female object of power: the mirror, tells us that this burial – the latest to be discovered on the Yorkshire Wolds – was that of another powerful woman (Figure 8.1; Hill 2001). It was found in 2001 at the edge of the village of Wetwang Slack, by the Guildhouse Consultancy (directed by the local archaeologist Rod Mackey, assisted by Kate Dennett). The importance of the burial and quality of the grave goods soon led to the involvement of the British Museum and English Heritage (Hill 2004). The valley is famous for its three chariot burials to the west, on the opposite side of the valley (Dent 1985), and another from Garton Slack, to the east (Brewster 1971). Yet nothing was known of the prehistory of the main village, situated on the crest of the slack, along which runs the main thoroughfare connecting Driffield to Fridaythorpe and on to York. The impressive square barrow which marked this woman's grave was found in the grounds of the 'Great Garth': a medieval manor (Neave and Neave 2008, 240). Although there were no spectacular views from this site, it may have been deliberately sited just 50 m east of the village 'mere' which by the early 14th century was described as a rain-fed pond, frequently dry in the summer (*ibid.*, 241; Havercroft 2001). For those who knew where to look, the barrow would certainly have been visible from the major north–south 'Wolds Way' linear earthwork, on the northern side of the slack (Hill 2004).

What of the woman herself? She had been laid on her left-hand side, facing west, her head to the south: as if gazing inland towards the tapering mouth of the slack. Evidence for some form of matting or cloth was found as a rectangular

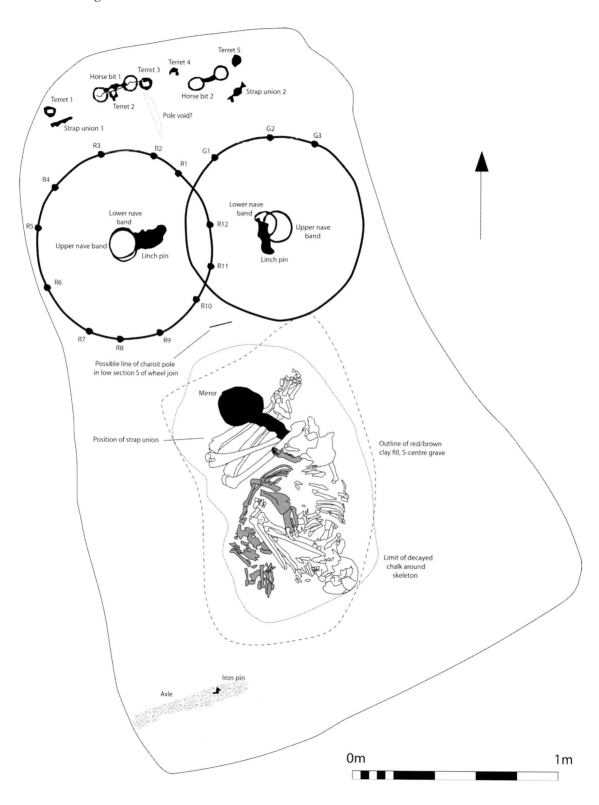

Terret 5

Terret 4

Horse bit 1   Terret 3

Terret 1

Terret 2

Strap union 1

Horse bit 2

Strap union 2

Pole void?

G2   G3

R3   R2   G1

R1

R4

R5   Lower nave
band

Lower nave
band

Upper nave
band

R12   Upper nave
band

Upper nave band   Linch pin

Linch pin

R11

R6

R10

R7   R8   R9

Possible line of charoit pole
in low section S of wheel join

Mirror

Position of strap union   Outline of red/brown
clay fill, S-centre grave

Limit of decayed
chalk around
skeleton

Iron pin

Axle

0m   1m

stain under the body (*ibid.*). The chariot wheels were laid below her feet, and the yoke (with its full complement of terrets) occupied the far northern end of the grave, running east–west and apparently laid on its side (*ibid.*). The axle meanwhile was below her head and suggestions of a soil stain at right-angles to this indicated this 'frame' of axle-pole shaft may have been laid as a single piece in the grave. From the soil stains around her body, it looked as if she may have been placed *within* the box of the chariot which had been removed from the main vehicle (Mackey, cited in Anthoons 2011): framed and contained by its sides. In contrast, Hill argues it may have been laid *over* the corpse (2004). As previously discussed, she may also have been wrapped, as her wrist appears to have been fractured (post-mortem) from being bound back towards the body (*ibid.*). A further squat strap union at her knees may have been part of the tie or closure of a cloak or shroud (*ibid.*). The head and forelimbs of a young adult male pig had been split and placed over her thigh and under/in front of her elbows: the forelimbs were not articulated and may have been defleshed before deposition. Parts of a second, younger pig were also present, suggesting multiple animals had been sacrificed or consumed by the mourners. The barrow over her grave had begun to erode, silting into the ditch, by the time mourners returned to the site, to leave further offerings of suckling pig … charred from a memorial feast, during which a portion had been once more set aside for the dead. Other fragmentary animal and human bones also appear to have been left on the mound or placed in the ditch, at an unspecified later date.

The new discovery attracted great interest in the local press as well as the archaeological community. Headlines alluded to her as a *'Warrior Queen'* (*Independent*, 7 April 2001) or Yorkshire *'Boadicea'* (*Yorkshire Post*, 19 February 2002), and she featured in a special edition of *Meet the Ancestors*, entitled *'Chariot Queen'* (BBC2, screened 19 February 2002, and revisited in the 2013 series). The initial programme suggested her skeletal remains had an intriguing story to tell. She was a senior or even elderly woman, at least 35–45 years old (though like the Wetwang woman, the good condition of her teeth belied her age). She was 5 ft 7½ inches (1.71 m) in height: significantly taller than most of the women from the other cemeteries, and also equal too or even taller than the average man (Chapter 4). Besides her respectable age and striking appearance, she had experienced a significant trauma in her life. Severe osteoarthritis and wear facets on her right shoulder suggest either vigorous over-use of that joint or more likely, a dislocated shoulder, sustained in a fall. This agonising injury seems to have been compounded by a serious jolt to the jaw on the same side of the body, causing the fracturing of flakes from several of her teeth (Hill 2004). The programme intimated this may well have resulted from a fall from the chariot, and given the risks involved in controlling such vehicles (as well as the feats of prowess which may have been attempted in them) this is not an unlikely suggestion! However, it is equally possible that this fall was sustained in other activities, since (as Chapter 4 has argued) many fractures and dislocations were the result of agricultural accidents.

FIGURE 8.1. The Wetwang Village chariot burial. Based on Hill 2001, fig. 1.

The facial reconstruction artist commissioned by the programme, Caroline Wilkinson, also argued that there was something deeply unsettling about the shape of her face. It was warped or twisted, resulting in significant asymmetry: the result, a Mr Hood of Manchester University argued, of something like a facial haemangioma … a misgrowth of the cells that line blood vessels (Hill 2004). It is important to note that the latest review of the evidence casts doubt upon this interpretation: the condition is extremely rare and the skull may simply have been deformed through post-depositional compression (S. Stead and Brothwell, cited in Hill 2004). However, we know from other famous examples such as the northern European bog bodies, that those marked by physical differences may well have been chosen as candidates for special roles (see Aldhouse-Green 2001; Giles 2009). If correct, the Wetwang woman would have been disfigured from birth by the lumpy red texture of the growth, covering the region from her cheek to eye socket. We say 'disfigured' but we know that in these communities red was a special, even sacred colour (Chapter 7). It is possible that this was seen by her community as a distinguishing mark: that she had somehow been 'enamelled' by the gods at birth, and chosen to be set apart for a special path in life.

Whether or not this element of her biography is true, her burial is extraordinary, and crystallizes many of the key themes in this book. Here we have a senior woman, who has probably come through her child-bearing years to become a respected elder. The mirror indicates the status she held in life, perhaps as a revered or even feared, seer, or else she was equipped to become a powerful ancestor in the afterlife. Mineralised impressions of hide and fur on the plate suggest the mirror was protected in a bag or covering made from a distinctive pelt: quite possibly, an otter (Hill, pers. comm.). The water-repelling nature of such a hide may have helped 'care' for the surface of this valuable and precious artefact, prone to rusting. Yet the ambiguous behaviour of this animal – a creature which moves with fluid ease between the realms of land and water – may also have been symbolically significant, as an emissary or denizen of these unpredictable yet life-giving waters. The location of the burial near to the mere was thus surely important. As a rare and vital source of drinking water in this notoriously dry valley (Chapter 3), the pond (like the mirror's reflective surface) could also have been seen as a portal to the underworld, from which life came, and into which the dead may have been thought to depart to be regenerated (see Chapter 7). The raising of her barrow a few hundred metres away may have been an attempt by her community to consolidate their rites to this water, which from henceforth were legitimated through, and protected by, the presence of a powerful ancestor. In addition, the mirror was decorated with a miniature version of the blue glass bead necklaces which adorned the necks of several older women in the valley below: women who became the preferred focus for several of their descendents' graves (Chapter 3). Yet whatever this suite of beads represents … a tassel tied to the mirror's handle, a decorative tie for the bag in which it was protected … these beads are so far unique. Given that their nearest parallels are to be found in Ireland, these apparently diminutive objects are deceptively important and may have spoken of far-distant relations. The involuted brooch which seems to form part of this bag tie, may have been decorated with coral, like the beads on some of the horse-gear: a substance which evoked contact with the distant Continent. Hill argues this may represent the largest volume of coral in any burial from the Wolds (2004). Yet at least some of this gear was old: repaired with the local equivalent substance of red glass, a material also used on the horse-bits. This colour and texture evoked the broader repertoire of objects of power: sword hilts and scabbard fittings, the bronze box of the Wetwang Slack female chariot burial, as well as some of the magnificent involuted brooches such as the one interred at Ferry Fryston. The notion of a long biography for some of the chariot parts is reinforced by the horse-bits, which were also worn and in one case, damaged (Hill 2004).

Complex crafting, local and long-distance relations, inherited heirlooms, colour and power, water and regeneration, feasting and memory, gender and age: her burial condenses many of the themes that have emerged in this book from the wider analysis of the landscape, settlement and burials. Together, they create a sense of the distinctive character of these later prehistoric communities in eastern Yorkshire 400–100 BC, and the important relationships which shaped their identity. Whilst family and genealogy defined the place of both living and dead, it has been suggested that the individuals buried with chariots may have been set apart from these ties, and came instead to epitomise an authority grounded not only in age and sex but distinctive skills, practical or ritual knowledge and significant life-histories. It was the ability of such individuals to manipulate not just local relations but deal with people, substances and ideas from more distant origins (either through direct travel or exchange) which also consolidated their power. Such an ego-centred society, defined by strong 'grid' rather than strong 'group' identity, characteristically valorises leaders renowned for their 'courage, determination and cunning' (Sharples 2010, 294, after Douglas 1970). It is interesting that either through birth or life-events, many of the East Yorkshire individuals were physically different, like the Garton Slack chariot male who Brewster argues had significant leg asymmetry (1971, 291) as well as a possible abscess or brain tumour (1975, 113), or the Wetwang Slack chariot male who survived the severe sword injury to the back of his head (Dent 1985). The Wetwang Village woman takes her place amongst those distinguished by their appearance and fortitude. It is clear from these accounts that such status could be achieved by either men or women, as the antiquarian Greenwell argued at the turn of the last century, in relation to the 'Arras Lady' – distinguished by both mirror and chariot:

> the woman occupied an important place in their polity, not only in relation to the family, but in a wider connexion [sic] being at times even in the position of the ruling power
>
> Greenwell 1906, 293–4.

Composite objects and relational identity

Greenwell's use of the term 'connection' is unwittingly astute, for what the most complex artefacts found in these burials epitomise is a web of relations: past and present, near and distant. In particular, the chariot can be thought of as the most elaborate of a range of composite artefacts (including swords, mirrors, containers, bead necklaces and brooches) whose crafting deliberately evoked this world of the local *and* the exotic, through design and decoration. Such items may well have had the status of 'sacred items' held by community leaders: accompanied by detailed biographical histories linked to prestigious owners and events ... even origin myths (Sharples 2010, 95). Sharples goes on to argue this is a defining attribute of societies who invest in 'the acquisition of rare and precious materials that can only be manipulated by specialist craftsmen and which can only be used by individuals set apart from the community' (2010, 312). They are extravagant objects: destined for a life of performance, wedded to distinctive people.

Such composite objects are defined by the diversity of components and materials involved in their making, as well as their multiple authorship: they are the product of networks of social obligations, skills and resources. Their meaning will vary with context and time, particularly different stages in the artefact's life-cycle, as well as the biographies of those associated with it (Finlay 2003, 170). Whilst such objects may appear to 'crystallise' momentarily in the hands of one individual, as embodiments of collective effort they are also exemplars of family or community identity. In contrast to previous interpretations which tend to present them as the personal possessions of an elite, chariots in particular can be seen as an ideal vehicle of communal aspiration and investment: strategically used in funerary rites to create a well-connected and well-travelled ancestor. Indeed, the 'making' of a chariot such as Ferry Fryston, may well have relied on the donation of different components from several sponsors. In East Yorkshire, the composite nature of this assemblage was revealed for all to see in the distinctive disassembling of the chariots during the funeral ceremony. This 'making and taking apart' motif arguably enabled onlookers to witness and commemorate the broader web of relations such artefacts embodied. It also made for a memorable technology of remembrance (Williams 2006), various components of which, as heirlooms, brought other times and people to mind. These properties make composite objects highly significant, socially charged objects in their own time, but also invaluable archaeological artefacts in the present day. As this book has shown, we can 'explode' such objects outwards, in terms of their crafting and life-story, to reveal the broader social and technological taskscape ... the landscape of the chariot ... through which they came into being (Ingold 1993).

We may imagine then, that a woman stitching the leather-work for the Wetwang harness knew the horse-gear to which it would be attached was old: decorated with exotic substances which were exchanged with distant communities across the sea. In contrast, the timber was felled locally, from saplings which the previous generations' carpenters had watched grow: singled out for their form as fit for an axle or hub stock. Other exchanges would have been made with communities in the surrounding vales, for iron and bronze or red glass. When she lifted her eyes to the horizon of the slack, she would see the stock being brought down into the valley: the herd from which her hides were stripped, cleaned and stretched. These cattle and sheep sustained and nourished the families she grew up with, whilst left-overs fattened the pigs who were ear-marked for special funeral feasts. All of this to-and-fro, of people and stock, created trackways along which the cemeteries clustered, so that inhabitants as well as visitors passing through were impressed by the amassed community of the dead. This craftswoman was bound into the rhythms of labour which defined the Iron Age landscape: not just the immediate project of making the vehicle and its trappings, of training ponies and drivers, but the broader tasks of stock-raising, producing food, building houses. Yet her work also bound her into a social landscape, of families, peers, elders, ancestors and strangers. In the moment of her stitchwork, she reached back into the past, outwards into the network of exchange relationships (near and distant) and forward into the moment of assembly and use. Stitch by stitch, she threaded those relationships into being.

Conclusion

In this last chapter, I have singled out the most iconic object made by these communities, to epitomise the approach taken in this book, arguing that the chariot was literally and metaphorically a vehicle of relations. Its multiple construction, and frequent amalgamation of old and new parts, appeared to crystallise authority in the hands of an impressive individual, forming an indissoluble bond with a charismatic figure. Yet as this book has tried to conjure, that power derived from family relations, community support and long-distance connections. These attributes were further cross-cut by aspects of age, gender and often an impressive individual biography, distinguished by courage in the face of dramatic events, fearful individual power (martial or spiritual) or spectacular skill. At times, this authority was exercised at the end of a sword or spear, but the lower levels of violence seen in these overtly martial communities (compared with regions like Wessex, King 2010; Sharples 2010) suggest its leaders wielded their power effectively, and were successful in negotiating disputes and feuds. Their bodies now held further capital for the bereaved, giving the living an opportunity to transform the deceased into a powerful ancestor.

Why inter the chariot rather than pass it on? The vehicle brought to that moment its own life-history and multiple roles: it was the ultimate stage for performance (Pare 1989), drawing attention to the skill and union of person, objects and animals, able to speed passage between realms. It condensed relations with the past and present, local and exotic, in a blur of intimidating motion. Stilled forever, as it became first a hearse and then a coffin, dramatically conveying its inhabitant to their last encounter and on into the afterlife. We do not know why other communities in Iron Age Britain and Ireland (who clearly had access to such technology) did not utilise it in funeral rites, but in East Yorkshire at least, this bestowed upon such vehicles a sacred, even a hallowed role (Piggott 1992, 20). It certainly created a distinctive aspect of cultural life which must have been renowned by the inhabitants of neighbouring districts who did things rather differently. Whether any individuals actually came from the Continent is an issue that still has to be resolved, but the different strands of evidence discussed here favour an interpretation of a largely indigenous population, in rare and sporadic contact with regions from the Champagne to Ireland: a model which helps explain the significance and cachet of exotic ideas and materials within these communities.

This account of later prehistoric Eastern Yorkshire has been based in the firm belief that archaeology is a powerful tool for investigating humanity, as it can analyse the social, material and historical conditions through which certain ways of being were made possible (after Barrett 1994). Through this analysis, we have apprehended some of the values which shaped Iron Age life and the ways in which different spheres of practice were interwoven, creating powerful worlds of metaphor which crossed different contexts. It has used this evidence to investigate *how* peoples' sense of identity, role and authority was forged. The importance of the places they dwelt in, the people and animals they worked with and the objects they made, bring us back to the key themes of the book: landscape, identity, material culture. They also return us to Mark Doty's poem, revealing the 'forged glamour' through which Iron Age people mocked death: making themselves memorable to us, through the remarkable remains of their lives.

Bibliography

Abbink, J. G. (1999) Violence, Ritual and Reproduction: Culture and Context in Surma Duelling. *Ethnology* 38(3), 227–242.

Abramson, P. (1996) Excavations along the Caythorpe Gas Pipeline, North Humberside. *Yorkshire Archaeological Journal* 68, 1–88.

Aldhouse-Green, M. (2001) *Dying for the Gods. Human Sacrifice in Iron Age and Roman Europe*. Stroud, Tempus.

Aldhouse-Green, M. (2004) Crowning Glories: Languages of Hair in Later Prehistoric Europe. *Proceedings of the Prehistoric Society* 70, 299–325.

Alès, C. (2000) Anger as a marker of love: the ethic of conviviality among the Yanomami. In J. Overing and A. Passes (eds), *The Anthropology of Love and Anger: the aesthetics of conviviality in Native Amazonia*. London, Routledge, 133–151.

Allison, K. J. (ed.) (1974) *A History of the County of the York. (East Riding Volume 2)*. London, Victoria County Histories.

Anon. (1897) The Recent Opening of the 'Danes' Graves' near Driffield. *The Yorkshire Weekly Post*. Saturday 7 August 1897, 11.

Anthoons, G. (2011) *Migration and elite networks as modes of cultural exchange in Iron Age Europe: a case study of contacts between the Continent and the Arras Culture*. Unpublished PhD thesis, University of Bangor.

Arnold, B. (2005) Mobile Men, Sedentary Women? Material culture as a marker of regional and sub-regional interaction in early Iron Age southwest Germany. In H. Dobrzansak, J. V. S. Megaw and D. Poleska, *Celts on the Margins: Studies in European Cultural Interaction, 7th c. BC–1st c. AD. Essays in Honour of Zenon Wozniak*. Institute of Archaeology and Ethnology of the Polish Academy of the Sciences, 17–26.

Arnold, B. and Gibson, D. B. (eds) (1995) *Celtic Chiefdom, Celtic State*. Cambridge, Cambridge University Press.

Arnold, C. J. (1995) The archaeology of inter-personal violence. *Scottish Archaeological Review* 9–10, 71–9.

Aylwin, E. and Ward, R. C. (1969) *Development and Utilisation of Water Supplies in the East Riding of Yorkshire*. Occasional Papers in Geography 10. Hull, University of Hull.

Bachelard, G. (1994) (reprint and translation of 1958) *The Poetics of Space*. Boston, Beacon Press.

Bailey, D. W. (2005) *Prehistoric Figurines: representation and corporeality in the Neolithic*. London, Routledge.

Barrett, J. (1989) Food, gender and metal: questions of social reproduction. In M. L. Sørensen and R. Thomas (eds), *The Bronze Age–Iron Age Transitions in Europe: Aspects of continuity and change in European societies c. 1200 to 500 BC*. Oxford, British Archaeological Report S483, 304–320.

Barrett, J. C. (1994) *Fragments from Antiquity*. Oxford, Blackwells.

Barrett, J. C. (1999a) Chronologies of Landscape. In P. Ucko and R. Layton (eds), *The Archaeology and Anthropology of Landscape*. London, Routledge, 21–30.

Barrett, J. C. (1999b) Rethinking the Bronze Age Environment. In K. J. Edwards and J. P. Sadler (eds), *Holocene Environments of Prehistoric Britain. Journal of Quaternary Science* 14(6), Quaternary Proceedings 7, 493–500.

Barrett, J. C. (1999c) The Mythical Landscapes of the British Iron Age. In W. Ashmore and A. B. Knapp (eds), *Archaeologies of Landscape*. Oxford, Blackwell, 253–268.

Barrett, J. and Fewster, K. (2000) Intimacy and Structural Transformation. Giddens and Archaeology (with a comment by Lesley McFadyen). In C. Holtorf and H. Karlsson (eds), *Philosophy and Archaeological Practice*. Göteborg, Bricoleur Press, 25–38.

Barrett, J., Freeman, P. W. M. and Woodward, A. (2000) *Cadbury Castle, Somerset: the later prehistoric and early historic archaeology*. London, English Heritage.

Barth, F. (ed.) (1969) *Ethnic Groups and Boundaries. The Social Organisation of Cultural Difference.* London, Allen and Unwin.

Barth, F. (1987) *Cosmologies in the Making. A generative approach to cultural variation in New Guinea.* Cambridge, Cambridge University Press.

Barth, F. (2002) An Anthropology of Knowledge. *Current Anthropology* 43(1), 1–18.

Bartlett, J. E. and Mackey, R. W. (1972) Walkington Wold Excavations. *East Riding Archaeologist* 1 (2), 1–100.

Basso, K. (1984) 'Stalking with Stories': Names, Places, and Moral Narratives among the Western Apache. In E. Bruner (ed.), *Text, Play and Story: the Construction and Reconstruction of Self and Society.* Washington, Proceedings of the American Ethnological Society, 19–55.

Basso, K. (1996) Wisdom sits in places: notes on a Western Apache landscape. In S. Feld and K. Basso (eds), *Senses of Place.* Sante Fe, New Mexico, School of American Research Press, 53–90.

Battaglia, D. (1990) *On the Bones of the Serpent. Person, Memory and Mortality in Sabarl Island Society.* London, University of Chicago Press.

BBC2 (2002a) *Meet the Ancestors: Chariot Queen.* (Series 5, Episode 1). Originally broadcast 19/02/2002.

BBC2 (2002b) *Timeflyers: Between the Lines. Series 1, Episode 1.* Originally broadcast 31/10/2002.

Beach, S. (2008) Villagers tell of flood nightmare after downpour. 7th August 2008. *Driffield Times.* Available at: http://www.driffieldtoday.co.uk/floods/Villagers-tell-of-floods-nightmare.4369044.jp (Accessed 12/08/2010).

Bendry, R., Hayes, T. E. and Palmer, M. R. (2005) Patterns of Iron Age Horse Supply: an analysis of Strontium Isotope Ratios in Teeth. *Archaeometery* 51(1), 140–150.

Berger, J. (1996a) *Pages of the Wound.* London, Bloomsbury.

Berger, J. (1996b) *Photocopies.* London, Bloomsbury.

Bevan, W. (1994) *Death, Landscape and Society: The Landscape Context of the East Yorkshire Iron Age Square Barrow Cemeteries.* Unpublished MA Dissertation, Sheffield University.

Bevan, W. (1997) Bounding the landscape: place and identity during the Yorkshire Wolds Iron Age. In A. Gwilt and C. Haselgrove (eds), *Reconstructing Iron Age Societies.* Oxford, Oxbow Monograph 71, 181–191.

Bevan, W. (1999a) Land-Life-Death-Regeneration: interpreting a middle Iron Age landscape in eastern Yorkshire. In W. Bevan (ed.), *Northern Exposure: interpretative devolution and the Iron Ages in Britain.* Leicester, Leicester University Press, 123–148.

Bevan, W. (1999b) The dead can dance: the landscape context of square barrow cemeteries in the East Yorkshire Iron age. In J. Downes and T. Pollard (eds), *The Loved Body's Corruption: archaeological approaches to mortuary practices.* Glasgow, Cruithne Press.

Bird-David, N. (1999) 'Animism' revisited: personhood, environment, and relational epistemology. *Current Anthropology* 33, 25–47.

Bloch, M. and Parry, J. (1982) *Death and the Regeneration of Life.* Cambridge, Cambridge University Press.

Bourdieu, P. (1970) The Berber House or the World reversed. *Social Science Information* 9(2), 151–70.

Bourdieu, P. (1977) *Outline for a Theory of Practice.* Cambridge, Cambridge University Press.

Bourdieu, P. (2002) (reprint of 1984 edition) *Distinction. A Social Critique of the Judgement of Taste.* Cambridge, Massachusetts, Harvard University Press.

Bowler, P. (1989) *The Invention of Progress.* Oxford, Blackwell.

Boyd Dawkins, W. (1880) *Early Man in Britain and His Place in the Tertiary Period.* London, Macmillan.

Boyle, A., Evans, T., O'Connor, S., Spence, A. and Brennand, M. (2007) Site D (Ferry Fryston) in the Iron Age and Romano-British Periods. In F. Brown, C. Howard-Davis, M. Brennand, A. Boyle, T. Evans, S. O'Connor, A. Spence, R. Heawood and A. Lupton (eds), *The Archaeology of the A1(M) Darrington to Dishforth DBFO Road Scheme.* Lancaster, Lancaster Imprints 12, 121–160.

Bradley, R. (2007) *The Prehistory of Britain and Ireland.* Cambridge, Cambridge University Press.

Bradley, R., Entwhistle, R. and Raymond, F. (1994) *Prehistoric Land Divisions On Salisbury Plain.* London, English Heritage Research Report 2.

Bradley, R. and Yates, D. (2007) After Celtic fields. The social organisation of Iron Age agriculture. In C. Haselgrove and R. Pope (eds). *The Earlier Iron Age in Britain and the near Continent.* Oxford, Oxbow, 94–102.

Bradley Foster, H. (1998) African American Jewellery Before the Civil War. In L. D. Sciama and J. B. Eicher (eds), *Beads and Bead Makers. Gender, Material Culture and Meaning.* Oxford, Berg, 177–192.

Brailsford, J. W. (1953) *Later Prehistoric Antiquities of the British Isles.* London, Trustees of the British Museum.

Brewster, T. C. M. (1963) *The Excavation of Staple Howe*. Wintringham, East Riding Archaeological Research Committee.

Brewster, T. C. M. (1971) The Garton Slack chariot burial, East Yorkshire. *Antiquity* 45, 289–292.

Brewster, T. C. M. (1975) Garton Slack. *Current Archaeology* 51, 104–116.

Brewster, T. C. M. (1980) *The Excavation of Garton and Wetwang Slacks*. Malton, Yorks., East Riding Archaeological Research Committee. (Microfiche).

British Museum. (2010) The Celtic Art Database (Technologies of Enchantment: Early Celtic Art in Britain Project). http://www.britishmuseum. org/research/research_projects/project_archive/ technologies_of_enchantment/the_celtic_art_ database.aspx (Accessed 02/06/2011).

Brück, J. (1999) Houses, lifecycles and deposition on Middle Bronze Age settlements in southern England. *Proceedings of the Prehistoric Society* 65, 145–66.

Brück, J. (2001) Body metaphors and technologies of transformation in the English Middle and Late Bronze Age. In J. Brück (ed.), *Bronze Age landscapes. Tradition and Transformation*. Oxbow, Oxford, 149–160.

Brück, J. (2004) Material metaphors: the relational construction of identity in Early Bronze Age burials in Ireland and Britain. *Journal of Social Archaeology* 4(3), 307–333.

Brück, J. and Goodman, M. (1999) Introduction: themes for a critical archaeology of prehistoric settlement. In J. Brück and M. Goodman (eds), *Making Places in the Prehistoric World: themes in settlement archaeology*. London, University College London Press, 1–19.

Buckland, P., Donohue, R., Fenton-Thomas, C. and Henderson, J. (1992) *Recent Fieldwork on the Yorkshire Wolds*. Unpublished interim report, University of Sheffield.

Buckland, P., Donohue, R., Fenton-Thomas, C. and Henderson, J. (1993) Recent fieldwork on the Yorkshire Wolds *Council for British Archaeology Group 4 Annual Report*.

Burgess, C. (1968) *Bronze Age Metalwork in Northern England: c. 1000 to 700 BC*. Newcastle upon Tyne, Oriel.

Busby, C. (1997) Permeable and partible persons: a comparative analysis of gender and the body in South India and Melanesia. *Journal of the Royal Anthropological Institute* 3(2), 261–78.

Bush, M. B. and Ellis, S. (1987) The sedimentological and vegetational history of Willow Garth. In S.

Ellis (ed.). *East Yorkshire Field Guide*. Cambridge, Quaternary Research Association, 42–52.

Butler, J. (1990) *Gender Trouble*. London, Routledge.

Butler, J. (1993) *Bodies That Matter*. New York, Routledge.

Caesar. (n.d.) *The Conquest of Gaul*. (translated by S. A. Handford, 1982 [1951 original translation]). London, Penguin Books.

Cardwell, P. (1989) Excavations at Cat Babbleton Farm, Ganton, North Yorkshire, 1986. *Yorkshire Archaeological Journal* 61, 15–27.

Carey, M. (1998) Gender in African Beadwork: An Overview. In L. D. Sciama and J. B. Eicher (eds), *Beads and Bead Makers. Gender, Material Culture and Meaning*. Oxford, Berg, 83–94.

Carsten, J. (2000) Introduction: cultures of relatedness. In J. Carsten (ed.), *Cultures of Relatedness. New Approaches to the Study of Kinship*. Cambridge, Cambridge University Press, 1–36.

Carsten, J. and Hugh-Jones, S. (1995) *About the House. Lévi-Strauss and Beyond*. Cambridge, Cambridge University Press.

Carter, S., Hunter, F. and Smith, A. (2010) A 5th Century BC Iron Age Chariot Burial from Newbridge, Edinburgh. *Proceedings of the Prehistoric Society* 76, 31–74.

Carver, M. (2000) Burial as poetry: the context of treasure in Anglo-Saxon graves. In E. M. Tyler (ed.), *Treasure in the Medieval West*. York and Woodbridge, York Medieval Press/ Boydell, 25–48.

Casey, E. S. (1996) How to Get from Space to Place in a Fairly Short Stretch of Time. In S. Feld and K. Basso (eds), *Senses of Place*. Sante Fe, School of American Research Press, 13–52.

Chadwick, A. (2007) Trackways, hooves and memory-days – human and animal movements and memories around the Iron Age and Romano-British rural landscapes of the English north midlands. In V. Cummings and B. Johnston (eds), *Prehistoric Journeys*. Oxford, Oxbow, 131–152.

Challis, A. J. and Harding, D. W. (1975) *Later Prehistory from the Trent to the Tyne. Part i: Discussion*. Oxford: British Archaeological Report 20.

Chamberlain, A. (2006) *Demography in Archaeology. Cambridge Manuals in Archaeology*. Cambridge, Cambridge University Press.

Chamberlain, A. and Parker Pearson, M. (2001) *Earthly Remains*. London, British Museum Press.

Champion, S. (1976) Coral in Europe. In P. M. Duval and C. F. C. Hawkes (eds). *Celtic Art in Ancient Europe*. London, Seminar Press, 29–37.

Childe, V. G. (1929) *The Danube in Prehistory.* Oxford, Clarendon Press.

Childe, V. G. (1940) *Prehistoric Communities of the British Isles.* London, Chambers.

Childe, V. G. (1956) *Piecing Together the Past: the interpretation of archaeological data.* London, Routledge and Kegan Paul.

Childe, V. G. (1958) *The Prehistory of European Society.* London, Penguin Books.

Clark, A. (1997) *Being There. Putting Brain, Body and World Together Again.* Massachusetts, MIT Press.

Clark, A. (2008) Where Brain, Body and World Collide. In C. Knappet and L. Malafouris (eds), *Material Agency. Towards a Non-Anthropocentric Approach.* New York, Springer.

Clark, J. G. D. (1948) (reprint of 1941 edition). *Prehistoric England.* London, Batsford.

Clark, J. G. D. (1966) The invasion hypothesis in British archaeology. *Antiquity* 40, 172–189.

Clark, J. G. D. (1968) Response to C. F. C. Hawkes. Notes and News: response to 'British Prehistory: the invasion hypothesis'. *Antiquity* 40, 298–299.

Clark, M. A., Worrell, M. B. and Pless, J. E. (1997) Postmortem Changes in Soft Tissues. In Haglund, W. D. and M. H. Sorg (eds), *Forensic Taphonomy. The Postmortem Fate of Human Remains.* London and New York, CRC Press, 151–164.

Clarke, D. L. (1968) *Analytical Archaeology.* London, Methuen.

Clay, B. (1992) Other Times, Other Places: Agency and the Big Man in Central New Ireland. *Man NS* 27, 719–33.

Cohen, A. P. (1982) A sense of time, a sense of place – the meaning of close social association in Whalsay, Shetland. In A. P. Cohen (ed.), *Belonging; Identity and Social Organisation in British Rural Cultures.* Manchester, Manchester University Press.

Cohen, A. P. (1985) *The Symbolic Construction of Community.* London, Routledge.

Coles, B. (1990) Anthropomorphic Wooden Figures from Britain and Ireland. *Proceedings of the Prehistoric Society* 56, 315–333.

Coles, J. (2002) Chariots of the Gods? Landscape and Imagery at Frännarp, Sweden. *Proceedings of the Prehistoric Society* 68, 215–246.

Collis, J. (2001) Coral, Amber and Cockle Shells: Trade in the Middle La Tène Period. *Past* 38, 3–4.

Cooper, A. N. (1920) *The Curiosities of East Yorkshire.* Scarborough, A. Brown and Sons/Hull, E. T. W. Dennis.

Coote, J. (1992) 'Marvels of Everyday Vision': The Anthropology of Aesthetics and the Cattle-Keeping Nilotes. In J. Cote and A. Shelton (eds), *Anthropology, Art and Aesthetics.* Oxford, Clarendon Press, 245–273.

Council for British Archaeology (1948) *Survey and Policy of Field Research in the Archaeology of Great Britain.* London, Council for British Archaeology.

Creighton, J. (2000) *Coins and Power in Late Iron Age Britain.* Cambridge, Cambridge University Press.

Crowther, D., Willis, S. and Creighton, J. (1989) Excavations at Redcliff. In P. Halkon (ed.), *New Light on the Parisi. Recent Discoveries in Iron Age and Roman East Yorkshire.* Hull, East Riding Archaeological Society/University of Hull School of Adult and Continuing Education, 6–9.

Cummings, V. and Johnston, B. (eds) (2007) *Prehistoric Journeys.* Oxford, Oxbow.

Cunliffe, B. (1978a) *Hengistbury Head.* London, Paul Elek.

Cunliffe, B. (1978b) (2nd edition) *Iron Age Communities in Britain.* London, Routledge and Kegan Paul.

Cunliffe, B. (1983) *Danebury: Anatomy of an Iron Age Hillfort.* London, Batsford.

Cunliffe, B. (1991) (3rd edition) *Iron Age Communities in Britain.* London, Routledge and Kegan Paul.

Cunliffe, B. (1992) Pits, Preconceptions and Propitiation in the British Iron Age. *Oxford Journal of Archaeology* 11, 69–83.

Cunliffe, B. (1995a) *Danebury: a hillfort community in perspective. Volume 6.* York, Council for British Archaeology.

Cunliffe, B. (1995b) *Iron Age Britain.* London, Batsford/English Heritage.

Cunliffe, B. (2000) *The Danebury Environs Programme: the prehistory of a Wessex landscape, vol. 1: Introduction.* Oxford, English Heritage and Oxford University Committee for Archaeology.

Cunliffe, B. (2003) (reprint 1983). *Danebury Hillfort.* Stroud, Tempus.

Cunliffe, B. (2009). (4th edition) *Iron Age Communities in Britain.* London, Routledge and Kegan Paul.

Dakyns, J. R. and Fox-Strangways, C. (1886) *The Geology of the Country around Driffield. Memoirs of the Geological Survey.* London, HMSO.

Davis, J. B. and Thurnham, J. (1865) *Crania Britannica: Delineations and Descriptions of the Skulls of the Aboriginal and Early Inhabitants of the British Islands.* London, privately published.

Dean, W. T. (2007) Yorkshire jet and its links to Pliny

the Elder. *Proceedings of the Yorkshire Geological Society* 56(4), 261–265.

Demarez, L. and Leman-Delerive, G. (2001) A linch-pin of British type found at Blicquy (Hainaut, Belguim). *Antiquaries Journal* 81, 391–5.

Dent, J. S. (1979) Bronze age burials from Wetwang Slack. *Yorkshire Archaeological Journal* 51, 23–39.

Dent, J. S. (1982) Cemeteries and Settlement Patterns of the Iron Age on the Yorkshire Wolds. *Proceedings of the Prehistoric Society* 48, 437–457.

Dent, J. S. (1983) Weapons, Wounds and War in the Iron Age. *Archaeological Journal* 140, 120–8.

Dent, J. S. (1984a) *Wetwang Slack: an Iron Age cemetery on the Yorkshire Wolds.* Unpublished MPhil thesis, University of Sheffield, Dept. of Archaeology and Prehistory.

Dent, J. S. (1984b) Two chariot burials at Wetwang Slack. *Current Archaeology* 93, 302–6.

Dent, J. S. (1985) Three cart burials from Wetwang, Yorkshire. *Antiquity* 59, 85–92.

Dent, J. S. (1995) *Aspects of Iron Age Settlement in East Yorkshire.* Unpublished PhD Thesis, University of Sheffield.

Dent, J. S. (2009) Examination of an Earthwork at Leconfield in 1989. In D. H. Evans (ed.), *An East Riding Miscellany.* Hull, East Riding Archaeologist 12, 67–69.

Dent, J. S. (2010) *The Iron Age in Eastern Yorkshire.* Oxford, British Archaeological Report 508.

Didsbury, P. (1990) *Aspects of Late Iron Age and Romano-British Settlement in the Lower Hull Valley.* Unpublished MPhil, Durham University.

Dietler, M. (1990) Driven by drink: the role of drinking in the political economy and the case of early Iron Age France. *Journal of Anthropological Archaeology* 9, 352–406.

Dietler, M. (1996) Feasts and commensal politics in the political economy: food, power and status in prehistoric Europe. In P. W. Wiessner and W. Schiefenhövel (eds), *Food and the Status Quest. An Interdisciplinary Perspective.* Oxford, Berghahn, 87–125.

Dietler, M. and Hayden, B. (2001) *Feasts: Archaeological and Ethnographic Perspectives on Food, Politics and Power.* Washington, Smithsonian Institution Press.

Dinnin, M. (1995) Palaeoenvironmental Programme. In R. Van der Noort and S. Ellis (eds), *Wetland Heritage of Holderness.* Hull, Humber Wetlands Project, 27–149.

Douglas, M. (1970) *Natural Symbols: Explorations in Cosmology.* London, Cresset Press.

Downes, J. (1997) Cremation: a spectacle and a journey. In J. Downes and T. Pollard (eds), *The Loved Body's Corruption.* Glasgow, Cruithne Press, 19–29.

Dransart, P. (1998) A Short History of Rosaries in the Andes. In L. D. Sciama and J. B. Eicher (eds), *Beads and Bead Makers. Gender, Material Culture and Meaning.* Oxford, Berg, 129–146.

Earle, T. (1978) *Economic and Social Organisation of a Complex Chiefdom: the Halelea District, Kaua'I, Hawaii.* Ann Arbor, Michigan, University of Michigan.

Edmonds, M. (1999) *Ancestral Geographies of the Neolithic. Landscapes, Monuments and Memory.* Routledge, London.

Ehrenberg, M. and Caple, C. (1983) Excavations at Fimber, Yorkshire. Interim Report. *Yorkshire Archaeological Society Prehistoric Research Bulletin* 20, 7–8.

Ehrenberg, M. and Caple, C. (1985) Excavations at Fimber, Yorkshire. Interim Report. *Yorkshire Archaeological Society Prehistoric Research Bulletin* 22, 7–8.

Eicher, J. B. (1998) Beaded and Bedecked Kalabari of Nigeria. In L. D. Sciama and J. B. Eicher (eds), *Beads and Bead Makers. Gender, Material Culture and Meaning.* Oxford, Berg, 95–116.

Evans, D. H. (2009) *An East Riding Miscellany.* Hull, East Riding Archaeologist 12.

Evans, D. H. and Atkinson, R. A. (2009) Recent Archaeological Work in the East Riding. In D. H. Evans (ed.), *An East Riding Miscellany.* Hull, East Riding Archaeologist 12, 249–403.

Evans, D. H. and Steedman, K. (2001) Recent Archaeological Work in the East Riding. In D. H. Evans (ed.), *An East Riding Miscellany.* Hull, East Riding Archaeologist 12, 67–156.

Evans, R. (1992) Erosion in England and Wales – the Present the Key to the Past. In M. Bell and J. Boardman (eds), *Past and Present Soil Erosion: Linking Archaeology and Geomorphology.* Oxford, Oxbow Monograph 22, 53–66.

Fabian, J. (1983) *Time and the Other: How Anthropology Makes Its Object.* New York, Columbia University Press.

Fajans, J. (1985) The Person in Social Context: The Social Character of Baining 'Psychology'. In H. M. White and J. Kirkpatrick (eds), *Person, Self and Experience: Exploring Pacific Ethnopsychologies.* Berkeley, University of California Press, 367–397.

Feeley-Harnik, G. (1989) Cloth and the creation of Ancestors in Madagascar. In A. B. Weiner and

J. Schneider (eds), *Cloth and Human Experience.* Washington, Smithsonian Books, 73–116.

Fenton Thomas, C. (1999) *Forgotten Wolds: Late Prehistoric and Early Historic Landscapes on the Yorkshire Chalk.* Unpublished PhD thesis, University of Sheffield.

Fenton Thomas, C. (2003) *Late Prehistoric and Early Historic Land-Use on the Yorkshire Wolds.* Oxford, British Archaeological Report 350.

Fenton Thomas, C. (2008) Mobile and Enclosed Landscapes in the Yorkshire Wolds. In A. Chadwick (ed.), *Recent Approaches to the Archaeology of Land Allotment.* Oxford, British Archaeological Report S1875, 252–273.

Fenton Thomas, C. (2009) *A Place By the Sea. Excavations at Sewerby Farm Cottage, Bridlington, Yorkshire.* York, On Site Archaeology.

Fenton Thomas, C. (2011) *Where Sky and Yorkshire and Water Meet. The Story of the Melton Landscape from Prehistory to the Present.* York, On Site Archaeology.

Ferguson, R. B. (1990) *Explaining War.* In J. Haas (ed.). *The Anthropology of War.* Cambridge, Cambridge University Press, 26–55.

Field, N., Parker Pearson, M. and Rylatt, J. (2003) In S. Catney and D. Start (eds), *Time and Tide: the Archaeology of the Witham Valley.* Sleaford, The Witham Valley Archaeology Research Committee (Heritage Trust of Lincolnshire), 16–32.

Finch, J. and Mason, J. (2000) *Passing On. Kinship and Inheritance in England.* London, Routledge.

Finlay, N. (2003) Microliths and Multiple Authorship. In L. Larsson, H. Kindgren, K. Knutsson, D. Loeffler and A. Åkerlund (eds), *Mesolithic on the move: papers presented at the 6th International Conference on the Mesolithic in Europe, Stockholm 2000.* Oxford, Oxbow: 167–176.

Fitzpatrick, A. (1994) Outside in: the structure of an Early Iron Age house at Dunston Park, Thatcham, Berkshire. In A. Fitzpatrick and E. Morris (eds), *The Iron Age in Wessex: Recent Work.* Salisbury, Trust for Wessex Archaeology, 68–72.

Fitzpatrick, A. (2008) Dancing with dragons: fantastic animals in the earlier Celtic art of Iron Age Britain. In C. Haselgrove and T. Moore (eds), *The Later Iron Age in Britain and Beyond.* Oxford, Oxbow, 339–357.

Fletcher, J. S. (1900) *Picturesque History of Yorkshire.* London, Caxton Publishing.

Fontijn, D. (2005) *Sacrificial Landscapes. Cultural Biographies of Persons, Objects and 'Natural' Places in the Bronze Age of the Southern Netherlands, c.*

2300–600 BC Analecta Prehisorica Leidensia. Leiden, University of Leiden.

Foster, S. W. (1987) The dry drainage system on the northern Wolds escarpment. In S. Ellis (ed.), *East Yorkshire: A Field Guide.* Cambridge, Quaternary Research Association, 36–38.

Fowler, C. (2004) *The Archaeology of Personhood.* London, Routledge.

Fox, C. (1923) *The Archaeology of the Cambridge region: a topographical study of the bronze, early iron, Roman and Anglo-Saxon ages, with an introductory note on the neolithic age.* Cambridge, Cambridge University Press.

Fox, C. (1943) *The Personality of Britain. Its Influence on Inhabitant and Invader in Prehistoric and Early Historic Times.* Cardiff, National Museum of Wales.

Fox, C. (1949) A Bronze Pole-Sheath from the Charioteers Barrow, Arras, Yorks. (Note). *Antiquaries Journal* 28, 123–137.

Fox, C. (1958) *Pattern and Purpose. A survey of Early Celtic Art in Britain.* Cardiff, National Museum of Wales.

Frankenstein, S. and Rowlands, M. J. (1978) Early Iron Age society in southwest Germany. *Bulletin of the Institute of Archaeology* 15, 73–112.

Fried, M. H. (1967) *The Evolution of Political Society: an essay in political economy.* New York, Random House.

Fukai, K. (1996a) Co-evolution between humans and domesticates: The cultural selection of animal coat-colour diversity among the Bodi. In R. Ellen and K. Fukai (eds), *Redefining Nature: ecology, culture and domestication.* Oxford, Berg, 319–386.

Fukai, K. (1996b) Conflict as a Levelling Mechanism – Analysis of Cattle Composition and Raiding among the Narim in Southern Sudan. *Nilo-Eithiopian Studies* 3–4, 1–23.

Furness, R. R. and King, S. J. (1978) *Soils in North Yorkshire IV, Sheet SE 63/73 (Selby), Soil Survey Record 56.* Rothamsted, Harpenden.

Galaty, J. G. and Bonte, P. (1991) *Herders, Warriors and Traders. Pastoralism in Africa.* Oxford, Westview Press.

Garcia Marquez, G. (2000) *A Hundred Years of Solitude.* (reprint of 1972 translation). London, Penguin Books.

Garrow, D., Beadsmoore, E. and Knight, M. (2005) Pit clusters and the temporality of occupation: an earlier Neolithic site at Kilverstone, Thetford, Norfolk. *Proceedings of the Prehistoric Society* 71, 139–57.

Gell, A. (1992) The technology of enchantment and

enchantment of technology. In J. Coote and A. Shelton (eds). *Anthropology, Art and Aesthetics.* Oxford, Clarendon Press, 40–67.

Gell, A. (1996) Vogel's Net: Traps as Artworks and Artworks as Traps. *Journal of Material Culture* 1, 15–38.

Gell, A. (1998) *Art and Agency. An Anthropological Theory.* Oxford, Clarendon Press.

Giddens, A. (1984) *The Constitution of Society. Outline of the theory of structuration.* Cambridge, Polity Press.

Gilchrist, R. (1999) *Gender and Archaeology. Contesting the Past.* London, Routledge.

Gilchrist, R. and Sloane, B. (2005) *Requiem: the Medieval Monastic Cemetery in Britain.* London, Museum of London Archaeological Service.

Giles, K. and Giles, M. (2007) The writing on the wall: the concealed communities of the East Yorkshire horselads. *Special Edition: Concealed Communities. International Journal of Historical Archaeology* 11(4), 326–357.

Giles, M. (2000) *Open-weave, Close-knit: archaeologies of identity in the later prehistoric landscape of East Yorkshire.* Unpublished PhD thesis, University of Sheffield.

Giles, M. (2006) Collecting the past, constructing identity: the antiquarian John Mortimer and the Driffield Museum of Antiquities and Geological Specimens. *Antiquaries Journal* 86, 279–316.

Giles, M. (2007a) Good fences make good neighbours? Exploring the ladder enclosures of late Iron Age East Yorkshire. In C. Haselgrove and T. Moore (eds), *The Later Iron Age in Britain and Beyond.* Oxford, Oxbow, 235–249.

Giles, M. (2007b) Making metal and forging relations: ironworking in the British Iron Age. *Oxford Journal of Archaeology* 26(4), 395–413.

Giles, M. (2007c) Refiguring rights: later Bronze Age and early Iron Age landscapes of East Yorkshire. In C. Haselgrove and R. Pope (eds), *The Earlier Iron Age in Britain and the near Continent.* Oxford, Oxbow, 103–118.

Giles, M. (2008a) Identity, Community and the Person in Later Prehistory. In J. Pollard (ed.), *Prehistoric Britain: Studies in Global Archaeology.* Oxford, Blackwells, 330–350.

Giles, M. (2008b) 'Seeing red': the aesthetics of martial objects in the Iron Age of East Yorkshire. In D. Garrow, C. Gosden and J. D. Hill (eds), *Rethinking Celtic Art.* Oxford, Oxbow, 59–77.

Giles, M. (2009) Iron Age Bog Bodies of north-western Europe: representing the dead. *Archaeological Dialogues* 16(1), 75–101.

Giles, M. and Joy, J. (2007) Mirrors in the British Iron Age: performance, revelation and power. In M. Anderson (ed.), *The Book of the Mirror: An Interdisciplinary Collection Exploring the Cultural Story of the Mirror.* Cambridge, Cambridge Scholars Press, 16–31.

Goffman, E. (1969) *The Presentation of the Self in Everyday Life.* Harmondsworth, Penguin.

Goffman, E. (1999) On Face-Work: an Analysis of Ritual Elements in Social Interaction. In A. Jaworski and N. Coupland (eds), *The Discourse Reader.* London, Routledge, 306–320.

Gohil, A. E. (2006) *Ancient Celtic and non-Celtic place-names of northern continental Europe.* Mémoires de la Société Belge d'Etudes Celtiques 27.

Gosden, C. (2005) What do objects want? *Journal of Archaeological Method and Theory* 12(3), 193–211.

Gowland, R. and Knüsel, C. (eds) (2006) *Social Archaeology of Funerary Remains.* Oxford, Oxbow.

Grantham, C. and Grantham, E. (1965) An Earthwork and Anglian Cemetery at Garton–on-the-Wolds, East Riding, Yorkshire. *Yorkshire Archaeological Journal* 41, 355–360.

Grasseni, C. (2004) Skilled vision. An apprenticeship in breeding asesthetics. *Social Anthropology* 12(1), 41–55.

Green, M. (1996) *Celtic Art. (Everyman Art Library).* London, Weidenfeld Nicholson.

Greenwell, W. (1865) Notices of the examination of ancient grave-hills in the North Riding of Yorkshire. *Archaeological Journal* 22, 97–117 and 241–64.

Greenwell, W. (1867) On the inhabitants of Yorkshire in pre-Roman times. *Proceedings of the Yorkshire Geological and Polytechnic So*ciety 4, 512–544.

Greenwell, Rev. W. (1877) *British Barrows. A Record of the Examination of Sepulchral Mounds in Various Parts of England.* Oxford, Clarendon Press.

Greenwell, W. (1906) Early Iron Age Burials in Yorkshire. *Archaeologia* 9, 251–324.

Guido, C. M. (1978) *The Glass Beads of the Prehistoric and Roman Periods in Britain and Ireland.* Report of the Research Committee of the Society of Antiquaries of London 15, Oxford.

Guilbert, G. C. (1975) Planned hillfort interiors. *Proceedings of the Prehistoric Society* 41, 203–221.

Gwilt, A. (1996) Ageing structures and shifting ideologies. *Antiquity* 70, 699–702.

Gwilt, A., Joy, J. and Hunter, F. (2010) The Celtic Art Database. Available at: http://www.britishmuseum.

org/research/research_projects/project_archive/
technologies_of_enchantment/the_celtic_art_
database.aspx (Accessed 03/07/2011).

Haldane, A. R. B. (1997) *The Drove Roads of Scotland.*
Edinburgh, Birlinn.

Halkon, P. (2008) *Archaeology and Environment in a
Changing East Yorkshire Landscape. The Foulney Valley
800 BC to c. AD 400.* Oxford, British Archaeological
Report 472.

Halkon, P., Healey, E., Innes, J. and Manby, T. (2009)
Change and Continuity within the Prehistoric
Landscape of the Foulney Valley. In D. H. Evans
(ed.), *An East Riding Miscellany.* Hull, East Riding
Archaeologist 12, 1–66.

Halkon, P. and Millett, M. (1999) *Rural Settlement
and Industry; Studies in the Iron Age and Roman
Archaeology of Lowland East Yorkshire.* Otley,
Yorkshire Archaeological Society.

Hamilakis, Y. (2003) The sacred geography of hunting:
wild animals, social power and gender in early
farming societies. In E. Kotjabopoulou, Y. Hamilakis,
P. Halstead, C. Gamble and P. Elefanti (eds),
Zooarchaeology in Greece. Athens, British School at
Athens, 239–247.

Hammerton, J. A. (1931) *Manners and Customs of
Mankind.* London, Amalgamated Press.

Harding, D. (2004) *The Iron Age in Northern Britain:
Celts and Romans, Natives and Invaders.* London,
Routledge.

Harding, D. (2007) *The Archaeology of Celtic Art.*
London, Routledge.

Härke, H. (1990) 'Warrior Graves'? The Background
of the Anglo–Saxon Weapon Burial Rite. *Past and
Present* 126, 22–43.

Harrell, K. (2009) *Mycenaean Ways of War: The Past,
Politics and Personhood.* Unpublished PhD Thesis,
University of Sheffield.

Harrell, K. (2012) The Weapon's Beauty: A Re-
consideration of the Ornamentation of the Shaft
Grave Swords. In M.-L. B. Nosch and R. Laffineur
(eds), *KOSMOS: Jewellery, Adornment and Textiles
in the Aegean Bronze Age.* Liège, Université de Liège,
799–806.

Harris, A. (1961) *The Rural Landscape of the East Riding
of Yorkshire 1700–1850.* London, Oxford University
Press/University of Hull.

Harris, A. (1996) A 'rage of ploughing': the reclamation
of the Yorkshire Wolds. *Yorkshire Archaeological
Journal* 68, 209–223.

Harrison, S. (1995) Transformations of identity in Sepik

Warfare. In M. Strathern (ed.), *Shifting Contexts:
Transformations in anthropological knowledge.*
London, Routledge, 81–98.

Harrison, S. (2001) The Mortimer Museum of
Archaeology and Geology at Driffield (1878–1918),
and its transfer to Hull. *East Riding Archaeologist*
10, 47–61.

Hart, E. (2005) The craft of hefting. (Rural Skills). *Rural
Wales* (summer 2005), 12–13.

Hartfield, G. (1965) *Horse Brasses.* London, Abelard-
Schuman.

Hartley, M and Ingilby, J. (1990) *Life and tradition in
the Moorlands of North-East Yorkshire.* Otley, J. M.
Dent.

Haselgrove, C., Armit, I., Champion, T., Creighton,
J. and Gwilt, A. (2001) *Understanding the British
Iron Age: an agenda for action.* Salisbury, Iron Age
Research Seminar and Prehistoric Society.

Haughton, C. and Powesland, D. (1999) *West Heslerton.
The Anglian Cemetery.* Yedingham, Landscape Research
Centre Archaeological Monograph Series 1.

Havercroft, A. (2001) *The Wetwang Chariot Burial.*
Unpublished interim report, The Guildhouse
Consultancy.

Hawkes, C. (1940) *The Prehistoric Foundations of Europe
to the Mycenean Age.* London, Methuen.

Hawkes, C. (1959) The ABC of the British Iron Age.
Antiquity 33, 170–182.

Hawkes, C. (1968) Notes and news: response to 'British
Prehistory: the invasion hypothesis'. *Antiquity* 40,
297–298.

Hawkes, C. with Hawkes, J. (1958) (reprint of 1944)
Prehistoric Britain. London, Penguin Books.

Hayfield, C., Pouncett, J. and Wagner, P. (1995) Vessey
Ponds: a 'prehistoric' water supply in East Yorkshire?
Proceedings of the Prehistoric Society 61, 393–408.

Hayfield, C. and Wagner, P. (1995) From dolines to
dewponds: a study of water supplies on the Yorkshire
Wolds. *Landscape History* 17, 49–64.

Helms, M. (1988) *Ulysses' Sail. An Ethnographic Odyssey
of Power, Knowledge and Geographic Distance.*
Princeton, New Jersey Press.

Helms, M. W. (1993) *Craft and the Kingly Ideal. Art,
Trade, and Power.* Austin, University of Texas Press.

Henderson, J. (1991) Industrial specialisation in late
Iron Age Britain and Europe. *Archaeological Journal*
148, 104–148.

Hendry, J. (1995) *Wrapping Culture.* Oxford, Oxford
University Press.

Henshall, A. S. (1950) Textile and weaving appliances

in prehistoric Britain. *Proceedings of the Prehistoric Society* 10, 130–157.

Herbert, E. W. (1993) *Iron, Gender and Power. Rituals of Transformation in African Societies.* Bloomington and Indianapolis, Indiana University Press.

Hertz, R. (2004) (reprint of 1960 edition) *Death and the Right Hand.* London, Routledge.

Hetherington, K. and Law, J. (2000) After networks. *Environment and Planning D: Society and Space* 18, 1–6.

Hicks, J. D. (1978) *A Victorian Boyhood on the Wolds. The Recollections of J. R. Mortimer.* Bridlington, East Yorkshire Local History Series 34.

Higham, N. (1987) Brigantia Revisited. *Northern History* 23, 1–19.

Hill, J. D. (1995a) How should we understand Iron Age societies and hillforts? A contextual study from southern Britain. In J. D. Hill and C. Cumberpatch (eds), *Different Iron Ages: studies on the Iron Age in temperate Europe.* Oxford, British Archaeological Report 602, 45–66.

Hill, J. D. (1995b) *Ritual and Rubbish in the Iron Age of Wessex.* Oxford, British Archaeological Report 242.

Hill, J. D. (1995c) The pre-Roman Iron Age in Britain and Ireland (c. 800 BC to AD 100): an overview. *Journal of World Prehistory* 9(1), 47–98.

Hill, J. D. (1997) 'The end of one kind of body and the beginning of another kind of body?' Toilet instruments and 'Romanization' in southern England during the first century AD. In A. Gwilt and C. Haselgrove (eds), *Reconstructing Iron Age Societies.* Oxford, Oxbow, 96–107.

Hill, J. D. (2001) A New Cart/Chariot Burial from Wetwang, East Yorkshire. *Past* 38, 2–3.

Hill, J. D. (2002) Wetwang Chariot Burial. *Current Archaeology* 178: 410–412.

Hill, J. D. (2004) *Excavation of an Iron Age Chariot in the Village of Wetwang, East Yorkshire in March/April 2001: Interim Report.* Unpublished report. London, British Museum.

Hill, J. D. (2006) Are we any closer to understanding how later Iron Age societies worked (or did not work)? In C. Haselgrove (ed.), *Les Mutations de la fin de l'age du fer; Celts et Gaulois IV Bibracte* 12/4, 169–180.

Hingley, R. (1997) Iron, ironworking and regeneration: a study of the symbolic meaning of metalworking in Iron Age Britain. In A. Gwilt and C. Haselgrove (eds), *Reconstructing Iron Age Societies.* Oxford, Oxbow, 9–18.

Hodder, I., Shanks, M., Alexandri, A., Buchli, V., Carmen, J., Last, J., and Lucas, G. (1995) *Interpreting Archaeology: finding meaning in the past.* London, Routledge.

Hodson, F. R. (1960) Reflections on 'The ABC of the British Iron Age'. *Antiquity* 34, 138–140.

Hodson, F. R. (1964) Cultural grouping within the British pre-Roman Iron Age. *Proceedings of the Prehistoric Society* 30, 99–110.

Hood, J. D. (1892) *Waterspouts on the Yorkshire Wolds: Cataclysm at Langtoft and Driffield.* Driffield, Frank Fawcett.

Hoskins, J. (1998) *Biographical Objects. How Things Tell the Stories of People's Lives.* London, Routledge.

Hotson, A. R. (1985) *An Investigation of Fossil Snail Fauna from Dry Valley Infill in the Yorkshire Wolds.* Unpublished BSc Dissertation No. 2292, University of Birmingham.

Howe, L. (2000) Risk, Ritual and Performance. *Journal of the Royal Anthropological Institute* NS 6, 63–79.

Hughes-Brock, H. (1998) Greek Beads of the Mycenaean Period (c. 1650–1100 BC): The Age of Heroines of Greek Tradition and Mythology. In L. D. Sciama and J. B. Eicher (eds), *Beads and Bead Makers. Gender, Material Culture and Meaning.* Oxford, Berg, 247–272.

Humber Field Archaeology (2000a) *Prehistory in the Humber Region.* Hull, Humber Field Archaeology.

Humber Field Archaeology (2000b) *BP Teeside to Altend Ethylene Pipeline. Assessment of results of archaeological excavations in the East Riding of Yorkshire. Report 6 – Sites 218, 222 and 908.* Hull, Humber Field Archaeology.

Humphrey, J. (2003) The utilization and technology of flint in the British Iron Age. In J. Humphrey (ed.). *Researching the Iron Age.* Leicester, Leicester Archaeology Monograph 11, 17–23.

Hunt, J. (1997) *Small-scale Sheep Keeping.* London, Faber and Faber.

Hunter, F. (2005) The image of the warrior in the British Iron Age – coin iconography in context. In C. Haselgrove and D. Wigg-Wolf (eds), *Iron Age Coinage and Ritual Practices. Studien zu Fundmünzen der Antike 20.* Mainz, Von Zabern, 43–68.

Huntingdon, R. and Metcalf, P. (1991) *Celebrations of death: the anthropology of mortuary ritual.* Cambridge, Cambridge University Press.

Hurford, R. (n.d.) Chariots. http://www.chariotmaker.co.uk/chariots.htm (Accessed 25/11/2011).

Ingold, T. (1993) The temporality of landscape. *World Archaeology* 25 (2), 152– 174.

Ingold, T. (1994) Introduction to culture. In T. Ingold (ed.), *Companion Encyclopaedia of Anthropology: humanity, culture and social life.* London and New York, Routledge, 329–349.

Ingold, T. (2000a) Ancestry, generation, substance, memory, land. In T. Ingold, *The Perception of the Environment. Essays in Livelihood, Dwelling and Skill.* London, Routledge, 132–151.

Ingold, T. (2000b) General introduction. In T. Ingold, *The Perception of the Environment. Essays in Livelihood, Dwelling and Skill.* London, Routledge, 1–11.

Ingold, T. (2004) Beyond biology and culture: the meaning of evolution in a relational world. *Social Anthropology* 12(2), 209–221.

Ingold, T. (2008) When Ant Meets Spider. Social Theory for Arthropods. In C. Knappet and L. Malafouris (eds), *Material Agency: towards a non-anthropocentric approach.* New York, Springer, 209–216.

Ito, K. L. (1985) Affective Bonds: Hawaiian Interelationships of self. In H. M. White and J. Kirkpatrick (eds), *Person, Self and Experience: Exploring Pacitfic Ethnopsychologies.* Berkeley, University of California Press, 201–227.

Jackson, K. (1948) On some Romano-British Place-names. *Journal of Roman Studies* 38, 57.

Jackson, K. H. (1964) *The Oldest Irish Tradition: a window onto the Iron Age.* Cambridge, Cambridge University Press.

Jackson, S. A. (1996) Remembering to Forget: Memory, Burial, and Self-Similarity in Sursuranga, New Ireland, Papua New Guinea. *Anthropology and Humanism* 21(2), 159–170.

James, S. (1993) *Exploring the World of the Celts.* London, Thames and Hudson.

James, S. (1999*) The Atlantic Celts: ancient people or modern invention?* London, British Museum Press.

James, S. (2007) A bloodless past: the pacification of the Iron Age. In C. Haselgrove and R. Pope (eds), *The Earlier Iron Age in Britain and the near Continent.* Oxford, Oxbow, 160–173.

James, S. and Rigby, V. (1997) *Britain and the Celtic Iron Age.* London, British Museum Press.

Janowski, M. (1998) Beads, Prestige and Life Among the Kelabit of Sarawak, East Malaysia. In L. D. Sciama and J. B. Eicher (eds), *Beads and Bead Makers. Gender, Material Culture and Meaning.* Oxford, Berg, 213–246.

Jay, M. (2008) Prehistoric Diet on the Yorkshire Wolds: Isotopes and Skeletons. *Prehistory Research Section Bulletin* 45, 68–70

Jay, M., Fuller, B. T., Richards, M. P., Knüsel, C. and

King, S. S. (2008) Iron Age Breastfeeding Practices in Britain: Isotopic Evidence from Wetwang Slack, East Yorkshire. *American Journal of Physical Anthropology* 136, 327–337.

Jay, M., Haselgrove, C., Hamilton, D., Hill, J. D. and Dent, J. (2012) Chariots and Content: New Radiocarbon Dates from Wetwang and the Chronology of Iron Age Burials and Brooches in East Yorkshire. *Oxford Journal of Archaeology* 31(2), 161–189.

Jay, M. and Richards, M. P. (2006) Diet in the Iron Age cemetery population at Wetwang Slack, East Yorkshire, UK: carbon and nitrogen stable isotope evidence. *Journal of Archaeological Science* 33, 653–662.

Jay, M. and Richards, M. P. (2007) British Iron Age Diet: Stable Isotopes and Other Evidence. *Proceedings of the Prehistoric Society* 73, 169–190.

Jenkins, R. (1996) *Social Identity.* London, Routledge.

Jones, O. and Cloke, P. (2008) Non-human agencies: Trees in Place and Time. In C. Knappett and L. Malafouris (eds), *Material Agency. Towards a Non-Anthropocentric Approach.* New York, Springer, 79–96.

Jones, S. (1997) *The Archaeology of Ethnicity.* London, Routledge.

Jones, S. (2000) Discourses of identity in the interpretation of the past. In J. Thomas (ed.), *Interpretive Archaeology: a reader.* Leicester, Continuum Press, 445–57.

Jope, M. (1995) A gold finger-ring found at Arras, Gone Missing Long Since. In B. Raftery, J. V. S. Megaw and V. Rigby (eds), *Sites and Sights of the Iron Age.* Oxbow, Oxford, 113–17.

Jope, M. (2000) *Early Celtic Art in the British Isles.* Oxford, Clarendon Press.

Judd, M. and Roberts, C. A. (1999) Fracture trauma in a Medieval British farming village. *American Journal of Physical Anthropology* 109(2), 229–243.

Jundi, S. and Hill, J. D. (1998) Brooches and identities in first century A.D. Britain: more than meets the eye? In C. Forcey, J. Hawthorne and R. Witcher (eds), *TRAC 97. Proceedings of the Seventh Annual Theoretical Roman Archaeology Conference.* Oxford, Oxbow, 125–137.

Karl, R. (2005) Master and Apprentice, Knight and Squire: Education in the 'Celtic' Iron Age. *Oxford Journal of Archaeology* 24(3), 255–271.

Kent, P. (1980) *British Regional Geology; From the Tees to the Wash.* Institute of Geological Sciences. London, HMSO.

Kerr, B. (1968) *Bound to the Soil. A Social History of Dorset 1750–1818.* Tiverton, Dorset Books.

King, S. (2010) *What makes War? Assessing Iron Age warfare through mortuary behaviour and osteological patterns of violence.* Unpublished PhD thesis, University of Bradford.

Kinsella, T. (transl.) (1970) *The Táin.* Oxford, Oxford University Press.

Knapp, B. J. (1979) *Elements of Geographical Hydrology.* London, Allen and Unwin.

Knight, B. (1991) *Simpson's Forensic Medicine.* (10th edition). London, Edward Arnold.

Kopytoff, I. (1986) The cultural biography of things: commoditization as process. In A. Appadurai (ed.), *The social life of things. Commodities in perspective.* Cambridge, Cambridge University Press, 64–91.

Kus, S. (1992) Towards an archaeology of Body and Soul. In J. C. Gardin and C. S. Peebles (eds), *Representation in Archaeology.* Bloomington, Indiana University Press, 168–77.

Lally, M. (2008) *Bodies of difference.* In K. Waddington and N. Sharples (eds). *Changing Perspectives on the First Millennium BC.* Oxford, Oxbow, 119–138.

Lambert, H. (2000) Village Bodies? Reflections on Locality, Constitution and Affect in Rajasthani Kinship. In M. Böck and A. Rao (eds), *Culture, creation and procreation. Concepts of Kinship in South Asian Practice.* Oxford, Berghahn Books, 81–100.

Larick, R. (1986) Age grading and ethnicity in the style of Loikop (Samburu) spears. *World Archaeology* 18(2), 269–283.

Latour, B. (1993) *We Have Never Been Modern.* (transl. by C. Porter from 1991 original). Cambridge, Massachusetts, Harvard University Press.

Law, J. and Mol, A. (2008) The Actor-Enacted: Cumbrian Sheep in 2001. In C. Knappett and L. Malafouris (eds), *Material Agency. Towards a Non-Anthropocentric Approach.* New York, Springer, 57–77.

Lawson, A. J. (ed.) (2000) *Potterne 1982–5: Animal husbandry in later prehistoric Wiltshire.* Salisbury, Wessex Archaeology Report 20.

Lawson, B. (2001) *The Language of Space.* Oxford, Architectural Press.

Lawton, I. (1992) *Duggleby Lodge.* York, York Survey and Research (unpublished report).

Layton, R. (1995) Relating to the Country in the Western Desert. In E. Hirsch and M. O'Hanlon (eds), *The Anthropology of Landscape.* Oxford, Clarendon Press, 210–231.

Leach, E. (1979) Discussion. In B. C. Burnham and J. Kinsbury (eds), *Space, Hierarchy and Society: interdisciplinary studies in social area analysis.* Oxford,

British Archaeological Report Supplementary Series 59, 119–24.

Lee-Thorp, J. A. (2008) On Isotopes and Old Bones. *Archaeometry* 50, 6, 925–950.

Lemert, C. and Branaman, A. (eds) (1997) *The Goffman Reader.* Oxford, Blackwell.

Lenerz-de Wilde, M. (1977) *Zirkelornamentik in der Kuntz der Laténezeit. Müchner Beiträge zur vor-und Frühgeschichte* 25. München, Beck.

Lewin, J. (1969) *The Yorkshire Wolds: a study in geomorphology.* Hull, University of Hull Occasional Papers in Geography 11.

Lienhardt, R. G. (1961) *Divinity and Experience: the religion of the Dinka.* Oxford, Oxford University Press.

LiPuma, E. (1988) *The Gift of Kinship: Structure and Practice in Maring Social Organisation.* Cambridge, Cambridge University Press.

LiPuma, E. (1998) Modernity and forms of personhood in Melanesia. In M. Lambek and A. Strathern (eds), *Bodies and Persons: Comparative Views from Africa and Melanesia.* Cambridge, Cambridge University Press, 53–79.

Littauer, M. A. and Crouwel, J. H. (2001) The Earliest Evidence for Metal Bridle Bits. *Oxford Journal of Archaeology* 20(4), 329–338.

Loades, M. (2005) Building an Iron Age British Chariot. http://www.mikeloades.co.uk/cms/images/British_Chariot.pdf (Accessed 25/07/2010).

Lock, G., Gosden, C. and Daly, P. (2005) *Segsbury Camp: excavations in 1996 and 1997 at an Iron Age hillfort on the Oxfordshire Ridgeway.* Oxford, Oxford University School of Archaeology.

Lorimer, H. (2006) Herding memories of humans and animals. *Environment and Planning D: Society and Space* 24(4), 497–518.

Lynch, K. (1989) Solidary labour: its nature and marginalisation. *Sociological Review* 37, 1–14.

MacGrail, S. (1990) Early boats of the Humber Basin. In S. Ellis and D. R. Crowther (eds), *Humber Perspectives: a region through the ages.* Hull, Hull University Press, 109–130.

Mack, J. (2008) *The Art of Small Things.* London, Trustees of the British Museum.

Manby, T. (1980) Bronze Age Settlement in Eastern Yorkshire. In J. Barrett and R. Bradley (eds), *Settlement and Society in the British Later Bronze Age.* Oxford, British Archaeological Report 83, 307–370.

Manby, T. (1985) The Thwing Project. *Prehistory Research Bulletin, Yorkshire Archaeological Society* 22.

Manby, T. (1986) The Thwing Project. *Prehistory Research Bulletin, Yorkshire Archaeological Society* 23, 1–8.

Manby, T. (1990) Hillforts in Yorkshire No. 3b: Yorkshire Wolds. *Prehistory Research Bulletin, Yorkshire Archaeological Society* 27, 3–7.

Manning G. W. and Saunders, C. (1972) A socketed iron axe from Maids Moreton, Buckinghamshire, with a note on the type. *Antiquaries Journal* 52, 276–292.

Mant, A. K. (1984) *Post-mortem changes.* In A. K. Mant (ed.), *Taylor's Principles and Practice of Medical Jurisprudence.* (13th edn). Edinburgh, Churchill Livingstone, 128–55.

Markey, M., Wilkes, E. M. and Darvill, T. (2002) Poole Harbour: An Iron Age Port. *Current Archaeology* 181, 7–11.

Marsden, B. M. (1999) [repr. of 1974] *The Early Barrow Diggers.* Stroud, Tempus.

Maschner, H. D. G. and Reedy-Maschner, K. L. (1998) Raid, Retreat, Defend (Repeat): The Archaeology and Ethnohistory of Warfare on the North Pacific Rim. *Journal of Anthropological Archaeology* 17, 19–51.

Matthew, W. M. (1993) Marling in British Agriculture: A Case of Partial Identity. *The Agricultural History Review.* 41(2), 97–110.

Maule Cole, E. (1897) Notes on the Danes Graves near Driffield. *Proceedings of the Yorkshire Geological Polytechnic Society* 13, 299–301.

Mays, S., Harding, C. and Heighway, C. (2007) *Wharram XI: The Churchyard.* York, York University Department of Archaeology.

McCabe, J. T. (2004) *Cattle Bring Us To Our Enemies. Turkana Ecology, Politics and Raiding in a Disequilibrium System.* Ann Arbor, University of Michigan Press.

McGarry, T. (2008) *Irish Late Prehistoric Burials.* Unpublished PhD thesis, University College Dublin.

Megaw, J. V. S. and Megaw, R. (1996) Ancient Celts and modern ethnicity. *Antiquity* 70, 175–181.

Megaw, R. and Megaw, J. V. S. (1994) Through a window on the European Iron Age darkly: fifty years of reading early Celtic art. *World Archaeology* 25(3), 287–303.

Megaw, R. and Megaw, J. V. S. (2001) *Celtic Art. From its beginnings to the Book of Kells.* London, Thames and Hudson.

Meisch, L. A. (1998) Why Do They Like Red? Beads, Ethnicity and Gender in Ecuador. In L. D. Sciama and J. B. Eicher (eds), *Beads and Bead Makers. Gender, Material Culture and Meaning.* Oxford, Berg, 147–176.

Millett, M. and McGrail, S. (1987) The Archaeology of the Hasholme Boat. *Archaeological Journal* 144, 69–155.

Milner, N., Craig, O. E., Bailey, G. N., Pederson, K. and Anderson, S. H. (2004) Something fishy in the Neolithic? A re-evaluation of stable isotope analysis of Mesolithic and Neolithic coastal populations. *Antiquity* 78, 9–22.

Mines, D. and Weiss, B. (1993) Materialisations of memory: the substance of remembering and forgetting. Introduction. *Anthropological Quarterly* 70, 161–3.

Mizoguchi, K. (1992) A historiography of a linear barrow cemetery: a structurationist's point of view. *Archaeological Review From Cambridge* 11(1), 19–49.

Montgomery, J., Cooper, R. E. and Evans, J. A. (2007) Foragers, farmers or foreigners? An assessment of dietary strontium isotope variation in Middle Neolithic and Early Bronze Age East Yorkshire. In M. Larssson and M. Parker Pearson (eds), *From Stonehenge to the Baltic: living with cultural diversity in the third millennium BC.* Oxford, British Archaeological Report S1692, 65–82.

Montgomery, J. and Jay, M. (2008) *Beaker People: Diet and Mobility.* Unpublished lecture presented at the Bronze Age Forum, University of Sheffield. November 2008.

Morgan, D. (1996) *Family Connections. An Introduction to Family Studies.* Cambridge, Polity Press.

Morris, B. (2000) *Animals and Ancestors: An Ethnography.* Oxford, Berg.

Morris, C. E. (1990) In Pursuit of the White Tusked Boar. Aspects of Hunting in Mycenean Society. In R. Hägg and G. C. Nordquist (eds), *Celebrations of Death and Divinity in the Bronze Age Argolid. Skrifter Utgivna Av Svenska Institutet I Athen 4, XL.* Stockholm, Swedish Institute at Athens, 149–156.

Morse, M. (1999) Craniology and the Adoption of the Three-Age System in Britain. *Proceedings of the Prehistoric Society* 65, 1–16.

Morse, M. (2005) *How the Celts Came to Britain: Druids, Ancient Skulls and the Birth of Archaeology.* Stroud, Tempus.

Mortimer, J. R. (1869) Notice of the opening of an Anglo-Saxon grave at Grimthorpe, Yorkshire. *Reliquary* 9, 180–2.

Mortimer, J. R. (1889) Prehistory of the village of Fimber

part I–II. *Proceedings of the Yorkshire Geological and Polytechnic Society* 11, 217–30 and 445–57.

Mortimer, J. R. (1895) The opening of Six Mounds at Scorborough, near Beverley. *Transactions of the East Riding Antiquarian Society* 3, 21–3.

Mortimer, J. R. (1897) A summary of what is known of the so-called 'Danes Graves' near Driffield. *Proceedings of the Yorkshire Geological and Polytechnic Society* 13, 286–98.

Mortimer, J. R. (1898) Report on the opening of a number of the so-called 'Danes Graves' at Kilham, East Riding, Yorkshire, and the discovery of a chariot burial of the early Iron Age. *Proceedings of the Society of Antiquaries*, 2nd series 17, 119–28.

Mortimer, J. R. (1899) A summary of what is known of the so-called 'Danes Graves' at Kilham, E. R. Yorks., and the discovery of a chariot burial of the Early Iron Age. *Proceedings of the Yorkshire Geological and Polytechnic Society* n.s. 13, 1895–9, 286–98.

Mortimer, J. R. (1905a) *Forty Years Researches in British and Saxon Burial Mounds of East Yorkshire.* London, A. Brown and Sons.

Mortimer, J. R. (1905b) Notes on the British remains found near Cawthorne Camps, *The Naturalist*, 264–5.

Mortimer, J. R. (1911a) Danes Graves. *Transactions of the East Riding Antiquarian Society* 18, 30–52.

Mortimer, J. R. (1911b) Notes on the stature etc. of our ancestors in East Yorkshire. *The Naturalist*, 313–17.

Mulhall, I. (2010) The Peat Men from Cloneycavan and Oldcroghan. *British Archaeology* 110, 34–41.

Mulhall, I., and E. K. Briggs (2007) Presenting a past society to a present day audience. Bog bodies in Iron Age Ireland. *Museum Ireland* 17, 71–81.

Munn, N. (1986) *The Fame of Gawa. A Symbolic Study of Value Transformation in a Massim (Papua New Guinea) Society.* Durham and London, Duke University Press.

Myers, F. R. (1991) *Pintupi Country, Pintupi Self: sentiment, place and politics amongst Western Desert Aborigines.* Oxford, University of California Press.

Nairn, C. (1974) *Ongka's Big Moka. (The Kawelka of Paupua, New Guinea).* Disappearing World. London, Granada Television.

Neal, C. (2010) *People and the environment: a geoarchaeological approach to the Yorkshire Wolds landscape.* Unpublished PhD thesis, University of York. (Available at: http://archaeologydataservice. ac.uk/archives/view/neal_phd_2011/)

Neave, D. and Neave, S. (2008) *A History of the County of York: East Riding. Volume 8.* London, Victoria County Histories.

Nicholson, J. (1998) *Folklore of East Yorkshire.* [Reprint of 1890 original]. Felinfach, Llanerch Publishers.

Nilsson Stutz, L. (2003) *Embodied Rituals and Ritualised Bodies. Acta Archaeologica Ludensia* 46. Lund, Almquiest and Wiksell Intl.

Norbeck, E. N. (1971) *Anthropology Today. An Introduction: Rites of Reversal.* Del Mar (California), CRM Books.

O'Hanlon, M. and Frankland, L. H. F. (2003) 'Co-present landscapes': routes and rootedness as sources of identity in Highlands New Guinea. In P. Stewart and A. Strathern (eds), *Landscape, Memory and History: Anthropological Perspectives.* London, Pluto Press, 166–188.

O'Hear, A. (1998) Lantana Beads: Gender Issues in their Production and Use. In L. D. Sciama and J. G. Eicher (eds) *Beads and Bead Makers.* Oxford, Berg, 117–128.

Oliver, G. (1829) *History and Antiquities of the Town and Minster Beverley in the County of York.* Beverley, M. Turner.

Osborn, A. J. (1996) Cattle, Co-wives, Children and Calabashes: Material Context for Symbol Use among the II Chamus of West-Central Kenya. *Journal of Anthropological Archaeology* 15, 107–136.

Osgood, R. (1999) Britain in the age of warrior heroes. *British Archaeology* 46, 8–9.

Oswald, A. (1997) A doorway onto the past: practical and mystic concerns in the orientation of roundhouse doorways. In A. Gwilt and C. Haselgrove (eds), *Reconstructing Iron Age Societies.* Oxford, Oxbow, 87–95.

Overing, J. and Passes, A. (eds) (2000) *The Anthropology of Love and Anger: the aesthetics of conviviality in Native Amazonia.* London, Routledge.

Page, W. (ed.) (1907) *The Victoria History of the County of York. Volume 1.* London, Archibald Constable.

Palk, N. (1984) *Iron Age Bridle Bits from Britain.* Edinburgh, Department of Archaeology.

Pare, C. (1989) From Dupljaja to Delphi: the ceremonial use of the wagon in later prehistory. *Antiquity* 63, 80–100.

Parker Pearson, M. (1994) Kings, Cattle and Social Change in Southern Madagascar. *Archaeological Review from Cambridge* 13(1), 75–82.

Parker Pearson, M. (1996) Food, fertility and front doors in the first millennium BC. In T. Champion and J. Collis (eds), *The Iron Age in Britain and Ireland: Recent Trends.* Sheffield, J. R. Collis Publications, 117–132.

Parker Pearson, M. (1999a) Food, Sex and Death: Cosmologies in the British Iron Age with Particular Reference to East Yorkshire. *Cambridge Archaeological Journal* 9(1), 43–69.

Parker Pearson, M. (1999b) *The Archaeology of Death and Burial.* Stroud, Alan Sutton.

Parker Pearson, M., Chamberlain, A., Craig, O., Marshall, P., Mulville, J., Smith, H., Chenery, C., Collins, M., Cook, G., Craig, G., Evans, J., Hiller, J., Montgomery, J. Schwenniger, J. -L., Taylor, G. and Wess, T. (2005) Evidence for mummification in Bronze Age Britain. *Antiquity* 79, 529–546.

Parker Pearson, M. and Richards, C. (1994) *Architecture and Social Order.* London, Routledge.

Parker Pearson, M. and Thorpe, N. (eds) (2005) *Warfare, Violence and Slavery. Proceedings of a Prehistoric Society conference at Sheffield University.* Oxford, British Archaeological Report S1374.

Parkes, P. (2006) Celtic fosterage: adoptive kinship and clientage in northwest Europe. *Comparative Studies in Society and History* 48, 359–95.

Pauli, L. (1975) *Keltische Volksglaube. Amulette und Sonderbestattungen am Dürrnberg bei Hallein und im Eisenzeitlichen Mitteleuropa.* München, C. H. Beck Vorlag.

Phillips, J. E. (2005) 'To make the dry bones live'. Amédée Forestier's Glastonbury Lake Village. In S. Smiles and S. Moser (eds), *Envisioning the Past.* Oxford, Blackwells, 72–91.

Piggott, S. (1950) Swords and Scabbards of the British Early Iron Age. *Proceedings of the Prehistoric Society* 15, 1–28.

Piggott, S. (1992) *Wagon, Chariot and Carriage. Symbol and Status in the History of Transport.* London, Thames and Hudson.

Pliny the Elder (n.d.) *Natural History* (transl. by J. Healey 2005). London, Penguin.

Pollard, A. M. (2009) Diagenetic and Isotopic Studies of Bones and Teeth. Editorial. *Archaeometry Virtual Issue* (2009).

Pope, R. (2007) Ritual and the roundhouse: a critique of recent ideas on domestic space in later British prehistory. In C. Haselgrove and R. Pope (eds), *The Earlier Iron Age in Britain and the near Continent.* Oxford, Oxbow Books, 204–228.

Porter, V. (1991) *Caring for Cows.* London, Whittet Books.

Powlesland, D. J. (1986) Excavations at Heslerton North Yorkshire 1978–82. *Archaeological Journal* 143, 53–173.

Prichard, J. Cowles. (1843) *The Natural History of Man:*

Comprising Inquiries into the Modifying Influence of Physical and Moral Agencies on the Different Tribes of the Human Family. London, H. Bailliere.

Proctor, W. (1855) Report of the proceedings of the Yorkshire Antiquarian Club, in the excavation of barrows from the year 1849. *Proceedings of the Yorkshire Philosophical Society*, 176–189.

Pryor, F. (2003) *Britain BC.* London, Harper Collins.

Ptolemy. (n.d.) *Geographia. Book II.* Available at: http://ahds.ac.uk/catalogue/collection.htm?uri=lll-2422–1 (Accessed 26/02/09).

Raftery, B. (1994) Reflections on the Irish Scabbard Style. In C. Dobiat (ed.), *Festschrift für Otto-Herman Frey zum. 65. Geburtstag.* Marburger Studien Zur Vor-Und Frühgeschichte 16. Marburg, Hitzeroth, 475–492.

Ramm, H. (1971) The Yorkshire Philosophical Society and Archaeology, 1822–55. *Yorkshire Philosophical Society Report* 1971, 66–73.

Ramm, H. (1978) *The Parisi.* London, Duckworth.

Rapport, N. and Overing, J. (2000) *Social and Cultural Anthropology: the Key Concepts.* London, Routledge.

Redfern, R. (2008) New Evidence for Iron Age Secondary Burial Practice and Bone Modification from Gussage All Saints and Maiden Castle (Dorset, England). *Oxford Journal of Archaeology* 27 (3), 281–301.

Redfern, R. (2009) Does Cranial Trauma Provide Evidence for Projectile Weaponry in Iron Age Dorset? *Oxford Journal of Archaeology* 28(4), 399–424.

Reid, C. (1885) *The Geology of Holderness.* London, HMSO.

Reynolds, P. (1979) *Iron Age Farm: The Butser Experiment.* London, British Museum Publications.

Rigby, V. (2004) *Pots and Pits: the British Museum East Yorkshire Settlements Project, 1988–1992.* Hull, East Riding Archaeologist 11.

Roberts, J. (2007) Short journeys, long-distance thinking. In V. Cummings and B. Johnston (eds), *Prehistoric Journeys.* Oxford, Oxbow, 102–109.

Robinson, P. (1995) Miniature socketed bronze axes from Wiltshire. *Wiltshire Archaeological and Natural History Magazine* 88, 60–68.

Rose, W. (2001)[repr. of 1937] *The Village Carpenter.* Pontyclerc, Stobart Davies.

Royston, P. (1893) *History of Rudston.* Bridlington Quay, George Fuby.

Ryan, K., Munene, K., Munyiri, S. K. and Kunoni, P. N. (1991. Cattle Naming: the Persistence of a Traditional Practice in Modern Maasailand. In P. J. Crabtreee and K. Ryan (eds), *Animal Use and Culture Change.* Philadelphia, MASCA, 91–96.

Rylatt, J. and Bevan, B. (2007) Realigning the world: pit alignments and their landscape context. In C. Haselgrove and T. Moore (eds), *The Later Iron Age in Britain and Beyond*. Oxford, Oxbow, 219–234.

Sahlins, M. D. and Service, E. (1965) *Evolution and Culture*. (3rd edition). Ann Arbor, Michigan, University of Michigan Press.

Saunders, N. J. (1998) Stealers of light, traders in brilliance: Amerindian metaphysics in the mirror of conquest. *RES: Anthropology and Aesthetics* 33(1), 225–252.

Saunders, N. (2001) A Dark Light: Reflections on Obsidian in Mesoamerica. *World Archaeology* 33(2), 220–236.

Scarry, E. (1985) *The Body in Pain. The Making and Unmaking of the World*. Oxford, Oxford University Press.

Schieffelin, E. L. (1985) Performance and the Cultural Construction of Reality. *American Ethnologist* 12(4), 707–724.

Schieffelin, E. L. (1996) On Failure and Performance. In C. Laderman and M. Roseman (eds), *The Performance of Healing*. London, Routledge, 59–85.

Schneider, J. and Weiner, A. B. (1988) Introduction. In A. B. Weiner and J. Schneider (eds) 1989, 1–29.

Sciama, L. D. (1998) Gender in the Making, Trading and Uses of Beads: An Introductory Essay. In L. D. Sciama and J. B. Eicher (eds), *Beads and Bead Makers. Gender, Material Culture and Meaning*. Oxford, Berg, 1–46.

Sciama, L. D. and Eicher, J. B. (eds) (1998) *Beads and Bead Makers. Gender, Material Culture and Meaning*. Oxford, Berg.

Scoggins, R. D. (1989) Bits and Mouth Injuries. *Veterinary Review* 9(2), 101–102.

Shanks, M. and Pearson, M. (2001) *Theatre/Archaeology. Disciplinary Dialogues*. London, Routledge.

Sharples, N. (2008) Comment I. Contextualising Iron Age art. In D. Garrow, C. Gosden and J. D. Hill (eds), *Rethinking Celtic Art*. Oxford, Oxbow, 203–213.

Sharples, N. (2010) *Social Relations in Later Prehistory. Wessex in the First Millennium BC*. Oxford, Oxford University Press.

Shaw, T. (1970) Methods of earthwork building. *Proceedings of the Prehistoric Society* 36, 280–281.

Sheahan, J. J. and Whellan, T. (1856) *History and Topography of the City of York; The Ainsty Wapentake and the East Riding of Yorkshire*. Beverley, John Green.

Sheppard, T. (1907) Note on a British chariot-burial at Hunmanby in East Yorkshire. *Yorkshire Archaeological Journal* 19, 482–488.

Sheppard, T. (1923) Roman Remains at Middleton-on-the-Wolds. *Transactions of the East Riding Antiquarian Society* 24, 80–84.

Sheppard, T. (1929) *Catalogue of the Mortimer Collection of Prehistoric Remains from East Yorkshire Barrows*. Hull, Hull Museums Publications 162.

Sheppard, T. (1939) Excavations at Eastburn, East Yorkshire. *Yorkshire Archaeological Journal* 34, 35–47.

Skeates, R. (1993) Mediterranean Coral: Its use and Exchange in and around the Alpine Region during the later Neolithic and Copper Age. *Oxford Journal of Archaeology* 12(3), 281–292.

Smith, A. H. (1937) *The Place-Names of the East Riding of Yorkshire and York*. Cambridge, Cambridge University Press.

Smith, D. J. (1979) *Discovering Horse-Drawn Vehicles*. Princes Risborough, Shire.

Smith, K. P. (2002) Through a Clouded Mirror: Africa at the Pan-American Exposition. Buffalo Museum of Science. http://www.sciencebuff.org/africa_at_the_pan_am_introduction.php (accessed September 13, 2005).

Smith, R. A. (1994) [repr. of 1925] *British Museum Guide to Early Iron Age Antiquities*. London, Trustees of the British Museum (reprint Ipswich, Anglia Publishing).

Smith, R. A. (1927) Pre-Roman Remains at Scarborough. *Archaeologia* 77, 179–200.

Smith, W. (1923) *Ancient Springs and Streams of the East Riding of Yorkshire. Their Topography and Traditions*. London, A. Brown and Sons.

Sofaer, J. (2006) *The Body as Material Culture: a theoretical osteoarchaeology*. Cambridge, Cambridge University Press.

Sørensen, M. L. (2000) *Gender Archaeology*. Cambridge, Polity Press.

Spratling, M. (2008) On the aesthetics of the ancient Britons. In D. Garrow, C. Gosden and J. D. Hill (eds), *Rethinking Celtic Art*. Oxford, Oxbow, 185–202.

Spriggs, M. (1990) Review of Hodder 1987. *Australian Archaeology* 30: 103.

Stacey, R. (2004) Evidence for the use of Birch-bark tar from Iron Age Britain. *Past* 47, 1–2.

Stead, I. (1965) *The La Tène Cultures of East Yorkshire*. Hull, Yorkshire Philosophical Society.

Stead, I. M. (1968) An Iron Age Hillfort at Grimthorpe, Yorkshire, England. *Proceedings of the Prehistoric Society* 34, 148–190.

Stead, I. M. (1979) *The Arras Culture*. York, York Philosophical Society.

Stead, I.M. (1980) *Rudston Roman Villa*. Leeds, Yorkshire Archaeological Society.

Stead, I. M. (1986) A Group of Iron Age Barrows at Cowlam, North Humberside. *Yorkshire Archaeological Journal* 58, 5–15.

Stead, I. M. (1988) Chalk Figurines of the Parisi. *Antiquaries Journal* 68, 9–29.

Stead, I. M. (1991) *Iron Age Cemeteries in East Yorkshire*. London, English Heritage.

Stead, I. M. (1996) *Celtic Art*. London, British Museum.

Stead, I. M. (2006) *British Iron Age Swords and Scabbards*. London, The British Museum Press.

Stead, I. M., Flouest, J-L. and Rigby, V. (2006) *Iron Age and Roman Burials in Champagne*. Oxford, Oxbow.

Steedman, K. (1991) *An Archaeological Evaluation at Home Farm, Sewerby*. Hull, Humberside County Council.

Stephens, M. R. (1986) *Devil's Hill, Heslerton. Interim Report*. Malton, ERARC.

Stevans, F. (2007) Identifying the Body: Representing Self. Art, Ornamentation and the Body in Prehistoric Europe. In J. Sofaer (ed.), *Material Identities*. Oxford, Blackwell, 82–98.

Stilllingfleet, Rev. E. W. (1847) Account of the Opening of Some Barrows on the Wolds of Yorkshire. Transcript of letter read at the Monthly Meeting of the Archaeological Institute, London: January (1847) (Beverley Archives ref. YE/571.92/226, 233). (Also published in *Proceedings of the Archaeological Institute York* 1846: 26–32).

Stocking, G. W. (1971) What's in a name? The origins of the Royal Anthropological Institute. *Man* 6, 369–390

Stoertz, C. (1997) *Ancient Landscapes of the Yorkshire Wolds*. Swindon, RCHME.

Strathern, M. (1988) *The Gender of the Gift*. Berkeley, University of California Press.

Sturt, G. (2000) [repr. of 1923] *The Wheelwright's Shop*. Cambridge, Cambridge University Press.

Swiss, A. J. and McDonnall, G. (2007a) Metallurgical Analysis of the Iron Tyres from the Chariot Burial. In F. Brown, C. Howard-Davis, M. Brennand, A. Boyle, T. Evans, S. O'Connor, A. Spence, R. Heawood and A. Lupton (eds), *The Archaeology of the A1(M) Darrington to Dishforth DBFO Road Scheme*. Lancaster, Lancaster Imprints 12: Appendix 2 (CD Rom).

Swiss, A. J. and McDonnall, G. (2007b) X-Ray Fluorescence of Artefacts from the Chariot Burial. In F. Brown, C. Howard-Davis, M. Brennand, A. Boyle, T. Evans, S. O'Connor, A. Spence, R. Heawood and A. Lupton (eds), *The Archaeology of the A1(M) Darrington to Dishforth DBFO Road Scheme*. Lancaster, Lancaster Imprints 12: Appendix 3 (CD Rom).

Tacitus (n.d.) a *The Agricola and The Germania*. (translated by H. Mattingley and revised by S.A. Handford 1970). London, Penguin.

Tacitus (n.d.) b *The Annals of Imperial Rome*. (translated by M. Grant 1996 [original translation 1956]). London, Penguin.

Târlea, A. (2004) Playing By The Rules: Swords and Swordfighters in the Mycenaean Society. *Dacia* 48–9, 125–150.

Tarlow, S. (1999) *Bereavement and Commemoration: an archaeology of mortality*. Oxford, Blackwell.

Taussig, M. (1999) *Defacement. Public Secrecy and the Labour of the Negative*. Stanford, Stanford University Press.

Taylor, C. (1993) To follow a rule ... In C. Calhoun, E. LiPuma and M. Postne (eds), *Bourdieu: Critical Perspectives*. Cambridge, Polity Press, 45–60.

Thomas, J. (ed.) (2000) *Interpretive Archaeology: A Reader*. London, Continuum.

Thomas, N. (1995) *Oceanic Art*. London, Thames and Hudson.

Thomas, N. (1998) Foreword. In A. Gell. *Art and Agency. An Anthropological Theory*. Oxford, Clarendon Press, vii–xiii.

Thompson, A. (2005) *Native British Trees*. Glastonbury, Wooden Books.

Thompson, E. P. (1991) *Customs in Common*. London, Merlin Press.

Thrift, N. and Dewsbury, J.-D. (2000) Dead geographies – and how to make them live. *Environment and Planning D: Society and Space* 18, 411–432.

Tomalin, S. (1998) Don't get your Necklaces in a Twist! Often-used Specialist Bead Terms and their Definitions for Researchers and Collectors. In In L. D. Sciama and J. B. Eicher (eds), *Beads and Bead Makers. Gender, Material Culture and Meaning*. Oxford, Berg, 299–306.

Trigger, B. (1978) *Time and Tradition: essays in archaeological interpretation*. Edinburgh, Edinburgh University Press.

Trigger, B. (1989) *A History of Archaeological Thought*. Cambridge, Cambridge University Press.

Tsetan, (1995) Tibetan art of divination. Tibetan Bulletin March–April 1995. http://www.tibet.com/Buddhism/divination.html (accessed April 16, 2006).

Tullett, A. (2010) Information Highways – Wessex linear ditches and the transmission of community. In M. Sterry, A. Tullett and N. Ray (eds), *In Search of the Iron Age. Proceedings of the IARSS 2008. University of Leicester.* Leicester, Leicester Archaeology Monograph 18, 111–126.

Tylor, E. B. (1871) *Primitive Culture: Researches into the Development of Mythology, Philosophy, Religion, Art, and Custom.* London, John Murray.

Tylor, E. B. (1888) On a method of investigating the development of institutions: applied to laws of marriage and descent. *Journal of the Royal Anthropological Institute* 18, 245–269.

Tyrell, A. (2000) Skeletal non-metric traits and the assessment of inter- and intra-population diversity: past problems and future potential. In S. Mays and M. Cox (eds), *Human Osteology in Archaeology and Forensic Science.* London, Greenwich Medical Media, 289–306.

Van der Noort, R. and Ellis, S. (eds) (1995) *Wetland Heritage of Holderness. An Archaeological Survey.* Hull, Humber Wetlands Project.

Van der Noort, R. and Ellis, S. (eds) (2000) *Wetland Heritage of the Hull Valley.* Hull, Humber Wetlands Project.

Van der Noort, R. and O'Sullivan, A. (2006) *Rethinking Wetland Archaeology.* London, Duckworth.

Van Gennep, A. (1960) *Rites of Passage* (transl. by M. Vicedom and S. Kimball). Chicago, University of Chicago Press.

Vince, J. (2010) *Discovering Horse-Brasses.* (2nd edn). Princes Risborough, Shire.

Wacher, J. (1966) Excavations at Riplingham, East Yorkshire, *Yorkshire Archaeological Journal* (1961–1966) 41, 608–669.

Waddington, K. E. (2007) The poetics of scale: the miniature axes from Whitchurch. In V. O. Jorge and J. Thomas (eds), Overcoming the modern invention of material culture. *Journal of Iberian Archaeology* 9/10, 187–206.

Waddington, K. E. and Sharples, N. (2007) Pins, Pixies and thick dark earth. *British Archaeology* 94, 28–33.

Wagner, P. (1992) *Late Holocene Environments and Man in East Yorkshire.* Unsubmitted PhD thesis, University of Sheffield.

Weiner, A. B. (1988) *The Trobrianders of Papua New Guinea.* Orlando, Harcourt College Publishers.

Weiner, A. B. (1989) Why Cloth? Wealth, Gender, and Power in Oceania. In A. B. Weiner and J. Schneider (eds) *Cloth and Human Experience.* Washington, Smithsonian Books, 3–72.

Weiner, A. B. and Schneider, J. (eds) (1989) *Cloth and Human Experience.* Washington, Smithsonian Books.

Wells, P. (2001) *Beyond Celts, Germans and Scythians: Archaeology and Identity in Iron Age Europe.* London, Duckworth.

Whimster, R. (1981) *Burial Practices in Iron Age Britain: A Discussion and Gazetteer of the Evidence, c. 700 BC–AD 43.* Oxford, British Archaeological Report 90.

White, R. (1991) *The Middle Ground. Indians, Empires, and the Republics in the Great Lakes Region, 1650–1815.* Cambridge, Cambridge University Press.

Whitehead, N. L. (2004) Introduction: Cultures, Conflicts, and the Poetics of Violent Practice. In N. L. Whitehead (ed.), *Violence.* Santa Fe, School of American Research Press, 3–24.

Wigley, A. (2007) Pitted histories: early first millennium AD pit alignments in the central Welsh Marches. In C. Haselgrove and R. Pope (eds), *The Earlier Iron Age in Britain and the near Continent.* Oxbow, Oxford, 119–134.

Williams, H. (2006) *Death and Memory in Early Medieval Britain.* Cambridge, Cambridge University Press.

Williams, R. (1989) *People of the Black Mountains. 1. The Beginning.* London, Chatto and Windus.

Williams, S. (1987) An 'archea-ology' of Turkana beads. In I. Hodder (ed.), *The Archaeology of Contextual Meanings.* Cambridge, Cambridge University Press, 31–8.

Wilson, D. (1851) *The Archaeology and Prehistoric Annals of Scotland.* Edinburgh, Sutherland and Knox.

Woodward, A. (2000) *British Barrows. A Matter of Life and Death.* Stroud, Tempus.

Woodward, A. (2002) Beads and Beakers: heirlooms and relics in the British Early Bronze Age. *Antiquity* 76, 1040–1047.

Woodward, D. (1984) *The Farming and Memorandum Books of Henry Best of Elmswell 1642.* Oxford, Oxford University Press.

Woodward, D. (ed.) (1985) *Descriptions of East Yorkshire: Leland to Defoe.* Beverley, East Yorkshire Local History Society.

Worsaae, J. J. A. (1849) *The Primeval Antiquities of Denmark: translated and applied to the illustration of similar remains in England.* (trans. and enlarged by W. J. Thoms). London, John Henry Parker.

Wright, D. (2000) Come Rain, Come Shine – The Langtoft Floods. In A. Whitworth (ed.), *Aspects of the Yorkshire Coast. Discovering Local History 2.* Barnsley, Wharncliffe Books, 123–134.

Wright, E. (1990) *The Ferriby Boats. Seacraft of the Bronze Age.* London, Routledge.

Wright, E. V. and Churchill, D. M. (1965) Prehistoric boats from North Ferriby, Yorkshire, England. *Proceedings of the Prehistoric Society* 31, 1–24.

WYAS. (2007) *Natural Gas Terminal, Easington. Archaeological Investigations. Report 1637.* Morley, West Yorkshire Archaeological Services.

Wylie, A. (1985) The Reaction Against Analogy. In M. Schiffer (ed.). *Advances in Archaeological Method and Theory* 8. New York, Academic Press, 63–111.

Young, G. (1828) *A Geological Survey of the Yorkshire Coast: describing the strata and fossils occurring between the Humber and the Tees, from the German Ocean to the Plain of York.* Whitby, R. Kirby.